MW01470956

WORLD WAR II AT SEA:
A Bibliography of Sources in English

by

MYRON J. SMITH, JR.

VOL. II: THE PACIFIC THEATER

With Forewords by
E. H. Simmons, Brig. Gen., U.S.M.C. (Ret.)
and Edward L. Beach, Capt., U.S.N. (Ret.)

The Scarecrow Press, Inc.
Metuchen, N.J.   1976

Library of Congress Cataloging in Publication Data

Smith, Myron J
    World War II at sea.

        Includes indexes.
        CONTENTS: v. 1.   The European theater. --v. 2.   The
Pacific theater. --v. 3.   General works, naval hardware, and
the All hands chronology (1941-1945).   Home fronts and spe-
cial studies.
        1.   World War, 1939-1945--Naval operations--Bibli-
ography. I. Title.
Z6207. W8S57   [D770]   016. 94054'5   75-34098
ISBN 0-8108-0884-6 (v. 1)
ISBN 0-8108-0969-9 (v. 2)
ISBN 0-8108-0970-2 (v. 3)

FOR MYRON J. SMITH, SR.

The Big War veteran
who made this all possible

"Among the men who fought . . .
Uncommon valor was a common virtue."

SUMMARY TABLE OF CONTENTS, 3 VOLUMES

FOREWORD TO VOLUME II

The war in the Pacific was peculiarly a naval war, a complex war, a war of technological and tactical change, a war of great distances reduced in time by modern communications and air power, a war of high drama with a readily discernible rhythm and strategic pattern.

The literature in the field is so vast and varied as to almost defy comprehensive collection and evaluation. The matrix and rubrics provided by Myron J. Smith, Jr., should therefore be particularly useful to those seeking to find their way through the labyrinth of things in print (and to a limited extent, directions to unpublished primary sources) on this theater. Mr. Smith cites something like 3200 references and in most cases provides signposts to their content and usefulness.

Users of this bibliography are urged to read the Introduction in which he describes his approach, methodology, and annotation system. Users should also read the internal introductions which precede each of the major sections. These provide context and the narrative glue needed to hold the bibliography together.

Edwin H. Simmons
Brig. Gen., U. S. Marine Corps (Ret.)
Director of Marine Corps History
   and Museums
Washington, D. C.

PREFACE TO VOLUME II

Between the Pearl Harbor attack in 1941 and the final termination of hostilities in 1945, the United States actually fought two completely separate and distinct wars. Our national policy, formulated by the Allied Combined Chiefs of Staff, supported by the U.S. Joint Chiefs of Staff and sealed by approval of the Allied Leaders, placed first priority in the war in the Atlantic. By logical consequence, the Pacific war was where America's naval might was put to its greatest test--because it had the lesser support from the home arsenal. And it was in the Pacific where the destiny for which our maritime forces had been forged was finally, and so superlatively, achieved.

Extending into 1944, as those of us who participated knew so well, the Pacific war was fought as a second-class action. The great priority was to save Europe from imminent destruction by Hitler's Nazi Germany. To do this, Hitler had to be beaten immediately, and decisively; to wait would have been disastrous to our allies and, even had the ultimate outcoming been the same, delay would have had incalculable results on the world of today.

So, no strategist that I know of holds that our priorities were not the correct ones. And I have often speculated as to what might have been the result if Hitler, on December 7th or 8th, 1941, had declared his everlasting solidarity with America and wished us all success in the war so suddenly and viciously begun by the naval and air forces of the Empire of Japan. Had Hitler, instead of declaring war upon the United States, seized the moment to mount an all-out effort to turn our full attention toward the Pacific, it is possible he might have succeeded. Certainly, pressures from our West Coast states and the territory of Hawaii would have strongly supported such a development. So also, I feel rather certain, would nearly all of our fighting men in the Pacific (excepting only, and always, those leaders possessed of superior strategic insight or information). The point is that

we did not declare war on Germany until after Germany declared war on us. Would we have done so if Germany had
not?

It was, of course, a monumental miscalculation by Hitler. For about its first three years the Pacific war had to
take second place so far as the United States and her allies
were concerned, while Hitler, to his surprise, got first bill-
ing. New ships, new equipment, improved weapons, went
eastward instead of westward. All were slow in coming to
the Pacific. Come they did, of course, but it was not until
the fourth year of the war that the Pacific fleet sailors--and
their comrades on shore and in the air--were able to achieve
a full appreciation of what they had been missing.

For then it was, with the war in Europe clearly on
the way to victory, that the ponderous weight of America's
strength was turned to the west. Then is when we realized
we had been holding Japan back almost as a rear-guard action while the real effort had been going somewhere else.
But when the turn-around came, it came with suddenness and
extraordinary power. The coiled steel spring, which our
Pacific forces had become, expanded rapidly under the pressures of support of all kinds suddenly lavished upon it. That
we were able to seize upon and make good use of this sudden
largesse, as it arrived, can only be ascribed to excellent
planning by those who knew what to look forward to.

And then, as every student of the history of World
War II knows, our forces simply exploded against an already
badly shaken enemy. There was no denying the all-consum-
ing power of the holocaust we then launched upon the perpetra-
tor of the Pearl Harbor atrocity.

The atom bomb clearly was not necessary; Japan was
already beaten to her knees in August of 1945. We in the
Pacific, who had experienced the whole four years of the war,
now saw the noose we had painfully drawn around Japan tight-
ened to the choking point. We knew the end must be near.
We could not, of course, know Japan was already trying to
surrender--but it took no genius to understand that Japan,
with no ships to ply the seas, no aircraft to fly the skies, no
means of supporting abandoned and starving troops, had come
to the end of her rope.

Much has already been written and much will undoubtedly continue to be written about this greatest of all modern
wars. I believe it was the last great general war the world

will see, for its conclusion ushered in the era of the balance of atomic terror. One result of this has been the creation of limited wars, the resort to "undeclared" wars which can be stopped more easily than declared ones, and the elimination, as evermore too frightful, of the total rupture of intercourse between nations which has characterized warfare for the last century or so. Whole libraries are already devoted to the accumulation of studies about this war. The mind of no man can hope to encompass even all that has already been written. And assuredly more will be added to the list as more old records are unearthed and new scholars make their contributions. To the naval buff, as well as to the serious naval historian, a scholarly compendium of naval source material is of vital importance. To writers of history and to writers of fiction as well, the publication of Myron Smith's World War II at Sea bibliography must rank as a Godsend.

Edward L. Beach
Capt., U. S. Navy (Ret.)
Washington, D. C.

CONTENTS OF VOLUME II

INTRODUCTION

World War II really began for most Americans as the result of the Japanese bombing of their Pacific naval base at Pearl Harbor, Hawaii. What went before had often been regarded as strictly a European conflict or a Sino-Japanese squabble which, except for occasional incidents at sea, seemed far removed. In fact, this was not quite so as is pointed out in The American Navy, 1918-1941, the final volume of the American Naval Bibliography Series (ANBS: five volumes, Scarecrow Press, 1972-1974, covering 1770-1941). The path had been chosen by both the Allies and Japan and in the end, there was nothing left to do but walk it.

In the introduction to The European Theater, Volume I of the World War II at Sea bibliography, the problems of bibliographic control for sea forces and other materials related to the conflict were examined. Such control for English language materials has not been very complete as many well know. [1]

I have long been interested in changing this situation. It seemed unfair and inaccurate to attempt a continuation of the ANBS, segregating Yankee activities from those of other nations in such an all-encompassing holocaust. No longer was it a simple case, in operational terms, of fighting one enemy; America was engaged on a number of fronts against three enemies while at the same time aiding and cooperating with a host of Allies. Thus the decision was taken to concentrate on an entirely new and comprehensive effort. I adopted as my motto the words of Admiral Sir Andrew B. Cunningham, R. N. , before the British attack on Taranto in November 1940: "We are so outnumbered there's only one thing to do. We must attack. "

The result, World War II at Sea: A Bibliography of Sources in English, in three volumes, is intended to provide aid to those seeking information on the sea forces (navies, marines, coast guards, amphibious and special units) of all

the belligerents.   I expect that this set will stand as the most
comprehensive bibliography on any aspect of World War II
ever published in the United States.

The criteria for selections in this compilation are the
same as those employed for the ANBS.   The following types
of published materials are represented: books and monographs,
scholarly papers, and periodical and journal articles.   Numerous U.S. as well as other government documents are cited,
regardless of size, as are doctoral dissertations, masters'
theses, and publications of the various armed services.   A
considerable amount of spade work has also been done in the
area of the yearbook-type unit histories produced by many
ex-servicemen in various Allied nations and those which are
relevant are cited.

A vast amount of printed but not strictly "published"
material exists concerning operations, training, etc., of sea
forces in the war.   Literally thousands of such items were
produced during and after the war, especially in the 1944-
1948 period.   Most of the primary source material of the
war might also be considered in this light, as the bulk of it,
at least that produced by Britons and Americans, was at
least typewritten.

Frankly, it is not possible to include all of these
items here.   I have made a selection of those deemed most
important by authorities and of some, such as the (American)
Cincpac-Cincpoa Bulletins, that had a relatively large circu-
lation.   I have, however, made an effort to demonstrate the
type of material which is available by giving close attention
to one area alone--reports by the U.S. Navy and Marine
Corps on the Guadalcanal campaign.   Those seeking lists of
primary materials on other campaigns, especially in the Pacific, are urged to pay close attention to the bibliographies
in the official U.S. Marine Corps histories and monographs
which are cited in each section of this volume.

Much has been included in this work, but it was necessary to draw the line somewhere.   Excluded materials were:
fiction, obvious childrens' works, newspaper articles (unless
reprinted in anthologies or free standing as special supple-
ments), poetry, and book reviews.   Almost all of these are
worthy of special bibliographies outside the scope of this
set.[2]

What is here is not offered strictly as an aid in cor-

recting deficiencies in our knowledge of certain sources,
though as such it may serve, but primarily as a non-subjec-
tive means of control. Towards this end, annotations of a
non-critical nature will often be supplied to clarify the content or titles of references.

Because of the mass of material available in English
and the excellence of foreign-language bibliographies, it was
early decided to limit coverage to items written in English.
This may seem a folly to some, but I suspect that the bulk
of the users of this work will appreciate this necessary re-
striction. The thousands of entries herein provided come
from the period 1939 through December 1973. If in the future
these volumes are revised, the cut-off date will of course be
extended.

Other features of the ANBS have also been incorporated
here. Each reference receives an entry number. These
numbers will be continued consecutively throughout the three
volumes. The first two volumes each receive an author index
and a name index (people, places, ships). Comprehensive
author and name indexes are then provided for all three volumes at the end of the final volume. The latest imprint date
of published works is indicated by the symbol, "Rpr." As
before, these abbreviations have been used: CurrBio for
Current Biography; SciAmer for Scientific American; and
USNIP for United States Naval Institute Proceedings.

This volume's appendix explores a little-known English-
language source telling of the war from the Japanese viewpoint: The Japanese Monographs.

Within this volume, items will be covered in a series
of alphabetically arranged sections and subsections, each of
these in turn will receive an historical introduction and will
finish with a note guiding the reader, in general, to other
sources of related material within the set.

No tool of this nature, with its inevitable omissions,
can hope to include the efforts of everyone who has ever
written in English on this large topic. To keep abreast of
the newest naval and sea service research, a periodic search
of the latest issues and editions of the following is recommended:

Air University Index to Military Periodicals. Maxwell Air
    Force Base, Ala.: Air University Library, 1949-. V. 1-.

Monthly.
Especially useful for foreign English language naval citations.

Albion, Robert G. Naval and Maritime History: An Annotated
Bibliography. 4th ed. Mystic, Conn.: Marine Historical
Association, 1972. 370p.
As with earlier editions of this subjective work, supple-
ments will undoubtedly be forthcoming from time to
time.

America: History and Life--A Guide to Periodical Literature.
Santa Barbara, Calif.: ABC-CLIO Press, 1964-. V. 1-.
Quarterly.

British Museum. Department of Printed Books. General
Catalog of Printed Books: Additions. London: Clowes,
1963-.
A subject index is published every four years.

Dissertation Abstracts International. Ann Arbor, Mich.:
University Microfilms, 1969-.
Begun over 30 years ago as Dissertation Abstracts; re-
fer to the "A" schedule, "The Humanities and Social
Sciences."

Historical Abstracts: A Quarterly, Covering the World's
Periodical Literature, 1775-1945. Santa Barbara, Calif.:
ABC-CLIO Press, 1955-. V. 1-.
Contains coverage of the United States to 1964 when
America: History and Life was begun. An excellent
source of non-American sea forces references.

"The Military Library." Military Affairs. Washington:
American Military Institute, 1937-. V. 1-. Quarterly.
An excellent source for book reviews and new periodical
article citations, this work now provides an annual up-
dating of Frank Cooling and Alan Millett's Doctoral Dissertations in Military Affairs: A Bibliography (Manhat-
tan: Kansas State University Library, 1972).

"Notable Naval Books of the Year." United States Naval Institute Proceedings. Annapolis: U.S. Naval Institute,
1950-. V. 76-.
Although book reviews are printed in each monthly issue, this outstanding summation is presented only in the
December number.

Readers' Guide to Periodical Literature.   New York: H. W.
Wilson, 1900-.
   It should be noted that any of the Wilson publications of
   a similar nature, such as The Social Science and Humanities Index, are exceptionally useful to students of
   World War II. The Cumulative Book Index is another
   example.

United States. Library of Congress. Library of Congress
Catalog. Books: Subjects. A Cumulative List of Works
Represented by Library of Congress Printed Cards. Wash-
ington: U. S. Government Printing Office, 1950-.
   Quarterly with annual cumulation. Exceedingly useful.

_____. Navy Department. Naval History Division. U. S.
Naval History: A Bibliography, 6th ed. Washington: U. S.
Government Printing Office, 1972. 91p.

Writings on American History: A Bibliography of Books and
Articles on United States History Published During the
Year --. Various publishers, 1902-.
   Unfortunately, no volumes have been compiled for the
   years 1941-1947. At this writing, with one appearing
   almost every year, the latest year covered is 1960.
   Without exception, when available, it must be regarded
   as the preferred tool on American sea forces.

      For those interested in books which will be published,
attention is directed to Forthcoming Books (New York: R. R.
Bowker, 1966-, v. 1-) as well as the preview sections in
that publisher's two periodicals, Library Journal and Publishers Weekly.

      For their advice, assistance, or encouragement in the
formulation, research, and completion of this endeavor, the
following persons and libraries are gratefully acknowledged:

      Dr. K. Jack Bauer, Rensselaer Polytechnic Institute
      Dr. Arthur Funk, University of Florida, Chairman of
         the American Committee on the History of the Second
         World War
      Mr. Fred Meigs, Assistant Librarian, Navy Department
         Library
      Dr. Dean C. Allerd, Head, Operational Archives Divi-
         sion, U. S. Navy Department, Naval History Division
      Mr. Donald Judge, Librarian, G. W. Blunt White Li-
         brary, Mystic Seaport, Connecticut

Mr. Robert H. Land, Chief, Reference Division, Libra-
ry of Congress
Captain T. McDonald, Public Information Section, U.S.
Coast Guard
Dr. Allen R. Millett, Ohio State University
Oberlin College (Ohio) Library
Manchester College (Indiana) Library
Miss Judy Greeson, Librarian, Huntington College (Indi-
ana) Library
Dr. John T. Mason, Jr., Oral History Director, U.S.
Naval Institute
The New York Public Library
Mjr. John C. Short, Jr., Head, Reference Section,
History and Museums Division, Headquarters, U.S.
Marine Corps
Mr. James Scheetz, Editor, Challenge Publications
Rear Admiral Ernest M. Eller, U.S. Navy (Ret.),
Annapolis, Md.
Dr. E. Mowbray Tate, Wake-Forest University
Rear Admiral Frederic Withington, U.S. Navy (Ret.),
Washington, D.C.
Mr. Alexander Kent, Esher, Surrey, England

In compiling this work, I have been in and out of
many libraries and corresponded with others. Most have
been exceptionally courteous and helpful. Dr. B. Franklin
Cooling, Chief of Research Studies, and Miss Joyce L. Eakin,
Assistant Director, Libraries, both of the U.S. Army Military History Research Collection at Carlisle, Pa., deserve
special thanks in this regard.

Special appreciation is reserved for my colleagues
here in Indiana without whose aid this project would still be
awaiting Admiral Cunningham's directive, "attack." Ms.
Martha Braun, Librarian of the Reference and Loan Division
of the Indiana State Library, and her staff have helped me
solve a number of ticklish bibliographic questions. Mr. Fred
J. Reynolds, Director of the Public Library of Ft. Wayne and
Allan County, has continued to provide the gracious encour-
agement and aid which helped me launch earlier efforts.

For their devoted help and understanding, the staff
and board of the Huntington Public Library stand deserv-
ing of my deepest commendation. Former President
Robert E. Smart, a veteran of the New Guinea-Philippine
operations, has been the source of much information,
while former Board President, Mr. Edwin DeWald, a student

of nautical affairs, has also been most helpful.

Myron J. Smith, Jr.
Huntington, Indiana

NOTES

1   I am pleased to note that even as the present work is being prepared, Robin Higham, a bibliographer of illustrious merit, has edited a work called <u>A Guide to the Sources of American Military History</u> (Hamden, Conn. :   Archon, 1975).   It will be a selective work with chapters written by such distinguished colleagues as Dean Allard and Frank Cooling.

2   Works on the naval fiction of the conflict will be found in the forthcoming book, Myron J. Smith, Jr. and Robert C. Weller, <u>Sea Fiction Guide</u> (Metuchen, N. J. :   Scarecrow Press, scheduled for late 1976).

IIA   GENERAL WORKS: PACIFIC THEATER, 1941-1945

Introduction. Confronted in the late 1930's with Japanese ambitions for a New Order in Asia, the United States rearmed at home and endeavored politically to halt what it considered a decline in the Far East. In spite of American opposition, the Japanese pushed ahead with their plans and eventually as we all know, attacked Pearl Harbor on December 7, 1941.

Even before the United States entered the conflict officially, she had held several planning sessions with the British, her probable ally. When--not necessarily if--war broke out in the Pacific, it was agreed that first resources would go to the defeat of the European Axis with the remainder left over committed against the Japanese.

The war in the far Pacific was the largest naval/sea forces campaign undertaken in man's history. The geography of the area being as immense as it is, the forces involved depended on their fleets in almost every detail. Although the fighting ashore was just as intense or more so, nowhere were the battles so huge as in the European Theater.

Following early reverses, the Allies, with the aid of carrier-borne air power, were able to reestablish their "sea power." Following Midway and Guadalcanal, they employed the sea--and their growing strength upon it--to push forcefully towards the island empire of Japan.

The references in this first section encompass the whole of the Pacific Theater. Most are too general or obscure for inclusion in a specific section or subsection.

2680   Abercrombie, Laurence A.   "The Blue Beetle."   USNIP, LXX (1944) 1197-1204.

2681   _____.   "Pacific Life Line: Further Action of the Blue Beetle." USNIP, LXX (1944), 1339-1347.

2682   _____, and Fletcher Pratt.   My Life to the Destroyers.   New York: Holt, 1944.   157p.

As with the citations above, this work constitutes reminiscences by an American destroyer commander concerning "work horse" operations in the Pacific, as told to the noted naval writer.

2683 Adams, Henry H., jt. author. See Nimitz, Chester W., no. 2999.

2684 "Admiral Bull [Halsey] Is Weary." Newsweek, XXVI (October 8, 1945), 60.

2685 "Admiral Halsey Is a Sailor's Sailor." Life, XIV (January 11, 1943), 37-38+.

2686 "Admiral William Halsey Is a Task Force Commander." Life, XII (June 29, 1942), 26-27.
          Halsey was probably the best-known operational officer in the American navy during World War II. It was he who commanded several of the early Allied naval/air raids (cited in IIB-6 below) and later successfully took over command of the Guadalcanal operation. Always an exponent of carrier air power, he employed it brilliantly during the Island Hopping campaigns of 1944, culminating with the giant Battle of Leyte Gulf. A number of his decisions have been questioned since the war, but by-and-large while it was being fought, most Yankee bluejackets were proud to serve with "Bull."

2687 Agnew, Dwight M. "The 'Tireless Tee' Goes Forth to War." USNIP, LXX (1944), 831-841.

2688 Air Group 3. N.p., 1945. 14p.

2689 Air Group 7. N.p., 1945. 132p.

2690 "Air Group 9 Comes Home." Life, XVI (May 1, 1944), 91-97.

2691 Air Group 9 Second Pacific Cruise, March 1944-July 1945, U.S.S. Lexington and U.S.S. Yorktown. Allentown, Pa.: Miers-Bachman, 1945. 88p.

2692 Air Group 20, an Unofficial Portrayal of Carrier Air Group Twenty U.S. Pacific Fleet from Commissioning to Completion of Combat Cruise, 1943-1945: Compiled from Private and Naval Sources in 1949. N.p., 1949. 84p.

2693 Air Squadron Two. Interpron Two, the Record of Our
      Squadron, How We Worked, Lived, and Played.
      N.p., 1945. 140p.
          Cruise book of Photographic Interpretation Squad-
      ron Two based on Guam. All of the last half dozen
      citations are unit "cruise books."

2694 Alexander, Jack. "They Sparked the Carrier Revolu-
      tion: Flying Officers Recently Made Admirals."
      Saturday Evening Post, CCXVII (September 16, 1944),
      9-11.
          Includes portraits and brief biographies.

2695 Allen, Gwenfred E. Hawaii's War Years, 1941-45.
      Honolulu: University of Hawaii Press, 1950. 418p.
      Repr. 1971.
          Before and after Pearl Harbor Sunday.

2696 Allied Forces. Southwest Pacific Area. The Reports
      of MacArthur: Prepared by His General Staff. 2
      vols. in 1. Washington: U.S. Government Print-
      ing Office, 1966.

2697 "American and Allied Strategy in the Far East." Mili-
      tary Review, XXIX (November-December 1949), 22-
      41.
          Quite comprehensive!

2698 Anderson, Orvil A. "Air War in the Pacific." Air-
      power Historian, IV (October 1957), 216-227.
          It should be noted from the outset that despite
      overshadowing in the European Theater Allied army
      and air force units played an important role in the
      war in the Pacific.

2699 Anderson, Robert E., ed. Was This Pastel? N.p.,
      1947. 16p.
          The brief "cruise book" of Navy Air Squadron
      16.

2700 Andrews, Adolphus J. "Admiral With Wings: The
      Career of Joseph Mason Reeves." Unpublished B.A.
      Senior Paper, Princeton University, 1943.

2701 Andrieu d'Albas, Emmanuel M. A. Death of a Navy:
      The Fleets of the Mikado in the Second World War,
      1941-1945. Translated from the French by Anthony

Rippon. London: Robert Hale, 1957. 224p.
Published in America simultaneously by the New
York firm of Devin-Adair in a 362-page edition
under the title, Death of a Navy: Japanese Naval
Action in World War II.

2702 Army Times, Editors of. Pearl Harbor and Hawaii:
A Military History. New York: Walker, 1971.
184p.
Covers the islands' history throughout the war
years.

2703 Arthur, Robert A. and Kenneth Cohlmia. The Third
Marine Division. Washington: Infantry Journal
Press, 1948. 399p.
Action on Bougainville, Guam, and Iwo Jima.

2704 Asprey, Robert B. Semper Fidelis. New York:
Norton, 1967. 293p.
The U.S. Marines in the Pacific War.

2705 Australia. Royal Australian Air Force. R.A.A.F.
Log. Canberra: Australian War Memorial, 1943.
200p.

2706 Avison, George. Uncle Sam's Marines. New York:
Macmillan, 1944. 40p.

2707 Ayling, Keith. Semper Fidelis: The U.S. Marines
in Action. Boston: Houghton, Mifflin, 1943.
194p.

2708 _____. They [Marines] Fly for Victory. New York:
Nelson, 1943. 215p.

2709 Baclagon, Uldarico S. Philippine Campaigns. Manila:
Graphic House, 1952. 388p.
Both the Japanese and American. Should be
used with sections IIB-5 and IIE-3 below.

2710 Bacon, Mary A., editor. See Hunter, Kenneth E.,
no. 2890.

2711 Bahrenburg, Bruce. The Pacific Then and Now: A
Revisiting of the Great Pacific Battlefields of
World War II. New York: G. P. Putnam, 1971.
318p.

2712 Baldwin, Hanson W. "Six Weeks of Naval War." <u>Sea</u>
      <u>Power</u>, (February 1942), 15-16.
      Primarily in the Pacific.

2713 Barnes, William W. "Carrier Pilot." In: William
      H. Fetridge, ed. <u>The Second Navy Reader</u>. In-
      dianapolis: Bobbs-Merrill, 1944. p. 252-259.
      Rpr. 1971.

2714 Bartlett, Donald. "Vice Admiral Chuichi Hara: Un-
      forgetable Foe." <u>USNIP</u>, XCVI (1970), 49-55.
      A Japanese carrier admiral active in the Coral
      Sea and Guadalcanal campaigns.

2715 Bateson, Charles. <u>The War With Japan: A Concise</u>
      <u>History</u>. East Lansing: Michigan State University
      Press, 1968. 417p.

2716 Batten, Loring W., 3rd. "Lest We Forget." <u>USNIP</u>,
      LXXIII (1947), 948-951.
      An account of the American escort carrier <u>Long</u>
      <u>Island</u> (CVE-1), which saw considerable action in
      the Pacific.

2717 <u>Battle Diary of</u> [U. S. Navy] <u>Patrol Bombing Squadron</u>
      <u>121, 5 September 1944 to 5 September 1945</u>. San
      Diego, Calif. Frye & Smith, 1945. 55p.
      That unit's "cruise book."

2718 "Battle of the Pacific." <u>Time</u>, XLI (January 18, 1943),
      26-29.
      A roundup of operations then underway.

2719 Befeler, Murray, jt. editor. <u>See</u> Hodge, Clarence L.,
      no. 2873.

2720 Bell, Frederick J. <u>Condition Red: Destroyer Action</u>
      <u>in the South Pacific</u>. New York: Longmans,
      Green, 1943. 274p.
      A combination of personal experiences and in-
      formation on the routine, crews, and operations of
      American destroyers in the early days of the
      Pacific War, with special emphasis on the Solomons
      campaign.

2721 Bergamini, David. <u>Japan's Imperial Conspiracy</u>. New
      York: Pocket Books, 1972. 1,364p.

A huge paperback telling the war from the
Japanese viewpoint.

2722 The Best Damn Heavy Bomber Unit in the World, the
      Jolly Rogers, Southwest Pacific, 1942-1944. Syd-
      ney, Australia: John Sands, 1944. 112p.
      "Cruise book" of an American Army Air Force
      group.

2723 "The Black Panthers. " Air Classics, II (March-April
      1965), 32-38.
      The story of Navy Attack Squadron 35 flying off
      carriers in the Pacific war.

2724 Bliven, Bruce. From Pearl Harbor to Okinawa: The
      War in the Pacific, 1941-1945. Landmark Books.
      New York: Random House, 1960. 192p.

2725 Boswell, Rolfe. Leathernecks: Our Marines in Fact
      and Picture. New York: Crowell, 1943. 194p.

2726 Bradshaw, Harvey D. "Marine Corps Aviation: Cun-
      ningham to Cu Lai. " USNIP, XCII (1966), 106-123.

2727 Brady, Parke H. "A Fighting Crew Wins Softer
      Bunks With Admiral Nimitz's Assent. " Navy, XII
      (April 1969), 17-19.

2728 Braun, Saul. Seven Heroes: Medal of Honor Stories
      of the War in the Pacific. New York: G. P.
      Putnam, 1965. 224p.
      The seven include: Capt. Henry Elrod, Marine
      Fighter Squadron 211; Sgt. Mitchell Paige on Gua-
      dalcanal; Lt. Cmdr. Bruce McCandless, U.S.S.
      San Francisco, off Guadalcanal; Lt. Robert Hanson,
      Marine Fighter Squadron 215; Lt. Arthur M. Pres-
      ton, PT Squadron 33; Lt. Cmdr. Eugene Fluckey,
      of the submarine U.S.S. Barb; and Fr. Joseph
      O'Callahan, of the carrier Franklin.

2729 Brodie, Bernard. "The Naval Strategy of the Pacific
      War. " Infantry Journal, LVII (August 1945), 34-39.

2730 _____. "Our Ships Strike Back. " Virginia Quarterly
      Review, XXI (April 1945), 186-206.

2731 _____. "The Revolution in the Pacific. " Virginia
      Quarterly Review, XX (October 1944), 496-510.

2732   "The Brood of Noisy Nan: The Marine Air Force."
       Time, XLIII (June 12, 1944), 71.

2733   Bryan, Joseph, 3rd. "Four-Star Sea Dog: The Com-
       mander of Our South Pacific Fleet." Saturday
       Evening Post, CCXVI (December 25, 1943-January
       1, 1944), 28-29+, 26+.
       Admiral Halsey.

2734   The Buccaneers of [U. S. Navy] Bombing Squadron 104:
       The Story of Its First Tour, 10 April 1943-15 April
       1944. Wichita, Kansas: McCormick-Armstrong,
       1944. 38p.
            The story of this unit's second tour, covering
       June 1, 1944-June 1, 1945, was published by an
       unknown printer in a 36-page booklet in 1945.

2735   Buchanan, A. R., ed. The Navy's Air War, a Mis-
       sion Completed. New York: Harper, 1946. 432p.
            Written with the aid and co-operation of the
       Aviation History Unit, OP-5198, in the Office of
       the Assistant Chief of Naval Operations (Air).

2736   Buggy, Hugh. Pacific Victory: A Short History of
       Australia's Part in the War Against Japan. Issued
       Under the Direction and by Authority of the Austral-
       ian Minister for Information. North Melbourne:
       Victorian Railway Print Works, 1945. 301p.

2737   Burke, Arleigh A. "An Evening with Admiral Burke."
       Unpublished paper, Individual Personnel File, U. S.
       Navy Department, Naval History Division, Opera-
       tional Archives, 1968. 43p.
            An interview conducted by Professor Langdon of
       the U. S. Naval Academy which touches on many
       aspects of the noted destroyer commander's service
       in the Pacific.

2738   Burrus, L. D., ed. The Ninth Marines: A Brief
       History of the Ninth Marine Regiment. Washington:
       Infantry Journal Press, 1946. 375p.
            Action on Bougainville, Guam, and Iwo Jima.

2739   Caidin, Martin, jt. author. See Okumiya, Masatake,
       no. 3008.

2740   _____., jt. author. See Sakai, Saburo, no. 3083.

2741   Cant, Gilbert. The Great Pacific Victory from the
       Solomons to Tokyo. New York: John Day, 1946.
       422p.

2742   _____. "Nimitz." Asia, XLV (July 1945), 339-342.
       In the high-command shuffle which followed
       Pearl Harbor, Texas-born Chester W. Nimitz was
       appointed C-in-C of the Pacific Fleet. In that
       position, and later as chief of the Pacific Ocean
       Area (making him an equal of General Douglas
       MacArthur), the admiral demonstrated strategic
       brilliance in directing the American drive toward
       Japan via the Central Pacific. Despite his awe-
       some responsibilities, this soft-spoken sailor was
       not without a sense of humor. When asked one
       day why a ship is always referred to in the femi-
       nine, he replied: "A ship is always referred to
       as 'she' because it costs so much to keep her in
       paint and powder." When Japan surrendered in
       1945, Nimitz signed the instruments of capituala-
       tion as America's representative. According to
       Admiral Morison, the admiral "probably inspired
       a greater personal loyalty than did any other ad-
       miral in the war."

2743   _____. War on Japan. I. P. R. Pamphlets. New
       York: American Council, Institute of Pacific Re-
       lations, 1945. 64p.
       A brief review of American battles, campaigns,
       and strategy in the Pacific, 1941-1945.

2744   Carlisle, Norman V. The Marines in Review. New
       York: E. P. Dutton, 1943. 192p.

2745   Carmichael, George K. "The Strategical Employment
       of Allied Naval Forces in the Pacific During World
       War II." Unpublished paper, Individual Personnel
       File, U. S. Navy Department, Naval History Divi-
       sion, Operational Archives, 1950. 20p.
       A March 1950 lecture delivered before students
       of the Naval War College on the strategic back-
       ground and execution of the war in the Pacific.

2746   Carnegie, Dale. "He Knows How to Handle Ships,
       Japs, and Wives." In: his Dale Carnegie's Bio-
       graphical Roundup. New York: Greenberg, 1944.
       p. 127-132.
       Admiral Nimitz.

2747 Carrier Air Group 86. New York: North River Press,
      1946. 140p.
      This and the next two citations are "cruise
      books. "

2748 Carrier Air Group 9, U.S.S. Essex: The Record of
      the First Two Years from Forming the Air Group
      in March 1942 to the Return from Action Against
      the Enemy in March 1944. Chicago: Lakeside
      Press, 1945. 119p.

2749 Carrier Air Group Ten, September 15, 1944 to Novem-
      ber 26, 1945, Aboard U.S.S. Intrepid, February
      18, 1945 to October 14, 1945. Los Angeles:
      Metropolitan Engravers, 1946. 174p.

2750 Casey, Robert J. This Is Where I Came In. India-
      napolis: Bobbs-Merrill, 1945. 307p.
      Sequel to the next entry.

2751 _____. Torpedo Junction: With the Pacific Fleet
      from Pearl Harbor to Midway. Indianapolis:
      Bobbs-Merrill, 1942. 423p.
      A correspondent's account, in diary form, of
      the seven months following December 7.

2752 Catton, Bruce. "The Marine Tradition. " American
      Heritage, X (February 1959), 24-35, 68-90.

2753 Cave, Hugh B. , jt. author. See Morris, Colton G. ,
      no. 2982.

2754 Chamberlain, John, jt. author. See Willoughby,
      Charles A. , no. 3263.

2755 Chapin, John C. "The Fourth Marine Division in
      World War II. " Unpublished paper, USMC File,
      U. S. Navy Department, Naval History Division,
      Operational Archives, 1945. 53p.
      Contains command and staff personnel and or-
      ganizational tables, as well as battle accounts of
      the outfit on Kwajalein, Saipan, Tinian, and Iwo
      Jima. A printed version of 89 pages was issued
      by the Historical Division of the Marine Corps
      the same year.

2756 _____. "History of the 4th Marine Division. "

Leatherneck, XXIX (April 1946), 20-21+.
A condensation of the above account.

2757 "Chester W. Nimitz. " CurrBio:III:39-41.

2758 Chevigny, Herbert. "Brother Leatherneck: The Monk
      Who Became a Marine. " Collier's, CXVI (Septem-
      ber 8, 1945), 24+.
      Abridged in Catholic Digest, IX (October 1945),
      87-93.

2759 "The Chief Shot a Seagull While Sharing a Life Raft
      With His Captain in the Pacific. " A. F. Times,
      XVI (February 4, 1956), 48.

2760 Childs, F. N. "Reap the Whirlwind. " USNIP,
      LXVIII (1942), 1552-1554.
      Naval air combat.

2761 Churchill, Allen. "Square-Cut Diamond. " In: Louis
      L. Snyder, ed. Masterpieces of War Reporting.
      New York: Julian Messner, 1962. p. 306-309.
      The story of Marine Master Gunnery Sergeant
      Leland Diamond as told by a Navy reporter in the
      November 7, 1943, issue of Yank, the Army
      Weekly.

2762 Churchill, Winston S. "Full Aid to the United States
      Against Japan: Address Before Congress, May
      19, 1943. " Vital Speeches, IX (June 1, 1943),
      482-487.
      Reprinted in Current History, New Series IV
      (June 1943), 262-270.

2763 Clark, Joseph J. and Clark G. Reynolds. Carrier
      Admiral. New York: David McKay, 1967. 333p.
      The autobiography of "Jocko" Clark, of whom
      Admiral Morison has said: ". . . part Cherokee
      Indian and part Southern Methodist, but all fighter.
      A picturesque character who looked more like a
      western desperado than a naval officer, he knew
      his business thoroughly and had more than his
      share of energy and dogged determination. "

2764 Coffey, Thomas M. Imperial Tragedy: Japan in
      World War II, The First Days and the Last.
      Cleveland: World Publishing, 1970. 531p.

2765 Cohlmia, Kenneth, jt. author. See Arthur, Robert A.,
      no. 2650.

2766 Collier, Basil. The War in the Far East, 1941-1945.
      New York: William Morrow, 1969. 530p.

2767 Columbia Broadcasting System. From Pearl Harbor
      Into Tokyo. New York, 1945. 22p.
      Excerpts from documented broadcasts of the
      Pacific war as transmitted into American homes,
      taken verbatim from the company's records.

2768 Composite Squadron Sixty-Three Cruise Book, August
      1944-October 1945. Baton Rouge, La.: Army &
      Navy Publishing Co., 1946. 47p.

2769 Condit, Kenneth W. and Edwin T. Turnbladh. Hold
      High the Torch: A History of the 4th Marines.
      Washington: Historical Branch, U.S. Marine
      Corps, 1960. 330p.
      Action from Bataan to Okinawa.

2770 Congdon, Donald, ed. Combat: The War With Japan.
      New York: Dell, 1962. 384p.
      Part of a larger set cited in Volume III.

2771 Conley, Cornelius W. "The Great Japanese Balloon
      Offensive." Air University Review, XIX (1968),
      68-83.
      A useless attempt to bomb the American main-
      land by launching large balloons, carrying high
      explosive, into the air currents circulating from
      Japan.

2772 Conner, Howard M. The Spearhead: The World War
      II History of the 5th Marine Division. Washington:
      Infantry Journal Press, 1950. 325p.

2773 Conner, John. "Cannoneers Post!" Leatherneck,
      XXVII (December 1944), 40-44.
      A brief history, to that time, of Marine artillery
      in the Pacific.

2774 Corkin, Frank R. Pacific Postmark: A Series of
      Letters from Abroad and Aboard a Fighting De-
      stroyer in the War Waters of the Pacific. Hart-
      ford, Conn.: Case, 1945. 172p.

The author was a lieutenant aboard U.S.S.
Ellet (DD-398).

2775 Craig, William. The Fall of Japan. New York: Dial
Press, 1967. 368p.
Contains excellent information relative to the
last two sections of this work.

2776 Craige, John H. "The Marines." In: William H.
Fetridge, ed. The Second Navy Reader. Indianapolis: Bobbs-Merrill, 1944. p. 311-319. Rpr.
1971.

2777 _____ . What the Citizen Should Know About the Marines. New York: Norton, 1941. 211p.

2778 Crane, Aimée, ed. Marines at War. New York:
Scribner, 1943. 124p.
Paintings and sketches by men of the Corps,
preceded by a biographical index.

2779 Crowell, Philip A., jt. author. See Isely, Jeter A.,
no. 2894.

2780 Crowley, Leo T. "Arms Across the Sea." Leatherneck, XXVII (May 1944), 18-19.

2781 Crump, Irving. Our Marines. New York: Dodd,
Mead, 1944. 236p.

2782 Daniel, Hawthorne. Islands of the Pacific. New
York: G. P. Putnam, 1943. 228p.

2783 Davis, Burke. Marine: The Life of Lt. Gen. Lewis
B. (Chesty) Puller, U.S.M.C. (Ret.). Boston:
Little, Brown, 1962. 230p.
The general was noted for his commands on
Guadalcanal, New Britain, and Peleliu.

2784 Davis, Russell. Marine at War. Boston: Little,
Brown, 1961. 258p.
Memoirs of service with the 2nd Battalion, 1st
Marines, especially during the Peleliu and Okinawa
campaigns.

2785 DeChant, John A. "Devilbirds." Marine Corps Gazette,
XXXI (February-November 1947), 10-16, 18-26, 32-
40, 20-32, 27-35, 52-58, 34-45, 36-46, 46-57, 32-38.

2786 _____. Devilbirds: The Story of United States Marine
        Corps Aviation in World War II. New York: Harp-
        er, 1947. 265p.

2787 _____., jt. author. See Hubler, Richard G., no.
        2889.

2788 "The Decisive Role of the U.S. Navy in Destroying the
        Japanese Fleet." U.S. News & World Report, XX
        (May 10, 1946), 18-19.

2789 De M. C. Crane, John. The United States Marines.
        Baton Rouge, La.: Army & Navy Publishing Co.,
        1952. 72p.
        A pictorial history offered under the auspices
        of the Marine Corps War Memorial Foundation.

2790 Dickinson, Clarence E. The Flying Guns: Cockpit
        Record of a Naval Pilot from Pearl Harbor Through
        Midway. In Collaboration With Boyden Sparkes.
        New York: Scribner's, 1942. 196p.
        The naval lieutenant-author was aboard the
        American carrier Enterprise, absent from Pearl
        Harbor at the time of the December 7 attack;
        however, in the next six months, he saw action in
        the raids on the Marshall Islands, Wake and
        Marcus, and in the great battle of Midway.
        Abridged in the Saturday Evening Post, the book
        records only events the pilot saw with little refer-
        ence to grand strategy.

2791 Dieckmann, Edward A. "Manila John Basilone."
        Marine Corps Gazette, XLVII (October 1963), 28-
        32.
        Biography of Gunnery Sergeant Basilone, who
        was awarded the Congressional Medal of Honor for
        gallantry on Guadalcanal and the Navy Cross (post-
        humously) for his service on Iwo Jima.

2792 Dobbin, J. F. "What Counts: Excerpts from a
        Letter." Scholastic, XLI (January 18, 1943), 2.
        The correspondent was the author's son, a
        Marine serving "somewhere" in the South Pacific.

2793 Doe, Jens A. "Notes on Jungle Warfare." Marine
        Corps Gazette, XXVIII (February 1944), 31-36.
        Written by a Marine Brigadier General who had
        seen much of it.

2794 Doll, Thomas E. Flying Leathernecks of World War
       II. Fallbrook, Calif.: Aero Publishers, 1971.
       94p.

2795 "The Domain of the U.S. Navy: On the Beachhead
       with the Marines." Navy, III (May 1960), 27+.
       With many examples drawn from and relative
       to this volume.

2796 Douglas-Allison, A. J. "Voyage of the Fukkai Maru,
       a Japanese Prison Ship." Blackwood's, CCLIX
       (February 1946), 135-143.

2797 Drake, Francis V. Vertical Warfare. Garden City,
       N.Y.: Doubleday, Doran, 1943. 141p.
       A heavily-illustrated work containing consider-
       able information on U.S.A.A.F. operations against
       Japanese shipping and bases in the Pacific.

2798 Driscoll, Joseph. "The Admiral of the Reopened Sea."
       Saturday Evening Post, CCXVI (April 8, 1944),
       24-25+.
       Admiral Nimitz.

2799 _____. Pacific Victory. Philadelphia: Lippincott,
       1944. 297p.
       Reminiscences of the New York Herald-Tribune
       correspondent accredited to the Pacific Fleet.
       Written with a distinct U.S.N. bias, the author
       has little good to say about the American Army,
       and General MacArthur in particular. Many hu-
       morous, human-interest stories are included, such
       as the story of the destroyer ficticiously named
       Frustrate, which always seemed to miss impending
       actions.

2800 Dyer, George C. The Amphibians Came to Conquer:
       The Story of Admiral Richmond Kelly Turner. 2
       vols. Washington: U.S. Government Printing
       Office, 1972.
       Although he made several errors, the admiral
       was a "prince" of amphibious warfare. After see-
       ing action in the Solomons, he became chief of
       "VPhib" and thereafter directed many of the land-
       ing operations of Nimitz's command. Of him, Ad-
       miral Morison has written: "Kelly Turner was an
       amazingly meticulous, thorough and accurate planner

for his own amphibious operations, and oversaw
every detail himself. Once Turner gave the word
to 'Land the Landing Force!' everything went like
clockwork...."

2801 Edmonds, Walter E.   They Fought With What They
      Had. Boston: Little, Brown, 1951. 532p.
      U. S. A. A. F. operations in the Pacific war,
      which as viewed during the Guadalcanal campaign
      for example, were often undertaken in support of
      "naval" objectives.

2802 Eichelberger, Robert L.   Dear Miss 'Em: General
      Eichelberger's War in the Pacific, 1942-1945.
      Edited by Jay Luvaas.   Contributions in Military
      History, no. 2. Westport, Conn.: Greenwood
      Press, 1972. 322p.
      From his post as Superintendent of the Military
      Academy, the general went to the Pacific in 1942
      to serve under MacArthur. During 1943, he saw
      service in New Guinea where he won victory at
      Buna. In September 1944, he was given command
      of the American 8th Army and led it during the
      reconquest of the Philippines.

2803 Eyre, James K. , Jr.   The Roosevelt-MacArthur Con-
      flict. Chambersburg, Pa.: Craft Press, 1950.
      234p.
      An account of the general's struggles to gain his
      own views in Pacific strategy.

2804 _____. "The Sea Campaign from Australia to the
      Philippines. " USNIP, LXXII (1946), 538-551.

2805 Fahey, James J.   Pacific War Diary, 1942-1945.
      Boston: Houghton, Mifflin, 1963. 404p. Rpr.
      1973.
      Based on the author's experiences aboard the
      U. S. S. Montpelier (CL-57).

2806 Falk, Edwin A.   From Perry to Pearl Harbor, the
      Struggle for Supremacy in the Pacific. New York:
      Doubleday, 1943. 362p.
      Contains limited data on the sea war from Pearl
      Harbor through Midway.

2807 Falk, Stanley L.   "Japanese Strategy in World War II."
      Military Review, XLII (June 1962), 70-81.

2808   Farley, Edward I.   P. T.   Patrol: Wartime Adventures
         in the Pacific and the Story of PT's in World War
         II.   New York: Exposition Press, 1957.   106p.

2809   Ferre, Edward, Jr.   "Trade Winds: On Active Duty
         With the Marines in the Pacific."   Saturday Review
         of Literature, XXVIII (June 2, 1945), 18.

2810   Field, J. A., Jr.   "Admiral [Isoroku] Yamamoto."
         USNIP, LXXV (1949), 1105-1113.
            A study of the man most Americans still hold
         responsible for the Pearl Harbor attack.   As
         C-in-C of the Japanese fleet, it was he who order-
         ed the advance on Midway in June 1942, which
         ended in disaster for the Imperial Navy.   This
         admiral also ordered the active defense of Guadal-
         canal--at times a very "iffy" affair for both sides.
         On April 17, 1943, American forces picked up
         radio signals which indicated that Yamamoto would
         be making an inspection tour in the forward area
         the following day.   A flight of P-38's was duly dis-
         patched and shot down the enemy naval leader.
         In the end, the thesis which this intelligent Japanese
         sailor put forth in 1940 came to pass, namely that
         because of American production rates, Japan would
         lose the war.

2811   The 5th [U. S. A. A. F.] Over the Southwest Pacific.
         Los Angeles: A. A. F. Publications, 1947.   40p.

2812   Finch, Percy, jt. author.   See Smith, Holland M.,
         no. 3105.

2813   "The First Marine Division."   Marine Corps Gazette,
         XLV (June 1961), 50-54.
            A brief history of this unit which first gained
         fame on Guadalcanal.

2814   "The Flying Grease-Monkeys of the Navy."   Popular
         Mechanics, LXXIX (March 1943), 56-61.

2815   Forester, Cecil S.   "Miracle in the Pacific: The Of-
         fice of Naval Operations."   Saturday Evening Post,
         CCXVII (December 30, 1944-January 6, 1945), 18-
         19+, 35+.

2816   Forgy, Howell M.   "... and Pass the Ammunition."
         D. Appleton-Century, 1944.   242p.

The lives and fights of the men aboard the
cruiser New Orleans (CA-32), from Pearl Harbor
through the Solomons campaign.

2817 Forrestel, Emmet P. Admiral Raymond A. Spruance,
      U. S. N. : A Study in Command. Washington: U. S.
      Government Printing Office, 1966. 276p.
         A brilliant tactical leader, this Hoosier-born ad-
      miral won two of the three most decisive naval
      battles of the Pacific war. At Midway, when Ad-
      miral Frank J. Fletcher's carrier Yorktown was
      put out of action, Spruance took charge of battle
      operations and launched his planes at just the right
      time to do maximum damage to Yamamoto's fleet.
      For the next year, the admiral served as Admiral
      Nimitz's Chief of Staff, where he helped plan much
      of the "island-hopping" strategy. After successful
      operations in the Gilberts, Marshalls, Task Force
      58 of his Central Pacific Fleet, under another able
      leader, Marc Mitscher, won the overwhelming
      victory of the June 19-20, 1944, Battle of the
      Philippine Sea, or "The Great Marianas Turkey
      Shoot. " In February 1945, this soft spoken sailor
      directed the first carrier air strike on Tokyo and
      off Okinawa, he never faltered in the face of Japa-
      nese kamikazes. Of him, Admiral Morison has
      said: "When we come to the admirals who command-
      ed at sea, and who directed a great battle, there
      was no one to equal Spruance. " For the latest
      biography of Spruance readers should note T. B.
      Buell's The Quiet Warrior (Boston: Little, Brown,
      1974).

2818 Foster, John M. Hell in the Heavens. New York:
      G. P. Putnam, 1961. 320p.
         The author served with Marine Fighter Squadron
      (VMF) 222.

2819 Francillon, René J. U. S. Army Air Forces in the
      Pacific. Fallbrook, Calif. : Aero Publishers,
      1969. 96p.
         Largely pictorial.

2820 Frank, Gerold, jt. editor. See Horan, James D. ,
      no. 2877.

2821 From Dobodura to Okinawa: History of the 308th

Bombardment Wing [U. S. A. A. F.] San Angelo,
Texas: Newsfoto, 1946. 98p.
A "cruise book. "

2822 Fujila, Nobuo. "I Bombed the U. S. A. " USNIP,
LXXXVII (1961), 64.

2823 Fukuda, Teizaburo. "A Mistaken War. " USNIP,
XCIV (1968), 42-48.
On the opposition of some Japanese naval lead-
ers to war with the United States.

2824 Fuller, Curtis. "Air Marines. " Flying, XXXIII
(December 1943), 24-25+.

2825 Gallagher, Barrett. Flattop. Garden City, N. Y.:
Doubleday, 1959. 126p.
Pacific aircraft carrier operations.

2826 Gallagher, James P. "Operation 'Save-a-Jack. '"
American Aviation Historical Society Journal, XVIII
(Summer 1973), 115-116.
Carried out in the South Pacific.

2827 Gault, Own. "How [Navy] Bombing 17 Tamed the
Beast. " Air Classics, VIII (April 1972), 10-15,
48-53.
The use of the Curtiss SB2C "Helldiver" dive-
bomber in the Pacific war, 1943-1945.

2828 Genda, Minoru. "Tactical Planning in the Imperial
Japanese Navy. " Naval War College Review, XXII
(October 1969), 45-50.
A March 7, 1969 talk given before students of
the U. S. Naval War College, Newport, R. I.

2829 Gilbert, Price, Jr. , comp. The Escort Carriers in
Action: The Story in Pictures of the Escort Car-
rier Force, U. S. Pacific Fleet, 1945, With a
Supplement for the Flagship U. S. S. Makin Island
[CVE-93]. Atlanta: Ruralist Press, 1946. 228p.

2830 Gill, George H. Royal Australian Navy, 1939-1942.
Canberra: Australian War Memorial, 1957. 686p.
Contains data on its cooperation with Allied
fleet units in 1942 against hopeless odds, as well
as the exploits of individual units in the Mediterranean (Volume I, Section ID-1).

2831 Gillespie, Oliver A. The Pacific: Official History of
      New Zealand in the Second World War, 1939-45.
      Wellington: War History Branch, Department of
      Internal Affairs, 1952. 395p.
         Contains, for example, much data on NZ armed
      forces association with American naval and marine
      forces during the Solomons campaign, as well as a
      section on the famed "Coastwatchers."

2832 Glover, Cato D. Command Performance--With Guts!
      New York: Greenwich Book Publishing Co., 1969.
      215p.
         The admiral's autobiography in which he describes
      his role in the Pacific war--executive commander
      of U.S.S. Saratoga during the Guadalcanal campaign,
      commander of the escort carrier Barnes, Admiral
      Nimitz's Assistant War Plans Officer, 1943-1944,
      commander of the "Big E," U.S.S. Enterprise,
      1944, and Head of the Pacific Planning Section,
      Plans Division of Headquarters COMINCH (Admiral
      Ernest J. King), 1945.

2833 Goodman, Warren H. "The First Marine Aircraft
      Wing." Unpublished paper, U.S.M.C. File, U.S.
      Navy Department, Naval History Division, Opera-
      tional Archives, n.d. 9p.
         The unit's actions at Guadalcanal, New Georgia,
      Bougainville, and Rabaul.

2834 _____. "Marine Corps Aviation in World War II:
      December 7, 1941-December 7, 1944." Unpub-
      lished paper, U.S.M.C. File, U.S. Navy Depart-
      ment, Naval History Division, Operational Archives,
      1945. 15p.

2835 _____. "One Job--One Corps." Marine Corps
      Gazette, XXVIII (November 1944), 22-24.
         Marine close air support of "dirt" Marines.

2836 _____. "The Second Marine Aircraft Wing." Unpub-
      lished paper, U.S.M.C. File, U.S. Navy Depart-
      ment, Naval History Division, Operational Archives,
      n.d. 11p.
         The unit saw action at Wake, Midway, Guadal-
      canal, and New Georgia.

2837 Goodwin, Hal. "SCAT! The South Pacific Combat Air
      Transport." In: Norman Carlisle, ed. The Air

Forces Reader. Indianapolis: Bobbs-Merrill,
1944. p. 380-385.
Reprinted from the March 1944 issue of Skyways.

2838 Gordon, Gary. The Rise and Fall of the Japanese
Empire. Derby, Conn.: Monarch Books, 1962.
236p.

2839 Gordon, Oliver L. Fight It Out. London: Kimber,
1957. 238p.
Reminiscences of the Pacific war.

2840 Great Britain. Admiralty. Ocean Front: The Story
of the War in the Pacific, 1941-1944. London:
H. M. Stationery Office, 1945. 65p.

2841 _____. _____. Naval Intelligence Division. The
Netherlands East Indies. Geographical Handbook
Series. 2 vols. London: H. M. Stationery Office,
1944.

2842 _____. _____. _____. Pacific Islands. Geographical
Handbook Series. 3 vols. London: H. M. Stationery Office, 1942-1945.

2843 _____. Colonial Office. Among Those Present: The
Official Story of the Pacific Islands at War. London: H. M. Stationery Office, 1946. 95p.
Concerns only those under British or Commonwealth
jurisdiction.

2844 Greene, F. T. "Mess Boy of Squadron X." In:
William H. Fetridge, ed. The Second Navy Reader.
Indianapolis: Bobbs-Merrill, 1944. p. 259-265.
Rpr. 1971.
Reprinted from a 1943 issue of This Week maga-
zine.

2845 Griffin, Alexander. Here Come the Marines: The
Story of the Devil Dogs from Tripoli to Wake Island. New York: Howell, Soskin, 1942. 219p.

2846 Guevara, Edith. "Paramarines Hit Hard and Hit
Often." Travel, LXXXI (September 1943), 26-30.

2847 Gunnison, R. A. "Postgrad All Americans, Pacific
Chapter: Footballers in PT's." Collier's, CXIV
(December 16, 1944), 27.

2848 Hailey, Foster B. "Fighting Marines." New York
      Times Magazine, (November 7, 1943), 11+.

2849 _____. "Master of the Pacific Chessboard." New
      York Times Magazine, (February 27, 1944), 9+.
      Admiral Nimitz.

2850 _____. Pacific Battle Line. New York: Macmillan,
      1944. 405p.
      A straightforward narrative of the Pacific War's
      first two years, especially Guadalcanal, as seen
      by the New York Times correspondent.

2851 _____. "Well Done, a Toast for Navy Day." New
      York Times Magazine, (October 24, 1943), 6-7.

2852 Hall, Basil. "The Mind and the Sword." Army
      Quarterly, XC (April 1965), 69-76.
      A British view of Japanese sea forces operations.

2853 Halsey, William F. Admiral Halsey's Story. New
      York: Whittlesey House, McGraw-Hill, 1947. 310p.

2854 _____. "Admiral Halsey Tells His Story." Saturday
      Evening Post, CCXIX (September 18-25, 1948),
      15-17+, 38-39+.
      Readers should also consult Benis M. Frank's
      new Halsey in Ballantine's Illustrated History of
      World War II (New York: Ballantine Books, 1974,
      160p.).

2855 _____. "Year of War in the South Pacific." USNIP,
      LXX (1944), 84-85.

2856 Hammel, Eric M. and John E. Lane. "Third Day on
      Red Beach." Marine Corps Gazette, LIV (Novem-
      ber 1970), 22-26.

2857 Hara, Tameichi, Fred Saito, and Roger Pineau. Jap-
      anese Destroyer Captain. New York: Ballantine
      Books, 1961. 311p.
      Autobiography of the former throughout the
      Pacific war.

2858 Hastings, Robert F. Privateer in the Coconut Navy.
      Los Angeles, 1946. 105p.
      Concerns Navy Air Squadron 106.

2859 Haugland, Vern. The A. A. F. Against Japan. New
       York: Harper, 1948. 515p.

2860 Hayashi, Saburo with Alvin D. Cox. Kogun: The
       Japanese Army in the Pacific War. Quantico, Va.:
       Marine Corps Association, 1959. 249p.
       Contains appropriate comments on sea forces
       activities, both Japanese and Allied, as well as a
       study of what the Allies were up against as they
       reconquered the Pacific.

2861 Hayes, Grace P. "The History of the Joint Chiefs of
       Staff in World War II: The War Against Japan."
       Unpublished paper, JCS File, U. S. Navy Depart-
       ment, Naval History Division, Operational Archives,
       1954. 952p.

2862 Hayes, John D. "Admiral Joseph Mason Reeves,
       U. S. N. (1872-1948)." Naval War College Review,
       XXIII (November 1970), 48-57; XXIV (January
       1972), 50-64.

2863 Heinl, Robert D. Soldiers of the Sea: A Definitive
       History of the U. S. Marine Corps, 1775-1962.
       Annapolis: U. S. Naval Institute, 1962. 693p.

2864 Hendryx, Gene. Semper Fi! The Story of the 9th
       Marines. New York: Pageant Press, 1959.

2865 Hess, Gary R. America Encounters India, 1941-47.
       Baltimore: Johns Hopkins University Press, 1971.
       211p.

2866 Hessler, William H. "The Carrier Task Force in
       World War II." USNIP, LXXI (1945), 1271-1281.

2867-2868 [No entries.]

2869 High, Stanley. "Nimitz Fires When He Is Ready."
       Rotarian, LXII (April 1943), 29-30+.
           Abridged in Reader's Digest, XLII (April 1943),
       58-62.

2870 _____. "Why a Marine is a Secret Weapon." Read-
       er's Digest, XLIV (January 1944), 104-109.

2871 "High Admiral." Newsweek, XX (November 30, 1942),
       23.

William F. Halsey.

2872 "History of the Far East Air Forces." Unpublished
      paper, Files of the Air University Library, Max-
      well Air Force Base, Alabama, n. d.

2873 Hodge, Clarence L. and Murray Befeler, eds. Pearl
      Harbor to Tokyo. Honolulu: Tongg, 1945. 156p.
      A pictorial history of the Pacific war.

2874 Holcomb, Thomas. "The Amazing Marines: Their
      Own Story." Navy, (January 1, 1943), 22-24.

2875 "Holland M. Smith." CurrBio:VI:556-558.
      A top Marine general active from Tarawa
      through Iwo Jima.

2876 Hopkins, Harold. Nice to Have You Aboard: A Per-
      sonal Account of the War in the Pacific, 1943-1945,
      by a British Officer Attached to the U.S. Pacific
      Fleet. London: Ian Allan, 1964. 217p.

2877 Horan, James D. and Gerold Frank, eds. Out in the
      Boondocks: Marines in Action in the Pacific, 21
      U.S. Marines Tell Their Stories. New York: G.
      P. Putnam, 1943. 209p.

2878 Horikoshi, Jiro, jt. author. See Okumiya, Masatake,
      no. 3008.

2879 "Hospital Plane Rescue." In: Norman Carlisle, ed.
      The Air Forces Reader. Indianapolis: Bobbs-Mer-
      rill, 1944. p. 320-321.
      The rescue of 20 downed Marines from a Douglas
      C-53 as related in the pages of Douglas Airview
      for December 1942.

2880 Hough, Frank O. The Island War: The United States
      Marine Corps in the Pacific. Philadelphia: Lip-
      pincott, 1947. 413p.

2881 _____., et al. Pearl Harbor to Guadalcanal. Vol. I
      of History of United States Marine Corps Operations
      in World War II. Washington: Historical Branch,
      U.S. Marine Corps, 1958. 439p.

2882 _____., jt. author. See Pierce, Philip N., no. 3032.

2883 "How Air Power Beat Japan." Flying, XXXVIII (February 1946), 52-82.
Includes naval air power.

2884 Howard, Clive and Joseph Whitley. One Damned Island After Another. Prepared by HQ, A. A. F., AFIPR, Personnel Narratives Division. Chapel Hill: University of North Carolina Press, 1946. 403p.

2885 Howard, Richard A. 999 Survived: An Analysis of Survival Experiences in the Southwest Pacific. ADTIC Publications. Maxwell Air Force Base, Ala.: Arctic, Desert, Tropic Information Center of the Air University, 1953. 60p.

2886 Howlett, R. A., comp. The History of the Fiji Military Forces, 1939-1945, Compiled from Official Records and Diaries. London: Published by the Crown Agents for the Colonies on Behalf of the Government of Fiji, 1948. 267p.
Published simultaneously by the Christchurch, New Zealand, firm of Whitcombe and Toombs. Contains very useful information on the Solomons and New Guinea campaigns.

2887 Hoyt, Edwin P. The Carrier War. Lancer's Photobook History of Modern Combat, no. 6. New York: Lancer Books, 1972. 176p.
"The exciting saga of our Navy's ordeal by fire in the Pacific."

2888 _____. How They Won the War in the Pacific: Nimitz and His Admirals. New York: Weybright and Talley, 1970. 554p.

2889 Hubler, Richard G. and John A. DeChant. Flying Leathernecks: The Complete Record of Marine Corps Aviation in Action, 1941-1944. Garden City, N.Y.: Doubleday, Doran, 1944. 225p.

2890 Hunter, Kenneth E. and Margaret E. Tackley, comps. The War Against Japan. Edited by Mary Ann Bacon. U.S. Army in World War II--Pictorial Record. Washington: Office of the Chief of Military History, Department of the Army, 1952. 471p.

2891 Hurlbut, James W. "Marines on Record." Marine

Corps Gazette, XXVIII (December 1944), 54.

2892 Icenhower, Joseph B. American Sea Heroes.   Maple-
wood, N. J.:   Hammond, 1970.   93p.
Contains brief biographies of Chester W. Nimitz,
Raymond A. Spruance, and William F. Halsey.

2893 Isby, David C.   "Tactical Naval Warfare in the Pacific,
1941-1943. " Strategy and Tactics, (May 1973),
5-19.

2894 Isely, Jeter A. and Philip A. Crowell.   The U.S.
Marine and Amphibious War: Its Theory and Its
Practice in the Pacific.   Princeton, N. J.:
Princeton University Press, 1951.   636p.

2895 "Isoroku Yamamoto. " CurrBio:III:57-59.

2896 _____. CurrBio:IV:57.

2897 Ito, Masauri, with Roger Pineau.   The End of the Imperial Japanese Navy.   Translated by Andrew Y.
Kuroda and Roger Pineau.   New York: Norton,
1962.   240p.

2898 James, David H.   The Rise and Fall of the Japanese
Empire.   New York: Macmillan, 1951.   409p.

2899 Jensen, Oliver O.   Carrier War.   New York: Simon
and Schuster, 1945.   172p.

2900 _____. "Carrier War: The Story of Mighty Task
Force 58. " Life, XVIII (March 26, 1945), 77-88.

2901 Joan of Arc, Sister.   My Name Is Nimitz.   New York,
1948.   115p.
Family history, including the American admiral.

2902 Johnston, Richard W.   Follow Me: The Story of the
Second Marine Division in World War II.   New
York: Random House, 1948.   305p.

2903 Jordan, Ralph B.   Born to Fight: The Life of Admiral
[William F.] Halsey.   Philadelphia: David McKay,
1946.   208p.

2904 Josephy, Alvin M. , Jr.   The Long and the Short and
the Tall: The Story of a Marine Combat Unit in

the Pacific. New York: Alfred A. Knopf, 1946.
221p.
A Marine combat correspondent's eyewitness account of the 3rd Marine Division on Guam and Iwo Jima.

2905 "Jungle War." In: Editors of Yank. The Best from Yank, the Army Weekly. New York: E. P. Dutton, 1945. p. 9-11.

2906 Kahn, Ely J. The Stragglers. New York: Random House, 1962. 176p.

2907 Kase, Toshikazu. Journey to the Missouri. Edited with a Foreword by David N. Rowe. New Haven: Yale University Press, 1950. 282p. Rpr. 1969.

2908 Kato, Masuo. The Lost War: A Japanese Reporter's Inside Story. New York: Alfred A. Knopf, 1946. 264p.
Some detail on Pearl Harbor and later naval events as recorded by one of the four Japanese newsmen present at the surrender aboard the battleship Missouri.

2909 Kenney, George C. General Kenney Reports: A Personal History of the Pacific War. New York: Duell, Sloan and Pearce, 1949. 594p.
The general commanded the U. S. A. A. F. in that theater during much of the conflict. Often, he found himself aiding Navy/Marine objectives as well as those of his own service.

2909a _____. The MacArthur I Knew. New York: Duell, Sloan and Pearce, 1951. 264p.

2910 _____. The Saga of Pappy Gunn. New York: Duell, Sloan and Pearce, 1959. 133p.
Tales and reminiscences concerning a legendary South Pacific airman.

2911 "King of the Cans: Arleigh A. Burke." Time, XLIV (July 17, 1944), 55.

2912 Kiralfy, Alexander. "Japanese Naval Strategy." In: Edward M. Earle, ed. Makers of Modern Strategy. Princeton, N. J.: Princeton University Press, 1943. p. 457-484. Rpr. 1972.

2913 _____. "The Pacific Campaigns. " In: William H.
       Fetridge, ed. The Second Navy Reader. Indiana-
       polis: Bobbs-Merrill, 1944. p. 279-291. Rpr.
       1971.
       Reprinted from a 1943 issue of Sea Power.

2914 _____. "Watch Japanese Air Power." Foreign Af-
       fairs, XXIII (October 1944), 66-78.

2915 Kirby, S. Woodburn. The War Against Japan. United
       Kingdom Military Series. 3 vols. London: H.
       M. Stationery Office, 1957-1961.
       The British official history.

2916 Kitaide, Daita. "The Last Flying Boat to Japan. "
       R. A. F. Flying Review, XV (September 1960), 16-
       17.

2917 Kiyoshi, I. "The Emperor and the Imperial [Japanese]
       Navy." Amerasia, VI (October 25, 1942), 371-375.

2918 Kuokka, Hubard. "Flying the Flak." Marine Corps
       Gazette, XXX (August 1946), 16-19, 47-49.
       U. S. Navy and Marine Corps aviators vs.
       Japanese anti-aircraft fire.

2919 Kuroda, Andrew Y., jt. trans. See Ito, Masauri, no.
       2842.

2920 Lane, John E., jt. author. See Hammel, Eric M.,
       no. 2802.

2921 Larkin, Claude A. "In the Air With Marine Air Group
       21." Marine Corps Gazette, LV (November 1971),
       33-35.

2922 Larsen, Colin R. Pacific Commandos: New Zealand-
       ers and Fijians in Action, a History of Southern
       Independent Commando and First Commando Fiji
       Guerrillas. Wellington, N. Z.: Reed, 1946. 161p.

2923 Leckie, Robert. Strong Men Armed: The United
       States Marines Against Japan. New York: Random
       House, 1962. 563p.

2924 Letcher, John S. One Marine's Story. Verona, Va.:
       McClure Press, 1970. 387p.

Follows the general's career from Nicaragua
in the late 1920's through the Pacific Theater of
World War II.

2925 Levin, Sol. "Historical Record of Group Pacific
Twelve. " Unpublished paper, U.S. Navy Department, Naval History Division, Operational Archives,
1945. 20p.
The story of Gropac 12's establishment and
maintenance of harbors and ports at advanced bases
from late 1944 through mid-1945.

2926 Lewis, Charles L. Famous American Marines. Bos-
ton: Page, 1950. 375p.
Chapters on those from the Pacific war include:
"Alexander Archer Vandegrift and the Solomons, "
"Holland McTyeire Smith: Tarawa, Saipan, and
Iwo Jima, " and "Roy Stanley Geiger, a Flying
Marine. "

2927 Lindley, Ernest K. "Britain's Pacific Commitment. "
Newsweek, XXI (May 31, 1943), 34.

2928 _____ . "MacArthur and the Navy. " Newsweek, XXV
(March 5, 1945), 44.

2929 Lippincott, Benjamin E. From Fiji Through the
Philippines With the Thirteenth [U.S. Army] Air
Force. San Angelo, Texas: Newsfoto, 1948.
193p.

2930 Little, Eric H. Action Pacific. Badger Books. London: Spencer, 1956. 189p.

2931 Litz, Leo M. Report from the Pacific. Indianapolis:
Indianapolis News, 1946. 427p.
The author was that paper's combat correspond-
ent.

2932 Livermore, Seward. "American Strategic Diplomacy
in the South Pacific. " Pacific Historical Review,
XII (March 1943), 42-49.

2933 Love, Edmund G. "Smith vs. Smith. " Infantry
Journal, LXIII (November 1948), 3-25.

2934 _____ . The 27th Infantry Division in World War II.
Washington: Infantry Journal Press, 1949. 677p.

An amphibious outfit which served with the
Marines in the Gilberts, on Saipan, and on Okinawa.

2935 Lucas, James. Combat Correspondent. New York:
      Reynal and Hitchcock, 1944. 210p.
      From Paris Island to service with the Marines
      in the Pacific on Guadalcanal, Espiritu Santo,
      New Georgia, Tarawa, and in New Zealand.

2936 Luvaas, Jay, editor. See Eichelberger, Robert L.,
      no. 2802.

2937 MacArthur, Douglas. Reminiscences. New York:
      McGraw-Hill, 1964. 438p.

2938 _____. A Soldier Speaks: Public Papers. New York:
      Praeger, 1965. 367p.
      The story of General MacArthur is familiar to
      almost everyone connected with or who has read
      of the Pacific war. Although his views on strategy
      led to some remarkable debates with his naval
      colleagues, his use of sea forces in hopping up
      New Guinea to the Philippines was excellent. His
      name will appear often throughout this volume in
      connection with the operations he led.

2939 McCahill, William P. First to Fight. Philadelphia:
      David McKay, 1943. 73p.
      A brief account of the Pacific operations of the
      Marines in 1941-1943.

2940 _____, ed. Hit the Beach! Your Marine Corps in
      Action: A Photographic Epic of Marine Corps
      Operations of World War II Told by the Intrepid
      Leaders Who Launched the Initial Offensive at
      Guadalcanal, Swept the Pacific, and Spearheaded
      the Occupation of the Japanese Empire. New
      York: Wise, 1948. 386p.

2941 McCarthy, Dudley. Southwest Pacific Area--First
      Year: Kokoda to Wau. Australia in the War of
      1939-1945: Series 1. Canberra: Australian War
      Memorial, 1959. 656p.

2942 Macdonnell, James E. Fleet Destroyer. Melbourne,
      Australia: The Book Depot, 1945. 102p.
      Reminiscences of a R.A.N. captain.

2943 Macintyre, Donald G. F. W. Aircraft Carrier: The
      Majestic Weapon. Ballantine's Illustrated History
      of World War II. New York: Ballantine Books,
      1972. 160p.
        More a study of Pacific carrier operations than
      a study of the ships themselves.

2944 _____. Sea Power in the Pacific: A History from the
      16th Century to the Present Day. New York:
      Crane, Russak, 1972. 281p.
        About a third of the volume deals with World
      War II.

2945 McJennet, John. "Air Power for Infantry." Marine
      Corps Gazette, XXIX (August 1945), 15-16+.
        In the Pacific.

2946 _____. "Marines Off the Carriers." Marine Corps
      Gazette, XXIX (December 1945), 7-10.

2947 McMillan, George. The Old Breed: A History of the
      First Marine Division in World War II. Washington:
      Infantry Journal Press, 1949. 483p.
        Action on Guadalcanal, New Britain, Peleliu,
      and Okinawa.

2948 _____, et al. Uncommon Valor: Marine Divisions
      in Action. Washington: Infantry Journal Press,
      1946. 256p.
        Brief histories of each of the six Marine Divi-
      sions.

2949 Macmillan, John and Joe O'Connell. "Cock of the
      Walk, the Pacific Sailor." New York Times Maga-
      zine, (November 22, 1942), 8-12.

2950 _____. _____. In: William H. Fetridge, ed. The
      Navy Reader. Indianapolis: Bobbs-Merrill, 1943.
      p. 30-36. Rpr. 1971.
        Written by two first-class seamen, this piece
      describes morale aboard a warship, musicians
      with the fleet, living conditions, letters from home,
      and girls!

2951 Maguire, William A. "Rig for Church: The Story of
      Father Maguire's Life as a Navy Chaplain." Com-
      monweal, XXXVI (June 12, 1942), 176-178.

2952 Maier, George. "From a Lookout in the Pacific: The
      Duty Days of a Pacific Coast Guardsman. " Etude,
      LXII (March 1945), 132.

2953 "Marc A. Mitscher. " CurrBio:V:36-38.
      One of the first American naval officers to
      adopt aviation as a career, Mitscher commanded
      the carrier Hornet in early 1942 when Col.
      James Doolittle's B-25 Army bombers left her deck to
      bomb Tokyo. After playing an important role at
      Midway under Admiral Spruance, the admiral for a
      time in 1943 commanded all air forces in the Solo-
      mon Islands. Given command of the famous Task
      Force 58, his command accounted for 796 Japanese
      ships and 4425 enemy planes between January and
      October 1944. In April and May 1945, his force
      took part in the Okinawa operation, taking many
      hits (mostly on picket ships) from the kamikazes.

2954 Marek, Stephen. Laughter in Hell: Being the True
      Experience of Lieutenant E. L. Guirey, U.S.N.
      and Technical Sergeant H. C. Nixon, U.S.M.C.
      and Their Comrades in the Japanese Prison Camps
      in Osaka and Tsuruga. Caldwell, Idaho: Caxton
      Printers, 1954. 256p.

2955 Marie, Louis E. "Paratroops. " In: Norman Carlisle,
      ed. The Air Forces Reader. Indianapolis: Bobbs-
      Merrill, 1944. p. 352-356.
      Actually, "Para-Marines, " as reprinted from
      the February 1943 issue of Flying.

2956 Marine Night Fighter Squadron 542. Baton Rouge, La.:
      Army & Navy Publishing Co., 1946. 71p.
      A "cruise book. "

2957 "The Marines Have Landed--. " Popular Mechanics,
      LXXVII (May 1942), 8-12.

2958 Marshall, Henry M. "Below Decks in Battle. " In:
      William H. Fetridge, ed. The Second Navy Reader.
      Indianapolis: Bobbs-Merrill, 1944. p. 349-355.
      Rpr. 1971.
      Reprinted from a 1943 issue of This Week maga-
      zine.

2959 Marshall, James. "Inshore Patrol. " In: William H.

Fetridge, ed. The Navy Reader. Indianapolis:
Bobbs-Merrill, 1943. p. 219-222. Rpr. 1971.
Life on and off the old "pickle boat," PE-57,
on the Pacific coastal patrol.

2960 Martin, Harold H. "The Big Hairy Dogfight." In:
Patrick O'Sheel and Glen Cook, eds. Semper
Fidelis: The U.S. Marines in the Pacific, 1942-
1945. New York: William Sloane Associates,
1947. p. 127-137.
U.S. Marine aviators vs. Japanese Zeroes
"somewhere" in the South Pacific.

2961 Martin, Ralph G. World War II: A Photographic
Record of the War in the Pacific from Pearl
Harbor to V-J Day. Greenwich, Conn.: Fawcett
Publications, 1965. 224p.

2962 Mattie, George H. "Flying Scouts: The Airborne
Eyes of the Boondocking Marines." Leatherneck,
XXVIII (July 1945), 24-25.

2963 Maxon, Yale C. Control of Japanese Foreign Policy:
A Study of Civil-Military Rivalry, 1930-1945.
Berkeley: University of California Press, 1957.
286p. Rpr. 1973.

2964 Mayer, Sydney L. MacArthur. Ballantine's Illustrated
History of World War II. New York: Ballantine
Books, 1971. 160p.

2965 Mears, Frederick. Carrier Combat. Garden City,
N.Y.: Doubleday, Doran, 1944. 156p.
Air action from Pearl Harbor through Guadalcanal as described by a Navy flier later killed in
action.

2966 Megee, Vernon E. "The Evolution of Marine Aviation:
Part II." Marine Corps Gazette, XLIX (September
1965), 55-60.
A study of the World War II years.

2967 Meigs, John F. "Japanese Sea Power." USNIP, LXX
(1944), 121-129.

2968 Metcalf, Clyde H. The Marine Corps Reader. New
York: G. P. Putnam, 1944. 600p.

Similar to the Navy Readers and the Air Force
Reader, from which excerpts are being cited.

2969 _____. "Peace and War With Japan." Marine Corps
Gazette, XXVII (June 1943), 10.

2970 Mikesh, R. C. Japan's World War II Balloon Bomb
Attacks on North America. Washington: Smith-
sonian Institution Press, 1973. 85p.

2971 Miller, Francis T. General Douglas MacArthur.
Philadelphia: Winston, 1944. 280p.
An expanded version of 295 pages was issued
by the same author and publisher in 1945.

2972 Miller, Max. Daybreak for Our Carrier. New York:
Whittlesey House, McGraw-Hill, 1944. 184p.
A heavily-illustrated account of life and work
aboard an American aircraft carrier in the Pacific,
aimed at "the folks back home."

2973 _____. It's Tomorrow Out Here. New York: McGraw-
Hill, 1945. 186p.
A photographic review of the Pacific naval war.

2974 Miller, Norman M. I Took the Sky Road. New York:
Dodd, Mead, 1945. 212p.
Concerns Navy Bombing Squadron 109.

2975 Miller, William. "The Forgotten Battalion." Leather-
neck, XXVIII (February 1945), 15-17.
The Guadalcanal, Tarawa, Eniwetok, Saipan, and
Guam service of the 2nd 155mm Howitzer Battalion,
U.S.M.C.

2976 Millington, Herbert. American Diplomacy and the
War of the Pacific. New York: Octagon, 1972.

2977 Moerler, William T., ed. Souvenir Battle Diary: A
Short History of the 1st Cavalry Division. Tokyo,
1945. 24p.
This U.S. Army unit saw considerable action,
alongside the Marines, during the Pacific war.

2978 Montross, Lynn. The United States Marines: A Pictorial History. New York: Rinehart, 1959. 242p.

2979 Morgan, Henry G. <u>Planning the Defeat of Japan: A</u>
<u>Study of Total War Strategy.</u> Washington: Office
of the Chief of Military History, Department of the
Army, 1961. 197p.

2980 Morison, Samuel E. "Pacific Strategy." <u>Marine Corps</u>
<u>Gazette</u>, XLVI (August 1962), 34-40.

2981 _____. "Theodore Stark Wilkinson." <u>Alumni Horae</u>,
XXVI (Spring-Summer 1946), 33-38.
This biography of the American admiral appeared
in the publication of St. Paul's School, Concord,
N. H.

2982 Morris, Colton G. and Hugh B. Cave. <u>The Fightin'est</u>
<u>Ship: The Story of the Cruiser Helena.</u> New York:
Dodd, Mead, 1944. 192p.
From Pearl Harbor through her torpedoing in the
1943 Battle of Kula Gulf.

2983 Morris, Frank D. "Beachboys." <u>Collier's</u>, CXI (May
1, 1943), 38+.
The Coast Guard's assignment during Pacific
landings.

2984 _____. "The Marines Have Landed and They Make
Quick Work of Fortifying Our Pacific Bases."
<u>Collier's</u>, CX (July 4, 1942), 12-13.

2985 Morrissey, Thomas L. <u>Odyssey of Fighting Two.</u>
Philadelphia: Lyon & Armor, 1945. 207p.
The author was air combat intelligence officer
of Navy Fighting Squadron Two.

2986 Morton, Louis. "Command in the Pacific, 1941-45."
<u>Military Review</u>, XLI (December 1961), 76-88.

2987 _____. "Japanese Policy and Strategy in Mid-War."
<u>USNIP</u>, LXXXV (1959), 52+.

2988 _____. "The Origins of the Pacific Strategy."
<u>Marine Corps Gazette</u>, XLI (August 1957), 36-43.

2989 _____. <u>Pacific Command: A Study of Interservice</u>
<u>Relations.</u> Harmon Memorial Lectures in Military
History, no. 3. Denver, Col.: U.S. Air Force
Academy, 1961. 29p.

2990 Mosley, Leonard. Hirohito: Emperor of Japan.
      Englewood Cliffs, N. J.: Prentice-Hall, 1966.
      371p.
          Traces his career before and after Pearl Har-
      bor, with considerable information on his role in
      Japanese military and naval matters.

2991 Myers, Martin L. Yardbird Myers, the Fouled-Up
      Leatherneck. Philadelphia: Dorrance, 1944.
      230p.
          Contains a useful glossary of contemporary
      Marine slang, mild in comparison with today's
      official usage.

2992 Nakayama, Sadayoshi and Norman Stanford. "The
      Importance of Seamanship in War." USNIP,
      LXXXVI (1960), 131.

2993 Navy Times, Editors of. Operation Victory: Winning
      the Pacific War. New York: G. P. Putnam,
      1968. 192p.

2994 Nelson, Frederick J. "Typhoons Over Guam."
      USNIP, LXVII (1941), 237-241.

2995 _____. "Yellow is the Color." USNIP, LXX (1944),
      981-983.

2996 Neumann, William L. American Encounters Japan:
      From Perry to MacArthur. Goucher College Series.
      Baltimore: Johns Hopkins University Press, 1963.
      353p. Rpr. 1969.

2997 New York. Museum of Modern Art. Power in the
      Pacific. New York: U. S. Camera, 1945. 144p.

2998 Nimitz, Chester W. "How One of the Society's Maps
      Saved a Precious Cargo." National Geographic,
      XCI (June 1947), 884.

2999 _____, Henry H. Adams, and Elmer B. Potter.
      Triumph in the Pacific: The Navy's Struggle
      Against Japan. Englewood Cliffs, N. J.: Prentice-
      Hall, 1963. 186p.
          A revision of the appropriate chapters from the
      authors' Sea Power: A Naval History.

3000 "Nimitz' Navy." Life, XVI (March 6, 1944), 41-44.

3001 Nofi, Albert. "War in the Pacific, 1941-1943." Strat-
      egy and Tactics, (1971), 15-31.

3002 O'Connell, Joe, jt. author. See Macmillan, John, no.
      2949.

3003 O'Connor, Raymond G., ed. The Japanese Navy in
      World War II. Annapolis: U.S. Naval Institute,
      1969. 147p.
          An anthology of articles by former Japanese
      naval and air officials telling their side of the story.
      Many of the pieces originally appeared in the pages
      of the USNIP.

3004 O'Connor, Richard. Pacific Destiny: An Informal
      History of the U.S. in the Far East, 1776-1968.
      Boston: Little, Brown, 1969. 505p.
          Contains several chapters relative to our period.

3005 Odgers, George. Air War Against Japan, 1943-1945.
      Australia in the War of 1939-1945-Series III. Can-
      berra: Australian War Memorial, 1957. 533p.

3006 O'Donnell, Edward U. "Hit the Deck." USNIP, LXXXIII
      (1957), 987-989.
          The grounding of a PCS off Guadalcanal in 1944.

3007 Ofstie, R. A. "War in the Pacific." Air Affairs, I
      (December 1946), 196-217.

3008 Okumiyu, Masatake, Jiro Horikoshi, and Martin Caidin.
      Zero! The Story of the Japanese Navy Air Force.
      London: Cassell, 1957. 364p. Rpr. 1968.

3009 Olds, Robert. Helldiver Squadron, the Story of Carrier
      Bombing Squadron 17, With Task Force 58. New
      York: Dodd, Mead, 1944. 225p.
          The Navy dive bomber, the "Helldiver," was
      first battle tested in the November 11, 1943, attack
      on Rabaul. This is an eyewitness report on the
      performance of the men and planes of the first
      Helldiver squadron from that date through February
      1944.

3010 O'Leary, Michael. "Pearl Harbor Avenger." Air
      Classics, IX (July 1973), 38-45.
          The Grumman TBF in the Pacific, beginning
      with Midway.

3011 Oliver, Edward F. "The Bombey Explosion." USNIP,
      LXXXIII (1957), 273-277.
         Catastrophe at the Bombey docks on April 14,
      1944.

3012 Oppenheimer, Harold L.   March to the Sound of the
      Drums: Marines in the South Pacific. Danville,
      Indiana: The Wabash Press, 1966. 333p.

3013 "Osami Naganto." CurrBio:III:56-58.
      Japanese carrier admiral.

3014 "Our Carriers in Action." New York Times Magazine,
      (January 17, 1943), 8-9.
      Illustrated.

3015 "Pacific Seadogs." New York Times Magazine, (June
      3, 1945), 10-11.
      Yankee admirals.

3016 Pacific Sweep: A Pictorial History of the Fifth Air
      Force Fighter Command. Sydney, Australia: F.
      H. Johnston, 1945. 112p.

3017 "The Pacific War as Recorded by American Artists."
      Life, XIX (October 8, 1945), 58-70.
      A pictorial.

3018 Pacini, John. With the R. A. N. to Tokio. Sydney,
      Australia: United Press, 1945. 52p.

3019 Palmer, Charles D. "You Can Take a Marine Away
      from Home, but You Can't Take Home Away from
      a Marine." American Home, XXXIV (July 1945),
      9-10.

3020 Paradise Parade: A Review of the XI Corps Campaigns
      from Finschafen, New Guinea, April 22, 1944 to
      Yokohama, Japan, September 2, 1945. Tokyo:
      Shyubido, 1945. 39p.
         Prepared under the direction of the public re-
      lations section of the Army Corps' G-2.

3021 Parker, William D. A Concise History of the United
      States Marine Corps, 1775-1969. Washington:
      U. S. Government Printing Office, 1971. 143p.

3022 Parkin, Ray. Into the Smother: A Journal of the

Burma-Siam Railway. London: Hogarth Press,
1963. 291p.
Reminiscences of Japanese POW camps, including a section on the survivors of H.M.A.S. Perth.

3023 Parrott, Marc. Hazard: Marines on Mission. Garden City, N.Y.: Doubleday, 1962. 225p.
Contains biographical sketches of Lou Diamond
on Guadalcanal and Ira Hayes on Iwo Jima.

3024 "Paul Sample's Naval Aviation." Life, XIV (January
4, 1943), 36-41.
Samples and comments on the artist's renderings
of early U.S. Pacific battles.

3025 Pearl, Jack. Admiral "Bull" Halsey. Derby, Conn.:
Monarch Books, 1962. 139p.

3026 Penfold, John B. "Japan's Rambling Balloon Barrage."
USNIP, LXXIII (1947), 963-965.

3027 Pettus, Francis. "A Four Day Patrol." Marine Corps
Gazette, XXVIII (June 1944), 28-32.

3028 Peyton, Green, pseud. See Wertenbaker, Green P.,
no. 3249.

3029 Pineau, Roger. "Japanese Carriers vs. Land-Based
Air in World War II." Unpublished paper, Individual
Personnel File, U.S. Navy Department, Naval History Division, Operational Archives, 1964. 38p.
A study of Japanese air attacks on land-based
targets in 1941-1942 which evaluates the effectiveness of carrier-based aircraft as opposed to land-
based planes.

3030 _____., jt. author. See Hara, Tameichi, no. 2857.

3031 _____., jt. trans. See Ito, Masauri, no. 2897.

3032 Pierce, Philip N. and Frank O. Hough. The Compact
History of the United States Marine Corps. New
York: Hawthorn, 1960. 326p.
Contains considerable data relative to our period.

3033 Poling, James. All Battle Stations Manned: The U.S.
Navy in World War II. New York: Grosset &

Dunlap, 1971. 249p.
An account of the reorganization and activities
of the U.S. Pacific Fleet after Pearl Harbor.

3034 Possony, Stefan T. "Japanese Naval Strategy. "
USNIP, LXX (1944), 515-524.

3035 "Postscript on Yamamato. " New York Times Magazine,
(January 13, 1946), 53.

3036 Potter, Elmer B. "Chester William Nimitz, 1885-
1966. " USNIP, XCII (1966), 30-55.
A biography of and tribute to the late Pacific
commander.

3037 _____. "The Japanese Navy Tells Its Story. " USNIP,
LXXIII (1947), 137-143.

3038 _____. "The Navy's War Against Japan--A Strategic
Analysis. " USNIP, LXXVI (1950), 824-837.

3039 _____., jt. author. See Nimitz, Chester W., no.
2999.

3040 Potter, John D. Yamamoto: The Man Who Menaced
America. New York: Viking, 1965. 332p.

3041 Pratt, Fletcher. Fleet Against Japan. New York:
Harper, 1946. 263p.

3042 _____. "The Marines in the Pacific War. " Marine
Corps Gazette, XXX (September-December 1946),
13, 31+, 23, 15; XXXI (January-December 1947),
33-42, 22-28, 42-53, 20-30, 32-43, 35-46, 42-49,
14-23, 46-58, 31, 38-58, 42-52; XXXII (January-
May 1948), 44-48, 38-50, 48, 32, 20.

3043 _____. The Marine's War: An Account of the
Struggle for the Pacific from Both American and
Japanese Sources. New York: Sloan, 1948. 446p.

3044 _____. The Navy Has Wings. New York: Harper,
1943. 224p.

3045 _____. "Nimitz and His Admirals. " Harper's Maga-
zine, CXC (February 1945), 209-217.
An abridged version appeared in Reader's Digest,
XLVI (April 1945), 70-75.

3046 _____. "Spruance: A Picture of the Admiral. "
Harper's Magazine, CXCIII (August 1946), 144-157.

3047 _____. "War in the Pacific. " New Republic, CXII
(May 28, 1945), 737-739.

3048 _____., jt. author. See Abercrombie, Laurence A. ,
no. 2682.

3049 Pratt, William V. "Airships Could Help Us in the
Pacific. " Newsweek, XXIII (January 24, 1944), 26.

3050 _____. "'From the Halls of Montezuma....':   168th
Anniversary. " Newsweek, XXII (November 15,
1943), 36.
The U. S. Marines.

3051 _____. "General MacArthur, A Service View. "
Newsweek, XXIII (May 1, 1944), 22.
Keeping in mind that the author was a retired
Chief of Naval Operations.

3052 _____. "MacArthur and the Battle of the Communi-
ques. " Newsweek, XXV (January 8, 1945), 28.

3053 _____. "The Man Who will Surprise the Japs. "
Newsweek, XXIII (February 21, 1944), 27.
Admiral Nimitz.

3054 _____. "The Mine as a Weapon Against Japan. "
Newsweek, XX (December 28, 1942), 21.

3055 _____. "A Navy Dive Bomber Delivers the Knockout."
Newsweek, XX (October 12, 1942), 26.

3056 _____. "Who Is This Man Nimitz?" Newsweek, XXV
(February 19, 1945), 34.

3057 _____. "Who Should Command the Pacific War?"
Newsweek, XXIV (December 11, 1944), 34.

3058 Proehl, Carl W. The Fourth Marine Division in
World War II. Washington: Infantry Journal Press,
1946.   238p.

3059 Raleigh, John M. Pacific Blackout. New York: Dodd,
Mead, 1943.   244p.

3060 Rankin, William H. The Man Who Rode the Thunder.
      Englewood Cliffs, N.J.: Prentice Hall, 1960.
      208p.
      An autobiography of Marine service since 1940.

3061 "Raymond A. Spruance." CurrBio:V:48-50.

3062 Regan, James F. "No Greater Love: Marine Raiders
      in the South Pacific." American Magazine, CXXXIX
      (June 1945), 17+.

3063 Reynolds, Clark G. "Day of the Night Carriers."
      Journal of the Royal United Service Institute, CXI
      (1965), 148-154.

3064 _____. The Fast Carriers: The Forging of an Air
      Navy. New York: McGraw-Hill, 1968. 498p.
      Based on the dissertation cited below.

3065 _____. "History and Development of the Fast Carrier
      Task Forces, 1943-1945." Unpublished PhD Disserta-
      tion, Duke University, 1964.

3066 Reynolds, Quentin J. Officially Dead: The Story of
      Commander C. D. Smith. New York: Random
      House, 1945. 244p.
      The capture, imprisonment, and escape of a
      former Yangtze River commercial skipper who
      joined the American Navy after Pearl Harbor.

3067 _____. "'Sara' Has a Birthday." Collier's, CXV
      (May 21, 1945), 21+.
      The carrier Saratoga.

3068 Richards, Guy. "Pacific Briefing." USNIP, LXXI
      (1945), 157-171.

3069 Richardson, David. "PT Boat Mission." In Editors
      of Yank. The Best from Yank, the Army Weekly.
      New York: E. P. Dutton, 1945. p. 253-255.

3070 "Richmond K. Turner." CurrBio:V:54-56.

3071 Rippon, Anthony, trans. See Andrieu d'Albas, Em-
      manuel M. A., no. 2701.

3072 Ritenour, J. Richmond. Meet VD-5. N. p., 1945.
      116p.

Navy Air Squadron Five, photographic.

3073 Row, David N., editor. See Kase, Toshikazu, no.
      2907.

3074 Ruark, Robert C. "The Return Trip: Homeward-
      Bound Troopships from the Southwest Pacific."
      Saturday Evening Post, CCXVII (October 14, 1944),
      20+.

3075 _____. "They Called 'em Fish Food: The Navy's
      Armed Guard." Saturday Evening Post, CCXVI
      (May 6, 1944), 24-25+.
      The professional contingents assigned to mer-
      chant ships.

3076 _____. "We Man the Deck Guns." Collier's, CXII
      (August 7, 1943), 11+.
      Navy sailors aboard merchant ships.

3077 _____. _____. In William H. Fetridge, ed. The
      Second Navy Reader. Indianapolis: Bobbs-Merrill,
      1944. p. 101-113. Rpr. 1971.
      The hectic life of naval gunners as reprinted
      from the 1943 issue of Collier's cited above.

3078 "SCAT: South Pacific Combat Air Transport Command."
      Flying, XXXV (October 1944), 118-119.

3079 St. George, Thomas R. c/o Postmaster. New York:
      Crowell, 1943. 194p.
      An American soldier's account of life aboard
      a troop transport bound for Australia. Excerpts
      first appeared in the San Francisco Chronicle.

3080 Saints: This is the Story of VC-27 Composite Squad-
      ron, U.S.N., After Months of Operating as a
      Group in the Combat Zone of the Southwest Pacific.
      N.p., 1946. 60 p.

3081 Saito, Fred, jt. author. See Hara, Tameichi, no.
      2857.

3082 Sakai, Saburo. "Fight to the Death." RAF Flying
      Review, XV (January 1960), 19-21+.
      Memoirs of a Japanese pilot.

3083 _____., with Martin Caidin and Fred Saito. Samurai!

New York: E. P. Dutton, 1957. 382p.
Memoirs of Japanese naval aviation throughout
the war, with particular emphasis on the kamikazes.

3084 Savage, Jimmie E. "Diary of a Sunsetter." Aero
      Album, III (1970), 40-43; IV (1971), 30-35.
      Journal of a pilot in VF-11, U.S.S. Hornet,
      September 5-November 5, 1944.

3085 Schuon, Karl, ed. The Leathernecks: An Informal
      History of the United States Marine Corps, Articles
      Selected from Leatherneck a Periodical. New York:
      Watts, 1963. 277p.
      Contains much data relative to the Pacific con-
      flict.

3086 Scrivner, Charles L. "Harpoon: On Patrol in a Lock-
      heed PV-2." Airpower, III (November 1973), 50-60.

3087 "Sea Power in Action: A Study of the Far Eastern
      War." Round Table, XXXV (March 1945), 111-116.

3088 Sears, Stephen W. Carrier War in the Pacific. Amer-
      ican Heritage Junior Library. New York: Ameri-
      can Heritage, 1966. 153p.
      Provides a useful introduction complete with the
      editorial assistance of Rear Admiral Ernest M.
      Eller and many color plates.

3089 Second Anniversary, Along the Way. N. p. , 1945.
      76p.
      Patrol Squadron 63 (air).

3090 Seventh Amphibious Force. N. p. , 1945. 32p.
      The outfit's cruise book.

3091 Shane, Theodore. Heroes of the Pacific. New York:
      Messner, 1944. 373p.
      From Pearl Harbor through the Solomons cam-
      paign.

3092 Sherman, Frederick C. Combat Command: The Amer-
      ican Aircraft Carriers in the Pacific War. New
      York: E. P. Dutton, 1950. 427p.

3093 Sherrod, Robert. "An Answer and Rebuttal to 'Smith
      vs. Smith.'" Infantry Journal, LXIV (January
      1949), 14-28.

3094   _____. History of Marine Corps Aviation in World
        War II. Washington: Combat Forces Press, 1952.
        496p.

3095   _____. On to the Westward: War in the Central
        Pacific. New York: Duell, Sloan and Pearce,
        1945. 333p.
        An account of the landings and battles on Tara-
        wa, Saipan, Iwo Jima, and Okinawa.

3096   _____. "With Nobility and Courage." Time, XLV
        (March 12, 1945), 33.

3097   Shigemitsu, Mamoru. Japan and Her Destiny. New
        York: E. P. Dutton, 1958.
        A former Japanese statesman's view of the road
        to Pearl Harbor.

3098   Shloss, Leon W. "The Secret Mission of the Mars."
        In Norman Carlisle, ed. The Air Forces Reader.
        Indianapolis: Bobbs-Merrill, 1944. p. 239-246.
        The first trip of a large Navy plane as reprinted
        from the March 18, 1944 issue of Liberty.

3099   Shoup, David M. "Shoup of the Marines." Life, LII
        (March 23, 1962), 49-61.
        Biographical, including his role in the Second
        World War.

3100   Sims, Edward H. Greatest Fighter Missions of the
        Top Navy and Marine Aces of World War II. New
        York: Harper, 1962. 250p.

3101   Sinton, Russell L., comp. The Menace from Moresby.
        San Angelo, Texas: Newsfoto, 1950. 109p.
        The Fifth U.S.A.A.F. in the Southwest Pacific.

3102   "Sketches of Naval Squadrons in World War II. Naval
        Aviation News (December 1947-December 1949).
        The various titles, with dates of publication
        in the NAN and page numbers, follow: 1. "Fight-
        ing One" (Dec. 1947, p. 8-9), 2. "VPB-8" (Jan.
        1948, p. 14-15), 3. "Torpedo Squadron Nine" (Feb.
        1949, p. 8-9), 4. "VPB-123" (March 1948, p. 16-
        17), 5. "VF-15" (April 1948, p. 28-29), 6. "Torpe-
        do Squadron Thirteen" (May 1948, p. 16-17),
        7. "Two-Ocean Raiders, VPB-128" (June 1948,

p. 26-27), 8. "Fighting Squadron Nineteen" (July
1948, p. 26-27), 9. "Torpedo Squadron 29" (Aug.
1948, p. 20-21), 10. "Fighting Seventeen" (Sept.
1948, p. 18-19), 11. "Torpedo Squadron Eleven"
(Oct. 1948, p. 26-27), 12. "Blackcats, VPB-52"
(Nov. 1948, p. 24-25), 13. "The Iron-Angels,
VF-14" (Dec. 1948, p. 26-27), 14. "Bombing
Squadron 109" (Jan. 1949, p. 12-13), 15. "Bombing Squadron 107" (Feb. 1949, p. 22-23), 16.
"Bombing Squadron 117" (March 1949, p. 16-17),
17. "VPB-119" (April 1949, p. 22-23), 18. "Bombing Squadron 118" (June 1949, p. 26-27), 19. "Fighting Squadron 9" (July 1949, p. 24-25), 20. "VT-14"
(Aug. 1949, p. 16-17), 21. "Air Group 6" (Sept.
1949, p. 14-15), 22. "Composite Squadron 42"
(Octo. 1949, p. 14-15), 23. "Utility Squadron 1"
(Dec. 1949, p. 14-15). All of these brief histories
are based on reports filed with the Aviation History
and Research Section of the Office of the Assistant
Chief of Naval Operations (Air).

3103 Smith, C. A. "The Shame of the Jap Navy." American Legion Magazine, LVIII (May 1955), 20-21.

3104 Smith, George H. "Survival in the South Seas." In
Norman Carlisle, ed. The Air Forces Reader.
Indianapolis: Bobbs-Merrill, 1944. p. 289-299.
Twenty days on a raft as reprinted from the
February 1944 issue of the Bureau of Naval Per-
sonnel Information Bulletin.

3105 Smith, Holland M. and Percy Finch. Coral and Brass.
New York: C. Scribner's, 1949. 289p.
Marines in the Pacific war, by one of their
noted commanders.

3106 Smith, Stanley E., ed. The United States Marine
Corps in World War II: The One Volume History
from Wake Island to Tsingtao, by the Men Who
Fought in the Pacific, and by Distinguished Marine
Experts, Authors, and Newspapermen. New York:
Random House, 1969. 1965p.

3107 Sondern, Frederic, Jr. "The Navy's Fliers Dish It
Out." In Norman Carlisle, ed. The Air Forces
Reader. Indianapolis: Bobbs-Merrill, 1944.
p. 149-153.

A discussion of carrier air tactics reprinted
from the April 1943 issue of Naval Affairs.

3108 _____. "The Navy's Fliers Dish It Out: A Combined
Dive-Bomber and Torpedo-Plane Attack." Reader's
Digest, XLII (May 1943), 69-72.

3109 South Pacific, 1943-44, U.S. Patrol Squadron 81. N.p.,
1945. 102p.
VP-81.

3110 Spagnola, James A. "'Never Forgotten.'" USNIP,
LXXV (1949), 590-591.
Admiral Nimitz.

3111 Spruance, Raymond A. "The Victory in the Pacific."
Journal of the Royal United Service Institute, CII
(November 1946), 539-555.

3112 Stanford, Norman, jt. author. See Nakayama, Sadayoshi, no. 2992.

3113 Stanton, Richard K. "Navy Minesweeper Lost."
Pacific Motor Boat, XXXV (April 1943), 11.
YMS-133 which capsized in Coos Bay, Oregon.

3114 Steel, Johannes. "Isaroku Yamamoto." In: his Men
Behind the War. Rev. ed. New York: Sheridan,
1943. p. 354-360.

3115 Steele, Theodore M. A Pictorial Record of the Combat
Duty of Bombing Squadron 109 in the Central Pacific,
28 December 1943-14 August 1944. N.p., 1944.
Unpaged.

3116 _____. A Pictorial Record of the Combat Duty of
Bombing Squadron 109 in the Western Pacific, 20
April 1945-15 August 1945. New York: General
Offset, 1946. Unpaged.

3117 Steichen, Edward, comp. Power in the Pacific, a
Pictorial Record of Navy Combat Operations on
Land, Sea, and in the Sky. New York: U.S.
Camera Publishing Company, 1945. 144p.
The 150 photographs, with explanatory text, were
originally assembled for an exhibition at New York's
Museum of Modern Art with the majority being
official U.S. Navy pictures.

3118 _____. U.S. Navy War Photographs: Pearl Harbor
       to Tokyo Bay. New York: U.S. Camera, 1946.
       108p.

3119 Stephan, S. L. "Ship to Shore and Island." Marine
       Corps Gazette, XXIX (July 1945), 20-24.

3120 Steward, Harold D. The First was First: The Story
       of the First Cavalry Division. Manila, Republic
       of the Philippines: Santo Tomas University Press,
       1945. 18p.

3121 Stockman, James R. "The Sixth Division." Leather-
       neck, XXIX (October 1946), 40-45.

3122 _____. "The Sixth Marine Division." Unpublished
       paper, USMC File, U.S. Navy Department, Naval
       History Division, Operational Archives, 1945. 19p.

3123 The Story of the XIII Bomber Command at Work,
       January 1943-July 1944. N.p., Reproduced by the
       Reproduction Platoon, 905th Engineer Air Force
       Headquarters Company, 1944. 160p.
       A unit history "conceived on Guadalcanal and
       prepared entirely in the combat area."

3124 Stump, Felix B. "An Evening with Admiral Felix B.
       Stump." Unpublished paper, Individual Personnel
       File, U.S. Navy Department, Naval History Divi-
       sion, Operational Archives, 1967. 32p.
       The admiral served as commander of the carrier
       Lexington (CV-16) during part of the Pacific war.

3125 Sullivan, W. E., Jr. "The History and Development
       of Close Air Support." Marine Corps Gazette, XL
       (November 1956), 20-24.
       Most of the examples are drawn from World
       War II in the Pacific.

3126 "The Sundowners," Air Group Eleven, Fighting Squadron
       Eleven. N.p., 1943. 14p.

3127 Swan, W. N. Spearheads of Invasion: An Account
       of the Seven Major Invasions Carried Out by the
       Allies in the Southwest Pacific Area During the
       Second World War, as Seen from a Royal Australian
       Naval Landing Ship Infantry. Sydney, Australia:
       Angus and Robertson, 1954. 307p.

3128 Tackley, Margaret E., jt. compiler. See Hunter, Kenneth E., no. 2890.

3129 Tallent, Robert W. "1937-1947." Leatherneck, XL (November 1957), 34-40.

3130 Tamura, Kyuzo. "History of Japanese Minesweeping-1937-1947." Unpublished paper, Individual Personnel File, U.S. Navy Department, Naval History Division, 1948. 66p.

3131 Taylor, Edwin J., Jr. "Memoirs, 1941-1946." Unpublished paper, Individual Personnel File, U.S. Navy Department, Naval History Division, Operational Archives, 1946. 29p.
      Memories of the rear admiral who served aboard the battleship Alabama and as executive officer of the South Dakota at Leyte Gulf.

3132 Taylor, Theodore. The Magnificent Mitscher. New York: Norton, 1954. 304p.

3133 Thacker, Joel D. "The Fifth Division." Leatherneck, XXIX (September 1946), 36-41.

3134 _____. "History of the 3rd Division." Leatherneck, XXIX (February 1946), 12-15+.

3135 _____. "Year of Fulfillment." Leatherneck, XXVIII (November 1945), 15-19.

3136 Theobald, Richard J. "The Maiden Voyage of LST 169." New Yorker, XIX (November 27, 1943-January 15, 1944), 58+, 112-115, 53-56, 65-69; XX (March 25, November 4, December 9, 1944), 80-82, 70-72, 74+.
      Manned by Coastguard sailors.

3137 Thomas, Lowell. These Men Shall Never Die. Philadelphia: John C. Winston, 1943. 308p.
      Tales of American heroes and heroships from Pearl Harbor through the Solomons campaigns.

3138 "Thomas C. Kinkaid." CurrBio:V:21-25.
      After losing the carrier Hornet in the Battle of the Santa Cruz Islands, Admiral Nimitz gave this commander another chance--and he did not fumble

again.   As chief of the Seventh Fleet, "MacArthur's
Navy, " he taught the controversial general the
meaning of sea power and helped him employ it
from New Guinea to the reconquest of the Philippines.

3139   Thursfield, Henry G.   "Seapower in the Pacific. "
National Review, CXXIII (September 1944), 202-
207.
A British view.

3140   _____. "War in the Pacific--a Retrospect. "   National
Review, CXXV (October 1945), 297-303.

3141   Toland, John.   The Rising Sun.   2 vols.   New York:
Random House, 1970.   Rpr. 1971.
U. S. -Japanese relations and war from the latter
viewpoint.

3142   Torpedo Squadron One, 1 October 1944-25 October
1945.   N. p. , 1945.   16p.
A squadron of aircraft aboard an American carrier.

3143   Torpedo Squadron 17.   San Francisco: James H.
Barry, 1945.   67p.
The above two references are unit "cruise
books. "

3144   "Tough Bill Halsey. "   Scholastic, XLI (November 9,
1942), 12.

3145   Tower, Herbert H.   Fighting the Devil with the Marines.
Philadelphia: Dorrance, 1945.   172p.
Memoirs of a Navy chaplain assigned to the
"devildogs. "

3146   Trumbull, Robert.   The Raft.   New York: Holt, 1942.
205p.
How three downed naval aviators spent 34 days
in a four-by-eight rubber lifeboat.

3147   Tupper, Fred Jr.   "Back-Seat [Navy] Heroes: The
Enlisted Technicians. "   Flying, XXXII (January
1943), 55-56.

3148   Turnbladh, Edwin T. , jt. author.   See Condit, Kenneth
W. , no. 2769.

3149 Ulanoff, Stanley M. Fighter Pilot. Garden City,
      N. Y. : Doubleday, 1962. 430p.

3150 "A U. S. Carrier Fights an Airplane Fire. " Life,
      XVII (December 4, 1944), 62-64.

3151 United States. Army. Far East Command. The Imperial
      Japanese Navy in World War II: A Graphic Pre-
      sentation of the Japanese Naval Organization and
      List of Combatant and Non-Combatant Vessels
      Lost or Damaged in the War. Japanese Operation-
      al Monograph Series, No. 116. Tokyo: Military
      History Section, Special Staff, General Headquarters,
      Far East Command, 1952. 279pp.

3152 _____. _____. Military Academy, Department of
      Military Art and Engineering. The War with Ja-
      pan. 3 pts. West Point, N. Y. , 1944-1946.

3153 _____. Department of Defense. "Secrets of
      the Pacific War: Excerpts from the Report Re-
      leased October 19, 1955. " U. S. News and World
      Report, XXXIX (October 28, 1955), 68-72+.

3154 _____. _____, Office of Public Information. "The
      Entry of the Soviet Union into the War Against
      Japan: Military Plans, 1941-1945. " Unpublished
      paper, Cabinet File, U. S. Navy Department, Naval
      History Division, Operational Archives, 1953. 107p.

3155 [No entry.]

3156 _____. Joint Army-Navy Assessment Committee.
      Japanese Naval and Merchant Shipping Losses During
      World War II by All Causes. Washington: U. S.
      Government Printing Office, 1947. Unpaged.
      Navexos P-468.

3157 _____. Marine Corps. Board to Reexamine the Adequacy
      of Present Concept of Mission and Functions of the
      Marine Corps. An Evaluation of Air Operations
      Affecting the U. S. Marine Corps in World War II.
      Quantico, Va. : Marine Corps Schools, 1945.
      Various paging.

3158 _____. _____. Division of Aviation. Flying with the
      Marine Corps. Washington, 1944.

3159   .   . Historical Branch. A Brief History
          of the United States Marine Corps. Marine Corps
          Historical Reference Series, no. 1. Rev. ed.
          Washington, 1964. 54p.

3160   .   .   . A Chronology of the United
          States Marine Corps. 4 vols. Washington, 1965-
          1970.
          The last two volumes, covering the years 1935-
          1946, are of interest here.

3161   .   .   . A History of Marine Corps
          Roles and Missions, 1775-1962. Marine Corps His-
          torical Reference Series, no. 30. Washington,
          1962. 36p.
          The duties assigned to the Corps by statute or
          regulation.

3162   .   .   . Marine Corps Lore. Marine
          Corps Historical Reference Series, no. 22. Wash-
          ington, 1963. 18p.

3163   .   . Marine Corps Schools, Quantico, Va.
          "Jungle Warfare." Marine Corps Gazette, XXVIII
          (September 1944), 1-124.
          A special issue on the subject.

3164   . Marine Corps Institute. Marines in Action:
          A Review of the U.S. Marine Corps' Operations in
          the Pacific Phase of World War II, from Samoa to
          Peleliu. Washington, 1945. 61p.

3165 "The United States Marine Corps in World War II. "
          USNIP, LXXIV (1948), 1013-1019.
          Pictorial.

3166   . Navy Department. Bureau of Aeronautics.
          South Pacific Air Command. "Administrative His-
          tory of Commander Aircraft South Pacific." Un-
          published paper, Type Commands File, U.S. Navy
          Department, Naval History Division, Operational
          Archives, n.d. 173p.
          In addition to dealing with aircraft, this report
          provides information on the establishment of advance
          airfields following the Japanese retreat toward their
          home islands in the war's last years.

3167   _____._____. Bureau of Medicine and Surgery,
        Hospital Corps Archives. "Rules and Regulations
        for Prisoners-of-War." Unpublished paper, Shore
        Establishment File, U.S. Navy Department, Naval
        History Division, Operational Archives, 1946. 21p.
        Twelve documents salvaged from the Bilibid
        Concentration Camp, Philippines, 1942-1944.

3168   _____._____. Naval Academy. Department of Eng-
        lish, History, and Government. Materials on Naval
        History. Annapolis: U.S. Naval Institute, 1952.
        109p.
        Contains Professor E. B. Potter's essay:
        "General Strategy: Pacific Theatre, 1941-1945."

3169   _____._____. Naval History Division. Chronology
        of the Navy's War in the Pacific, World War II.
        Washington, 1947. 116p.

3170   _____._____. Office of the Chief of Naval Opera-
        tions. "Battle Experiences." Unpublished papers,
        26 vols., CNO File, U.S. Navy Department, Naval
        History Division, Operational Archives, 1943-1945.
        3,022p.
        These bulletins were designed to provide reliable
        information concerning operations so that the lessons
        learned might be put to good advantage. Those
        concerning Pacific operations are as follows by
        bulletin number: (1) "Battle Experience from Pearl
        Harbor to Midway"--covers the period from Dec.
        1941 through June 1942, including the Makin Island
        Raid of August 17-18, 1942. (2) "Battle Experi-
        ence, Solomon Islands Actions"--from Aug. -Sept.
        1942, including the bombardment of Kiska on Aug.
        7, 1942. (3) "Battle Experience, Solomon Islands
        Actions"--Oct. 1942. (4) "Battle Experience, Sol-
        omon Islands Actions"--Nov. 1942. (5) "Battle
        Experience, Solomon Islands Actions"--Dec. 1942-
        Jan. 1943. (6) "Battle Experience, Solomon Island
        and Alaskan Actions"--Jan. -Feb. 1943. (7) "Bat-
        tle Experience, Solomon Island and Alaskan Ac-
        tions"--Mar. 1943. (8) "Battle Experience, Solo-
        mon Islands and Alaskan Area Bombardments"--
        May and July 1943. (9) "Battle Experience, As-
        sault and Occupation of Attu Island"--May 1943.
        (10) "Battle Experience, Naval Operations, Solomon
        Islands Area"--June 30-July 12, 1943. (11) "Battle

Experience, Naval Operations, Solomon Islands
Area"--July 12-Aug. 10, 1943. (12) "Battle Experience, Solomon Islands and Alaskan Areas"--
July-Oct. 1943. (13) "Battle Experience, Bombardment of Wake Island"--Oct. 5-6, 1943.
(14) "Battle Experience, Naval Operations, South
and Southwest Pacific Ocean Areas"--Oct. 6-Nov.
2, 1943. (15) "Battle Experience, Supporting Operations Before and During the Occupation of the
Gilbert Islands"--Nov. 1943. (16) "Battle Experience, Battle off Cape St. George, New Ireland"--
Nov. 24-25, 1943. (17) "Battle Experience, Supporting Operations for the Occupation of the Marshall Islands, Including Eniwetok"--Feb. 1944.
(18) "Battle Experience, Battleship, Cruiser, and
Destroyer Sweep Around Truk, 16-17 Feb. 1944.
Bombardments of Satawal and Ponape, 30 April-
1 May 1944." (20) "Battle Experience, Supporting
Operations for the Captures of the Marianas Islands
(Saipan, Guam, and Tinian"--June-Aug. 1944.
(21) "Battle Experience, Night Action and Subse-
quent Bombardment of Chichi Jima and Ani Jima,
Bonin Islands, 4-5 Augu 1944; Destruction of Japanese Convoy off Bislig Bay [Sept. 9, 1944]; Sup-
porting Operations for the Occupation of Palau and
Ulithi [Sept.-Oct. 1944]." (22) "Battle Experience,
Battle of Leyte Gulf: A) Battle of Surigao Strait,
B) Battle of Samar, C) Battle off Cape Engano"--
Oct. 23-27, 1944. (23) "Battle Experience, Bombardments of Iwo Jima, Nov. 1944-Jan. 1945; Third
Fleet Operations in Support of Central Luzon Landings, Including the South China Sea Sweep, 30 Dec.
1944-23 Jan. 1945." (24) "Battle Experience, Radar
Pickets and Methods of Combatting Suicide Attacks
off Okinawa"--Mar.-May 1945. (25) "Battle Ex-
perience, Encountering Typhoons or Storms"--June-
Aug. 1945 off Okinawa. (26) "Battle Experience,
Final Operations of Units of the Pacific Fleet off
the Shores of Japan"--July-Sept. 1945.

3171 _____. _____. _____. U.S. Naval Aviation in the
Pacific. Washington: U.S. Government Printing
Office, 1947. 56p.

3172 _____. _____. _____. Intelligence Division. "The
Japan Sea." Unpublished paper, CNO File, U.S.
Navy Department, Naval History Division, Opera-
tional Archives, 1945. 51p.

Stresses geography and the navigation of the area.

3173 _____ . _____ . Office of the Deputy Chief of Naval Operations (Air). "Air War Against Japan, April 1942 to August 1945." Unpublished papers, DCNO (Air) File, U.S. Navy Department, Naval History Division, Operational Archives, 1945. 200p.
Actually a series of bi-monthly intelligence summaries published during the period.

3174 _____ . _____ . Pacific Fleet and Pacific Ocean Area. Air Notes from Captured Documents and Prisoners-of-War. Cincpac-Cincpoa Bulletin 82-44. N.p., 1944.

3175 _____ . _____ . _____ . _____ . Cincpac-Cincpoa Bulletin 94-44. N.p., 1944.

3176 _____ . _____ . _____ . _____ . Cincpac-Cincpoa Bulletin 101-44. N.p., 1944.

3177 _____ . _____ . _____ . _____ . Cincpac-Cincpoa Bulletin 105-44. N.p., 1944.

3178 _____ . _____ . _____ . _____ . Cincpac-Cincpoa Bulletin 109-44. N.p., 1944.

3179 _____ . _____ . _____ . Biography of New Japanese Commander-in-Chief. Cincpac-Cincpoa Bulletin 76-44. N.p., 1944.
Admiral Mineichi Koga replaced Admiral Yamamoto when the latter was shot down.

3180 _____ . _____ . _____ . Change in the Japanese High Command. Cincpac-Cincpoa Bulletin 57-44. N.p., 1944.

3181 _____ . _____ . _____ . "Command History, World War II, 7 December 1941-August 1945." Unpublished paper, Fleets File, U.S. Navy Department, Naval History Division, Operational Archives, 1946. 445p.
Useful for understanding the command relationships and channels of communication to and from operating forces of CINCPAC-CINCPOA.

3182   _____ . _____ . _____ The Development of Japanese
        Seapower. Cincpac-Cincpoa Bulletin 93-45. N. p. ,
        1945.

3183   _____ . _____ . _____ Functions of the 1st Battalion
        Staff of the [Japanese] 1st Amphibious Brigade.
        Cincpac-Cincpoa Bulletin 97-44. N. p. , 1944.

3184   _____ . _____ . _____ A Guide to the Western Pacific
        for the Use of the Army, Navy, and Marine Corps.
        Cincpac-Cincpoa Bulletin 126-44. N. p. , 1944.
        140p.

3185   _____ . _____ . _____ History of the Japanese 1st
        Amphibious Brigade. Cincpac-Cincpoa Bulletin 88-
        44. N. p. , 1944.

3186   _____ . _____ . _____ Important Flag Officers of the
        Japanese Navy. Cincpac-Cincpoa Bulletin 93-44.
        N. p. , 1944.
        Brief but full biographies.

3187   _____ . _____ . _____ Japanese Amphibious Opera-
        tions. Cincpac-Cincpoa Bulletin 70-43. N. p. ,
        1943.

3188   _____ . _____ . _____ Japanese Army and Navy Land
        Forces. Know Your Enemy Series. N. p. , 1943.
        Supplement to Cincpac-Cincpoa Weekly Intelli-
        gence, Vol. I, no. 13.

3189   _____ . _____ . _____ Japanese Mobile Raiding Units.
        Cincpac-Cincpoa Bulletin 90-44. N. p. , 1944.

3190   _____ . _____ . _____ Japanese Naval Ground Forces.
        Cincpac-Cincpoa Bulletin 11-45. N. p. , 1945.

3191   _____ . _____ . _____ Japanese Naval Personnel
        from Information to Date. Cincpac-Cincpoa Bulletin
        50-44. N. p. , 1944.

3192   _____ . _____ . _____ Japanese Navy Staff and Com-
        mand List. Cincpac-Cincpoa Bulletin 90-45. N. p. ,
        1945.

3193   _____ . _____ . _____ Postal Addresses of Naval
        Units, 11 May 43 to 29 May 44. Special Trans-

lation No. 48. Cincpac-Cincpoa Bulletin 44-45.
N. p. , 1945.

3194 _____._____._____. Reference Manual of Japanese
Naval Postal Addresses. Special Translation No.
13. N. p. , 1944.

3195 _____._____._____._____. Cincpac-Cincpoa Bulletin 73-45. N. p. , 1945.
Supplement to Special Translation No. 13.

3196 _____._____._____. Register of Japanese Naval
Officers. Cincpac-Cincpoa Bulletin 43-45. N. p. ,
1945.

3197 _____._____._____. "Report of Operations in the
Pacific Ocean Areas. " Unpublished paper, Fleets
File, U. S. Navy Department, Naval History Divi-
sion, Operational Archives, 1942-1945. 3, 000p.
A month-by-month detailed narrative by the
Fleet commander covering all battles.

3198 _____._____._____. Revised Register of Japanese
Naval Officers. Cincpac-Cincpoa Bulletin 124-45.
N. p. , 1945.

3199 _____._____._____. Secret Sailing Directions.
Cincpac-Cincpoa Bulletins, as follow: 13-42,
(n. p. , 1942); 31-43 (North Pacific), (n. p. , 1943);
55-44 (South Pacific), (n. p. , 1944); and 60-44
(Central Pacific), (n. p. , 1944).

3200 _____._____._____. Supplement No. 1 to Special
Translation No. 10--Data on Special Naval Landing
Forces. Cincpac-Cincpoa Bulletin 32-45. N. p. ,
1945.

3201 _____._____._____. Supplement No. 1 to Special
Translation No. 20--Data on Japanese Naval Air
Groups. Cincpac-Cincpoa Bulletin 25-45. N. p. ,
1945.

3202 _____._____._____. Tables of Organization and
Tables of Equipment--Jap Forces. Know Your
Enemy Series. N. p. , 1944.
Supplement to Cincpac-Cincpoa Weekly Intelli-
gence, Vol. I, no. 26.

3203   .   .   . Tables of Organization and
         Tables of Equipment of Japanese Forces.   Know
         Your Enemy Series.   Cincpac-Cincpoa Bulletin 6-
         45.   N. p. , 1945.

3204   .   .   . Amphibious Group 5.   "The
         History of Amphibious Group Five, June 1944 to
         August 1945. " Unpublished paper, Type Commands
         File, U.S. Navy Department, Naval History Divi-
         sion, Operational Archives, ca. 1945.   70p.
            This unit served at Guadalcanal, Saipan, Guam,
         Okinawa, Peleliu, Manus, and the Philippines.

3205   .   .   . Amphibious Group 7.   "Com-
         mand History of Amphibious Group Seven. "   Un-
         published paper, Type Commands File, U.S. Navy
         Department, Naval History Division, Operational
         Archives, 1945.   36p.
            This report follows the unit through the Western
         Pacific, including the Philippine and Okinawa cam-
         paigns, from September 21, 1944 to August 14,
         1945.

3206   .   .   .   . "History. " Unpublished
         paper, Type Commands File, U.S. Navy Depart-
         ment, Naval History Division, Operational Archives,
         n. d.   63p.
            A general account of the command's World War
         II operations, particularly in New Guinea and the
         Philippines.

3207   .   .   .   . "Seventh Amphibious
         Force Command History, 10 January 1943-23 Decem-
         ber 1945. " Unpublished paper, Type Commands
         File.   U.S. Navy Department, Naval History Divi-
         sion, Operational Archives, 1945.   109p.
            One of the basic sources employed by Admiral
         Barbey in preparing his MacArthur's Amphibious
         Navy cited elsewhere in this volume.

3208   .   .   . Amphibious Group 11.   "Com-
         mand History of Amphibious Group Eleven. "   Un-
         published paper, Type Commands File, U.S. Navy
         Department, Naval History Division, Operational
         Archives, 1945.   8p.
            This report follows the unit through the Western
         Pacific, including the Philippine and Okinawa cam-
         paigns, from mid-1944 to the end of the war.

3209 _____._____._____. Amphibious Group 14. "Command History: Staff of Commander, Amphibious Group Fourteen. " Unpublished paper, Type Commands File, U.S. Navy Department, Naval History Division, Operational Archives, 1945. 11p.
The group was formed late in April 1945 for a possible invasion of Japan.

3210 _____._____._____. Amphibious Group 13. "Command History: Amphibious Group Thirteen. " Unpublished paper, Type Commands File, U.S. Navy Department, Naval History Division, Operational Archives, 1945. 18p.
This unit participated in the early training for the Okinawa landings, but was recalled to Pearl Harbor before it could participate.

3211 _____._____._____. Amphibious Group 12. "Command History--Amphibious Group Twelve. " Unpublished paper, Type Commands File, U.S. Navy Department, Naval History Division, Operational Archives, 1945. 15p.
Follows the unit from October 1944 to August 1945, with particular reference to the Okinawa campaign.

3212 _____._____._____. Analytical Division. "Unit of Command as It Functioned in the Pacific Ocean Areas in World War II. " Unpublished paper, U.S. Navy Department, Naval History Division, Operational Archives, n.d. 35p.

3213 _____._____._____. Central Pacific Forward Area. "History of Military Government Section. " Unpublished paper, U.S. Navy Department, Naval History Division, Operational Archives, 1945. 2p.
Very concise!

3214 _____._____._____._____. "Sub-Area Commands. " Unpublished paper, U.S. Navy Department, Naval History Division, Operational Archives, 1945. 32p.
Island and atoll commands in the area.

3215 _____._____._____._____. "Utility Air Group. " Unpublished paper, U.S. Navy Department, Naval History Division, Operational Archives, 1945. 5p.
Activities from late 1943 to late 1944.

3216   .   .   .   Communications Division.
            "History of CINCPAC-CINCPOA Communications
            Division, 7 December 1941-15 August 1945. " Un-
            published paper, U.S. Navy Department, Naval
            History Division, Operational Archives, 1945.
            500p.

3217   .   .   . , Destroyer Squadron Fifty Six.
            "Combat History of Destroyer Squadron Fifty Six. "
            Unpublished paper, Type Commands File, U.S.
            Navy Department, Naval History Division, 1945.
            12p.
            From late 1944 through 1945 at Lingayen and
            Leyte Gulf, Philippines.

3218   .   .   . , Fighting Squadron Six. "The
            War Record of Fighting Squadron 6, 7 December
            1941-20 June 1942. " Unpublished paper, Type
            Commands File, U.S. Navy Department, Naval
            History Division, Operational Archives, 1963. 67p.
            The daily operations of an aviation unit assigned
            to the carrier Enterprise. Presented in log form,
            the work contains considerable data on the Battle
            of Midway.

3219   .   .   . , Fighting Squadron Twenty
            Three. "Story of 'Fighting 23.' " Unpublished
            paper, Type Commands File, U.S. Navy Department,
            Naval History Division, Operational Archives, n.d.
            30p.
            A daily chronology from November 16, 1942 to
            May 11, 1944.

3220   .   .   .   Intelligence Section. "A His-
            tory of the Combat Intelligence Section, Staff C-in-
            C Pacific Fleet, from December 7 1941 Until
            September 1945. " Unpublished paper, U.S. Navy
            Department, Naval History Division, Operational
            Archives, 1945. 450p.

3221   .   .   .   LST Flotilla 7. "History of
            LST Flotilla Seven. " Unpublished paper, Type
            Commands File, U.S. Navy Department, Naval His-
            tory Division, Operational Archives, 1946. 21p.
            The unit's operations included New Guinea, Ad-
            miralty Islands, and the Philippine reconquest.

3222 ___.___.___. LST Flotilla 13. "War History
of LST Flotilla Thirteen." Unpublished paper,
Type Commands File, U.S. Navy Department, Naval
History Division, Operational Archives, 1945. 20p.
This unit saw action at Guadalcanal, Eniwetok,
Saipan, Tinian, Peleliu, Guam, the Philippines,
and in Japan.

3223 ___.___.___. Marshalls-Gilberts Patrol and
Escort Group. "Wartime History of Task Group
96. 3." Unpublished paper, U.S. Navy Department,
Naval History Division, Operational Archives, 1945.
7p.
The unit which provided convoy protection between
the Marshalls and forward area ports.

3224 ___.___.___. Military Government Section.
"CINCPAC-CINCPOA Command History, Military
Government Section." Unpublished paper, U.S.
Navy Department, Naval History Division, Opera-
tional Archives, n.d. 225p.

3225 ___.___.___. Operations Division. "History
of the Operations Division." Unpublished paper,
U.S. Navy Department, Naval History Division,
Operational Archives, 1945. 225p.

3226 ___.___.___. Philippine Sea Frontier. "Nar-
rative History of the Philippine Sea Frontier."
Unpublished paper, Sea Frontiers File, U.S. Navy
Department, Naval History Division, Operational
Archives, 1945. 27p.
From mid-1944 to mid-1945.

3227 ___.___.___. Public Information Office.
"History of CINCPAC Public Information." Un-
published paper, U.S. Navy Department, Naval
History Division, Operational Archives, n.d. 60p.
Includes information on the problems of censor-
ship.

3228 ___.___.___. War Plans Division. "History
of the War Plans Division, During World War II."
Unpublished paper, U.S. Navy Department, Naval
History Division, Operational Archives, 1945. 13p.

3229 ___.___.___. Welfare and Recreation Section.

"History. " Unpublished paper, U. S. Navy Department, Naval History Division, Operational Archives, n. d.   9p.

3230 _____._____. Samoan Defense Group. "United States Naval History of the Samoan Defense Group. " Unpublished paper, U. S. Navy Department, Naval History Division, Operational Archives, 1945.   85p.

3231 _____._____. South Pacific Area and Forces. "History of New Zealand During World War II. " Unpublished paper, U. S. Navy Department, Naval History Division, Operational Archives, n. d.   567p.
An extensive three-part series: (1) manpower, (2) sea frontier organization, (3) shipbuilding and ship repair facilities.

3232 _____. Strategic Bombing Survey (Pacific). Naval Analysis Division. The Campaigns of the Pacific War. Washington, 1946. 389p. Rpr. 1969.

3233 _____._____._____. The Fifth Air Force in the War Against Japan. Washington: U. S. Government Printing Office, 1947.   114p.

3234 _____._____._____. Interrogations of Japanese Officials. 2 vols. Washington, 1946.
Questions as to the effectiveness of U. S. naval bombing.

3235 _____._____._____. "The Offensive Mine-Laying Campaign Against Japan. " Airpower Historian, V (July 1958), 161-171.
Reprinting of the report of the October 1942-August 1945 operation.

3236 _____._____._____. Summary Report (Pacific War). Washington, 1946. 32p.

3237 _____. War Department. Army Air Forces. Army Air Forces in the War Against Japan, 1941-1942. Washington: U. S. Government Printing Office, 1945.   171p.
The Doolittle Raid is featured.

3238 _____._____. Western Defense Command. "Japanese Free Balloons and Related Incidents. " Unpublished

paper, U.S. Army File, U.S. Navy Department,
Naval History Division, Operational Archives, 1945.
55p.

3239 An Unofficial History of the 500th Bombardment Group,
      One of the Four Combat Groups of the 73rd Wing
      Under 21st Bomber Command and 20th Air Force,
      Stationed for Overseas Operations at Saipan in the
      Marianas Islands. Riverside, Calif.: Rubidoux,
      1946. 100p.

3240 Updegraph, Charles L., Jr. U.S. Marine Corps
      Special Units of World War II. Historical Reference
      Pamphlet. Washington: Historical Division, U.S.
      Marine Corps, 1972. 105p.
      All were employed in the Pacific war.

3241 Utility [Air] Squadron 13, Odyssey, 1944-1945. San
      Diego, Calif.: Frye & Smith, 1945. 48p.

3242 Vandegrift, Arthur A. "From Guadalcanal to the
      Shores of Japan." New York Times Magazine,
      (August 5, 1945), 5+.

3243 Waite, Elmont. "He Opened the Airway to Japan:
      Vice Admiral [Marc] Mitscher." Saturday Evening
      Post, CCXVII (December 2, 1944), 1+.

3244 Walker, Wayne T. "Attack in the Pacific." World
      War II Magazine, III (October 1973), 11-17.
      The work of U.S. carriers.

3245 _____. "Battles on the Philippine Seas." World War
      II Magazine, II (December 1972), 6-22.

3246 Warnecke, G. W. "Suetsugu's Fence--Key to Pacific
      Strategy." Pacific Affairs, XV (December 1942),
      430-449.

3247 Weigley, Russell F. "The Strategic Tradition of A.
      T. Mahan: Strategists of the Pacific War." In
      his The American Way of War: A History of
      United States Military Strategy and Policy. The
      Wars of the United States Series. New York:
      Macmillan, 1973. p. 269-312.

3248 We'll Say Goodbye: A Story of the 307th Bombardment

Group (hv.), 13th Army Air Force, South and
Southwest Pacific. Sydney: F. H. Johnston, 1945.
56p.

3249   Wertenbaker, Green P. 5,000 Miles Toward Tokyo.
By Green Peyton, pseud. Norman: University of
Oklahoma Press, 1945. 173p.
Naval action in the Pacific, October 1943-Octo-
ber 1944, as seen from the decks of the small
carrier U.S.S. Suwannee.

3250   Wethe, W. G. "Marine Aviation in Support of Amphibious Troops." Marine Corps Gazette, XXXV (January 1951), 26-35.
Most of the examples are drawn from World
War II with particular emphasis on the Okinawa
operation.

3251   Wharton, Don. "Old Lou, the Marines' Marine."
Reader's Digest, XLIV (February 1944), 46-49.

3252   Wheeler, Keith. The Pacific is My Beat. New
York: Dutton, 1943. 383p.
Service of a Chicago Daily News correspondent
with the Pacific fleet in mid-Pacific and the
Aleutians.

3253   White, Lillian C. Pioneer and Patriot: George Cook
Sweet, Commander U.S. Navy, 1877-1953. Del-
ray Beach, Fla.: Southern Publishing Company,
1965.
A pioneer in naval aviation.

3254   Whitehouse, Arch. Squadrons of the Sea. Garden
City, N.Y.: Doubleday, 1962. 383p.
Carrier operations in the Pacific are covered
in Chapters IV-X.

3255   Whitley, Joseph, jt. author. See Howard, Clive,
no. 2884.

3256   Whitney, Courtney. MacArthur: His Rendezvous with
History. New York: Knopf, 1956. 547p.

3257   Wilhelm, Maria. The Man Who Watched the Rising
Sun: The Story of Admiral Ellis M. Zacharias.
Hidden Heroes Series. New York: Watts, 1967.
238p.

3258 Willard, W. Weyth. The Leathernecks Come Through.
      New York: Fleming H. Revell, 1944. 224p.
      A chaplain's memoirs of service in the Solomons
      and Gilberts.

3259 "William F. Halsey." CurrBio:III:31-33.

3260 Williams, R. C., Jr. "Jap Defensive Tactics--Attu
      to Okinawa." Infantry Journal, LVII (August 1945),
      28-32.

3261 Williams, Wesley R. "Officer Recalls Flying British
      Plane in Aid of Marines." AFTimes, XXIII
      (August 25, 1962), 11.

3262 Willock, R. Unaccustomed to Fear: A Biography of
      the Late [Marine] General Roy S. Geiger. Prince-
      ton, N. J., 1968.

3263 Willoughby, Charles A. and John Chamberlain. Mac-
      Arthur, 1941-1945: Victory in the Pacific. Lon-
      don: Heinemann, 1956. 414p.

3264 Wilson, Earl J., et al. Your Marine Corps in World
      War I. Atlanta: Albert Love, 1946. 98p.

3265 Winston, Robert A. Aircraft Carrier. New York:
      Harper, 1942. 88p.

3266 _____. Fighting Squadron: A Veteran Squadron Lead-
      er's First-Hand Account of Carrier Combat with
      Task Force 58. New York: Holliday House, 1946.
      182p.
      Fighting Squadron 31.

3267 Worden, William L. "There Was a Man, Admiral
      Raymond A. Spruance." Reader's Digest, LXX
      (April 1957), 117-121.

3268 Worthington, Joseph M. "The Story of Destroyer
      Squadron 57, World War II." Unpublished paper,
      Type Commands File, U.S. Navy Department,
      Naval History Division, Operational Archives,
      1968. 39p.
      All ships of the commodore's squadron saw
      action in the Aleutians late in 1944, as radar pick-
      ets off Okinawa, and in Japanese waters during 1945.

3269 Wright, Bertram C. The 1st Cavalry Division in
      World War II. Tokyo: Toppan Printing Co.,
      1947. 245p.
          This U.S. Army unit saw much Pacific service.

3270 Wylie, Joseph C. "Reflections on the War in the
      Pacific." USNIP, LXXVIII (1952), 351-361, 1256-
      1257.

3271 Yanaga, Chitoshi. Japan Since Perry. Series in His-
      tory. New York: MacGraw-Hill, 1949. 723p.
      Includes World War II.

3272 Yingling, James M. A Brief History of the 5th Ma-
      rines. Marine Corps Historical Reference Series,
      no. 36. Washington: Historical Branch, U.S.
      Marine Corps, 1963. 38p.

3273 Yokoi, Toshiyuki. "Thoughts on Japan's Naval Defeat."
      USNIP, LXXXVI (1960), 68-69.

3274 Yu, Te-jen. The Japanese Struggle for World Empire.
      New York: Vantage Press, 1967.

3275 Zahl, Harold A. "The Secret Everyone Knew." Signal,
      XXIV (April 1970), 39-43.
          Japanese balloon-bomb operations against Ameri-
      ca.

3276 Zehnpfennig, Gladys. Melvin J. Maas, Gallant Man
      of Action. Men of Achievement Series. Minneap-
      olis: T. S. Denison, 1967. 296p.
      Marine aviator.

3277 [No entry.]

3278 Ziesing, Hibben. History of Fighting Squadron 46: A
      Log in Narrative Form of Its Participation in World
      War II. New York: Plantin Press, 1946. 43p.

          Further References: Readers will find additional
      data relative to this section in some of the general works cited
      in Volume III, Part 1.

IIB THE JAPANESE TRIUMPHANT

(1) GENERAL WORKS

Introduction. Japan began down the long road to
World War II the earliest of any of the Axis. Her conquest
of Manchuria in late 1931 was only a taste of what was to
come as moderate leaders of that nation were removed, often
violently, and replaced by military extremists.

The first six months after Pearl Harbor, that
"infamous act" which put America officially into the war,
saw the Japanese triumphant everywhere in the Pacific. The
few Allied forces, naval or otherwise, available in the area
could not stand against them for long.

The references gathered into this section are often
quite specific. Unfortunately in many cases, there is an
insufficient number on any one topic to justify a sub-section
below. In addition to these and the general citations, one
should note that the majority of the material available on the
diplomatic/naval developments leading to Pearl Harbor are
not being repeated here. Although we have added a few of
the more important works, most of this literature has already been listed in Vol. V of Myron J. Smith, Jr., American Naval Bibliography Series, The American Navy, 1918-
1941 (Metuchen, N.J.: Scarecrow Press, 1974). Those
interested in the maneuvering before the event, as opposed
to the actual operational aspects, are urged to consult that
work.

3279 Abend, Hallett. Ramparts of the Pacific. Garden
      City, N.Y.: Doubleday, Doran, 1942. 332p.

3280 Abernethy, E. P. "The Pecos Died Hard." USNIP,
      XCV (1969), 74-83.
      When Japan attacked Pearl Harbor, the oiler
      Pecos (AO-6) was in the Philippines. On Decem-
      ber 8, she departed Cavite Navy Yard, headed

south to pick up oil in Borneo, and then succored
U.S. warships attempting to hold back the Japanese.
Early in 1942, near Christmas Island, she stopped
to take aboard survivors from the sunken Langley
which had been rescued by destroyers. After trans-
ferring these and fighting off a Japanese land-based
bomber attack, she was subjected to three carrier
strikes from I.J.N. Soryu on March 1st. The last
of these sent the verteran to the bottom, although
232 survivors were picked up.

3281 "Admiral at the Front: [Thomas] Hart." Time,
      XXXVIII (November 24, 1941), 36-38.
        In 1939, this American naval leader was appoint-
      ed C-in-C of the U.S. Asiatic Fleet. Shortly after
      Pearl Harbor, all Allied warships in the Pacific
      were placed under his command in an A.B.D.A.
      force. He retired from the service following the
      disasters to that fleet; however, because of his
      vast experience, he was called upon to sit on the
      naval board. He held that post until 1945, when
      he again retired.

3282 Baldridge, Harry A. "The United States Navy in a
      Tight Fix." American Collector, XI (1942), 6-7,
      21.
        In the Pacific following Pearl Harbor.

3283 Ballantine, Joseph W. "Mukden to Pearl Harbor."
      Foreign Affairs, XXVII (July 1949), 651-664.
        The road to war.

3284 Bisson, Thomas A. American Policy in the Far East,
      1931-1941. I.P.R. Inquiry Series. Rev. ed.
      New York: Institute of Pacific Relations, 1941.
      206p.
        Contains a supplementary chapter by Miriam S.
      Farley with considerable information on naval
      problems.

3285 _____. America's Far Eastern Policy. I.P.R. In-
      quiry Series. New York: Published for the Inter-
      national Secretariat, Institute of Pacific Relations,
      by Macmillan, 1945. 235p.

3286 Blakeney, Benjamin B., jt. editor. See Togo,
      Shigenori, no. 3379.

3287 Bowers, Faubion. "Twenty-Five Years Ago--How
      Japan Won the War." New York Times Magazine
      (August 30, 1970), 5-7, 35-44.

3288 Bryant, Arthur. "Events in the Pacific: A Lesson
      on Sea Power." Illustrated London News, CC
      (February 14, 1942), 196.

3289 Buss, Claude A. War and Diplomacy in Eastern Asia.
      New York: Macmillan, 1941. 570p.

3290 Butow, Robert J. C. "The Hull-Nomura Conversations:
      A Fundamental Misconception." American Histori-
      cal Review, (1960), 822-836.

3291 _____. Tojo and the Coming of the War. Princeton,
      N. J. : Princeton University Press, 1961. 584p.

3292 Byas, Hugh. The Japanese Enemy, His Power and
      His Vulnerability. New York: Alfred A. Knopf,
      1942. 107p.
      The views of a New York Times correspondent.

3293 Bywater, Hector C. The Great Pacific War, a Histori-
      cal Prophecy Now Being Fulfilled. Boston: Hough-
      ton, Mifflin, 1942. 319p.
      A slight revision of the work cited in my The
      American Navy, 1918-1941: A Bibliography.

3294 _____. "The Great Pacific War: An Imaginary Con-
      flict Described by an Expert in 1925 Now Proves
      Prophetic." Life, XI (December 22, 1941), 74-77.

3295 Caidin, Martin. The Ragged, Rugged Warriors: The
      Story of American Pilots in the Early Air War
      Against Japan. New York: Dutton, 1966. 384p.

3296 Chamberlin, William H. Japan Over Asia. Rev. and
      enl. ed. Garden City, N. Y. : Blue Ribbon Books,
      1942. 463p.

3297 Codman, Charles. "Twenty-Four Hours on Carrier
      Patrol: Dive-Bombing With a Carrier-Based Navy
      Squadron." Saturday Evening Post, CCXIV (Janu-
      ary 10, 1942), 12-13+.

3298 Cohn, David L. "The Battle of Makassar Straits."

Unpublished paper, Individual Personnel File, U.S.
Navy Department, Naval History Division, Operational Archives, 1945. 16p.
The action of January 24, 1942, in which four
American four-stacker destroyers surprised a
Japanese transport squadron off Borneo, sinking a
number of enemy vessels. According to notations
on the margins, the account was related to the
author by Admiral William Glassford, Jr., who
commanded the U.S. warships.

3299 Craigie, Robert. Behind the Japanese Mask. London
and New York: Hutchinson, 1946. 174p.
Memoirs of the British ambassador to Japan
concerning the road to war in the Far East. For
the record, it might be noted here that, unlike
America, the United Kingdom did not receive any
"notes" and Japanese forces were pushing towards
Malaya some hours before Pearl Harbor.

3300 Crozat, Victor J. "Japan Drives Southwest." Army,
XVII (June 1967), 65-73.

3301 De Haas, J. Anton. Our Allies: The Netherlands
East Indies. New York: Oxford University Press,
1942.
A 10¢ pamphlet.

3302 De Wilde, C. J. M. Kretschmer. "'All Ships Follow
Me': The Operations of the Royal Netherlands
Navy in the Pacific War." Military Review, XXXI
(December 1951), 106-109.
After the Battle of the Java Sea in early 1942,
there were few ships of this brave force left!

3303 Droste, Chris B. Till Better Days. London and New
York: Hurst and Blackett, 1946. 104p.
The fall of the Dutch East Indies.

3304 "Dutch MTB's in the Far East in 1942." Warship
International, V (Spring 1968), 156.

3305 Engel, L. "Japan's Losses in the Southwest Pacific."
Far Eastern Survey, XI (March 9, 1942), 60-62.

3306 _____. "United Nations' Losses in the Pacific." Far
Eastern Survey, XI (April 20, 1942), 101-102.

One should not rely too closely on these early figures.

3307 Eyre, James K., Jr. "The Background to Japanese Naval Treachery in the Pacific." USNIP, LXX (1944), 874-884.

3308 Ferraby, Hubert C. "Sea Power in the Pacific." 19th Century, CXXXI (February 1942), 56-60.

3309 Fleisher, Wilfrid. Our Enemy Japan. Garden City, N.Y.: Doubleday, Doran, 1942. 236p.
Primarily devoted to the period before Pearl Harbor, with copies of President Roosevelt's messages and speeches following the attack appended.

3310 Fumihiko, Tojo, jt. editor. See Togo, Shigenori, no. 3379.

3311 Gallagher, O'Dowd. Retreat in the East: A War Book. London: Harrap, 1942. 190p. Rpr. 1956.

3312 Gayn, Mark J. The Fight for the Pacific. New York: William Morrow, 1942. 378p.

3313 Gervasi, Frank. "Thunder Over the Pacific." Collier's, CIX (January 3, 1942), 8-10.

3314 Goggins, William B. "U.S.S. Marblehead (CL-12): The Ship That Wouldn't Give Up." All Hands, no. 558, (July 1963), 58-63.
Following the January 24, 1942, Battle of Makassar Straits, which this light cruiser covered, she was badly damaged in air attacks on February 4. Unable to obtain repairs of a lasting nature at Tjilatjap in the East Indies or at Trincomalee, Ceylon, she sailed via South Africa and Brazil for New York. There she arrived and was immediately placed in drydock on May 4 where she was extensively rebuilt. She then served in the South Atlantic patrol, in the support of the invasion of Southern France, and as a training ship before decommissioning in 1945.

3315 Gordon, C. V. "H.N.M.S. Tjerk Hiddes, Timor Ferry." USNIP, LXXXVI (1960), 31-35.
On the Dutch destroyer's evacuation of Allied

fighting men from Timor to Darwin, Australia, in
December 1941.

3316 Grew, Joseph C. Report from Tokyo: A Message to
the American People. New York: Simon and
Schuster, 1942. 88p.
Advises that the Japanese not be underestimated.

3317 _____. Ten Years in Japan: A Contemporary Record
Drawn from the Diaries and Private and Official
Papers of Joseph C. Grew, United States Ambassa-
dor to Japan, 1932-1942. New York: Simon and
Schuster, 1944. 554p.
Should be compared with British Ambassador
Craigie's account, no. 3299 above.

3318 Harkness, Albert, Jr. "Retreat in the Southwest
Pacific. " Unpublished paper, U.S. Navy Department, Naval History Division, Operational Archives,
1949. 121p.
Based on the next citation, this work is primarily
concerned with the command, administrative, and
strategic implications of the topic.

3319 _____. "Retreat in the Southwest Pacific, December
8, 1941-March 4, 1942. " Unpublished PhD Dissertation, Brown University, 1949.

3320 Helfrich, C. E. L. "The Royal Netherlands Navy and
the War in the Far East. " Asiatic Review, New
Series XXXIX (October 1943), 381-384.

3321 Herzog, James H. Closing the Open Door: American-
Japanese Diplomatic Negotiations, 1936-1941.
Annapolis: U.S. Naval Institute, 1973. 296p.
Based on the dissertation cited next.

3322 _____. "The Role of the United States Navy in the
Evolution and Execution of American Foreign Policy
Relative to Japan, 1936-1941. " Unpublished PhD
Dissertation, Brown University, 1963.

3323 Higgins, Trumbull. "Japanese Strategy in 1941. "
USNIP, LXXXII (1956), 1330-1331.

3324 Hill, Max. Exchange Ship. New York: Farrar &
Rinehart, 1942. 312p.

Relates the author's experiences as a POW in
Japan and as a passenger on an exchange ship.

3325 Hill, Norman L. "Was There an Ultimatum Before
Pearl Harbor?" American Journal of International
Law, XLII (April 1948), 355-367.

3326 "Hirohito's Aces: Credit for Japanese Victories Be-
longs to Three Navy Leaders." Newsweek, XVIII
(December 22, 1941), 39.
Starting with Yamamoto.

3327 "The Jap Threat in the Pacific Grows Despite the
New Punch of the Allies." Newsweek, XIX (February 9, 1942), 17-22.

3328 "Japan Suffers Her Greatest Naval Defeat of the War:
The Battle of Macassar Straits." Illustrated Lon-
don News, CC (February 7, 1942), 180-181.
The destroyer raid on Japanese shipping off
Balikpapan, Borneo, on January 24, 1942.

3329 "Japanese Landing Force, Supported by Warships and
Planes." Illustrated London News, CC (April 4,
1942), 410.

3330 Jones, Eli S. "Adventure in Failure: Behind the
Scenes Before Pearl Harbor." Asia, XLV (December 1945), 609-616.

3331 Kennedy, Paul. Pacific Onslaught: 7th Dec. 1941-
7th Feb. 1943. Ballantine's Illustrated History of
World War II. New York: Ballantine Books,
1972. 160p.
Japan triumphant.

3332 Kiralfy, Alexander. Victory in the Pacific: How We
Must Defeat Japan. New York: John Day, 1942.
283p.
Advocates an offensive aimed at Japanese political, military, and industrial centers.

3333 Konoye, Fumimaro. The Memoirs of Prince Fumimaro Konoye. Tokyo: Okuyama Service [195?].
62p.
The English-language reminiscences of General
Tojo's immediate predecessor as Japanese premier.

3334 Layton, Edwin T. "Rendezvous in Reverse. " USNIP,
      LXXIX (1953), 478-485.
      The second Japanese attack on Pearl Harbor,
      May 4, 1942, supposedly based on a story by Alec
      Hudson. Hudson's reply to this article was printed
      on pages 896-899 of the same volume of the USNIP.

3335 Leighton, Isabel, jt. author. See Perry, George S.,
      no. 3357.

3336 Lewis, Winston B. "The Period of Japanese Expan-
      sion. " In: Elmer B. Potter, ed. Sea Power:
      A Naval History. Englewood Cliffs, N. J. : Pren-
      tice-Hall, 1960. p. 646-669.

3337 "The Loss of the Langley. " Newsweek, XIX (April
      13, 1942), 22.
      After her reclassification from CV-1 to AV-3
      in the late 1930' s, the former carrier, now a
      seaplane tender, was assigned to the Pacific. In
      late February, she, together with two destroyers,
      were assigned to deliver a cargo of P-40 aircraft
      to Tjilatjap, Java. On February 27, the three
      were attacked off that East Indies harbor, the
      Langley was hit, and it proved impossible to save
      her. She was destroyed by gunfire from her es-
      corts, after all but 16 of her crew was rescued.

3338 Lu, David J. From the Marco Polo Bridge to Pearl
      Harbor: Japan's Entry Into World War II. Wash-
      ington: Public Affairs Press, 1961. 274p.

3339 Mack, William R. "Macassar Merry-go-Round. "
      USNIP, LXIX (1943), 669-673.
      The January 24, 1942 destroyer attack on Japa-
      nese transports.

3340 Martin, Pete, jt. author. See Morrill, John, no.
      3343.

3341 Merrifield, Robert B. "Japan's Amphibious Bid. "
      Marine Corps Gazette, XXXVIII (May 1954), 40-47.
      Early World War II operations.

3342 Mill, Edward W. "The War in the Pacific. " Current
      History, New Series I (February 1942), 487-494;
      III (November 1942), 187-190.

3343 Morrill, John and Pete Martin. South from Corregi-
        dor. New York: Simon and Schuster, 1943. 249p.
        The dangerous voyage of the American mine-
        sweeper Quail's (AM-15) crew to Australia in an
        open boat through waters controlled by the Japanese.

3344 Morton, Louis. "The Japanese Decision for War. "
        USNIP, LXXX (1954), 1324-1335.

3345 _____. "Japanese Strategy in 1941. " USNIP, LXXXII
        (1956), 202-204.

3346 _____., ed. "The Evolution of Japanese Landing Op-
        erations. " Marine Corps Gazette, XL (April
        1956), 44-53.

3347 Moyes, John F. Scrap-Iron Flotilla. Sydney, Austral-
        ia: N. S. W. Bookstall Co. , 1943. 218p.
        A first-hand account of the A. B. D. A. fleet sent
        to oppose the Japanese in early 1942.

3348 "The Muddle in the Pacific. " New Statesman & Nation,
        XXII (December 27, 1941), 519.

3349 "Naval War in the Pacific. " Engineering, CLIII (March
        20, 1943), 231-232.

3350 "Navy Task Force Shoots Down 16 Jap Bombers in a
        Pacific Air-Sea Battle. " Life, XII (March 16,
        1942), 38-39.

3351 Neumann, William L. "How American Policy Toward
        Japan Contributed to War in the Pacific. " In:
        Harry E. Barnes, ed. Perpetual War for Perpetual
        Peace. Caldwell, Idaho: Caxton Printers, 1953.
        p. 231-269.

3352 Nimitz, Chester W. "Letter. " American Mathematical
        Monthly, XLIX (March 1942), 212-214.

3353 "1942: Diversion in the Pacific. " National Review,
        CXVIII (January 1942), 1-8.
        A British look at Allied strategy.

3354 Nomura, Kichisaburo. "Stepping Stones to War. "
        USNIP, LXXVII (1951), 926-931.

3355 "The Pacific Arena: The A. B. D. A. Defenders Slow

the Japs After the Initial Blitz Gains. " Newsweek,
XVIII (December 22, 1941), 17-20.

3356 Pelzer, K. J. "Japan's Drive Against the Netherlands
East Indies. " Far Eastern Survey, XI (February
9, 1942), 37-40.

3357 Perry, George S. and Isabel Leighton. Where Away,
a Modern Odyssey. New York: Whittlesey House,
McGraw-Hill, 1944. 249p.
      The battles of the light cruiser Marblehead and
her epic voyage from the Dutch East Indies to New
York in early 1942.

3358 "Planes vs. Ships: Air Power Grabs the Spotlight in
U. S. and British Sinkings. " Newsweek, XVIII
(December 22, 1941), 20.
      This entry is considered general as it concerns
both Pearl Harbor and the loss of H. M. ships
Repulse and Prince of Wales.

3359 Pratt, William V. "Postscript on the Battle of
Macassar Strait. " Newsweek, XIX (February 23,
1942), 16.

3360 _____. "Sea Strategy of the Japanese Thrust. "
Newsweek, XIX (February 9, 1942), 19.

3361 _____. "The Significance of Japan's Strategy. " Newsweek, XVIII (December 29, 1941), 15.

3362 _____. "Why the Fleet Could Not Retreat to the
West Coast. " Newsweek, XXVI (December 3, 1945),
36.
      Following Pearl Harbor.

3363 Puleston, William D. The Armed Forces of the Pacific: A Comparison of the Military and Naval Power
of the United States and Japan. New Haven, Conn. :
Yale University Press, 1941. 274p.
      Although published prior to Pearl Harbor, the
value of this work shows through during the period
of this section.

3364 Reeves, G. A. "Aircraft Carriers in the Pacific
War Arena. " Canadian Aviation, XV (April 1942),
24-27.

3365   Richards, David K. K.   "The Beginning of Pearl Harbor,
          July 1909 to December 7, 1941." USNIP, LXX
          (1944), 536-545.

3366   Richmond, Herbert W.   'Naval Strategy in the East."
          Fortnightly, CLVI (December 1941), 566-569.

3367   _____.   "War in the Far East." Fortnightly, CLVII
          (January 1942), 71-75.

3368   Spiro, David.   "Philistines: Adventures of H.M.S.
          Maru." Blackwood's, CCXLVIII (November 1940),
          459-463.

3369   Steiger, George N.   "Awaiting a Far Eastern Show-
          down." Current History, New Series I (November
          1941), 261-265.
          Little did the author know Japan would deliver
          it in spades beginning early in the month following
          the publication of his article!

3370   Stove, G. W.   "The Queen's Navy at War: Operations
          of the Royal Netherlands Navy in the Southwest
          Pacific During the Invasion of the Philippines,
          Malacca, and the East Indies." USNIP, LXXVI
          (1950), 288-301.
          During which time the R.N.N. served as part
          of the A.B.D.A. fleet.

3371   "Strategicus," pseud.   "Far Eastern Dangers." Spec-
          tator, CLCVII (December 19, 1941), 573.

3372   Taylor, George E.   America in the New Pacific.   New
          York: Macmillan, 1942.   160p.
          Primarily concerned with American policy before
          and after Pearl Harbor.

3373   "The Third Sea Power in the World: The Imperial
          Japanese Navy." Illustrated London News, CXCIX
          (December 13, 1941), 752-753.
          In all honesty, when this issue hit the streets
          the I.J.N. was the premier sea power!

3374   "Thomas C. Hart." CurrBio:III:21-22.

3375   Thursfield, Henry G.   "In the Pacific: Air Power and
          Sea Power." National Review, CXVIII (March
          1942), 245-250.

3376 _____. Navies of the United States and Japan. Lon-
      don: Rolls House Publishing Co., 1942. 35p.
      A comparison.

3377 _____. "Naval War Commentary: Sea and Air in the
      Indian Ocean. " National Review, CXVIII (May
      1942), 445-451.
      How Admiral Sir James Somerville's fleet sur-
      vived the Japanese onslaught in that area is worthy
      of much greater research and publication than it
      has received.

3378 _____. "War in the Pacific. " National Review,
      CXVIII (January 1942), 23-28.

3379 Togo, Shigenori. The Cause of Japan. Translated
      and Edited by Togo Fumihiko and Benjamin B.
      Blakeney. New York: Simon and Schuster, 1956.
      372p.

3380 Toland, John. But Not In Shame: The Six Months
      After Pearl Harbor. New York: Random House,
      1961. 427p.
      Recommended as the first stopping place among
      secondary materials for students of this section.

3381 _____. "Defenses Crumble. " Look, XXV (October
      10. 1961), 90-98.
      An excerpt from the above citation.

3382 Tolley, Kemp. "The Cruise of the Lanikai. " USNIP,
      XCIX (1973), 76-79.

3383 _____. _____. Annapolis: U.S. Naval Institute,
      1973. 356p.

3384 _____. "The Strange Assignment of the Lanikai. "
      USNIP, LXXXVIII (1962), 70-83.
      This small schooner, commanded by the author,
      was to have been placed before any advancing
      Japanese fleet intent on war. Her sinking would
      then provide America with an excuse to enter the
      war officially. Pearl Harbor foiled this plan and
      the vessel was forced to escape from the area
      rapidly being overrun by the enemy.

3385 _____. "The Strange Mission of the Lanikai. "

American Heritage, XXIV (October 1973), 56-61,
93-95.

3386 "Tommy Hart Speaks Out." Time, XL (October 13,
1942), 67-70.

3387 "Tommy Hart's Gold Star." Time, XXXIX (June 1,
1942), 48.

3388 "U.S.A. and Japan: Two Navies in a Chart Silhou-
ette." Illustrated London News, CXCIX (October
25, 1941), 532.

3389 "U.S. Admiral is Far Eastern Boss." Scholastic,
XL (February 2, 1942), 15.
On Admiral Hart's command of the A.B.D.A.
forces.

3390 "U.S. Aircraft Carriers of Hawaii: Photographs."
Illustrated London News, CXCIX (December 13,
1941), 754.

3391 "The U.S. Navy Lays Down Lines in the Pacific."
Scholastic, XL (March 23, 1942), 6.

3392 Van Beers, Ton. "With One Stove-Pipe and Bags of
Cheek." Fifteen Nations, VI (August-September
1961), 104-106.
Adventures with the Royal Netherlands Navy.

3393 Van Der Klaauw, B. "Dutch Against Nippon: The
Story of the Dutch East Indies Air Force and Its
Fight Against Japan in 1941-1942." Air Pictorial,
XXIV (December 1962), 370-374.

3394 Van Hook, J. Q. "Genesis of the War in the Pacific
Area." Southwestern Social Science Quarterly,
XXIII (March 1943), 381-398.

3395 Varg, Paul. "Alternatives in the Far East." World
Affairs, XXVI (1955), 247-254.
At and just before the time of Pearl Harbor.

3396 "Views of American Strategic Strong Points in the
Pacific." Illustrated London News, CXCIX (December 13, 1941), 759.

3397 Vogel, Bertram.   "Diplomatic Prelude to Pearl Har-
         bor. " USNIP, LXXV (1949), 414-421.

3398 "War in the Far East Hinges on Manila and on Singa-
         pore. " Life, XII (January 5, 1942), 30-31.

3399 "The War in the Pacific. " Life, XII (January 5, 1942),
         24-27.

3400 "War in the Wind. " Newsweek, XXVII (February 11,
         1946), 25-26.
         The days just before Pearl Harbor.

3401 "Ward, J. A.   "More Aircraft Carriers Needed in the
         Pacific. " Aero Digest, XL (February 1942), 74.

3402 Wavell, Archibald.   Despatch by the Supreme Com-
         mander of the A. B. D. A. Area to the Combined
         Chiefs of Staff on the Operations in the Southwest
         Pacific, 15 January-25 February 1942.   London:
         H. M. Stationery Office, 1948.   22p.

3403 Wigmore, Lionel.   The Japanese Thrust.   Australia
         in the War of 1939-1945: Series I.   Canberra:
         Australian War Memorial, 1957.   715p.

         Further References: Readers will find addition-
al information relative to this section in section IIA above,
as well as in the general histories cited in Volume III,
Part 1.

                (2) SURPRISE AT PEARL HARBOR

         Introduction.   The success of the British carrier
raid on Taranto, Italy, in mid-November 1940 (see Volume
I, section ID-2) was not lost on Japan's naval leaders.
Early the following year, Admiral Isoroku Yamamoto, C-in-
C of the Imperial Navy, proposed attacking the American
battle fleet at Pearl Harbor.   That learned sailor, who had
fostered the rapid growth of his fleet's air arm in the late
1930's, hoped that such an assault would immobilize U. S.
Navy units while Japan conquered her so-called "Southern
Resources Area. "   Details of his proposal were worked out
during the summer and fall, with the decision for war--ac-

tually a gamble on Axis success in Africa and Russia--made
in early December.   If Germany could carry the ball unas-
sisted in Europe (co-ordination on this was so poor that
Japanese leaders did not even inform Hitler that Pearl Harbor was coming!), then Southeast Asia could be overrun and
the Americans handed a fait accompli.

On Sunday morning, December 7, 1941, 360 offensive Japanese aircraft lifted off Vice Admiral C. Nagumo's
carriers for the "infamous" raid on the Yankee fleet at Pearl
Harbor, and on military and air installations on Oahu, Territory of Hawaii.   When they were finished, four battleships,
a minelayer, and a target ship were sunk, four battleships,
three cruisers, three destroyers, a seaplane tender and a
repair ship were damaged.   Nearly 200 U.S. Army and Navy
aircraft were destroyed and over 2300 Americans were dead.
The Japanese lost five midget submarines, 28 aircraft, and
fewer than 100 men.

Despite the apparent success of the attack, Nagumo's
people missed a number of important targets.   The American
carriers, not in port that day, were undamaged as were all
American submarines.   Surprisingly, they also failed to take
out the island's oil supply, which was entirely above ground
in storage tanks.   These omissions would return to haunt
the raiders many times over.

The references in this section concern, with a few
exceptions, the operational aspects of the Japanese mission.
Such diplomatic maneuvering as occurred before the event is,
for the most part, covered in Volume V of my American
Naval Bibliography series, The American Navy, 1918-1941:
A Bibliography (Metuchen, N.J.:   Scarecrow Press, 1974).
A considerable body of "Pearl Harbor literature" grew up
during the late stages of the war and early days of the peace
centered on attempting to assess "blame" for the incident.
Most of this is cited here.

3404   Adams, Val.   "That Sunday Twenty-Five Years Ago I
          Was on a Tower Overlooking All of Pearl Harbor."
          Esquire, LXVI (December 1966), 252+.

3405   "Admiral vs. Admiral."   Time, XLVI (December 31,
          1945), 18.
          Concerning blame for the attack.

3406   Alcott, C. D.   "Why Remember Pearl Harbor?"   An-
          tioch Review, II (March 1942), 6-25.

3407   Alden, John D.   "Up From Ashes--The Saga of Cassin
       and Downes. "   USNIP, LXXXVII (1961), 33-35, 102,
       331.
           DD-372 and DD-375 were both damaged in the
       raid, but were repaired and sent forth to battle.

3408   "The Attack on Hawaii: First Pictures Show the Death
       and Destruction at the American Base. "   Life, XI
       (December 29, 1941), 11-19.

3409   Baker, Leonard.   Roosevelt and Pearl Harbor.   New
       York: Macmillan, 1970.   352p.

3410   Barker, A. J.   Pearl Harbor.   Ballantine's Illustrated
       History of World War II.   New York: Ballantine
       Books, 1970.   160p.

3411   Barnes, Harry E.   Pearl Harbor After a Quarter of
       a Century.   New York: Arno, 1972.   132p.
           Reprinted from Left and Right, IV (1968).

3412   _____.   "Where Was the General?"   Chicago Tribune
       Special Supplement, (December 7, 1966), 8-9.
           Contends that General George C. Marshall was
       not out horseback riding that morning as legend
       says and thus could have gotten a warning message
       off to Pearl Harbor.

3413   _____, et al.   "The Mystery of Pearl Harbor. "
       National Review, XVIII (December 13, 1966), 1260-
       1272.

3414   Bergen, John J.   "The Lessons of Pearl Harbor. "
       Navy, I (December 1958), 5+.

3415   Biemiller, Carl L.   "The Long Day of Pearl Harbor. "
       Holiday, XX (December 1956), 88-91+.

3416   "The Blame for Pearl Harbor: Newspaper Editorials."
       Forum, DIV (October 1945), 182-185.

3417   "Blitz Chronology. "   Newsweek, XVIII (December 15,
       1941), 19-21.

3418   Boehm, William R.   "The Nevada's Navagational
       Nimbleness. "   USNIP, LXXXIV (1958), 107.
           Hit and aflame, but under steam, the old battle-

wagon beached herself rather than blocking the
port's channel.

3419 Borg, Dorothy, et al. Pearl Harbor as History:
      Japanese-American Relations, 1931-1941. Studies
      of the East Asian Institute. New York: Columbia
      University Press, 1973. 801p.

3420 Bradley, Mark E. "Kimmel, Short Were Not Bad
      Guys." Electrical Warfare, IV (Winter 1972), 20-
      21+.
          Contends that the U.S. Navy and Army command-
      ers on Oahu were not responsible for the success
      of the Japanese endeavor.

3421 Brittin, Burdick H. "We Four Ensigns." USNIP,
      XCII (1966), 106-109.
          Comments on the attack.

3422 Brownlow, Donald G. The Accused: The Ordeal of
      Rear Admiral Husband Edward Kimmel, U.S. Navy.
      New York: Vantage Press, 1968. 190p.

3423 Burtness, Paul S. and Warren U. Ober. "Secretary
      [Henry L.] Stimson and the First Pearl Harbor
      Investigation." Australian Journal of Politics and
      History, XIV (January 1968), 24-36.
          The inquiry which placed all the blame on Ad-
      miral Kimmel and General Short.

3424 _____, eds. The Puzzle of Pearl Harbor. Evanston,
      Ill.: Row, Peterson, 1962. 244p.

3425 Cant, Gilbert. "What Happened at Pearl Harbor."
      Science Digest, XI (May 1942), 16-22.

3426 Chamberlain, J. "The Man Who Pushed Pearl Har-
      bor." Life, XX (April 1, 1946), 84-88.
          Yamamoto.

3427 Clark, Blake. Remember Pearl Harbor! New York:
      Modern Age Books, 1942. 127p.
          The suddenness and horror of the Japanese at-
      tack recalled by a University of Hawaii professor
      who was an eyewitness.

3428 _____. _____. Rev. ed. New York: Harper, 1943.
      300p.

Contains additional photographs, maps, and the
U.S. Army and Navy honor rolls.

3429 _____. "Remember Pearl Harbor: The Epic of
American Courage Against Treacherous Odds. "
Reader's Digest, XL (June 1942), 45-54.

3430 Cope, Harley F. "'Climb Mount Niitaka!'" USNIP,
LXXII (1946), 1515-1519.
The Japanese attack, set off by the code-words
of the author's title.

3431 Cort, David. "The Truth About the Truth About Pearl
Harbor. " Nation, CLXXVIII (April 17, May 22,
1954), 329-331, 451+.
Includes discussion.

3432 Coughlin, William J.   "The Great Mokusatsu Mistake:
Was This the Deadliest Error of Our Time?"
Harper's, CCVI (March 1953), 31-40.
Contending that Pearl Harbor was the beginning
of the end for the Japanese warlords, this article
was abridged in Reader's Digest, LXII (May 1953),
133-135, under the title "Was It the Deadliest
Error of Our Time?"

3433 Cranwell, John P.   "Did the Japanese Win at Pearl
Harbor?" USNIP, LXX (1944), 661-667.
Examines some of the attackers' omissions
cited in our introduction to this section.

3434 Crump, Irving. "They Fired the First Shots. " In:
his Our Marines. New York: Dodd, Mead, 1944.
p. 233-236.
U.S. Marines at Pearl Harbor.

3435 "Damaged Vessels at Pearl Harbor: West Virginia,
California, Oklahoma. " USNIP, LXIX (1943),
1086-1090.

3436 Day, A. Grove and Carl Stroven, eds. Hawaiian
Reader. New York: Appleton-Century-Crofts,
1959.
Contains a section on the Pearl Harbor attack.

3437 December 7, the First Thirty Hours, by the Correspondents of Time, Life, and Fortune. New York:
Alfred A. Knopf, 1942. 229p.

The reports of 50 reporters describing the re-
actions of the world's public to the assault. Relatively little data on the actual raid itself.

3438 "Did F. D. R. Needle the Japanese to Bomb Pearl Harbor: A Discussion. " Saturday Evening Post,
CCXXVI (May 15, June 19, 1954), 10+, 4+.

3439 Didion, John. "Hawaii: Taps at Pearl Harbor. "
Saturday Evening Post, CCXXXIX (December 17,
1966), 22-29.

3440 "Dorie Miller, First U. S. Hero of World War II. "
Ebony, XXV (December 1969), 132-134+.
A black sailor's stand during the attack.

3441 Duncan, R. L. "Without Warning. " American Legion
Magazine, LXIII (December 1957), 18-19.
The Japanese raid.

3442 Dupuy, Theodore N. "Pearl Harbor: Who Blundered?"
American Heritage, XIII (February 1962), 64-81.

3443 Emmons, Roger M. "Pearl Harbor. " Marine Corps
Gazette, XXVIII (February 1944), 3-9.

3444 Evans, William R. , Jr. "Remember Pearl Harbor!"
In: Gayle Thornbrough and Dorothy Riker, eds.
Readings in Indiana History. Indianapolis: Indiana
Historical Bureau, 1956. p. 593-594.
A letter home written by an ensign on the scene.
The author was later killed during the Battle of
Midway.

3445 "The Facts on Pearl Harbor: Text of the Navy Report. " Current History, New Series III (January
1943), 443-446.

3446 Featherman, Maurice. "The Ship That Sank From
Fright. " USNIP, XCVIII (1972), 84-86.
The loss of the minelayer Oglala.

3447 Feis, Herbert. The Road to Pearl Harbor: The Com-
ing of the War Between the United States and
Japan. Princeton, N. J. : Princeton University
Press, 1950. 356p.

3448 _____. "War Came at Pearl Harbor: Suspicions Con-
      sidered. " Yale Review, XLV (March 1956), 378-
      390.

3449 Fergusson, Erna. Our Hawaii. New York: Alfred
      A. Knopf, 1942. 304p.

3450 Ferrell, Robert H. "Pearl Harbor and the Revision-
      ists. " Historian, XVII (1955), 215-233.
      Considers the writings of the various "schools"
      of history writers relative to the attack and respon-
      sibility for same.

3451 "The Final Facts of Pearl Harbor. " U.S. News &
      World Report, XX (February 1, 1946), 19-21.

3452 "First Japanese Photographs of the Treacherous Attack
      on Pearl Harbor. " Illustrated London News, CC
      (June 20, 1942), 786.

3453 Flynn, John T. The Truth About Pearl Harbor. New
      York, 1944. 32p.

3454 Fox, Barry, pseud. See Stevens, Mrs. Albert M.,
      no. 3559.

3455 Fox, Leonard J. "Pearl Harbor. " Unpublished paper,
      Individual Personnel File, U.S. Navy Department,
      Naval History Division, Operational Archives, n.d.
      5p.
      Memoirs of a Chief Petty Officer aboard the
      cruiser Helena as the Japanese raid began.

3456 Fuchida, Mitsuo. From Pearl Harbor to Golgotha.
      San Jose, Calif.: Sky Pilots Press, 1953. 96p.

3457 _____. "I Led the Air Attack on Pearl Harbor. "
      USNIP, LXXVIII (1952), 939-952.

3458 Fukudome, Shigeru. "The Hawaii Operation. " USNIP,
      LXXXI (1955), 1314-1331.
      The above three references all present the
      Japanese side of the attack.

3459 "Full Text of the Official Reports Concerning the At-
      tack on Pearl Harbor. " U.S. News & World Re-
      port, Special Supplement, XIX (September 1, 1945),
      1-86.

3460 Gilbert, Daniel. What Really Happened at Pearl Har-
        bor. New York: Zondervan, 1943. 48p.

3461 Gillis, James M. "The Blame for Pearl Harbor. "
        Catholic World, CLXII (October 1945), 1-7.

3462 ____. "Footnote to Pearl Harbor. " Catholic World,
        CLXII (February 1946), 393-394.

3463 ____. "The Last Word on Pearl Harbor?" Catholic
        World, CLXIV (February 1947), 394.

3464 ____. "Pearl Harbor Reconsidered. " Catholic
        World, CLXIV (March 1947), 490-491.

3465 Greaves, Percy L. , Jr. "The Pearl Harbor Investi-
        gations. " In: Harry E. Barnes, ed. Perpetual
        War for Perpetual Peace. Caldwell, Idaho: Cax-
        ton Printers, 1953. p. 407-483.

3466 Hailey, Foster. "Their Mission Was to Begin a War:
        A Reconsideration of Events That Lead to Japan's
        Attack on Pearl Harbor. " New York Times Maga-
        zine, (December 2, 1945), 8-9+.

3467 Hale, William H. "After Pearl Harbor. " New Re-
        public, CV (December 15, 1941), 816-817.

3468 ____. "Trouble for the Admirals. " New Republic,
        CV (December 22, 1941), 845, 849-850.
        Blame--and the shakeup in the Pacific Command
        following the Japanese raid.

3469 "Havoc at Honolulu. " Time, XXXVIII (December 22,
        1941), 15-16.

3470 Hawaii at War. Honolulu Star-Bulletin, Special Supple-
        ments, 1942-1943.
        Two special issues, which contain some limited
        data on the Pearl Harbor attack.

3471 Hayter, Maurine K. "Hawaiian Retrospect. " USNIP,
        LXIX (1943), 1415-1417.

3472 Hibel, Franklin. "Caught With Our Planes Down. "
        Air Force, XXXIX (December 1956), 81-82+.

3473 Higgins, Trumbull. "East Wind Rain." USNIP, LXXXI
      (1955), 1198-1205.

3474 Hole, Theodore. "Pacific Anniversary." National Re-
      view, CXIX (December 1942), 490-494.

3475 Hollingshead, Billie. "The Japanese Attack of 7 Decem-
      ber 1941 on the Marine Corps Air Station at Ewa,
      Oahu, Territory of Hawaii." Unpublished paper,
      USMC File, U.S. Navy Department, Naval History
      Division, Operational Archives, 1945. 30p.

3476 Honan, William H. "Japan Strikes, 1941: Prophesies
      in Books by Hector C. Bywater." American Heri-
      tage, XXII (December 1970), 12-15+.

3477 "How Pearl Harbor Happened." Time, XXXIX (Febru-
      ary 2, 1942), 16.

3478 "Husband E. Kimmel." CurrBio:III:28-30.

3479 "Isaac C. Kidd." CurrBio:III:23.
          At the time of the Japanese attack, Rear Admiral
      Kidd was Commander of Battleship Division 1 and
      Chief of Staff and Aide, Commander, Battleship
      Battle Force. As the first enemy planes came in,
      he rushed to the bridge of his flagship, U.S.S.
      Arizona (BB-39). There, according to the certif-
      icate which accompanied his Congressional Medal
      of Honor and Purple Heart, he "courageously
      discharged his duties as Senior Officer Present
      Afloat until Arizona blew up from a magazine ex-
      plosion and a direct bomb hit on the bridge which
      resulted in the loss of his life."

3480 "Japan Launches Reckless Attack on the U.S." Life,
      XI (December 15, 1941), 27-33.

3481 "Japan's Wanton Raid on Hawaii's Air Base." Illustrat-
      ed London News, CXCIX (December 27, 1941), 819.

3482 "Judgment Day: The Court-Martial of Kimmel and
      Short a Knotty Legal and Military Puzzle." News-
      week, XXIII (April 24, 1944), 36+.

3483 "Killed in Action: 32 Portraits." Life, XI (December
      22, 1941), 22-23.

II The Pacific Theater 108

Victims of the Japanese raid.

3484 Kimmel, Husband E. "Admiral Kimmel: Why Was
He Not Warned?" U.S. News & World Report,
LXI (December 19, 1966), 20.
An excerpt from one of the admiral's speeches.

3485 _____. Admiral Kimmel's Story. Chicago: H.
Regnery, 1955. 206p.
The author was in command at the time of the
Pearl Harbor attack, a post he had held for ten
months, but was immediately relieved along with
General Short after the raid. The two were
strongly criticized for allegedly not taking the
necessary precautions to safeguard their ships and
installations in light of the dangerous tensions of
the times. Supporters of the men, led by the
admiral himself, have vigorously rebutted these
charges of culpability. They have maintained that
they were not kept posted on the diplomatic maneuvering nor urged to guard against surprise attack
on their facilities--a danger some in Washington
knew to exist. In the long run, however, it was
the shortcomings of both the basic military and
the naval system which came to be assessed.
No one knew the whole picture that intelligence was
attempting to tell and no one had overall responsi-
bility for the defense of the island.

3486 "Kimmel to the Attack." Newsweek, XXVII (January
28, 1946), 25-26.
The admiral's further defense of his situation on
December 7.

3487 Kittredge, Tracy B. "The Muddle Before Pearl Harbor." U.S. News & World Report, XXXVII (December 3, 1954), 52-63, 110-139.
See Admiral Theobald's reply cited below.

3488 "The Knock-Out Blow was No K.O.: Remember Pearl
Harbor." Illustrated London News, CCII (January
2, 1943), 11-13.

3489 Knox, Franklin. "The Pearl Harbor Report." In:
William H. Fetridge, ed. The Navy Reader.
Indianapolis: Bobbs-Merrill, 1943. p. 21-26.
Rpr. 1971.

3490 _____. "Secretary Knox Reports." New Republic, CV
     (December 22, 1941), 843.

3491 Korotkov, G. "Pearl Harbor." Soviet Military Re-
     view, VI (November 1971), 42-45.

3492 Krock, Arthur. "The Infamous Prelude to Pearl Har-
     bor: The Inside Story of the Kurusu Peace Mis-
     sion." New York Times Magazine, (November 8,
     1942), 3-5.

3493 Lauterbach, Richard E. "Secret Jap War Plans: Of-
     ficial Reports Reveal the Pearl Harbor Strategy."
     Life, XX (March 4, 1946), 16+.

3494 Leighton, Isabel, ed. The Aspirin Age, 1919-1941.
     New York: Simon and Schuster, 1949.
        Contains an interesting article, "1941, Pearl
     Harbor Sunday: The End of an Era."

3495 Lindley, Ernest K. "How Not to Get the Pearl Harbor
     Facts." Newsweek, XXVI (December 24, 1945),
     37.

3496 _____. "The Significance of the Report on Pearl
     Harbor." Newsweek, XIX (February 2, 1942), 24.

3497 Lockridge, Richard. "No Second Navyhood." New
     Yorker, XVII (January 10, 1942), 33.

3498 Lord, Walter. Day of Infamy. New York: Holt,
     1957. 254p.
        Often the first stopping point for operational
     aspects of the Japanese raid.

3499 _____. "Five Missed Chances at Pearl Harbor."
     Reader's Digest, LXXI (December 1957), 42-45.
        Summary of an address by the author.

3500 McElroy, J. W. "Fiction Foreshadows Fact."
     USNIP, LXXXV (1959), 112.
        Further comments on the work of Hector C.
     Bywater in the 1920's.

3501 Matsumoto, Toru, trans. See Sakamaki, Kazuo, no.
     3551.

3502 "Memories Still Fresh." Newsweek, LXVIII (December
      12, 1966), 38-42.

3503 Miles, Sherman. "Pearl Harbor in Retrospect." At-
      lantic, CLXXXII (July 1948), 65-72.

3504 Millis, Walter. This is Pearl!: The United States
      and Japan, 1941. New York: William Morrow,
      1947. 384p.

3505 _____. "Two Hours That Changed History." New
      York Times Magazine, (December 2, 1956), 15+.

3506 Mitchell, Donald W. History of the Modern American
      Navy from 1883 Through Pearl Harbor. New York:
      Alfred A. Knopf, 1946. 477p.
          Based on the next citation, with some revision
      to 1942.

3507 _____. "The History of the United States Navy."
      Unpublished PhD Dissertation, University of
      Southern California, 1938.

3508 _____. "Scapegoats and Facts." Nation, CLIV (Feb-
      ruary 7, 1942), 155-157.
          Who was to blame and what can consequently be
      done.

3509 _____. "What the Navy Can Do." Nation, CLIII
      (December 20, 1941), 633-635.

3510 Morgan, David J. "They Were Ready." USNIP, XCIX
      (1973), 80-81.
          A brief account of the opening of the Pearl Har-
      bor action by the U.S. destroyer Ward when she
      sank a Japanese mini-submarine.

3511 Morgenstern, George. "The Actual Road to Pearl
      Harbor." In: Harry E. Barnes, ed. Perpetual
      War for Perpetual Peace. Caldwell, Idaho: Cax-
      ton Printers, 1953. p. 315-407.
          Another entry into the "conspiracy theory" of
      the attack. All of these are debunked by Admiral
      Morison in the works by him cited in the general
      histories contained in Volume III.

3512 _____. Pearl Harbor: The Story of the Secret War.
      New York: Devin-Adair, 1947. 425p.

3513 Morison, Samuel E.   "The Lessons of Pearl Harbor."
         Saturday Evening Post, CCXXXIV (October 28, 1961),
         19-27.
            Also opposes the "conspiracy theory."

3514 Morton, Louis.   "Pearl Harbor in Perspective."
         USNIP, LXXXI (1955), 461-468.

3515 Muller, Edwin.   "The Inside Story of Pearl Harbor:
         How American Strategists Devised the Plan Used
         in the Sneak Jap Attack."   Reader's Digest, XLIV
         (April 1944), 25-27.
            Refers to American pre-war fleet maneuvers
         which did, indeed, correctly anticipate December 7.
         One should, however, give considerable thought to
         the statement contained in the memoirs of Admiral
         Sir Andrew B. Cunningham (cited in Volume I) that
         Nippon learned as much from the Taranto raid as
         from Bywater or the U.S. Navy.

3516 Murata, Kiyoaki.   "'Treachery' at Pearl Harbor."
         USNIP, LXXXII (1956), 904-906.
            Addresses the question of the "sneakiness" of
         the attack.

3517 "The Navy's View of Pearl Harbor: Catastrophe
         Through Errors."   U.S. News & World Report, XX
         (January 11, 1946), 22-24.

3518 Nevins, Allan.   "A Challenge to the Historic Truth:
         An Attempt is Being Made to Distort the Record
         of Why We Went to War."   New York Times Maga-
         zine, (December 16, 1945), 8+.

3519 Ober, Warren V., jt. author.   See Burtness, Paul S.,
         nos. 3423-3424.

3520 Oliver, Frederick L.   "The Danger of Unpreparedness."
         USNIP, LXXI (1945), 763-775.
            Comments on the Pearl Harbor raid.

3521 "Our Fleet Was Still There."   Newsweek, XXVI (De-
         cember 3, 1945), 36-38.
            Comments on the Japanese failure to take out
         American carriers and submarines during the at-
         tack.

3522 Parkinson, Roger.   Attack on Pearl Harbor.   Docu-

mentary History Series.   New York: Putnam,
1973.   128p.

3523   "Pearl Harbor. "   Time, XLVI (December 3, 1945),
       24-25.

3524   "Pearl Harbor: An Editorial. "   Commonweal, XCIX
       (November 16, 1973), 166-167.

3525   "Pearl Harbor and After. "   New Republic, CXIII
       (September 10, 1945), 303-305.

3526   "Pearl Harbor Blew Up Some Crusty Illusions. "   Sat-
       urday Evening Post, CCXVIII (February 9, 1946),
       124.
           Readers should also note David M. Armstrong's
       "Pearl Harbor: An Eyewitness Report, " in Ameri-
       can History Illustrated, IX (August 1974), 4-12,
       41-48.

3527   "Pearl Harbor Eve. "   Newsweek, XXVII (February
       25, 1946), 29.

3528   "Pearl Harbor Fog. "   Newsweek, XXVI (December 24,
       1945), 31.

3529   "Pearl Harbor: How America's Guard Was Dropped,
       With a Digest of the Report. "   Newsweek, XXVI
       (September 10, 1945), 40+.

3530   "The Pearl Harbor Report. "   Commonweal, XXXV
       (February 6, 1942), 379.

3531   _____ .   Scholastic, XLVII (September 24, 1945), 11.

3532   _____ .   Time, XLVI (September 10, 1945), 25-27.

3533   "The Pearl Harbor Report: Excerpts of the Army and
       Navy Pearl Harbor Reports and Secretary [Henry
       L.] Stimson's Statement. "   Current History, New
       Series IX (October 1945), 343-379.

3534   "Pearl Harbor Secrets. "   Newsweek, XXVI (November
       19, 1945), 37-39.

3535   "Pearl Harbor Survivors' Reminiscences. "   Newsweek,
       LXXVIII (December 13, 1971), 16-17.

3536 "Pearl Harbor: The Damage Revealed. " Life, XIII
      (December 14, 1942), 31-37.

3537 "Pearl Harbor: The Planning Stage. " U.S. Navy
      Weekly Intelligence Bulletin, I (December 8, 1944),
      1-22.

3538 "Pictures of the Nation's Worst Naval Disaster Show
      Pearl Harbor Hell. " Life, XII (February 16,
      1942), 30-32+.

3539 Pierce, Philip N. "Twenty Years Ago. " Leatherneck,
      XLI (December 1961), 24-29, 79.

3540 Pogue, Forrest C. "Pearl Harbor Blunders. " Look,
      XXIX (December 14, 1945), 34-39.
             An excerpt from the author's biography, George
      C. Marshall: The War Years.

3541 Prange, Gordon W. "Tora! Tora! Tora!" Reader's
      Digest, LXXXIII (October-November 1963), 251-
      258ff.
             The story of Pearl Harbor later made into a
      lavish Japanese-American movie. The title is
      Japanese for "Attack! Attack! Attack!"

3542 Pratt, William V. "The Japanese Onslaught: A Blend
      of Treachery and Skill. " Newsweek, XVIII (Decem-
      ber 15, 1941), 26.

3543 _____. "Our Fleet Still Retains Its Punch. " News-
      week, XVIII (December 15, 1941), 64-66.

3544 _____. "Some Plain Speaking About Pearl Harbor. "
      Newsweek, XXVI (September 10, 1945), 42.

3545 Ramsey, Logan C. "The 'Ifs' of Pearl Harbor. "
      USNIP, LXXVI (1950), 364-371.

3546 Richardson, Benjamin. "Dorie Miller. " In: his
      Great American Negroes. Rev. ed. New York:
      T. Y. Crowell, 1956. p. 317-326.
             The Black Pearl Harbor "hero" reported MIA
      in 1942.

3547 "Report on Pearl Harbor. " New Republic, CVI (Feb-
      ruary 2, 1942), 134.

3548 "The Roberts Report Sounds Death Knell of Franklin
      Field Mentality." Newsweek, XIX (February 2,
      1942), 23-25.

3549 Roosevelt, Franklin D. "After Pearl Harbor, an Un-
      published Story: First Reactions at the White
      House." U.S. News & World Report, XX (April
      19, 1946), 24a-24b+.
      Printed after the President's death.

3550 Rosenthal, Abraham M. "The Day the World Changed
      Forever." New York Times Magazine, (December
      3, 1961), 32-33+.

3551 Sakamaki, Kazuo. I Attacked Pearl Harbor. Trans-
      lated from the Japanese by Toru Matsumoto. New
      York: Association Press, 1949. 133p.

3552 Samson, George. "Japan's Fatal Blunder." Interna-
      tional Affairs, XXIV (October 1948), 543-554.

3553 Sasaki, Okino, as Told to Ellsworth Boyd. "Suicide
      Sub Attack." Sea Classics, V (January 1972), 36-
      41.
      The Japanese mini-submarine assault on Pearl
      Harbor which resulted in the loss of five of these
      small craft.

3554 Schroeder, Paul W. The Axis Alliance and Japanese-
      American Relations, 1941. Ithaca, N.Y.: Cornell
      University Press, 1958. 246p.

3555 "Second Guesses on Pearl Harbor: Was Effective De-
      fense Possible?" U.S. News & World Report, XX
      (February 22, 1946), 22-23.

3556 Shaw, Samuel R. "Marine Barracks, Navy Yard,
      Pearl Harbor, December 1941." Shipmate, XXXVI
      (December 1973), 16-20.

3557 Sokol, Anthony E. "Why Pearl Harbor?" USNIP,
      LXXI (1945), 401-409.

3558 Standley, William H. "More About Pearl Harbor."
      U.S. News & World Report, XXXVI (April 16,
      1954), 40-42+.

3559 Stevens, Mrs. Albert M.   "That Day at Pearl Har-
         bor." By Barry Fox, pseud. Harper's, CLXXXVI
         (January 1943), 214-220.

3560 Stimson, Henry L.   "Statement to the Congressional
         Joint Committee on the Investigation of the Pearl
         Harbor Attack, March 21, 1946." U.S. News &
         World Report, XX (March 29, 1946), 63-74.
            Excerpts were also printed in Newsweek, XXVII
         (April 1, 1946), 21; and Time, XLVII (April 1,
         1946), 20-21.

3561 "The Story of Pearl Harbor." New Republic, CXIII
         (December 10, 1945), 782-784.

3562 "The Story of Pearl Harbor: Excerpts From the
         Navy's Report." Newsweek, XX (December 14,
         1942), 38.

3563 Stowell, E. C.   "Japan Attacks the United States."
         American Journal of International Law, XXXVI
         (January 1942), 87-89.

3564 Strong, Mary K.   "Washington at Pearl Harbor."
         Current History, New Series X (February 1946),
         125-132.

3565 Stroven, Carl, jt. author. See Day, A. Grove, no.
         3436.

3566 Strum, Theodore R.   "Those Aging Ghosts of Pearl
         Harbor." Airman, XV (December 1971), 14-18.

3567 Sweeney, Charles. Pearl Harbor. Murray, Utah,
         1946.   74p.

3568 Taggard, Ernestine K.   "I Remember Pearl Harbor."
         Scholastic, XXXIX (January 5, 1942), 20+.

3569 Taussig, Joseph K., Jr.   "I Remember Pearl Harbor."
         USNIP, XCVIII (1972), 18-24.

3570 Taylor, Theodore. Air Raid--Pearl Harbor: The
         Story of December 7, 1941. New York: T. Y.
         Crowell, 1971.   185p.

3571 Theobald, Robert A.   "Admiral Theobald Replies to the

Kittredge Article. " U.S. News & World Report,
XXXVIII (January 28, 1955), 117-118.
The Kittredge article is cited above, no. 3427.

3572 _____. The Final Secret of Pearl Harbor: The
Washington Contribution to the Japanese Attack.
Forewords by Husband E. Kimmel and William F.
Halsey. New York: Devin-Adair, 1954. 202p.
A controversial "conspiracy" view of the raid
which pretty much lets Admiral Kimmel and Gener-
al Short off the hook.

3573 _____. _____. U.S. News & World Report, XXXVI
(April 2-7, 1954), 21-23, 48-93, 30-32, 48-50.
Excerpts from the above citation.

3574 Thomis, Wayne. "Pearl Harbor Is Attacked!: Brave
Men Fight and Die. " Chicago Tribune Special Supplement, (December 7, 1966), 2.

3575 Togo, Shigenori. "Why Japan Attacked Pearl Harbor. "
U.S. News & World Report, XLI (August 31, 1956),
122-151.

3576 Toland, John. "Death Watch in the Pacific. " Look,
XXV (September 12, 1961), 86-88+.
The Pearl Harbor story as excerpted from the
author's book, But Not in Shame.

3577 Tolley, Kemp. "Divided We Fell. " USNIP, XCII
(1966), 36-52.

3578 Trefousse, Hans L. , ed. What Happened to Pearl
Harbor?: Documents Pertaining to the Japanese
Attack of December 7, 1941 and Its Background.
New York: Twayne, 1958. 324p.

3579 "The True Story of Pearl Harbor: Interviews. " U.S.
News & World Report, LI (December 11, 1961),
56-67.

3580 Trumbull, Robert. "A Sunday That Seems Like Yes-
terday. " New York Times Magazine, (December
4, 1966), 162+.

3581 Tyson, David O. "The Story of the Battleship Arizona
[BB-39]. " Arizona History, XXIX (September
1953), 34-39.

A memorial now covers her hulk buried in the
mud of Pearl Harbor.

3582   "U.S. Naval Losses: Photographs. " Illustrated London
       News, CXCIX (December 27, 1941), 823.

3583   United States.   Commission to Investigate and Report
       the Facts Relating to the Attack Made by Japanese
       Armed Forces Upon Pearl Harbor in the Territory
       of Hawaii on December 7, 1941. Attack Upon
       Pearl Harbor: Report of the Commission Appointed
       by the President of the United States.   Washington:
       U.S. Government Printing Office, 1942.   21p.
           Also printed as Senate doc. 159, 77th Cong. ,
       2nd sess. Created by Executive Order, this group
       was known as the Roberts Commission, after its
       chairman, Supreme Court Justice Owen J. Roberts.
       Its concern was almost entirely with the efficiency--
       or lack of it--on the part of General Short, Admiral
       Kimmel, and their subordinates on Oahu.

3584   _____. Congress. Joint Select Committee. Hearings
       on the Pearl Harbor Attack.   39 vols. Washington:
       U.S. Government Printing Office, 1946. Rpr. 1972.

3585   _____. _____. _____. Report. Washington: U.S.
       Government Printing Office, 1946.   604p.
           Also printed as Senate doc. 244, 79th Cong. ,
       2nd sess. If available, one might want to examine
       the above two references during any research on
       the subject of this section.

3586   _____. Navy Department. Narrative Statement of
       Evidence at the Navy Pearl Harbor Investigation.
       3 vols. Washington, 1945.
           The Navy Court of Inquiry (NCI) appointed by
       Secretary Forrestal which held its hearings from
       July-October 1944.

3587   _____. _____. "Statement on Pearl Harbor. " USNIP,
       LXIX (1943), 279-281.
           Reprinted from the December 6, 1942 issue of
       the New York Herald Tribune.

3588   _____. _____. Office of the Chief of Naval Operations,
       Intelligence Division. "Combat Narrative: Pearl
       Harbor. " Unpublished paper, CNO-ONI File, U.S.

Navy Department, Naval History Division, Operational Archives, 1942. 37p.

3589 ____. War Department. Full Text of the Official Reports Concerning the Attack on Pearl Harbor. Washington: U.S. News, 1945.

3590 "Victory for Treachery: Pearl Harbour During and After the Attack of December 7." Illustrated London News, CC (February 21, 1942), 244-245.

3591 Villard, Oswald G. "Pearl Harbor Report." Current History, New Series II (March 1942), 11-15.

3592 Walker, Wayne T. "Tora, Tora: Pearl Harbor." World War II Magazine, II (August 1972), 34-38. Largely pictorial.

3593 Waller, George M., ed. Pearl Harbor: Roosevelt and the Coming of the War. Problems in American Civilization. Boston: D.C. Heath, 1953. 112p. Rpr. 1965.

3594 Wallin, Homer N. Pearl Harbor: Why, How, Fleet Salvage and Final Appraisal. Washington: U.S. Government Printing Office, 1968. 377p. A publication of the Naval History Division.

3595 "Wanted: The Truth About Pearl Harbor." Collier's, CXVI (October 27, 1945), 86.

3596 Ward, Robert E. "The Inside Story of the [Japanese] Pearl Harbor Plan." USNIP, LXXVII (1951), 1270-1283; LXXVIII (1952), 435-438.

3597 Whitehouse, Arthur G. J., "Arch." "The Greatest Carrier Attack." In: his Squadrons of the Sea. Garden City, N.Y.: Doubleday, 1962. p. 114-143. The Japanese raid of December 7.

3598 "Who Was to Blame at Pearl Harbor?" Christian Century, LXII (September 12, 1945), 1027.

3599 Wilkinson, J. Burke. "Sneak Craft Attack in the Pacific." USNIP, LXXIII (1947), 279-287. Allied and Japanese mini-sub employment beginning with Pearl Harbor.

3600 Wilson, Gill R.   "Fear of Aircraft Carriers Made
        Japan Waste Its Pearl Harbor Advantage. " USNIP,
        LXX (1944), 722-725.
            Reprinted from the April 23, 1944 issue of the
        New York Herald Tribune.

3601 Wohstetter, Roberta.   "Cuba and Pearl Harbor: Hind-
        sight and Foresight. "   Foreign Affairs, XLIII
        (July 1965), 691-707.
            The Missile Crisis of 1962 compared to Decem-
        ber 7.

3602 _____.   Pearl Harbor: Warning and Decision.   Stan-
        ford, Calif. : Stanford University Press, 1962.
        426p.
            Considers the operational as well as the political
        and intelligence aspects of the Japanese raid.

3603 _____.   "What Really Happened at Pearl Harbor?"
        U. S. News & World Report, LXI (December 12,
        1966), 46-47.

3604 Young, Stephen B.   "God, Please Get Us Out of This."
        American Heritage, XVII (April 1966), 48-51+.

3605 _____.   "Out of the Darkness. " USNIP, XCI (1965),
        86-95.
            Both of the above references constitute the
        reminiscences of a survivor of the Oklahoma, which
        was sunk during the attack.

            Further References: Readers are reminded that
additional information relative to this section will be found
in sections IIA and IIB-1 above, as well as in the general
histories cited in Volume III, Part 1 and the Intelligence-
Espionage section of Part 2.

              (3) GALLANTRY AT WAKE AND GUAM

            Introduction.   The Japanese began their Pacific
onslaught not only by attacking the American fleet at Pearl
Harbor, but by simultaneously assaulting U. S. , British, and
Dutch possessions as well.   Many of the operations under
discussion here in section IIB were underway at or about the
same time.

On December 8, in widely scattered assignments, enemy bombers dropped their deadly loads on Guam, Wake, Hong Kong, Singapore, and the Philippines. During their Guam attack, the American minesweeper <u>Penguin</u> (AM-33) was sunk by horizontal bombers. Two days later, a Japanese landing force stormed ashore on that little outpost in the Marianas Islands and obtained its surrender.

Wake Island, a little over 2000 miles from Pearl Harbor and north of the Japanese-held Marshall Islands, was a tougher nut. Three days before Pearl Harbor Sunday, a dozen F4F "Wildcat" fighters had been flown to that post from the carrier <u>Enterprise</u>--one of the main reasons she was not in Hawaii. In addition, somewhat fewer than 500 U.S. Marines under Major James P. S. Devereux manned a mixed defense of 3-inch and 5-inch anti-aircraft and coastal defense guns. More than a thousand civilian construction workers were on hand building an air-submarine base and many of these were to be exposed--often lending a hand in the fighting.

After the December 8 bombing, the Japanese confidently expected to capture the place on December 11. Accordingly they sent a lightly-escorted force of three light cruisers and six destroyers to accompany their troop transports. Acting on island commander Winfield S. Cunningham's orders, the Wake defenders "lay low." When their enemy came within comfortable range, the Marines opened fire and the Wildcats took to the air. In a little while it was all over--for the moment. The defenders had sunk the IJN destroyers <u>Hayate</u> and <u>Kisaragi</u>, damaged two others and two of the cruisers, and prevented the Japanese from putting a single man ashore.

Meanwhile in Pearl Harbor where confusion was still widespread, Admiral Husband E. Kimmel ordered Rear Admiral Frank J. Fletcher to take the carrier <u>Saratoga</u> and her escorts to the island's defense. Here tragic delays prevented the U.S. task group from getting off before December 16 and before it could come within effective range, it was too late.

The Japanese, stung by events on the 11th, did not bungle a second time. Borrowing two carriers from the Pearl Harbor striking force, they returned to the waters off Wake on December 21, That day and the next they bombarded the island and in the pre-dawn darkness of December 23, went ashore. After a struggle against overwhelming odds, Cunningham was forced to surrender.

Both sides learned important lessons out of these episodes. To a certain extent, the Japanese, as they would

demonstrate in Malaya and the Philippines, brought their full
weight to bear on their adversaries.   The Americans learned
the teachings of delay.   Additionally, it was found that the
enemy was not overly-kind to the construction workers, who
after all were civilians not supposed to be shooting at them.
To remedy this problem, or at the least obtain POW status
for captured workers, the Navy Department created the
famous U.S. Naval Construction Battalions, or "Seabees."

3606   "An Alumnus Tells of Experiences During the Wake
          Island Attack." Scholastic, XL (March 9, 1942),
          21.

3607   Armknecht, Richard F.   "This was Wake." Christian
          Science Monitor Magazine, (July 3, 1942), 7+.

3608   Baldwin, Hanson W.   "The Saga of Wake." Virginia
          Quarterly Review, XVIII (July 1942), 321-335.

3609   Bayler, Walter L. J.   "A Day at Wake Island."
          Marine Corps Gazette, XXVII (July 1943), 7.

3610   _____. "The Last Man Off Wake Island." Saturday
          Evening Post, CCXV (April 3-17, 1943), 12-13+,
          28-29+, 26-27+.

3611   _____, as told to Cecil Carnes. Last Man off Wake
          Island. Indianapolis: Bobbs-Merrill, 1943.   367p.
             A Marine aviator who served on Wake, at Midway
          and Ewa, and on Guadalcanal.

3612   Boyle, Martin. Yanks Don't Cry. New York: Bernard
          Geis, 1963.   249p. Rpr. 1966.
             Reminiscences of a Marine captured on Guam and
          sent to a Japanese POW camp, 1941-1945.

3613   Burroughs, J. R.   "The Siege of Wake Island." Ameri-
          can Heritage, X (June 1959), 65-76.

3614   Casey, Robert J.   "Field Day at Wake Island." In
          William H. Fetridge, ed.   The Navy Reader.
          Indianapolis: Bobbs-Merrill, 1943.   p. 187-200.
          Rpr. 1971.
             Reprinted from the author's Torpedo Junction,
          this excerpt describes the activities of a U.S.
          naval vessel off the island between 4-11 a.m. on
          February 28, 1942.

3615   Conner, John. "Return from Wake. " Leatherneck,
          XXVIII (October 1945), 20-22.

3616   Cunningham, Winfield S. Wake Island Command.
          Boston: Little, Brown, 1961. 300p.

3617   "Defenders of Wake. " Sea Power, (February 1942),
          7-11.

3618   Devereux, James P. S. The Story of Wake Island.
          Philadelphia: Lippincott, 1947. 252p.

3619   _____ . "This Is How It Was. " Saturday Evening
          Post, CCXVII (February 23, March 2-16, 1946),
          10-11+, 28-29+, 28-29+, 20+.
          Wake Island.

3620   "Flame of Glory: Wake's Hopeless, Gallant Fight. "
          Time, XXXIX (January 19, 1942), 20-24.

3621   Furnas, William J. "Leathernecks to the Last: The
          Heroic Defenders of Wake Island. " Collier's, CX
          (November 21, 1942), 100-101.

3622   Harwell, Ernie. "The Wake Story. " Leatherneck,
          XXVIII (November 1945), 22-26.

3623   Heinl, Robert D. , Jr. The Defense of Wake. Wash-
          ington: Historical Section, Division of Public In-
          formation, U.S. Marine Corps, 1947. 76p.
          By both U.S. and Japanese forces in turn.

3624   _____ . "Wake Island. " Navy, IX (December 1966),
          20-23.

3625   _____ . "We're Headed For Wake. " Marine Corps
          Gazette, XXX (June 1946), passim.
          An account of the abortive Wake relief expedition
          to which the author was assigned.

3626   Junghans, Earl A. "Wake: 1568-1946. " Unpublished
          paper, Individual Personnel File, U.S. Navy De-
          partment, Naval History Division, Operational
          Archives, n.d. 20p.
          Written shortly after the Japanese surrender,
          the bulk of the study concerns the World War II
          years.

3627 Lademan, Joseph A.   "U.S.S. Gold Star--Flagship of
      the Guam Navy. " USNIP, XCIX (1973), 67-79.
      The story of a tramp steamer converted to naval
      purposes and what happened to her in the early days
      of the war.

3628 "Remember Guam and Wake!" American Federationist,
      XLIX (January 1942), 7.

3629 Roosevelt, Franklin D.   "Citation of the Wake Island
      Detachment of the 1st Defense Battalion, USMC. "
      USNIP, LXXIV (1948), 750-751.

3630 "The Stand at Wake. " Time, XVIII (December 22,
      1941), 19.

3631 Stowers, H. B.   "Hell on a Horseshoe. " American
      Legion Magazine, LXVI (April 1959), 12-13+.
      The 1941 battle for Wake Island.

3632 Tweed, George R.   Robinson Crusoe, USN: The Ad-
      ventures of George R. Tweed on Jap-Held Guam,
      As Told to Blake Clark.   New York and London:
      Whittlesey House, McGraw-Hill, 1945.   267p.

3633 Votaw, Homer C.   "Wake Island. " USNIP, LXVII
      (1941), 52-55.

3634 Werstein, Irving. Wake: The Story of a Battle.   New
      York: Crowell, 1964.   145p.

3635 Wilds, Thomas.   "The Japanese Seizure of Guam,
      1941. " Marine Corps Gazette, XXXIX (July 1955),
      20-23.

3636 Wilhelm, Donald.   "What Happened at Wake Island. "
      Reader's Digest, XL (April 1942), 41-46.

3637 Williamson, Samuel T.   "From Montezuma's Halls to
      Wake Island. " New York Times Magazine, (Janu-
      ary 25, 1942), 10-11+.

      Further References: Additional data relative to
this part will be found in sections IIA and IIB-1 above, as
well as in the general works cited in Volume III, Part 1.

(4) SINGAPORE, ASIA, AND THE INDIAN OCEAN

Introduction. At the same time that American
ships in Pearl Harbor were taking the assault from Admiral
Nagumo's carriers, other Japanese forces were headed towards the Netherlands East Indies, Burma, and British Malaya. The great fortress of Singapore on the tip of that
latter peninsula, as well as the Crown Colony of Hong Kong
on the China coast, were soon to be attacked.

In late 1941, even before the outbreak of war,
Winston Churchill decided that the Royal Navy should put on
a show of strength in the waters off Malaya as a deterrent
to Japanese aggression. Consequently over strong Admiralty
anxiety, he ordered the new battleship Prince of Wales (fully
recovered from her bout with K.M. Bismarck) and the battle-
cruiser Repulse to proceed to the Far East. The new carrier Indomitable, which was to have gone with this "Force
Z," under Admiral Sir T. Phillips, ran aground off Jamaica
thus depriving the task group of its air cover.

Having arrived safely at Singapore, the admiral
was shocked like everyone else to learn of Pearl Harbor.
On the evening of December 8, he took his two capital ships
plus four destroyers to sea for an attack on Japanese transports which were even then reported landing men at Singora
on Malaya's northeast coast. Unable to obtain R.A.F. cover,
Force Z was a sitting duck when the Japanese discovered
it en route to Kuantan, early the next morning.

Shortly after 11 a.m. local time, the British ships
were attacked by 85 Japanese bombers and torpedo planes
from Saigon. Shortly thereafter, the British dreadnought and
her companion were on the sea bottom. Fortunately, casualties were few. With those two monsters out of the way, the
Japanese gained virtually undisputed command of the entire
western Pacific.

The loss of Repulse and Prince of Wales sealed the
fate of Allied colonies in the path of the advancing enemy.
Additionally, the confidence of the defenders of Singapore
was badly shaken. Hoping against hope, they attempted to
defend their strategically ill-located base from the armies
of General Yamashita gaily peddling their bicycles down the
spine of Malaya. What was left of the Royal Navy was put
under command of Admiral Thomas Hart's A.B.D.A. force
headquartered in Java.

Singapore surrendered on February 15, 1942. A
few weeks later, the enemy succeeded in taking all of the
Dutch East Indies (covered in section IIB-5) and began moving

into Burma.   On March 8, the great port of Rangoon fell
into their hands.

I should note here that this section also contains
the few references available concerning the Japanese raids
into the Indian Ocean in the spring of 1942.

Vice Admiral Sir James Somerville, who had
commanded the Royal Navy "Force H" at Gibraltar, arrived
at Ceylon at the end of March 1942, where he found a re-
spectable force of three carriers, five battleships, and a
number of cruisers and destroyers.   Shortly after his arrival,
he was tipped off that the Japanese were planning a raid on
Ceylon for April 1.   Heeding this warning, he took his fleet
to sea for a rendezvous at a secret base in the Maldive
Islands.

Sure enough, the Japanese came.   Employing virtually the same carrier force he had used on Pearl Harbor,
Admiral Nagumo launched his air assault on Colombo, Ceylon,
on Easter Sunday, April 5.   A little later his planes caught
H. M. cruisers Dorsetshire and Cornwall en route to join
Somerville and promptly ended their careers.   On April 9,
the cagey Japanese leader sent his air armada against the
other British base on Ceylon, Trincomalee.   On the rebound,
it found and sank the old carrier H. M. S. Hermes and an
accompanying destroyer.

While Nagumo's people were striking at Ceylon, a
heavy cruiser force detached from the main fleet and commanded by Vice Admiral Takeo Kurita entered the Bay of
Bengal.   In the first nine days of April, the six heavy cruisers and planes from his light carrier sank four British warships and some 135,000 tons of merchant shipping.

These disasters led Admiral Somerville almost to
abandon the Indian Ocean.   Sending his slow battleships to
east Africa, he kept only H. M. S. Warspite, the carriers
Indomitable and Formidable, and their screens as a mobile
force capable of covering British sea communications between
India and the Persian Gulf.   When it appeared that the enemy
would strike at Ceylon and India, Prime Minister Churchill
asked the Americans to send some of their vessels to reinforce the Home Fleet so that reinforcements could be rushed
to Somerville.   This done, the British were able to capture
Madagascar in May, an operation which is covered in Volume
I of this set, section ID-7.

The references which follow concern the events
above.   It should be pointed out, however, that this bibliography does not provide coverage on the Asian mainland.   A
few general references have been included as they relate to
the relatively few sea forces activities of the early Burma
campaign.

3638 Ash, Bernard. Someone Had Blundered: The Story of
        the Repulse and the Prince of Wales. London:
        Joseph, 1960. 267p.
            Published in America the following year by the
        Garden City, N. Y. , firm of Doubleday.

3639 Attiwill, Kenneth. The Singapore Story. London:
        Muller, 1959. 253p. Rpr. 1961.
            Published in America the following year by the
        Garden City, N. Y. , firm of Doubleday under the
        title, Fortress: The Story of the Siege and Fall
        of Singapore.

3640 Barber, Noel. A Sinister Twilight: The Fall of Singa-
        pore, 1942. Boston: Houghton, Mifflin, 1968.
        364p.
            Originally published in an edition of 319 pages
        by the London firm of Collins.

3641 Barclay, C. N. "The Fall of Singapore: A Reapprais-
        al. " Army, XVIII (April 1968), 44-53.

3642 Barker, A. J. [Tomoyuki] Yamashita. Ballantine's
        Illustrated History of World War II. New York:
        Ballantine Books, 1973. 160p.
            A biography of the Japanese general known as
        "The Tiger of Malaya. "

3643 Bennett, Geoffrey. Loss of the Price of Wales and
        Repulse. Sea Battles in Close-up, no. 7. Anna-
        polis: U. S. Naval Institute, 1973. 128p.
            Originally published by the London firm of Ian
        Allan.

3644 Booth, K. "Singapore, 1942: Some Warnings. " Army
        Quarterly, CII (January 1972), 191-200.

3645 Bowen, F. C. "A Century of the China Station. "
        Journal of the Royal United Service Institute,
        XCVII (February 1941), 57-65.

3646 Braddon, Russell. The Naked Island. London:
        Laurie, 1952. 266p.
            Singapore.

3647 Brown, Cecil. "How I Got the Story. " Collier's,
        CIX (May 16, 1942), 12.

By taking passage aboard H. M. S. Repulse as the entries below will illustrate.

3648 _____. "How Japan Wages War." Life, XII (May 11, 1942), 98-108.

3649 _____. "The Last of the Repulse." In: Curt Reiss, ed. They Were There: The Story of World War II and How It Came About, by America's Foremost Correspondents. New York: Putnam, 1944.

3650 _____. "Malay Jungle War: Jap Cunning and British Over-Confidence Have Endangered the Defense of Singapore." Life, XII (January 12, 1942), 32+.

3651 _____. "The Sinking of the Repulse and Prince of Wales: A Blow-by-Blow Account." Newsweek, XVIII (December 22, 1941), 18.

3652 _____. "Stand by for Torpedo: The Dramatic Story of the Aerial Torpedoing of the Repulse and the Prince of Wales." Collier's, CIX (January 17, 1942), 12+.
          An abridged version appeared in Reader's Digest, XL (March 1942), 1-5.

3653 _____. _____. In: Jacob H. Wise, et al. Meanings in Reading: 35 Essays and Articles. New York: Harcourt, 1943. p. 317-323.

3654 _____. Suez to Singapore. New York: Random House, 1942. 545p.
          The travels of this CBS newsman whose account of the sinking of H. M. battlecruiser Repulse, which he survived, was a radio "event" when broadcast.

3655 Caffrey, Kate. Out in the Midday Sun: Singapore, 1941-1945--The End of an Empire. New York: Stein and Day, 1973. 312p.

3656 Carew, John M. The Fall of Hong Kong. By Tim Carew, pseud. London: Blond, 1960. 228p. Rpr. 1963.

3657 _____. The Longest Retreat: The Burma Campaign, 1942. By Tim Carew, pseud. London: Hamilton, 1969. 276p.

3658   Carew, Tim, pseud. See Carew, John M. , nos. 3656-
       3657.

3659   Chaphekar, Shankarrao G. A Brief Study of the Malay-
       an Campaign, 1941-1942. 2nd and rev. ed. Poona,
       Malasia: Maharashtra Militarisation Board, 1960.
       121p.
           Published simultaneously in Great Britain by the
       London firm of Bailey and Swinfen.

3660   Chapman, Frederick S. The Jungle is Neutral. Lon-
       don: Chatto and Windus, 1949. 435p. Rpr. 1957.
           Published simultaneously in America by the New
       York firm of Norton in a 435-page edition.

3661   Clifford, Nicholas R. Retreat from China: British
       Policy in the Far East, 1937-1941. Seattle: Uni-
       versity of Washington Press, 1967. 222p.

3662   D'Albiac, J. H. "Ceylon. " Flying, XXXI (September
       1942), 95-96+.
           A target of the Japanese carrier thrust into the
       Indian Ocean.

3663   Dartford, Gerald P. A Short History of Malaya. New
       York: International Publications Service, 1963.
       218p.
           Contains some information on the fall of Singa-
       pore.

3664   Davidson, Nancy E. D. I. Winning Hazard. By Noel
       Wynyard, pseud. London: Low, 1947. 181p.
           Following the loss of Singapore, a number of
       raids were made by intrepid Allied seamen against
       enemy shipping in the harbor. This account was
       written by the widow of one of those who participated
       in a canoe assault from a fishing vessel backed up
       by H. M. submarine Porpoise.

3665   "The Destruction of H. M. S. Prince of Wales and H. M. S.
       Repulse: A Dramatic Air Battle off Malaya. " Il-
       lustrated London News, CXCIX (December 20, 1941),
       782-783.

3666   Elliott, Charles B. "Keys of the Indian Ocean. " Asia,
       XLII (April 1942), 216-217.
           Primarily the British forces based on Ceylon.

3667 Elsegood, A. G. "The Epic of the Dorsetshire."
      Society of Dorset Men in London Yearbook, XXXIX
      (1945-46), 70-76.
      Lost in the Indian Ocean.

3668 "Escape from Singapore: Letter of a Young American
      Officer." Infantry Journal, LII (February 1943),
      61-64.

3669 Eyre, Donald C., with Douglas Bowler. The Soul and
      the Sea. London: Hale, 1959. 192p.
      The fall of Singapore.

3670 "The Fall of Singapore Puts Java in the Jaws of the
      Jap Nutcracker." Newsweek, XIX (February 23,
      1942), 13-15.

3671 Gallagher, O'Dowd. Action in the East. Garden City,
      N. Y.: Doubleday, Doran, 1942. 300p.

3672 _____. "The Destruction of Force Z: South China
      Sea, 10th December 1941." In: John Winton, ed.
      The War at Sea: The British Navy in World War
      II.
         An excerpt from 3671 in which the author, Lon-
      don Daily Express correspondent in Singapore and
      a "shipmate" of Cecil Brown's aboard H. M. S.
      Repulse, tells how the Japanese planes sank the
      two British giants. Surviving to be picked up by
      a British destroyer, Gallagher filed his report
      which appeared in the pages of his newspaper about
      a week later.

3673 Glover, Edwin M. In 70 Days: The Story of the
      Japanese Campaign in British Malaya. London:
      Muller, 1946. 244p. Rpr. 1949.

3674 Grenfell, Russell. Main Fleet to Singapore. London:
      Faber, 1941. 231p.
      Still useful.

3675 "H. M. S. Dorsetshire Leaves Her Crew in the Indian
      Ocean." Life, XIII (September 14, 1942), 32.

3676 Hampshire, A. Cecil. "The Exploits of Force Viper."
      Journal of the Royal United Service Institute, CXIII
      (February 1968), 41-50.

The exploits of 106 Royal Marines operating in Burma in 1942.

3677 Hill, A. H. "The Japanese Invasion." Blackwood's, CCLV (February-March 1944), 130-144, 177-189. Into Malaya and their capture of Singapore.

3678 Hooker, Robert. "Japan's Lost Opportunity in the War: Her Failure to Take Madagascar." Yale Review, New Series XXXV (September 1945), 30-39.

3679 Hough, Richard A. Death of a Battleship. New York: Macmillan, 1963. 216p. This account of the sinking of the Repulse and Prince of Wales was published simultaneously in Britain by the London firm of Collins under the title, The Hunting of Force Z.

3680 Howe, H. V. , editor. See Tsuji, Masanobu, no. 3711.

3681 Jensen, Owen E. "Escape from Shanghai." Leatherneck, XXVI (January 1943), 24-25+.

3682 Kiralfy, Alexander. "Strategy of the Indian Ocean." Asia, XLII (June 1942), 353-357.

3683 Kirby, Stanley W. Singapore: The Chain of Disaster. London: Cassell, 1971. 270p. Published simultaneously in America by the New York firm of Macmillan, this is a forthright "unofficial" history by a British "official" historian. Its thesis is simple: without landward defenses, Singapore was lost before the foundations were laid in 1928.

3684 Lake, Margaret E. , trans. See Tsuji, Masanobu no. 3711.

3685 Layton, Geoffrey. "The Loss of H. M. Ships Prince of Wales and Repulse." Supplement 38214, London Gazette, February 26, 1948. Reprinting of a dispatch from the C-in-C, Eastern Fleet, originally dated December 17, 1941.

3686 Leasor, James. Singapore: The Battle That Changed History. The Crossroads of World History Series. Garden City, N. Y. : Doubleday, 1968. 325p.

3687   Lederer, William J.   "The American Navy is in the
       Middle of China. " USNIP, LXVIII (1942), 1142-
       1146.

3688   Little, Eric H.   The Luck of H. M. S. Dragon: A South
       African's Thrilling Sea Story Containing Numerous
       Incidents of the War in the Far East, Including the
       Evacuations of Singapore and Batavia.   Cape Town,
       S. A. : Stewart Printing Co. , 1944.   93p.
       The Dragon was a cruiser.

3689   Mant, Gilbert.   Grim Glory.   New and expanded ed.
       Sydney, Australia: Currawong, 1955.   95p.
       The fall of Singapore.

3690   Miller, Eugene E.   Strategy at Singapore.   New York:
       Macmillan, 1942.   145p.
       A study conducted by the American Council on
       Public Affairs, it appeared after that outpost was
       captured.

3691   Owen, Frank.   The Fall of Singapore.   London: Joseph,
       1960.   216p.   Rpr. 1962.

3692   Percival, Arthur E.   The War in Malaya.   London:
       Eyre and Spottiswoode, 1949.   336p.
       The British commander in the defense of Malaya
       and General Yamashita's direct opponent, the former
       surrendered to the latter in 1942, was held prisoner
       in Manchuria, but released in time to be present
       for Yamashita's surrender of the Philippines in
       1945.

3693   Playfair, Giles.   Singapore Goes Off the Air.   New
       York: E. P. Dutton, 1943.   273p.
       As recalled by a representative of the BBC.

3694   Prasad, Bisheshwar, ed.   The Retreat from Burma,
       1941-1942.   Official History of the Indian Armed
       Forces in the Second World War, 1939-1945: Cam-
       paigns in the Eastern Theater.   New Delhi, India:
       Combined Inter-Services Historical Section, 1952.
       501p.

3695   Pratt, William V.   "We Bomb Japan [The Doolittle
       Raid], but Don't Forget the Indian Ocean. " News-
       week, XIX (April 27, 1942), 20.

3696   "The Prince of Wales and Repulse." Aeronautics,
           XXXI (December 1954), 40-42.

3697   "Prince of Wales, Repulse: A Lesson." Time,
           XXXVIII (December 22, 1941), 20+.
               Capital ships minus air cover vs. airpower =
           0 capital ships.

3698   Richmond, Herbert W. "Singapore." Fortnightly,
           CLVII (March 1942), 237-243.

3699   _____. "Squandered Sea Power." Fortnightly, CLVII
           (April 1942), 323-327.

3700   Robinson, A. O. "The Malayan Campaign in the Light
           of the Principles of War." Journal of the Royal
           United Service Institute, CIX (1964), 224-232.

3701   Russell-Roberts, Denis. Spotlight on Singapore. Lon-
           don: Gibbs and Philips, 1965.   301p.   .

3702   Sansom, George B. "The Story of Singapore." Foreign
           Affairs, XXII (January 1944), 279-297.

3703   Sheehan, John M. "The Gorges of the Yangtze Kiang."
           USNIP, LXIX (1943), 1418-1424.

3704   _____. "Nanking." USNIP, LXIX (1943), 1189-1195.

3705   Simson, Ivan. Singapore, Too Little, Too Late:
           Some Aspects of the Malayan Disaster in 1942.
           London: Leo Cooper, 1970.   165p.

3706   "Sir Geoffrey Layton." CurrBio:III:25-26.
               Commander of the British Eastern Fleet. Stu-
           dents might also want to check the biography of
           Admiral Sir James Somerville in Volume I of this
           set.

3707   Stacey, C. P. "The Defense of Hong Kong." Canadian
           Army Journal, IV (November-December 1950), 5-13,
           18-31.

3708   Strabolgi, J. M. K., Lord. Singapore and After: A
           Study of the Pacific Campaign. London: Hutchin-
           son, 1942.   161p.

3709   Swinson, Arthur. Defeat in Malaya: The Fall of
       Singapore. Ballantine's Illustrated History of World
       War II. New York: Ballantine Books, 1970.   160p.

3710   Tomlinson, Henry M. Malay Waters: The Story of
       Little Ships Coasting Out of Singapore and Penang
       in Peace and War. London: Hodder and Stoughton,
       1950.   199p.

3711   Tsuji, Masanobu. Singapore: The Japanese Version.
       Translated by Margaret E. Lake and Edited by E.
       V. Howe. New York: St. Martin's Press, 1960.
       358p.
              Originally published by the Sydney, Australia,
       firm of Smith, this work was issued in Britain by
       Constable in 1962.

3712   Walker, Wayne T.   "The Sinking of the Repulse and
       the Prince of Wales." World War II Magazine, II
       (August 1972), 66.

3713   Weller, George. Singapore Is Silent. New York:
       Harcourt, 1943.   321p.
              The loss of the place as recorded by a Chicago
       Daily News correspondent, with some information
       on the sinking of the Repulse and Prince of Wales.

3714   Wettern, Desmond.   "Get Off My Bloody Ship." In:
       John Winton, ed. The War at Sea: The British
       Navy in World War II. New York: William Mor-
       row, 1967.   p. 162-164.
              In an excerpt from the next reference the author
       cites the reply of Lt. Stephen Polkingham of H. M.
       river gunboat Peterel when the Japanese demanded
       his surrender at Shanghai shortly after Pearl Har-
       bor.

3715   _____ . The Lonely Battle. London: Allen, 1960.
       223p.

3716   "With the Eastern Fleet: H. M. S. Prince of Wales at
       Singapore." Illustrated London News, CXCIX
       (December 13, 1941), 760.
              That ship was already four days on the bottom
       when this came out.

3717   Wynyard, Noel, pseud. See Davidson, Nancy E. D. I.,
       no.

Further References: Readers are reminded that
additional information relative to this section will be found
in sections IIA and IIB-1 above, as well as in the Appendix
to this volume and the general works cited in Volume III,
Part 1.

(5) THE NETHERLANDS EAST INDIES AND THE JAVA SEA

Introduction. At approximately the same time that
the Japanese were moving upon Singapore (section IIB-4) and
working over the Philippines (IIB-6) so were they advancing
in a series of amphibious operations into the oil-rich Netherlands East Indies. The eventual objective was Java, the
most highly developed island in the area with a population almost as large as Great Britain's.

By early January 1942, the American Asiatic Fleet
had fallen back from the Philippines to Java. There on the
10th, British General Sir Archibald P. Wavell arrived to
head up what became known as the A. B. D. A. forces--after
their American, British, Dutch, and Australian contingents.
Unfortunately a great number of unforeseen circumstances
were combined under the pressure of the Japanese thrust to
bring failure to the highest and lowest levels of that organization.

It is impossible in a short introduction like this to
explore the many landings and engagements in this area with
any degree of thoroughness. The Allies put up a good many
fights, usually for nought, against the Japanese. A calendar
of the larger of these actions--really skirmishes--will allow
us some look at the proceedings:

January 24 Action off Dalikpapan, Borneo, in which four
    flush-deck American destroyers attacked and sank four
    transports and a patrol craft of the Imperial Navy. This
    was the only successful surface action fought by the Allies
    during the entire campaign and the last successful night
    operation American forces would take part in for almost a
    year.
February 4 Engagement in Madoera Strait in which U. S. S.
    Houston's after turret was put out of commission and the
    U. S. S. Marblehead was battered to a point where she had
    to withdraw from the campaign.
February 13-14 The A. B. D. A. fleet was severely bombed
    by enemy aircraft near Banka Island off Sumatra. Several

vessels were severely shaken by near misses; none were
put out of action.

February 19-20   Dutch Rear Admiral Karel Doorman's fleet
caught an outnumbered Japanese landing force in Badoeng
Strait off Java, but lack of concentration wasted this advantage.   In the attack, the Dutch cruiser Tromp was
badly hit and a Netherlands destroyer sunk with no damage
to the enemy.

February 27-28   Battle of the Java Sea, described below.

        (It is recommended that anyone studying this cam-
paign or indeed any aspect of the Pacific conflict use a good
atlas or gazetteer, a favorite example being Webster's Geographical Dictionary.)   After the surrender of Singapore on
February 15, 1942, the Japanese were able to devote their
entire southern attention to closing the net on Java.   Admiral
Thomas Hart, who had headed the A.B.D.A. naval forces
ashore under General Wavell, turned over his command to a
Dutch Vice Admiral and returned to America shortly thereafter.   Wavell, himself convinced that Java's case was hopeless, closed shop on February 25, thereby dissolving his
command and turning over to the Dutch the continuing defense
of their colonies.

        While the A.B.D.A. force was officially ending
operations, Rear Admiral Jisaburo Osawa and Rear Admiral
Shoji Nishimura were approaching Java with a heavy naval
covering force and over 90 transports between them.   These
were discovered by Admiral Doorman's force, composed of
R.N.S. De Ruyter, H.M.S. Exeter of River Plate fame,
U.S.S. Houston, H.M.A.S. Perth, R.N.S. Java, and their
screen of three British, two Dutch, and four American destroyers.

        The first round in the Battle of the Java Sea
opened off Surabaya on the morning of February 27.   When
it ended, the Exeter was severely damaged and one of the
Dutch "tincans" sunk.   The Allies retreated.

        Steaming up the Java coast, Doorman again en-
countered the Japanese about 11 p.m. that same day.   After
a 20-minute exchange of gunfire, the Japanese launched some
of their "long lance" torpedoes which caught both Dutch
cruisers.   As the flagship De Ruyter sank, Doorman signalled
the Perth and Houston to retire.   These two cruisers plus
several destroyers reached safety the next day for a tempo-
rary respite.

        On the evening of February 28th, the Houston
and Perth plus a Dutch destroyer put to sea in a last desperate hope to find and sink an enemy landing force.   The

four American destroyers, thus far undamaged, were sent
to Australia--the only elements of Doorman's group that
would survive.   Meanwhile the two cruisers found their
quarry in Sunda Strait where they quickly moved in and sank
four transports.   This action attracted the Japanese covering
force which just as promptly came up, surrounded the Allied
units, and dispatched them.
      These heroic skirmishes in the Java Sea were
designed to purchase time for the defenders of Java, but they
actually had little effective influence on the outcome of events.
Batavia and Surabaya fell quickly and by March 9 the Japanese
had their Java prize.   The majority of the Allied warships
had gone down against overwhelming odds which, if nothing
else, kindled the spirit of revenge in their home countries.

3718   Baldwin, Hanson W.   "Saga of a Stout Ship, the Hous-
        ton. "   New York Times Magazine, (March 3, 1946),
        5-7+.

3719   "The Battle of Java. "   Time, XXXIX (March 9, 1942),
        16.

3720   "The Battle of the Java Sea: Photographs and Map. "
        Illustrated London News, CC (March 21, 1942),
        350-351.

3721   Cain, T. J. H. M. S. Electra.   London: Muller,
        1959.   282p.
        A British destroyer which participated with other
    Allied forces in the unsuccessful Battle of the Java
    Sea.

3722   Collins, J. A.   "The Battle of the Java Sea, 27 Feb-
        ruary 1942. "   Supplement 38346, London Gazette,
        July 7, 1948.
        Reprinting of a dispatch from the Commodore
    Commanding, China Force, originally dated March
    17, 1942.

3723   "The Death of the Houston. "   Time, XLVII (March 11,
        1946), 25.

3724   Eyre, James K. , Jr.   "Java Sea: A Memorable Naval
        Battle. "   USNIP, LXIX (1943), 516-523.

3725   "Heroic Action Against Hopeless Odds: Some Dramatic

Incidents in the Naval Battle of the Java Sea. "
Illustrated London News, CC (March 28, 1942),
382-383.

3726 "Java Showdown. " Newsweek, XIX (March 9, 1942),
11-12.

3727 Legge, John D. Indonesia. The Modern World in
Historical Perspective. Englewood Cliffs, N. J. :
Prentice-Hall, 1965. 184p.
A brief history with some data relative to this
section.

3728 Leighton, I. , jt. author. See Perry, George S. , no.
3738.

3729 "Lessons from Defeat: The Battle of Java. " Time,
XXXIX (March 23, 1942), 17.

3730 Mack, William R. "Battle at Bali. " USNIP, LXIX
(1943), 825-827.

3731 _____. "The Battle of the Java Sea. " USNIP, LXIX
(1943), 1052-1060.

3732 McKie, Ronald C. H. The Survivors. Indianapolis:
Bobbs-Merrill, 1953. 246p.
Published simultaneously in Britain and Australia
by the firm of Angus and Robertson under the title
Proud Echo, this work concerns the men of
H. M. A. S. Perth, the Battle of the Java Sea, and
the fate of the ship's "survivors. "

3733 'Naval Battle at Java. " National Review, CXVIII
(April 1942), 316-319.

3734 "[Netherlands East] Indies. " Newsweek, XIX (March 2,
1942), 13-17.

3735 Noble, J. Kendrick. "The Death of the Houston. "
American Legion Magazine, (January 1951), 22-23+.

3736 Parkin, Ray. "The Lower Steering Position. " In:
John Winton, ed. The War at Sea: The British
Navy in World War II. New York: William Morrow,
1967. p. 210-214.
An excerpt from the next citation in which the

author looks at the scene aboard H. M. A. S. <u>Perth</u> in the Java Sea, February 27-28, 1942.

3737   _____. <u>Out of the Smoke: The Story of a Sail</u>. London: Hogarth Press, 1960. 310p.

3738   Perry, George S. and I. Leighton. "The Ship That Wouldn't Sink: U. S. S. <u>Marblehead</u>. " <u>Collier's</u>, CXIV (November 11-25, 1944), 12-13+, 16-17+, 24+.

3739   Pratt, William V. "The Battle of Java: The Peril of Mixed Command. " <u>Newsweek</u>, XIX (March 23, 1942), 16.

3740   Schubert, Paul. "No Guns for the Black Gang: Bringing in the <u>Marblehead</u> After the Java Sea Battle. " <u>Collier's</u>, CX (August 29, 1942), 40-41.

3741   Tallantyre, Renée. "Against the Dutch East Indian Backdrop. " <u>Canadian Geographic Magazine</u>, XXIV (March 1942), 146-155.

3742   Thomas, David A. <u>The Battle of the Java Sea</u>. London: Deutsch, 1968. 260p.
        Published in America the following year by the New York firm of Stein and Day.

3743   "U. S. -Dutch Attack Shatters Jap Convoy: Ten Transports and One Warship Sunk. " <u>Knickerbocker's Weekly</u>, (February 2, 1942), 4-11.
        A very glowing report of the American destroyer action off Balikpapan on January 24.

3744   United States. Navy Department. Office of the Chief of Naval Operations, Intelligence Division. "Combat Narrative: The Java Sea Campaign. " Unpublished paper, CNO-ONI File, U. S. Navy Department, Naval History Division, Operational Archives, 1942. 92p.

3745   Van Heurn, J. N. C. "Battle in the Java Sea. " <u>Asiatic Review</u>, New Series XXXIX (October 1943), 385-388.

3746   _____. "The Battle of Bali. " <u>Asiatic Review</u>, New Series XXXIX (April 1943), 188-192.

3747   Walker, Wayne T.   "Java Sea Action."   World War II
       Magazine, II (December 1971), 42-50.

3748   Weller, George.   "The First Eye-Witness Account of
       the Java Sea Naval Battle."   Knickerbocker's Week-
       ly, (April 6, 1942), 19-24.

3749   _____.   "How One Man Saved a Cruiser."   USNIP,
       LXVIII (1942), 869-871.
              An account of the damage control operation
       aboard the Houston following the February 4 en-
       gagement in Madoera Strait as reprinted from the
       April 14, 1942 issue of the Baltimore Evening Sun.

3750   Winslow, Walter G.   "The 'Galloping Ghost.'"   USNIP,
       LXXV (1949), 154-163.

3751   _____.   U.S.S. Houston, Ghost of the Java Sea.   Bal-
       timore: Collins Litho. Company, 1971.   20p.

3752   _____._____.   Bethesda, Md.:   Winslow Books, 1971.
       20p.

          Further References: Readers will find additional
information relative to this section in sections IIA and IIB-1
above, as well as in the Appendix to this volume and the
general works cited in Volume III, Part 1.

               (6) THE LOSS OF THE PHILIPPINES

          Introduction.   News of the Pearl Harbor attack
reached Manila in the early morning hours of December 8.
On orders from Admiral Hart, Rear Admiral William A.
Glassford immediately gathered a small fleet around the
cruiser Houston and headed south.   The Army, expecting a
dawn air raid, sent its planes into the air but found nothing.
Returning to base on Luzon, they were parked in neat rows
where Japanese aircraft promptly destroyed most of them
when they flew over the scene around noon.
          On December 10, the same day that the Prince of
Wales and Repulse were lost, the Japanese substantially destroyed the Cavite Navy Yard near Manila in a heavy air
attack.   On December 21, Japanese transports entered the
Lingayen Gulf and shortly thereafter began landing on the

western side of Luzon above Manila. On Christmas Eve they
put another force ashore on the eastern side of the island.
General Douglas MacArthur declared Manila an open city
while Admiral Hart and the remainder of the U.S. submarine
fleet headed for the Netherlands East Indies. On January 2,
1942, Manila was occupied by the Japanese.

Following these disasters, MacArthur led his men,
including several U.S. Navy and Marine Corps contingents,
onto the Bataan peninsula where it was hoped that they could
fight a rear guard action against General Masaharu Homma's
army until relief could come from America. It was generally not known, except in the highest circles, that such aid
would not be forthcoming and that everything which became
available was being sent to Australia.

American and Filipino forces put up a heroic defense of Bataan which by early February had stalled Homma's
advance. Not until March when more Japanese reinforcements arrived on Luzon was Homma able to renew his attacks. Following a heavy bombardment on April 3 and 4,
Japanese soldiers pushed forward and shattered the American
lines. Bataan was surrendered on April 9.

Whatever American and Filipino personnel were
able to got across Manila Bay to the island fortress of Corregidor which still held out. General Jonathan Wainwright,
who took over command of the area when MacArthur was
ordered to Australia, could not stem the enemy drive. From
March 24, the Japanese pounded "The Rock" by air and with
various sized artillery from Bataan, only two miles away.
This constant bombardment crushed the defenders, most of
whose guns were in positions too exposed for counterbattery
fire--or which were knocked out. Just before midnight on
May 5, some 2000 Japanese landed on the island and were
met with a stiff man-to-man resistance. However, they
secured their foothold, introduced tanks, and obtained Wainwright's surrender at 10 a.m. the next morning. Under
the threat of massacre by Homma, the American general was
also forced to obtain the surrender of the entire Philippine
archipelago. On June 9, 1942, five days after the Battle of
Midway, all organized Allied resistance had ceased.

The references which follow reflect the entire campaign for the Philippines. It should be remembered that all
branches of the American and Japanese services were active
in this as in other areas of this section and the impossibility
of separating just "sea forces" activity here is just as difficult as it will be when other campaigns such as the Solomons
are examined.

3753   Agoncillo, Teodoro A.   The Fateful Years: Japan's
       Adventure in the Philippines, 1941-1945.   2 vols.
       Quezon City: R. P. Garcia, 1965.
       The most recent Filipino study.

3754   Babcock, C. Stanton.   "The Philippine Campaign."
       Cavalry Journal, LII (March-April 1943), 7-10.

3755   Baldwin, Hanson W.   "Corregidor: The Full Story."
       New York Times Magazine, (September 27, 1946),
       16+.

3756   _____.   "The Fall of Corregidor."   American Heri-
       tage, XVII (August 1966), 16-23.

3757   _____.   "The 4th Marines at Corregidor."   Marine
       Corps Gazette, XXX (November-December 1946),
       13-18, 50-54, 27-35; XXXI (January-February
       1947), 23-29, 39-43.

3758   "Bataan: Where Heroes Fell."   Time, XXXIX (April
       20, 1942), 18-21.

3759   "Bataan's End: American Troops Fall Back for a Last
       Stand at Corregidor."   Newsweek, XIX (April 20,
       1942), 19-23.

3760   "Battered Bataan."   Newsweek, XIX (March 2, 1942),
       17.

3761   "The Battle of the Philippines."   Time, XXXIX (March
       30-May 4, 1942), 25, 24, 26-27, 23.

3762   Beck, John J.   MacArthur and Wainwright: Sacrifice
       of the Philippines.   Albuquerque: University of
       New Mexico Press, 1973.

3763   Bell, J. Franklin.   "Corregidor."   Military Engineer,
       XXXIV (March 1942), 131-132.

3764   Belote, James H. and William M.   Corregidor: The
       Saga of a Fortress.   New York: Harper & Row,
       1967.   272p.

3765   "Bloody Bataan."   Newsweek, XIX (February 9, 1942),
       21-22.

3766   Braly, William C. "Corregidor: A Name, A Symbol,
        A Tradition. " Coast Artillery Journal, XC (July-
        August 1947), 2-9, 36-44.

3767   Buenafe, Manuel E. The Wartime Philippines. Manila:
        Philippine Education Foundation, 1950. 248p.

3768   Case, Homer. "War Damage to Corregidor. " Coast
        Artillery Journal, XC (May-June 1947), 37-42.

3769   Chynoweth, B. G. "Lessons From the Fall of the
        Philippines. " Military Engineer, XLVI (September-
        October 1954), 369-372.

3770   Colville, Cabot. "Our Two Months on Corregidor. "
        Saturday Evening Post, CCXIV (June 27, 1942),
        15+.

3771   Conroy, Robert. The Battle of Bataan: America's
        Greatest Defeat. New York: Macmillan, 1969.
        85p.

3772   Considine, Robert "Bob. " MacArthur, the Magnificent.
        Washington: David McKay, 1942. 126p.

3773   _____., editor. See Wainwright, Jonathan M. , no.
        3835.

3774   "Corregidor. " Field Artillery Journal, XXXII (July
        1942), 553-555.

3775   "Corregidor Finale. " Newsweek, XIX (May 18, 1942),
        21-22.

3776   Cross, Francis R. "Forgotten Island, an Episode of
        the Philippines. " USNIP, LXIX (1943), 833-840.

3777   "The Epic of Bataan: From Dispatches and Broadcasts
        of Men Who Were There. " Reader's Digest, XL
        (June 1942), 4-7.

3778   Fuqua, S. O. "Japanese Strategy in the Philippine
        Attacks. " Newsweek, XVIII (December 22, 1941),
        14-15.

3779   _____. "Taps for Bataan, an Epic of Valor. " News-
        week, XIX (April 20, 1942), 19.

3780   Futrell, Robert F.   "Air Hostilities in the Philippines,
        8 December 1941. " Air University Review, XVI
        (January-February 1965), 33-45.

3781   Gause, Damon J.   "Escape from Corregidor's Hell. "
        New York Times Magazine, (May 2, 1943), 12, 34-
        35.

3782   Gunnison, Royal A.   "Blitz Over the Philippines. "
        Collier's, CIX (January 17, 1942), 17+.

3783   _____.   "I Saw Our Flag Come Down. "   Collier's,
        CXIII (May 20, 1944), 79.

3784   _____.   "Manila Eye-Witness. "   Collier's, CIX (Jan-
        uary 10, 1942), 13+.

3785   _____.   "Surrender at Corregidor. "   Collier's, CXIII
        (March 18, 1944), 13, 56, 58-59.

3786   _____.   "This Man MacArthur. "   Collier's, CIX
        (January 31, 1942), 13+.

3787   Hawkins, Jack.   "Corregidor Falls. " In: Patrick
        O'Sheel and Gene Cook, eds. Semper Fidelis:
        The U. S. Marines in the Pacific, 1942-1945.
        New York: William Sloane Associates, 1947.   p.
        1-11.

3788   _____.   Never Say Die.   Philadelphia: Dorrance,
        1961.   196p.
              The author, no relation to the late, noted British
        actor, served on Corregidor, escape from a Japa-
        nese P. O. W. camp, fought with Filipino guerrillas
        on Mindanao, and eventually escaped to Australia.

3789   Hersey, John.   Men on Bataan.   New York: Alfred A.
        Knopf, 1942.   313p.
              A biography of General MacArthur and a study of
        the Philippine Defense Command through early
        1942, based on soldiers' letters and unpublished
        cables from correspondents on the scene.

3790   Hill, M. A.   "The Lessons of Bataan. "   Science Di-
        gest, XII (December 1942), 52-56.

3791   Ind, Allison.   Bataan, the Judgement Seat.   New York:

Macmillan, 1944. 395p.
"The saga of the Philippine Command of the U.S.
Army Air Force, May 1941 to May 1942. "

3792 Ingham, Travis. Rendezvous by Submarine: The Story
of Charles Parsons and the Guerrilla Soldiers in
the Philippines. Garden City, N. Y.: Doubleday,
1945. 255p.
Those wishing to check on other submarine operations in this area are urged to see section IID-6.

3793 Irwin, C. L. "Corregidor in Action. " Coast Artillery
Journal, LXXXVI (January-February 1943), 9-12.

3794 Jacoby, Melville J. "The Battle of Bataan. " Life,
XII (February 9, 1942), 35.

3795 _____. "Farewell to Bataan. " Life, XII (March 30,
1942), 44+.

3796 _____. "MacArthur's Men. " Life, XII (March 16,
1942), 14+.
Correspondent Jacoby was killed in action in
early May 1942. For an account of his daring,
see "Death in the Line of Duty, " Life, XII (May
11, 1942), 32; and "In the Line of Duty, " Time,
XXXIX (May 11, 1942), 55-57.

3797 Jenkins, E. J. "The Corregidor Operation. " Military
Review, XXVI (April 1946), 57-64.

3798 Keene, J. W. "Corregidor. " Marine Corps Gazette,
XLIX (November 1965), 65-69.
The role of the 4th Marines.

3799 Knickerbocker, H. R. "MacArthur's Dash. " In:
Louis L. Snyder, ed. Masterpieces of War Reporting. New York: Julian Messner, 1962. p. 156-
160.
This piece, reprinted from the Chicago Sun of
March 19, 1942, recalls the general's escape from
the Philippines by PT boat and B-17.

3800 Lardner, John. "Flashback to Bataan: The Epic of
the Last Days. " Newsweek, XX (July 6, 1942),
25.

3801   MacArthur, Douglas.   MacArthur on War.   New York:
          Duell, Sloan & Pearce, 1942.   419p.
          A collection of official writings, including com-
          muniques from the Philippines, designed to give
          evidence of the general's able military strategy and
          foresightedness.

3802   Marquez, Adalia.   Blood on the Rising Sun: A Factual
          Story of the Japanese Invasion of the Philippines.
          New York: De Tanko, 1957.   253p.

3803   Marshall, Walter L.   "The Japanese Treasure Hunt in
          Manila Bay."   USNIP, LXXXIV (1958), 37-47.
          The attempt using captured U.S. divers to re-
          cover the fortune in Filipino silver dumped into the
          waters off Corregidor in the last days of the siege.
          About half still remains on the ocean floor.

3804   "May 6, 1942."   Time, XLIII (May 8, 1944), 61-62+.
          The surrender of Corregidor.

3805   Mellnik, Stephen M.   "How the Japs Took Corregidor."
          Coast Artillery Journal, LXXXVIII (March-April
          1945), 2-11, 17.

3806   Miller, Ernest B.   Bataan Uncensored.   Long Prairie,
          Minn. :   Hart, 1949.   403p.

3807   Moore, George F.   "Report on Philippine Coast Artil-
          lery Command and the Harbor Defenses of Manila
          and Subic Bays, Corregidor, 14 February 1941 to
          6 May 1942. "   Unpublished paper, Individual Per-
          sonnel File, U.S. Navy Department, Naval History
          Division, Operational Archives, 1946.   148p.

3808   Morton, Louis.   The Fall of the Philippines.   United
          States Army in World War II--The War in the
          Pacific.   Washington: Office of the Chief of Mili-
          tary History, Department of the Army, 1953.   626p.
          A basic source.   Be sure to check the bibliog-
          raphy.

3809   Parker, Thomas C.   "The Epic of Corregidor-Bataan,
          December 24, 1941-May 6, 1942. "   USNIP, LXIX
          (1943), 9-22.

3810   _____.   "The Subterranean River of Palawan, Philippine

Islands. " USNIP, LXVIII (1942), 1530-1533.

3811   "Philippine Epic: General MacArthur and His Men
       Made a Thermopylae of Bataan. " Life, XII (April
       13, 1942), 25-37.

3812   "Philippine Slugfest: Corregidor Joins the Land Forces
       in Pounding the Jap Invaders. " Newsweek, XIX
       (February 16, 1942), 22-23.

3813   "The Philippines. " Newsweek, XIX (February 2,
       1942), 15-17.

3814   Pollock, Thomas F. "Operation Flight-Bridiron: 27
       April-3 May 1942. " Unpublished paper, Individual
       Personnel File, U.S. Navy Department, Naval
       History Division, Operational Archives, 1963.   12p.
            The mission of two PBY flying boats sent from
       Perth, Australia, to Corregidor with medicine and
       supplies plus orders to bring out passengers.   All
       flight personnel involved were subsequently awarded
       the Silver Star, including the author who was pilot
       of the lead plane.

3815   Prickett, William F.   "The Naval Battalion on Bataan."
       USNIP, LXXXVI (1960), 72-75.
            Under Commander Francis J. Bridget, January-
       February 1942.

3816   _____ . "The Naval Battalion at Mariveles. " Marine
       Corps Gazette, XXXIV (June 1950), 40-43.

3817   Quezon, Manuel L. The Good Fight. New York: D.
       Appleton-Century, 1946.   336p.
            Contains a dramatic section on his escape from
       Corregidor with MacArthur aboard an American PT
       boat.

3818   Rabekoff, Sidney.   "PT's are Potent. " In: William H.
       Fetridge, ed. The Second Navy Reader.   Indiana-
       polis: Bobbs-Merrill, 1944.   p. 52-71.   Rpr. 1971.
            Motor torpedo boat activities in the Philippines
       and Solomons as reprinted from a 1943 issue of
       True Magazine.

3819   Redmond, Juanita. I Served on Bataan. Philadelphia:
       Lippincott, 1943.   166p.

3820   _____. _____. Scholastic, XLIII (September 27, 1943),
        13-14.
             Reminiscences of a nurse from the first attacks
        through her evacuation by submarine from Corregi-
        dor.

3821   Romulo, Carlos P. I Saw the Fall of the Philippines.
        Garden City, N.Y.: Doubleday, Doran, 1942.
        323p.
             An account by MacArthur's aide.

3822   _____. "The Philippines Await Their D-Day. " New
        York Times Magazine, (October 22, 1944), 5+.

3823   Rutherford, Ward. Fall of the Philippines. Ballan-
        tine's Illustrated History of World War II. New
        York: Ballantine Books, 1971. 160p.

3824   Sackett, E. L. "U.S.S. Canopus Courageous. " All
        Hands, no. 521, (June 1960), 58-63.
             This submarine tender (AS-9) had served with
        the Asiatic Fleet since 1924. After the Japanese
        attack, she gallantly provided aid to those few
        American ships and submarines left on station as
        well as providing men, equipment, supplies, and
        gunboats converted from her launches for the Bataan
        campaign. In April as the Japanese closed in,
        she was scuttled by her own men to prevent her
        falling into enemy hands.

3825   Sayre, Francis B. "Corregidor. " Vital Speeches,
        VIII (May 15, 1942), 467-469.

3826   _____. "War Days on Corregidor. " Life, XII (April
        20, 1942), 94-98+.

3827   Shimada, Koichi, assisted by Clarke H. Kawakami and
        Roger Pineau. "Japanese Naval Air Operations in
        the Philippine Invasion. " USNIP, LXXXI (1955),
        1-17, 1048-1049.

3828   Stirling, Nora B. Treasure Under the Sea. Garden
        City, N.Y.: Doubleday, 1957.
             Contains an account of the Corregidor silver.

3829   "The Strategic Situation in the Philippines: Routes and
        Distances. " Illustrated London News, CC (January
        10, 1942), 41.

3830   "Tales From Bataan. " Time, XXXIX (March 9, 1942),
       20-21.

3831   "Torpedo Boats Strike in the Pacific and Sink Two
       Japanese Ships in Daring Philippine Raids. " Life,
       XII (February 9, 1942), 42+.

3832   Uno, George K. Corregidor, Isle of Delusion. Shang-
       hai, China: Mercury Press, 1942.
       An important work giving the Japanese version.

3833   "U. S. S. Pigeon Was No Sitting Duck. " All Hands, no.
       453, (November 1954), 16-20.
       The adventures of little AM-47 during the Japa-
       nese invasion.

3834   Volckmann, Russell W. We Remained: Three Years
       Behind the Enemy Lines in the Philippines. New
       York: Norton, 1954. 244p.

3835   Wainwright, Jonathan M. General Wainwright's Story.
       Edited by Robert "Bob" Considine. Garden City,
       N. Y. : Doubleday, Doran, 1946. 314p.

3836   Whitcomb, Edgar A. Escape From Corregidor. Chi-
       cago: Henry Regnery, 1958. 274p.
       Reminiscences by one of the few Americans to
       escape "The Rock. " The author has just recently
       completed a term as Governor of Indiana.

3837   White, William L. They Were Expendable. New York:
       Harcourt, 1942. 209p.
       This story of PT boat action during the Bataan
       and Corregidor operations, written on the testimony
       from four of the five survivors of MTB Squadron 3,
       is probably the most widely known naval account
       of this section. Of these men under Lt. Bulkeley's
       command, who pulled MacArthur and Quezon safely
       off "The Rock, " the author writes: "The sad young
       men back from battle wander as strangers in a
       strange land, talking a grim language of realism
       which smug citizenry doesn't understand, trying to
       tell of a tragedy which few enjoy hearing. "

3838   [No entry.]

3839   _____ . _____ . In: William H. Fetridge, ed. The

     Navy Reader. Indianapolis: Bobbs-Merrill, 1943.
     p. 169-172. Rpr. 1971.
     An excerpt from the above citation.

3840 Wolfert, Ira. American Guerrilla in the Philippines.
     New York: Simon and Schuster, 1945. 301p.
     Charles Parsons.

     Further References: Readers are reminded that
additional data relative to this section can be found in sections
IIA and IIB-1 above, as well as in the Appendix to this
volume and the general works cited in Volume III, Part 1.

(7) EARLY ALLIED PACIFIC RAIDS

     Introduction. In a time of Allied sorrow, there
was one ray of light: the American carriers had not been
caught at Pearl Harbor. While A. B. D. A. forces were
fighting a hopeless effort in the south Pacific, American officials on Oahu, fearful that the enemy might move from the
Marshall and Gilbert Islands upon Samoa, sent their carriers
to put an end to any such notion. On February 1, 1942, the
Yorktown-group of Rear Admiral Frank J. Fletcher struck
at Makin in the northern Gilberts plus two islands in the
southern Marshalls. Meanwhile Vice Admiral William F.
Halsey's command, centered around U. S. S. Enterprise (CV-
6), sallied deep into the Marshalls hitting Japanese bases at
Wotje, Maloelap, and Kwajalein. These Yankee strikes had
the effect of causing Nippon to divert two powerful carriers,
or about a third of her most important striking arm, for the
defense of the home islands. A third raid by the Lexington-
group under Vice Admiral Wilson Brown, which was scheduled
to hit the big enemy base of Rabaul in late February, was
abandoned when the Allied force was spotted and attacked.
     Two months later, shortly after the Japanese made
their sweep through the Indian Ocean, there occurred one of
the most famous raids in military or naval history, the Halsey-Doolittle assault on Tokyo. This event is so noted that
we shall mention its operation only briefly.
     On April 18, 1942, 16 U. S. Army B-25 "Mitchell"
medium-bombers lifted off the deck of the carrier Hornet
after being escorted to within 800 miles of Japan by Admiral
Halsey's force, which in addition to "Shangri-La," consisted
of the Enterprise and a cruiser/destroyer screen. Meeting

little resistance, Colonel James H. Doolittle's force dropped
its bombs on Tokyo and a few other Japanese cities--doing
only slight damage--and made for improvised landing fields
in China.   Fifteen of the sixteen planes were lost in crash
landings; the only one to make it safely was impounded by
Russia for landing at Vladivostok.   Although several of the
crewmen were captured and a few eventually executed by the
Japanese for "war crimes," 71 of the participating 80 airmen
survived.

The physical damage inflicted by these early raids
was negligible; however, on both sides the morale effect was
impressive.   Americans, depressed by defeat, were cheered
to know their forces were fighting back.   The Japanese, on
the other hand, were seriously alarmed and ordered a series
of defensive arrangements which were to have important
implications.

3841   "Admiral Bill [Halsey]: Destroyer Ace Led Raids on
       the Marshall and Gilbert Islands. " Newsweek, XIX
       (February 23, 1942), 18-19.

3842   "Bombers Over Tokyo. " Christian Century, LIX
       (April 29, 1942), 550-551.

3843   "Bombs on Japan. " Time, XXXIX (April 27, 1942),
       18-19.

3843a Caidin, Martin.   "Doolittle's Raid on Tokyo. " In:
       Philip Hirsch, ed. Fighting Generals. New York:
       Pyramid Books, 1960. p. 78-90.

3844   Considine, Bob, editor. See Lawson, Ted W. , no.
       3859.

3845   Courtney, W. B.   "Through Hell and High Brass: The
       Story of Jimmy Doolittle. " Collier's, CXXII (No-
       vember 13-December 18, 1948), 18-19+, 63-67,
       26-27+, 28+, 18-19+, 26+.

3846   Critchfield, John S.   "The Halsey-Doolittle Tokyo
       Raid. " Sea Power, XIV (December 1971), 25-29.

3847   Cutter, Slade D.   "We Raid the Coast of Japan. "
       American Magazine, CXXXV (March 1943), 26-27+.

3848   Dickinson, Clarence E.   "I Fly For Vengeance: The

Raid on the Marshall Islands. " Saturday Evening
Post, CCXV (October 17, 1942), 22-23+.

3849 "Doolittle's Deed. " Newsweek, XIX (June 1, 1942), 27.

3850 Eierman, Jacob. "I Helped Bomb Japan. " Popular
Science, CXLIII (July 1943), 64-68.

3851 "First Launching of Land Bombers at Sea: The Famous
[Doolittle] Raid on Tokyo. " Illustrated London News,
CCII (May 8, 1943), 509.

3852 Glines, Carroll V. "The Day (April 18, 1942) Doolittle Hit Tokyo. " Air Force and Space Digest, L
(April 1967), 84-85+.

3853 _____. Doolittle's Tokyo Raiders. Princeton, N. J. :
Van Nostrand, 1964. 447p.
Contains complete details on the U. S. Navy's
aid in the project.

3854 _____. Jimmy Doolittle: Daredevil Aviator and
Scientist. U. S. Air Force Academy Series. New
York: Macmillan, 1972. 183p.

3855 _____. "The Raid From 'Shangri-La': Interview. "
Airman, IX (April 1965), 32-35.
The author, who in this case is also the inter-
viewee, took part in the noted sortie.

3856 Hyde, C. C. "Japanese Executions of American Aviators. " American Journal of International Law,
XXXVII (July 1943), 480-482.

3857 "James H. Doolittle. " CurrBio:III:16-18.

3858 "Jimmy Did It: The Aid Raid on Japan. " Time,
XXXIX (June 1, 1942), 17.
One should note the interview with General Doo-
little which appeared in American Heritage, XXV
(April 1974), 48-57+, under the title "I Am Not A
Very Timid Type.... "

3859 Lawson, Ted W. Thirty Seconds Over Tokyo, ed. by
Bob Considine. New York: Random House, 1943.
221p.
An excellent view of the Doolittle Raid from the

fliers' point of view. The book was later made
into an exciting movie starring Spencer Tracy as
the valiant colonel.

3860 "Last Year's Raid on Tokyo: The 'Mitchells' Took Off
from the Hornet. " Illustrated London News, CCII
(May 1, 1943), 490.
To avoid informing the enemy that the raid had
originated from the carrier, President Roosevelt
borrowed the title of a popular novel and "christen-
ed" the warship "Shangri-La. "

3861 Mann, Carl. Lightning in the Air: The Story of Jimmy Doolittle. New York: McBride, 1943. 256p.

3862 Merrill, James M. Target Tokyo, the Halsey-Doolittle Raid. Chicago: Rand McNally, 1964. 208p.
Should be used jointly with the Glines work cited
above.

3863 Morris, Frank D. "Zero Weather. " Collier's, CXII
(December 18, 1943), 24+.
The February 1942 carrier raids.

3864 "The Navy Releases the First Pictures of the Daring
Raid on the Gilbert and Marshall Islands. " Life,
XII (February 23, 1942), 24-25.

3865 Powell, Henry. "Diving Artillery: What It Is Like to
Ride a Dive-Bombing Plane. " Popular Science, CXL
(April 1942), 90-96.
The February raids.

3866 Pratt, William V. "How the Attack on Tokyo was
Planned. " Newsweek, XXV (February 25, 1945),
28.

3867 Reynolds, Quentin. The Amazing Mr. Doolittle. New
York: Appleton-Century-Crofts, 1953.

3868 _____. "Jimmy Doolittle: Master of the Calculated
Risk. " Reader's Digest, LXII (May 1953), 159-167.
An excerpt from the above citation.

3869 Sherrod, Robert. "The Raid on Wake Island From the
Rear Seat of a Dive Bomber. Life, XV (October
25, 1943), 27-29.

3870 Sims, Jack A. "The Tokyo Raid--An Avenging Call. "
      Airpower Historian, IV (October 1957), 174-185.
      The Doolittle exploit.

3871 Strum, Ted R. "The Last Tokyo Raider. " Airman,
      XVII (December 1973), 22-23.
           On the retirement of Col. James H. Macia from
      the U.S. Air Force with a look at his most noted
      adventure.

3872 "Tokyo Is Bombed at Last. " Life, XII (April 27,
      1942), 34-36.

3873 "The Tokyo Raid, Bases Which Made It Possible. "
      Newsweek, XXIV (December 4, 1944), 32-34.

3874 "The U.S. Awards Medals to 80 Heroes of the Army's
      Bombing Raid on Japan. " Life, XII (June 1, 1942),
      28-29.

3875 United States. Navy Department. Office of the Chief
      of Naval Operations, Intelligence Division. "Com-
      bat Narrative: Early Raids in the Pacific Ocean,
      1 February-10 March 1942. " Unpublished paper,
      CNO-ONI File, U.S. Navy Department, Naval His-
      tory Division, Operational Archives, 1942. 71p.
           The raids were on the Marshall and Gilbert Is-
      lands, Wake and Marcus, Lae and Salamaua, and
      almost on Rabaul.

3876 _____._____._____. "Combat Narrative: The
      Navy's Share in the Tokyo Raid. " Unpublished
      paper, CNO-ONI File, U.S. Navy Department,
      Naval History Division, Operational Archives, 1942.
      8p.

3877 _____. War Department. "The First Raid on Japan,
      April 18, 1942. " In: Norman Carlisle, ed. The
      Air Forces Reader. Indianapolis: Bobbs-Merrill,
      1944. p. 163-168.

3878 _____._____. Army Air Forces, China, Burma, and
      India. "Final Report, First Special Aviation Proj-
      ect. " Unpublished paper, Army File, U.S. Navy
      Department, Naval History Division, Operational
      Archives, 1942. 342p.
           This June 1942 document is the final field report

on the Halsey-Doolittle raid.   In rough form, the
two parts provide thorough and well-documented
analysis of the achievements and shortcomings of
this joint-service venture.

3879   Walker, Wayne T.   "B-25's Over Tokyo. " World War
       II Magazine, III (October 1973), 30-40.
          A pictorial essay.

3880   White, Thomas R.   "The Hornet Stings Japan: Diary
       of the Raid on Japan and a Trek Through China to
       Safety. " Atlantic, CLXXI (June 1943), 41-46.
          This memoir of the Doolittle exploit was abridged
       in Scholastic, XLIV (April 10, 1944), 13-16.

3881   Woodward, Clark H.   "The Bomb Voyage to Tokyo:
       Speculative Sea-and-Air Attack From the Aleutian
       Islands. " Popular Mechanics, LXXVIII (July 1942),
       1-5.
          When this article appeared, it still was not known
       that the Hornet launched Doolittle.

          Further References: Readers will find additional
data relative to this part in section IIA above, as well as in
the general works cited in Volume III, Part 1.

(8)   AUSTRALIA'S DEFENSE

          Introduction.   As part of the British Commonwealth,
Australia had already been at war with Germany and Italy for
over two years when the Japanese bombed Pearl Harbor.
Units of her service had seen extensive service in the European Theater, particularly in the Mediterranean area.
          When the forces of the Rising Sun commenced their
Pacific conquests, the "Aussies" found themselves facing a
new foe almost on their back doorstep. By the spring of
1942, after the fall of Malaya and the loss of the Dutch East
Indies, that nation, already having lost 22,000 men in those
campaigns, appeared open for invasion. On February 19,
Admiral Nagumo's carriers raided Darwin, the major port
in the northern end of the country. Docks, warehouses, and
shipping, including the U.S. destroyer Peary, were destroyed
and the city evacuated.
          In the face of some considerable controversy, the

government of Prime Minister John Curtin transferred home
two battle-hardened divisions of Australian troops from the
Middle East to bolster defenses. Recognizing the impotence
of Great Britain in the Pacific, it also actively initiated a
closer policy of cooperation with the United States.   On March
17, 1942, General Douglas MacArthur transferred his headquarters from the Philippines to Australia.
        The Japanese, on the other hand, were moving
ahead in their attempts to isolate the continent.   The Naval
General Staff worked out a plan to accomplish this by moving
from Rabaul into Eastern New Guinea, capturing Lae, Sala-
mauna, and Port Moresby, as well as down the Solomons and
the New Hebrides to New Caledonia, the Fijis, and Samoa.
        Fortunately for the Allies, the enemy advance, as
shall be noted in later sections, did not succeed.   The Battles of the Coral Sea and Midway put an effective damper on
it and allowed Australia, together with the Americans, to
begin the ultimately victorious counterattack.
        Throughoüt the War in the Pacific, the armed
forces of Australia cooperated closely with those of other
Allied nations.   By late 1944, they had suffered, on a world-
wide basis, almost 85,000 casualties--truly a sizeable number
when one considers the total population.   The circumstances
of these tolls raised Australia to a strength and independence
in foreign relations that would change that nation's role in
international affairs for years to come.
        The references in this section are general works
applying broadly to Australia and New Zealand, and specific
works dealing with events that happened on or near their
soil.   Titles concerning their participation in various campaigns away from home will be found in other parts of this
compilation.

3882   Australia and New Zealand.   Theatres of War Series.
       New York: Columbia University Press, 1942.   16p.

3883   Australia.   Royal Australian Navy.   H. M. A. S. :   Writ-
       ten and Prepared by Serving Personnel of the
       R. A. N.   2 vols.   Canberra: Australian War Me-
       morial, 1942-1943.
            Volume I: 1939-1942.
            Volume II: 1942-1943.

3884   Australia Today.   2 vols.   Melbourne: United Com-
       mercial Travellers' Association of Australia, 1943-
       1945.

11-12.

86 "Australia's War." Time, XLVI (July 30, 1945), 28-
29.
A summary.

3887 Bateson, Henry. "IS Australia Threatened?" New
Statesman, XXIII (January 10, 1942), 19-20.

3888 Eliot, George F. "Australia, Keystone of Far Eastern
Strategy." Foreign Affairs, XX (April 1942), 402-
409.

3889 Evatt, Herbert V. The Foreign Policy of Australia.
Sydney and London: Angus and Robertson, 1945.
266p.

3890 Griffiths, Owen E. Darwin Drama. Sydney, Australia:
L. C. Publishing Co., 1947. 218p.
The February 19, 1942 Japanese carrier raid.

3891 Hayes, Robert C. "Return to the Islands: Melbourne."
Leatherneck, XLIII (June 1960), 50-52.
On the Australian city; part of a series.

3892 Hilder, Brett. "Jettison!" In: Gavin Lyall, ed. The
War in the Air: The Royal Air Force in World
War II. New York: William Morrow, 1968. p.
363-367.
On the mining activities of R.A.A.F. Catalinas
in the Far East during the first months of the
Pacific conflict.

3893 Holmes, John W., ed. Australia and New Zealand at
War. Pamphlets on World Affairs, no. C-9. New
York: Oxford University Press, 1940. 40p.

3894 Johnston, George H. Australia at War. Sydney and
London: Angus and Robertson, 1942. 265p.

3895 _____. Pacific Partners. London: Gollancz, 1944.
227p.
This account of Australia-American co-operation

was published in America simultaneously by the
New York firm of Duell, Sloan, and Pearce.

3896 Kahn, Ely J.   G. I. Jungle: An American Soldier in
      Australia and New Zealand.   New York: Simon &
      Schuster, 1943.   150p.
      The story of the first U.S. convoy of troops to
      those nations and the daily lives of Yanks while
      there.

3897 Lardner, John.   "Ringside Seat at a Darwin Air Raid."
      Newsweek, XIX (April 13, 1942), 26.

3898 _____. "The Sacking of Darwin. " New Yorker, XXII
      (July 13, 1946), 54+.

3899 Laytha, Edgar.   "Australia's Baby Singapore. " Satur-
      day Evening Post, CCXIV (February 14, 1942), 12-
      13+.
      Darwin.

3900 Lockwood, Douglas W.   Australia's Pearl Harbor:
      Darwin, 1942.   London: Cassell, 1966.   232p.

3901 "[MacArthur's] Mystery Trip to Australia. " Newsweek,
      XIX (March 30, 1942), 18.

3902 Murtagh, James G.   "Japan Over Australia. " Common-
      weal, XXXV (April 3, 1942), 582-583.

3903 Penton, Brian.   "Help Us Hold Australia. " Saturday
      Evening Post, CCXIV (April 11, 1942), 16-17+.

3904 Walker, Howell.   "Life in Dauntless Darwin. " Nation-
      al Geographic, LXXXII (July 1942), 122-138.

3905 _____. "Sydney Faces the War Front Down Under. "
      National Geographic, LXXXIII (March 1943), 358-
      374.

3906 Wolfe, Henry C.   "Pacific Springboard: Australia,
      Jumping-Off Place For Our Forces in the South
      Seas. " American Magazine, CXXXIII (May 1942),
      117-120.

      Further References: Readers are advised that
additional citations relative to this section will be found in

section IIA above, as well as in the general works section of Volume III, Part 1. References to the war service of Australian sea forces units are found throughout both Volumes I and II.

IIC THE TIDE SLOWLY TURNS

(1) GENERAL WORKS

Introduction. The first six months of the War in
the Pacific had seen the Japanese triumphant everywhere.
From Pearl Harbor through the Pacific islands, and from
China almost into India and Australia the men representing
the Rising Sun carried all before them.
Then, through a series of accidents as well as by
virtue of planning, the Allies first stopped the growth of the
enemy perimeter and then began slowly to push it back.
Some of the largest battles of sea forces in all recorded
history took place during those hopeful months: Coral Sea,
Midway, the Solomons, New Guinea. Of course, some of
the least epic battles also took place, as noted in the almost
totally-forgotten Aleutians campaigns waged by both the Japanese and Americans.
The titles which follow are presented because, for
the most part, they cover a span of time exceeding that in
any one of the various sub-sections in this category. A few
of these references have their beginnings in IIB or a sub-
section thereof, and carry on through the period here covered. All bear witness to that truism first expressed by
British Admiral Sir Roger Keyes in 1915: "In all operations
a moment arrives when brave decisions have to be made if
an enterprise is to be carried through." For Allies and
Axis alike, these were weeks of great enterprise.

3907 "The Allies Advance in the South Pacific." Life, XV
       (October 4, 1943), 27-33.

3908 "The Allies Bomb Rabaul: U.S. Marines Land on
       Bougainville." Life, XV (November 29, 1943),
       34-38.
            Entered here as this citation is to two separate
       events.

3909   "Battles in the Pacific." <u>National Review</u>, CXIX
       (July 1942), 5-7.

3910   Bayler, Walter L. J. <u>The Last Man Off Wake Island</u>.
       Indianapolis: Bobbs-Merrill, 1943. 367p.
       This title is somewhat misleading as it primarily
       concerns this Marine's activities at Midway and on
       Guadalcanal.

3911   "End of an Argument: Emphasis on Airplane Carriers
       and on Air-Borne Attack." <u>Time</u>, XXXIX (May
       25, 1942), 69.

3912   Forgy, Howard M. "...and Pass the Ammunition."
       Edited by Jack S. McDowell. New York: D. Ap-
       pleton-Century, 1944. 242p.
       The chaplain's account of the U.S.S. <u>New Orleans</u>
       in the Battles of the Coral Sea and Midway.

3913   "From the Snows of Alaska to the Shores of the Solo-
       mons, the Marines Carry on Their 167-Year Tradi-
       tion." <u>Newsweek</u>, XX (November 9, 1942), 30+.

3914   Gaskill, Gordon. "Night Patrol: An Account of a
       Typical PT-Boat Mission." <u>American Magazine</u>,
       CXXXVI (December 1943), 46-47+.

3915   Ghormley, Robert L. "South Pacific Command: Events
       Leading Up to the U.S. Attack on the Solomon Is-
       lands." Unpublished paper, Forces File, U.S.
       Navy Department, Naval History Division, Operation-
       al Archives, 1943. 23p.
       Largely a personal account of the author's experi-
       ence as Commander South Pacific, April-October
       1942.

3916   _____. "South Pacific Command History: The Early
       Period." Unpublished paper, Forces File, U.S.
       Navy Department, Naval History Division, Opera-
       tional Archives, 1943. 150p.
       An expanded version of the above reference.

3917   Hailey, Foster. <u>Pacific Battle Line</u>. New York:
       Macmillan, 1944. 405p.
       Pearl Harbor through the Aleutians campaign.

3918   _____. "Their Morale Is All Right, How's Yours?:

The Spirit of the Pacific Fleet Is Excellent. " New
York Times Magazine, (November 8, 1942), 6+.

3919   Horan, James. Out in the Boondocks: Marines in
       Action in the Pacific. New York: Putnam, 1943.
       209p.
           Covers only the first year of the war through the
       Guadalcanal offensive.

3920   Johnston, Stanley. The Grim Reapers. New York:
       и. P. Dutton, 1943. 221p.
           Concerns Navy VF-10 Squadron in action in Mid-
       way and in the Solomons.

3921   Kessing, Felix M. South Seas in the Modern World.
       Institute of Pacific Relations Research Series. Rev.
       ed. New York: Day, 1945. 391p.
           Useful for knowledge of the area in which the
       sea forces were fighting throughout the Pacific war.

3922   Lardner, John. Southwest Passage: The Yankees in
       the Pacific. Philadelphia: Lippincott, 1943. 302p.
           A report by Newsweek's correspondent in Austral-
       ia and New Guinea in 1942.

3923   Lee, Clark. They Call It Pacific: An Eyewitness
       Story of Our War Against Japan From Bataan to the
       Solomons. New York: Viking, 1943. 374p.
           As seen by an AP correspondent. Contains some
       comments on strategy, the enemy, and American
       fighting.

3924   Littrell, Gaither. "Pappy's Blacksheep: One of the
       Pacific's Deadliest Squadrons. " Flying, XXXV
       (December 1944), 25-26+.
           "Pappy" Boyington's air squadron, VMF-222.

3925   London, John J. "An Early World War II Troop Con-
       voy to New Caledonia Via Panama and Australia. "
       USNIP, LXXI (1945), 681-687.

3926   McDowell, Jack S. , editor. See Forgy, Howard M. ,
       no. 3912.

3927   McPherson, Irvin H. "I Fly For the Navy. " In:
       William H. Fetridge, ed. The Navy Reader.
       Indianapolis: Bobbs-Merrill, 1943. p. 172-180.
       Rpr. 1971.

Commentary on early U.S. naval air operations.

3928   Madden, George B.   "Loss of the Little and Gregory."
       Unpublished paper, Individual Personnel File, U.S.
       Navy Department, Naval History Division, Opera-
       tional Archives, n.d.   4p.
              APD-4 and APD-3 were both sunk in the Pacific
       in August 1942.

3929   Mitchell, Donald W.   "The Coming Offensive in the
       Pacific."   Nation, CLVI (April 3, 1943), 482-483.

3930   _____.   "The Pacific Offensive."   Nation, CLVII
       (July 24, 1943), 96-97.

3931   _____.   "Pushing the Japanese Back."   Nation, CLVII
       (September 18, 1943), 319-320.

3932   _____.   "Time Is On Our Side: The United Nations
       Pull Ahead of Japan."   Current History, New
       Series V (December 1943), 295-298.

3933   Moore, Thomas.   The Sky Is My Witness.   New York:
       Putnam, 1943.   135p.
              How a young Irishman from Brooklyn joined the
       Marines and saw service with Marine Scout Bombing
       Squadron (VMSB) 24 at Midway and with Marine
       Scout Bombing Squadron (VMSB) 232 during the
       Guadalcanal campaign.

3934   Nathan, R. S.   "Geopolitics and Pacific Strategy."
       Pacific Affairs, XV (June 1942), 154-163.
              As it relates to our period.

3935   "The Navy Chennault: [John S.] Thach, a Veteran Air-
       man Whom Navy Fliers Recognize as Their Best
       Fighter Tactician."   Time, XLI (June 14, 1943),
       66-68.

3936   "Navy Dive Bombing."   Life, XIII (November 2, 1942),
       87-95.
              An illustrated account of how it was practiced
       during our period.

3937   Oliver, Edward F.   "The Death of the President
       Coolidge."   Ships and the Sea, III (June 1953), 24-
       26.

She went down after running into an Allied mine-
field in the New Hebrides in 1942.

3938 "104 Days: Ended by the Yorktown Sinking. " Newsweek, XX (September 28, 1942), 20.

3939 Parsons, Robert P. "The Marines Have Landed. "
Atlantic, CLXXI (March 1943), 73-79.
An abridged version of this piece appeared in
Reader's Digest, XLII (June 1943), 105-108, under
the title, "Marines Land in Elysia. "

3940 Potter, Elmer B. "The Limited Offensive. " In: his
Sea Power: A Naval History. Englewood Cliffs,
N. J. : Prentice-Hall, 1960. p. 711-734.

3941 Pratt, William V. "The Dive Bomber Stars in Aerial
War at Sea. " Newsweek, XX (August 17, 1942),
28.
Coral Sea through Guadalcanal's initial landings.

3942 _____. "Four Actions That Illustrate New Naval
Tactics. " Newsweek, XXI (January 25, 1943), 21.
All fought during our period.

3943 _____. "It Wasn't Reprisal, the Japs Meant Business:
The Attacks in Unalaska and Midway. " Newsweek,
XIX (June 15, 1942), 20.

3944 _____. "Pacific Outlook: A Long War of Attrition. "
Newsweek, XX (November 9, 1942), 18.

3945 _____. "The Way Is Open for a U.S. Pacific Punch. "
Newsweek, XIX (June 22, 1942), 26.

3946 "Robert L. Ghormley. " CurrBio:III:25-27.

3947 Ryan, W. D. "I Fight with the Mosquito Fleet. "
American Magazine, CXXXIV (November 1942), 26-
27+.
Adventures with American PT-Boats.

3948 "Tell It To the Marines. " Independent Woman, XXII
(March 1943), 66.

3949 United States. Navy Department. Office of the Chief
of Naval Operations, Intelligence Division. "Combat

Narrative: Miscellaneous Actions in the South Pacific, 8 August 1942-22 January 1943. " Unpublished paper, CNO-ONI File, U.S. Navy Department, Naval History Division, Operational Archives, 1943. 70p.

3950 _____. _____. Pacific Fleet and Pacific Ocean Areas. Enemy Positions, Central Pacific. Cincpac-Cincpoa Bulletin 11-42. N.p. , 1942.

3951 _____. _____. _____. Enemy Positions, North Pacific. Cincpac-Cincpoa Bulletin 5-42. N.p. , 1942.

3952 _____. _____. _____. Enemy Positions, South Pacific. Cincpac-Cincpoa Bulletin 3-42. N.p. , 1942.

3953 _____. _____. _____. United Nations Bases, Central and South Pacific. Cincpac-Cincpoa Bulletin 7-42. N.p. , 1942.
       This and the previous three references are all intelligence reports.

3954 _____. _____. _____, Motor Torpedo Boat Squadron 13. "History. " Unpublished paper, Type Commands File, U.S. Navy Department, Naval History Division, Operational Archives, 1945. 19p.
       This unit saw action in the Aleutians and the South Pacific.

3955 Ward, J. A. "Air Power in the Pacific Conflict. " Aero Digest, XLI (May 1942), 54, 56, 58.

3956 White, William L. "The Eastern Sea Frontier. " Reader's Digest, XLI (October 1942), 102-107.

3957 Wolfert, Ira. Torpedo 8, the Story of Swede Larsen's Bomber Squadron. Boston: Houghton, Mifflin, 1943. 127p.
       A brief history of the group from its training through its decimation at Midway, and its reformation and action in the Solomons. After Midway, the squadron slogan was changed from "Attack" to "Attack--and Vengeance !"

       Further References: Readers will find additional citations relative to this section in IIA above, as well as in the general works cited in Volume III, Part 1.

(2) STANDOFF IN THE CORAL SEA

Introduction. As mentioned in the introduction to
section IIB-8 above, the Japanese Naval Staff in the spring of
1942 became increasingly interested in isolating Australia.
To do this, they would capture New Guinea, the Solomons,
and certain other island groups around the continent.
The Allies having gained information on these plans
via the enemy's own codes, it was decided that American and
such Allied (mostly Australian) naval forces which could be
brought together should attempt to stop the Japanese move on
Port Moresby. Putting the Lexington-group together with the
Yorktown-group in the southeast Coral Sea on May 1, its
commander, Rear Admiral Frank J. Fletcher soon found
action.
On May 4, planes from the U.S.S. Yorktown raided
Tulagi in the Solomons, while the Lexington and her escort
were refueled. Two days later, Fletcher formally merged
the two carriers into a single striking force within a single
screen of escorts. Rear Admiral Aubrey W. Fitch, commander of the "Lady Lex" and an old carrier hand, was
given tactical command to be exercised during air operations.
While Fletcher was making his arrangements, a
strong force, including the carriers Shokaku and Zuikaku,
under Vice Admiral Takeo Takagi, with Rear Admiral Tadaichi
Hara commanding the carriers, entered the Coral Sea. The
stage was being set for the first naval battle in history during
which the opposing forces would not even come in sight of
one another.
On May 7, Admiral Fletcher ordered Rear Admiral
J. C. Crace, R.N., to take three cruisers and the same
number of destroyers to the northwest to halt by surface
action the Japanese Port Moresby Invasion Force. The
Britisher's ships were attacked by Japanese aircraft and by
U.S.A.A.F. B-26's supposing them to be the enemy. Fortunately for the Allies, none of Crace's ships were sunk.
Meanwhile, on this day after the fall of Corregidor,
American pilots spotted the small carrier Shoho and in the
first U.S. attack on an enemy flattop, sent her to the bottom
under a baker's dozen of bomb hits.
The Japanese, in addition to assaulting Crace's
force, which was reported as a carrier force to Vice Admiral
Shigeyoshi Inouye's headquarters on Rabaul, learned of a third
Yankee "carrier" force in addition to Fletcher's. Rabaul-
based Imperial Navy planes hit the enemy group--and sank
the destroyer U.S.S. Sims and fatally damaged the "carrier,"

which turned out to be the oiler Neosho. Through a series
of errors, the Japanese failed to make contact with Fletcher's
main body.
     The following day both sides learned the location
of one another and launched almost simultaneous air strikes.
Planes from the American carriers located the enemy and
severely damaged the Shokaku, the Zuikaku having found
refuge in a rain squall. Japanese pilots were likewise successful, locating and damaging the Lexington. For awhile
it appeared that the "Lady Lex" would survive; in fact, she
began to recover her own returning planes. Then in the
early afternoon she was raked by a huge explosion, followed
two hours later by another one. Fire went out of control
and by early evening it was necessary to abandon her. After
removing the crew, a destroyer sent the proud old vessel to
the bottom with five torpedoes.
     Tactically, the Battle of the Coral Sea was a
Japanese victory, the American fleet having been forced to
retire. Strategically it was an Allied success as Admiral
Inouye postponed the Port Moresby invasion, thereby leaving
the American-Australian "lifeline" intact. Morally, it gave
the Americans a big boost: for the first time since Pearl
Harbor, Japanese expansion was effectively stalled.

3958 "After the Great Coral Sea Victory the U.S.S. Lexing-
         ton Blows Up: Photographs." Illustrated London
         News, CC (June 20, 1942), 707.

3959 "Aubrey Fitch." CurrBio:VI:190-192.

3960 "Battle of the Coral Sea: Photographs and Map."
         Illustrated London News, CC (May 16, 1942), 587.

3961 "The Coral Sea: Norman Bel Geddes' Models Reenact
         the Naval Battle." Life, XII (May 25, 1942), 21-25.

3962 "Coral Sea, the Battle and the Carrier." All Hands,
         no. 518, (March 1960), 59-63.

3963 "The First Carrier Battle." All Hands, no. 533,
         (June 1961), 27-31.

3964 Hoehling, Adolph A. The Lexington Goes Down.
         Englewood Cliffs, N.J.: Prentice-Hall, 1971.
         208p.

3965 "In the Coral Sea." Time, XXXIX (May 18, 1942),
      18-20.

3966 Johnston, Stanley. "The Battle of the Coral Sea."
      In: Louis L. Snyder, ed. Masterpieces of War
      Reporting. New York: Julian Messner, 1962.
      p. 169-174.
        Written by the only correspondent aboard, this
      account, reprinted from the June 17, 1942 issue of
      the Chicago Tribune, tells of the last days of the
      U.S.S. Lexington.

3967 _____. "Coral Sea, the Naval Battle Fought in the
      Air." Reader's Digest, XLI (August 1942), 77-82.

3968 _____. Queen of the Flat-Tops: The U.S.S. Lexing-
      ton and the Coral Sea Battle. New York: E. P.
      Dutton, 1942. 280p. Rpr. 1969.

3969 Karig, Walter and Welbourne Kelly. "The 'Old Lady's'
      Last Fight." USNIP, LXX (1944), 1489-1499.
      The Lexington.

3970 Kelly, Welbourne, jt. author. See Karig, Walter,
      no. 3969.

3971 "Last Moments of the Jap Aircraft Carrier Ryukaku,
      Sunk by U.S. Bombers in the Battle of the Coral
      Sea." Illustrated London News, CCI (July 11,
      1942), 50-51.
        Photographs correct; however, their subject was
      the Shoho, not the Ryukaku--which was not even
      engaged.

3972 Leming, Joseph. "The Battle of the Coral Sea." In:
      his Brave Ships of World War II. London: Nelson,
      1944. p. 156-170.

3973 "'Lest We Forget!'--The Battle of the Coral Sea."
      Navy, II (August 1959), 29-30.

3974 "Lexington (CV-2) Had a Short But Heroic Career in
      World War II." All Hands, no. 561, (October
      1963), 60-63.

3975 Mill, Edward W. "Hitting Back at Japan." Current
      History, New Series II (June 1942), 253-258.

3976 "Old Friendships Rekindled at Down Under Celebration--
      the Battle of the Coral Sea." Navy, III (September
      1960), 22-26.

3977 O'Neill, Herbert C. "Japan's Next Move." By
      "Strategicus," pseud. Spectator, CLCVIII (May 29,
      1942), 501.

3978 _____. "The Coral Sea Battle." By "Strategicus,"
      pseud. Spectator, CLXVIII (May 15, 1942), 457.

3979 Pratt, William V. "A Look Beyond the Battle of the
      Coral Sea." Newsweek, XIX (May 18, 1942), 16.

3980 Rawlings, Charles A. "Fat Girl: The U.S.S. Neosho,
      an Auxiliary Oiler Attached to the Pacific Fleet,
      Dies Gallantly in the Coral Sea." Saturday Evening
      Post, CCXV (February 6, 1943), 9-11+.

3981 Seasholes, Henry C. Adrift in the South Pacific; or,
      Six Nights in the Coral Sea. Boston: Baker, 1951.
      55p.
      By a survivor of the Neosho.

3982 "Strategicus," pseud. See O'Neill, Herbert C., nos.
      3977-3978.

3983 United States. Naval War College. "The Battle of
      the Coral Sea, May 1-11, 1942." Unpublished
      paper, Battle Analysis Series, Training Commands
      File, U.S. Navy Department, Naval History Divi-
      sion, Operational Archives, 1947. 128p.
      A detailed tactical analysis based on both Japanese
      and Allied sources.

3984 _____. Navy Department. Office of the Chief of
      Naval Operations, Intelligence Division. "Combat
      Narrative: The Battle of the Coral Sea, 4-8 May
      1942." Unpublished paper, CNO-ONI File, U.S.
      Navy Department, Naval History Division, Opera-
      tional Archives, 1942. 60p.
      Readers will note with pleasure the publication
      by the U.S. Naval Institute of Bernard Millot's
      Battle of the Coral Sea in the late Fall of 1974.
      It will stand as No. 11 in that firm's Sea Battles
      in Close-Up series.

3985 "U.S.S. Lexington, Pride of the U.S. Fleet, Sinks to
       a Hero's Grave in the Pacific." Life, XII (June
       22, 1942), 22-23.

3986 Walker, Gordon. "Prelude to Victory in the South
       Pacific: One of the Greatest Chapters in American
       Naval History." Christian Science Monitor Maga-
       zine, (April 24, 1943), 5+.

        Further References: Additional data relative to
this section will be found in sections IIA and IIC-1 above,
as well as in the general works cited in Volume III, Part 1.

                 (3) THE EPIC OF MIDWAY

        Introduction. When one considers the truly "de-
cisive" victories of World War II, the name of a tiny island
1135 miles west of Hawaii always comes to mind. This tiny
dot, housing an air- and seaplane base, was Midway.
        When the Imperial Naval High Command gave Ad-
miral Yamamoto the directive on May 5 to capture the spot
it had several objectives in mind. In addition to neutralizing
any further chances of surprise attacks like the Doolittle
adventure which might come from that area or the Aleutians
(which are covered in section IIC-4), the American base at
Pearl Harbor could be kept under constant surveillance. More
important, however, was the belief that the only sure way to
prevent a rapid enemy recovery was to lure its carriers and
otherwise weaker naval forces into a contest from which the
Imperial Navy would emerge as complete victor. In short,
the Japanese went fishing. With the exception of a few fleet
elements engaged elsewhere, Yamamoto would take his entire
available carrier and surface force on the expedition.
        Admiral Chester Nimitz was not taken by surprise
as his enemy expected. American intelligence deciphered
the Japanese codes and thus told him what to expect. Instead
of moving in cold to what surely would have been defeat,
"CincPac" was able to plan how best to handle the situation
with what resources were available.
        The Battle of Midway lasted the better part of a
workingman's week beginning on June 2, when the carrier
task forces of Rear Admiral Fletcher and Rear Admiral Raymond A. Spruance came together some 350 miles northeast
of Midway Island. The following day aircraft based on that

island located and attacked the transports of Yamamoto's
Combined Fleet about 600 miles west.

Early on June 4, Japanese carrier planes struck
the island installations of Midway Island, which were defended
by U.S.A.A.F. and Marine Corps warplanes. The U.S.
carriers Enterprise, Hornet, and Yorktown launched their
attack against the enemy carriers, sinking the Kaga and
Soryu. Planes from the Japanese fleet meanwhile located
and damaged the Yorktown. Stung by these events, Yamamoto scrapped the plan to occupy Midway and ordered the
Combined Fleet to retire westward.

Admiral Spruance pursued the enemy and the following day, American planes so damaged the Japanese carriers Akagi and Hiryu that they had to be abandoned and dispatched. The chase was continued into the next day. June 6
saw the Yankee pilots add the enemy heavy cruiser Mikuma
to the lost list. After recovering aircraft, the Americans
turned east to refuel, thus breaking contact and ending the
engagement.

In a postscript to the contest, the Japanese submarine service ended the careers of both the Yorktown and
the destroyer Hammann by torpedo on June 6-7.

In addition to the crippling loss of four aircraft
carriers, the Japanese suffered the loss of a huge percentage
of their most capable naval air pilots. The loss of the
Yorktown, while severe, would presently be amended by U.S.
shipyards. In this "high tide" battle of the War in the Pacific, the overconfident men of the Rising Sun gambled and
lost and the Allies were given a chance to assume the offensive.

3987   Barker, A. J. Midway: The Turning Point. Ballan-
        tine's Illustrated History of World War II. New
        York: Ballantine Books, 1971. 160p.

3988   "The Battle of Midway Island Is Recorded in Color by
        Navy Cameramen." Life, XIII (November 2, 1942),
        62-63.
             Reproduces some of those color prints.

3989   Bryan, Joseph, 3rd. "Never a Battle Like Midway."
        Saturday Evening Post, CCXXI (March 26, 1949),
        24-25+.

3990   "Carrier Pilot: Midway, From the Deck of a Carrier."
        Air Classics, III (July 1966), 4-8+.
             Reminiscences.

3991 Castillo, Edmund L. Midway: Battle for the Pacific.
      Landmark Books. New York: Random House,
      1968. 176p.

3992 "A Chapter of History. " Time, XL (July 27, 1942),
      25-26.

3993 "The Classic Dauntless and the Battle of Midway. "
      Airpower, III (January 1973), 24-38.

3994 Coale, Griffith B. Victory at Midway. New York:
      Farrar, 1944. 178p.
         The title here is a bit misleading as about two
      thirds of the book is devoted to the author's attempt
      to reconstruct the Pearl Harbor attack in pictures,
      with the remaining third given over to the subject
      of the title.

3995 Creasy, Edward, jt. author. See Mitchell, Joseph B.,
      no. 4039.

3996 D'Andrea, Thomas M. "Marines at Midway. " Marine
      Corps Gazette, XLVIII (November 1964), 27-31.

3997 Eller, Ernest M. "The Battle of Midway. " Ordnance,
      XL (September-October 1955), 237-240.

3998 Evans, William R., Jr. "Letter From a Navy Pilot. "
      In: William H. Fetridge, ed. The Navy Reader.
      Indianapolis: Bobbs-Merrill, 1943. p. 36-41.
      Rpr. 1971.
         The oft-reprinted letter from a Hoosier native,
      a member of the famed Torpedo Squadron 8 of
      U.S.S. Hornet, who was killed during the engage-
      ment.

3999 "The Face of Victory. " Time, XXXIX (June 15, 1942),
      16-17.

4000 Felt, Harry D. "An Evening With Admiral Harry D.
      Felt. " Unpublished paper, Individual Personnel
      File, U.S. Navy Department, Naval History Divi-
      sion, Operational Archives, 1968. 25p.
         An interview conducted by Professor Clark G.
      Reynolds which recalls the admiral's Pacific serv-
      ice, especially at Midway.

4001 Ferrier, H. H. "Torpedo Squadron 8: The Other

Chapter. " USNIP, XC (1964), 72-76.
Concerns six torpedo bombers of that unit detailed to Midway Island to guard it against the impending Japanese invasion.

4002   Field, John.   "The Life and Death of the U.S.S. Yorktown. " Life, XIII (November 16, 1942), 126-130.

4003   _____.   _____.   In: William H. Fetridge, ed. The
Navy Reader. Indianapolis: Bobbs-Merrill, 1943.
p. 149-162. Rpr. 1971.

4004   "The Fightingest Ship: The Carrier Yorktown Sank
Near Midway. " Time, XL (September 28, 1942),
36-37.

4005   Frank, Patrick H. H. and Joseph D. Harrington.
Rendezvous at Midway: U.S.S. Yorktown and the
Japanese Carrier Fleet. New York: Stein & Day,
1967.   252p.

4006   Fuchida, Mitsuo and Masatake Okumiya. Midway, the
Battle That Doomed Japan: The Japanese Navy's
Story. Annapolis: U.S. Naval Institute, 1955.
266p.

4007   _____. "Prelude to Midway. " USNIP, LXXXI (1955),
505-513.

4008   _____. "Two Fateful Minutes at Midway. " USNIP,
LXXXI (1955), 660-665.

4009   "The Full Story of Midway. " USNIP, LXVIII (1942),
1317-1321, 1347-1354, 1515-1517.

4010   Gay, George H. "Midway. " In: Louis L. Snyder,
ed. Masterpieces of War Reporting. New York:
Julian Messner, 1962. p. 179-182.
Reprinted from the June 9, 1942 issue of the
New York Times, this is an eyewitness account
by a torpedo plane pilot shot down in the midst
of the Japanese fleet.

4011   _____. "Torpedo Squadron 8: The Heroic Story of
30 Men Who Attacked the Jap Fleet. " Life, XIII
(August 31, 1942), 70-73.

4012   Gray, James S., Jr. "Decision at Midway. " Un-

published paper, Individual Personnel File, U.S.
Navy Department, Naval History Division, Operational Archives, n.d. 12p.
The participation of Fighting Squadron Six in
the battle as recalled by its commander.

4013 "The Great American Naval Victory Off Midway Island
on June 6 to 8, Reconstructed by Norman Bel
Geddes' Ship Models: Photographs." Illustrated
London News, CCI (July 25, 1942), 90-91.

4014 Harrington, Joseph D., jt. author. See Frank,
Patrick H. H., no. 4005.

4015 _____., jt. author. See Tanabe, Yahachi, no. 4054.

4016 Heinl, Robert D., Jr. Marines at Midway. Washington: Historical Section, Division of Public Information, U.S. Marine Corps, 1948. 56p.

4017 Hough, Richard A. The Battle of Midway: Victory in
the Pacific. New York: Macmillan, 1970. 90p.

4018 "How the [Japanese] Carriers Were Sunk: The Enemy
Overestimated." Time, XLII (November 22, 1943),
24.

4019 "Into the Valley of Death." Time, XL (August 17,
1942), 16-17.

4020 "The Jap Shellacking Thrills the U.S. After 6 Months
of Glum News." Newsweek, XIX (June 15, 1942),
17-19.

4021 "Japanese Aircraft Carriers at Midway." Sea Classics, III (March 1970), 15+.

4022 "The Japanese Debacle Off Midway Island: Photographs."
Illustrated London News, CCI (July 11, 1942), 49.

4023 Jones, Ken D. and Arthur F. McClure. Hollywood at
War. Cranbury, N.J.: A. S. Barnes, 1971.
Contains data on the U.S. Navy's request to the
movie industry to film the anticipated Battle of
Midway. How accurate was the U.S. intelligence
estimate of the fighting to come can be noted from
the fact that Hollywood was able to get set up on
the island in time to obtain the pictures desired.

4024 "June 4, 1942. " Time, LXIX (June 10, 1957), 26-29.

4025 "The Last Hours of the Yorktown Sunk Off Midway
      Island. " Illustrated London News, CCI (September
      26, 1942), 352.

4026 Leming, Joseph. "Yorktown, Enterprise, and Hornet
      at Midway. " In: his Brave Ships of World War
      II. London: Nelson, 1944. p. 171-185.

4027 Lewis, Winston B. "Midway and the Aleutians. " In:
      Elmer B. Potter, ed. Sea Power: A Naval His-
      tory. Englewood Cliffs, N. J. : Prentice-Hall,
      1960. p. 669-689.

4028 "Life on Midway. " Life, XIII (November 23, 1942),
      118-122.

4029 Lord, Walter. Incredible Victory. New York: Harp-
      er & Row, 1967. 331p.

4030 _____. "Midway. " Look, XXXI (August 8, 22, 1967),
      32-38+, 32-36+.
          Excerpts from the above citation. The author's
      work contains many anecdotes from interviews with
      participants in the battle on both sides.

4031 McBee, Frederick. "The Battle of Midway. " World
      War II Magazine, II (February 1972), 14-24.
          A pictorial essay.

4032 McClure, Arthur F. , jt. author. See Jones, Ken D. ,
      no. 4023.

4033 Maudlin, D. B. "Midway Today. " USNIP, LXXXVI
      (1960), 91-99.

4034 "The Midway Battle. " Life, XIII (July 27, 1942), 32-
      34.

4035 "Midway: Models Reconstruct the War's Decisive
      Battle. " Life, XX (February 18, 1946), 93-101.

4036 "Midway--the Battle That Turned the Tide. " All
      Hands, no. 561, (October 1963), 20-22.

4037 '"Midway to Our Objective': Admiral Nimitz's Great

Victory. " Illustrated London News, CC (June 13, 1942), 690.

4038 Mitchell, Donald W. "The Score After Midway. "
      Nation, CLIV (June 27, 1942), 732-734.

4039 Mitchell, Joseph B. and Edward Creasy. "The Battle
      of Midway, A. D. 1942. " In: their Twenty Deci-
      sive Battles of the World. New York: Macmillan,
      1964. p. 306-318.
      Creasy was given joint authorship in the work
      for his earlier contributions in the historiography
      of decisive battles.

4040 Moore, Thomas. "I Dive-Bombed a Jap Carrier. "
      Collier's, CXI (April 10, 1943), 20+.

4041 Morison, Samuel E. "Six Minutes That Changed the
      World. " American Heritage, XIV (February 1963),
      50-56, 102-103.

4042 Morris, Frank D. "Four Fliers From Midway, They
      Sprang a Brand-New Kind of Warfare on the Jap's
      Invasion Fleet: The Moonlight Torpedo Attack of
      the PBY Flying Boats or 'Catalinas. '" Collier's,
      CX (July 25, 1943), 11+.

4043 Nagumo, Chuichi. "Action Report by the C-in-C of
      the [Japanese] First Air Fleet. " ONI Review,
      (May 1947), passim.
      The Japanese view of Midway.

4044 Okumiya, Masatake, jt. author. See Fuchida, Mitsuo,
      no. 4006.

4045 Pate, Elbert W. "An Ill Wind From the East. "
      USNIP, LXXI (1945), 411-413.

4046 Powers, Thomas E. "Incredible Midway. " USNIP,
      XCIII (1967), 64-73.

4047 Prange, Gordon W. "Miracle at Midway. " Reader's
      Digest, CI (November 1972), 255-262+.

4048 Pratt, William V. "Midway is Still a Ranking Victory."
      Newsweek, XXIV (November 13, 1944), 50.

4049 Ray, Clarence C. "Personal Recollections of Certain

Events of the Battle of Midway. " Unpublished
paper, Individual Personnel File, U.S. Navy Department, Naval History Division, Operational
Archives, 1967. 17p.
A collection of anecdotes concerning the author's
experiences aboard the carrier Yorktown.

4050   "Report on Midway. " Newsweek, XX (July 27, 1942),
25.

4051   Smith, Chester L.   Midway, 4 June 1942.   Los
Angeles, Calif. :   Bede Press, 1967.   65p.
The work comes complete with a 33-1/3 rpm
phonograph record.

4052   Smith, Ward.   Midway: Turning Point of the Pacific.
New York: Thomas Y. Crowell, 1966.   174p.
By the commander of the escort force charged
with the protection of the Yorktown.

4053   Spruance, Raymond A.   "Foreword for Midway. "
USNIP, LXXXI (1955), 658-659.
Comments on the Fuchida works cited above.

4054   Tanabe, Yahachi and Joseph D. Harrington.   "I Sank
the Yorktown at Midway. " USNIP, LXXXIX (1963),
58-65.
The first author was skipper of the Japanese
submarine I-168 which did in the American carrier.

4055   Thach, John S.   "The Red Rain of Battle: The Story
of Fighter Squadron Three. " Collier's, CX (December 12, 1942), 16-17+.

4056   Tuleja, Thaddeus V.   Climax at Midway.   New York:
W. W. Norton, 1960.   248p.

4057   "Turning Point in the Pacific. " All Hands, no. 546,
(July 1962), 59-63.

4058   "U.S. Naval Victory: The Battle of Midway Island. "
Illustrated London News, CCI (August 1, 1942),
117.

4059   United States.   Naval War College.   "The Battle of
Midway, Including the Aleutian Phase, June 3-14,
1942. " Unpublished paper, Battle Analysis Series,

Training Commands File, U.S. Navy Department,
Naval History Division, Operational Archives,
1948. 239p.
A detailed tactical analysis based on both
Allied and Japanese sources.

4060 _____. Navy Department.   Office of Naval Intelligence.   The Japanese Story of Midway, a Translation.   Opnav P32-1002.   Washington: U.S.
Government Printing Office, 1947.   68p.

4061 _____. _____. Office of the Chief of Naval Operations, Intelligence Division.   "Combat Narrative:
The Battle of Midway, 3-6 June 1942. "   Unpublished
paper, CNO-ONI File, U.S. Navy Department,
Naval History Division, Operational Archives, 1942.
60p.

4062 "U.S.S. Yorktown Is Sunk at Sea. "   Life, XIII (September 28, 1942), 34-35.

4063 Wadleigh, John R.   "Memories of Midway, Thirty
Years Ago. "   Shipmate, (June 1972), 3-8.

4064 "The War in the Pacific: The Great Turning Point. "
Newsweek, XIX (June 22, 1942), 23-27.

4065 Warner, Oliver.   "Midway. "   In: his Great Sea Battles.   London: Spring Books, 1963.   p. 282-292.

4066 Werstein, Irving.   The Battle of Midway.   New York:
Thomas Y. Crowell, 1961.   145p.

Further References: Readers are reminded that
additional data relative to this section will be found in sections
IIA and IIC-1 above, as well as IIC-4 below.   The general
works cited in Volume III, Part 1, in many instances contain
appropriate information, while the general works on military
intelligence in Part 2 also contain references.

(4) THE FORGOTTEN ALEUTIANS CAMPAIGN

Introduction.   The Japanese decision to move into
the Aleutians chain of islands off Alaska was taken at the

same time as the design for the decisive Battle of Midway; indeed, the northern operation was a "prong" of the over-all strategy.   Because of the geographical distances involved, however, the two segments have been separated within this volume.

The Imperial Navy's decision on the Aleutians is readily understood.   Those islands are the shortest route from Tokyo to San Francisco on the map and could be looked upon as the most obvious line of Yankee counterattack.   In fact, both the Americans and the Japanese feared that one or the other would, despite the region's terrible weather, attack via that direction.   For that reason, both tied up a goodly number of air and ground resources in that frigid climate for most of the war.

The same intelligence sources which warned of the Midway clash also told Admiral Nimitz of the impending enemy move to the north.   Scraping up a motley collection of five cruisers, 14 destroyers, and half a dozen submarines, he sent them under Rear Admiral Robert A. Theobald to prevent the Aleutians from falling by default.   He would be opposed by Vice Admiral Boshiro Hosogaya's Northern Area Force of four groups, and Rear Admiral Kakuji Kakuta's Second Mobile Group, which included the carriers Ryujo and Junyo.

Space does not permit an examination in detail of Theobald's defense.   Dutch Harbor was bombed and the Japanese occupied both the islands of Attu and Kiska.   For nearly a year afterward, Allied operations in this theater consisted mainly in attempting to isolate those two enemy-held islands by air or submarine action.

One should not forget the role played by the U.S. and Canadian armies and air forces.   During the 1942-1943 winter, the islands of Adak and Amchika were occupied, air fields constructed, and missions flown to the extent that Kiska was cut off from surface contact with Japan.

To cut off the more westerly island of Attu demanded aggressive naval action.   To that end, Rear Admiral Charles H. McMorris bombarded Attu in mid-February 1943 and disrupted its supply.   Admiral Hosogaya, who managed to get a convoy to the outpost in March, attempted the ploy a second time later in the month, only to be engaged by the Americans in the last of the classic daylight surface actions, the Battle of the Komandorski Islands.

The March 26 encounter, which saw the Yankee cruiser Salt Lake City badly damaged, forced Hosogaya to retire--an act which resulted in his own loss of command. The convoy did not get through and thereafter Attu and Kiska were only meagerly supplied by submarine.

The isolation of the enemy did not appease the
Americans, who simply did not enjoy the thought of any U.S.
territory--useless or not--in Japanese hands. Thus it was
that American forces assaulted Attu on May 11, 1943, under
the over-all direction of Rear Admiral Thomas C. Kinkaid.
In a bloody month-long campaign, which witnessed a massive
"banzai" charge on May 29, the island was recaptured. On
August 13, the battle-tested Americans struck at Kiska--only
to find that the Japanese garrison had been spirited away
three weeks earlier.

With Attu and Kiska no longer any sort of "threat,"
the North Pacific lapsed into a backwater of interest, public
and military. Thomas Kinkaid, his reputation started and
promotion won, went south to command the U.S. Seventh
Fleet, better known as "MacArthur's Navy."

4067 "Action in Alaska." Leatherneck, XXV (September
        1942), 15-18.

4068 "The Aleutian Advance." Newsweek, XX (October 12,
        1942), 26-28.

4069 "Aleutian Attack: U.S. Armada Occupies Andreanofs."
        Life, XIII (October 19, 1942), 38-39.

4070 "Aleutians Windup: Americans Recover Kiska." News-
        week, XXII (August 30, 1943), 24-25.

4071 "Allied Troops Retake Deserted Kiska." Life, XV
        (September 13, 1943), 25-31.

4072 "Attu Aftermath." Newsweek, XIV (June 14, 1943),
        24.

4073 "Attu: From Its Snowy Peaks the Japs Are Dug Out."
        Life, XIV (June 14, 1943), 70-71.

4074 "Attu: The U.S. Retakes the Aleutians." Life, XV
        (October 11, 1943), 85.

4075 Bishop, John. "My Speed Zero." In: Saturday Even-
        ing Post, Editors of. True Stories of Courage and
        Survival. Cleveland: World Publishing Co., 1963.
        p. 111-121. Rpr. 1966.
        A look at the Battle of the Komandorski Islands.

4076 Blackford, Charles M., 3rd. "Kiska Dry-Run."

USNIP, XCIII (1967), 64-73.

4077   Burhans, Robert D. The First Special Service Force,
       a War History of the North Americans, 1942-1944.
       Washington: Infantry Journal Press, 1947. 376p.
       Yanks and Canadians in the Aleutians.

4078   Chikaya, Masatake. "The Mysterious Withdrawal From
       Kiska." USNIP, LXXXIV (1958), 30-47.
       Explained from the Japanese viewpoint.

4079   Danver, James A. "Early History of Motor Torpedo
       Boat Squadron Thirteen." Unpublished paper, Type
       Commands File, U.S. Navy Department, Naval
       History Division, Operational Archives, 1944.
       125p.
           Written by the executive officer of the unit, this
       personal account covers the training of the PT-Boat
       group at New Orleans and its deployment in the
       Aleutians during the winter of 1943-1944.

4080   Deacon, Kenneth J. "Attu, May 1943." Military
       Engineer, LIX (January-February 1967), 25.

4081   Donahue, Ralph J. Ready on the Right: The True
       Story of a Naturalist-Seabee on the Islands of
       Kodiak, Unalaska, Tanga, Oahu, Entwetok, Guam,
       Ulithi, and Okinawa. Kansas City, Mo.: Smith,
       1946. 194p.

4082   Driscoll, Joseph. The War Discovers Alaska. Phila-
       delphia: Lippincott, 1943. 352p.

4083   Ellsworth, Lyman R. Guys on Ice. New York: David
       McKay, 1952. 277p.

4084   Eyre, James K., Jr. "Alaska and the Aleutians:
       Cockpit of the North Pacific." USNIP, LXIX (1943),
       1287-1297.

4085   Ford, Corey. Short Cut to Tokyo: The Battle for the
       Aleutians. New York: Scribner's, 1943. 141p.

4086   Garfield, Brian W. The Thousand-Mile War: World
       War II in Alaska and the Aleutians. Garden City,
       N.Y.: Doubleday, 1969. 351p.

4087 Gilman, William. Our Hidden Front. New York:
      Raynal & Hitchcock, 1944. 266p.

4088 Glines, Carroll V. "The Forgotten War in the
      Aleutians. " Air Force and Space Digest, LI
      (March 1968), 30-33+.

4088a Griffin, D. F. First Steps to Tokyo: The Royal
      Canadian Air Force in the Aleutians. London:
      Dent, 1944. 50p.
          The RCAF helped the Americans work over
      Japanese sources of supply.

4089 Hailey, Foster. "Cold, Fog, Mud, Life in the Aleu-
      tians: Our Soldiers, Sailors, and Airmen Find the
      Billet a Tough One. " New York Times Magazine,
      (August 22, 1943), 4-5+.

4090 Hall, M. S. "Cold Weather Combat Clothing, 1942-
      1948. " Marine Corps Gazette, XXXII (May 1948),
      50-56.

4091 Handleman, Howard. Bridge to Victory: The Story
      of the Reconquest of the Aleutians. New York:
      Random House, 1943. 275p.

4092 Hatch, F. J. "The Aleutian Campaign. " Roundel, XV
      (May-June 1963), 18-23, 18-23.

4093 Karig, Walter and Eric Purdon. "The Komandorskis--
      a Little Known Victory. " USNIP, LXXII (1946),
      1411-1415.

4094 Kiralfy, Alexander. "Japan's Alaskan Strategy. " New
      Republic, CVI (June 29, 1942), 889-890.

4095 McCandless, Bruce. "The Battle of the Pips. " USNIP,
      LXXXIV (1958), 49-56.
          The night action against non existent enemy ships
      off Kiska, July 25-26, 1943, which was fought by the
      Americans due to faulty radar.

4096 McMillan, Ira E. "The Battle for Attu--Proving
      Ground for Cold Weather Operations. " USNIP,
      LXXV (1949), 662-671.

4097 Mills, Stephen. Arctic War Birds. Seattle, Wash. :

Superior Publications, 1971.   191p.
Subtitled, "A Pictorial History of Bush Flying
With the Military in the Defense of Alaska and
America.

4098   Morgan, Murray C.   Bridge to Russia: Those Amazing Aleutians.   New York: E. P. Dutton, 1947.
222p.

4099   "The Occupation of Amchitka. "   U.S. Coast Guard
Academy Alumni Association Bulletin,   V (August
1943),   83.

4100   Paneth, Philip.   Alaskan Backdoor to Japan.   London:
Alliance Press, 1943.   108p.

4101   [No entry.]

4102   Potter, Jean C.   Alaska Under Arms.   New York:
Macmillan, 1942.   200p.

4103   Pratt, Fletcher.   "The Campaign Beyond Glory: The
Navy in the Aleutians, 1942-1943. "   Harper's,
CLXXXIX (November 1944), 558-569.

4104   Pratt, William V.   "Japs in the Aleutians Are Not to
Be Ignored. "   Newsweek, XXI (May 3, 1943), 24.

4105   _____.   "What the Japanese Are Up to in Attu. "
Newsweek, XIX (June 29, 1942), 20.

4106   Purdon, Eric, jt. author.   See Karig, Walter, no.
4093.

4107   Sherrod, Robert.   "Burial in the Aleutians. "   Time,
XLI (June 28, 1943), 62+.

4108   Sutherland, Mason.   "A Navy Artist Paints the Aleutians: W. F. Draper. "   National Geographic,
LXXXIV (August 1943), 157-176.

4109   Underbrink, Robert L.   "The Day the Navy Caught a
Zero. "   USNIP, XCIV (1968), 136-138.
In the Aleutians in mid-1942.

4110   United States.   Naval War College.   "The Battle of the
Komandorski Islands. "   Unpublished paper, Battle

Analysis Series, Training Commands File, U.S.
Navy Department, Naval History Division, Operational Archives, 1943. 19p.

4111 _____. Navy Department. Office of the Chief of
Naval Operations, Intelligence Division. "Combat
Narrative: The Aleutians Campaign, June 1942-
August 1943." Unpublished paper, CNO-ONI File,
U.S. Navy Department, Naval History Division,
Operational Archives, 1943. 105p.

4112 _____. _____. Pacific Fleet, North Pacific Naval
Forces. "Command History." Unpublished paper,
Naval Forces File, U.S. Navy Department, Naval
History Division, Operational Archives, 1945.
170p.

4113 _____. _____. _____. LST Flotilla Three. "Early
History of LST Flotilla 3." Unpublished paper,
Type Commands File, U.S. Navy Department,
Naval History Division, Operational Archives, n.d.
2p.
The unit saw action in the Aleutians.

4114 _____. _____. _____. North Pacific Advanced Intelli-
gence Center. "The Aleutian Campaign: A Brief
Historical Outline to and Including the Occupation
of Kiska, August 1943." Unpublished paper, Naval
Forces File, U.S. Navy Department, Naval History
Division, Operational Archives, 1944. 159p.

4115 Wright, W. A. "In the Aleutians." U.S. Coast Guard
Academy Alumni Association Bulletin, V (January
1944), 171.

Further References: Readers will find additional
information relative to this section in sections IIA, IIC-1 and
IIC-3 above, as well as in the general works cited in Volume
III, Part 1.

(5) TRAUMA IN THE SOLOMONS

Introduction. Following their defeat at Midway, a
shocked Imperial Headquarters cancelled most of its further

aggression and elected instead to concentrate on strengthening the empire's defense perimeter. A comparatively minor cog in this machinery would set off the next dramatic explosion of the Pacific war.

Still anxious to obtain Port Moresby on New Guinea, the Japanese began constructing a bomber and seaplane base on Tulagi and Guadalcanal in the nearby Solomon Islands. When completed, these could be expected to provide the foot soldiers of the Rising Sun the necessary air cover for their task.

Having knocked the enemy off balance at Midway, Admiral Nimitz and General MacArthur urged that an Allied counteroffensive be launched as quickly as possible, especially in light of the potential danger represented by the Japanese presence in the Solomons. After a bit of interservice command reshuffling and the selection of Nimitz's plans, the Joint Chiefs of Staff on July 2, 1942, issued orders for the recovery of the New Britain-New Ireland-New Guinea area, beginning with the occupation of the lower Solomon Islands. Here is a chronology of these several separate operations:

1942

August 7 American Marines land on Guadalcanal and Tulagi. The battle is joined.

August 8 American Marines capture the Japanese airfield and rename it Henderson Field.

August 8-9 In a surprise attack aimed at the U.S. landing force, a Japanese task force sinks three American and one Australian cruiser in the Battle of Savo Island. Allied naval units retire from Guadalcanal.

August 16 Rear Admiral Raizo Tanaka leaves Rabaul with a transport group thus beginning to run the "Tokyo Express." Later he would employ primarily destroyers.

August 21 The Battle of the Tenaru River on Guadalcanal sees the first Japanese assault on Henderson Field repulsed.

August 24 In another attempt on the American operation, the Japanese lose the carrier Ryujo in the aerial Battle of the Eastern Solomons.

August 20-30 U.S. Navy, Marine Corps, and Army Air Force planes begin landing at Henderson Field and commence offensive operations as the "Cactus Air Force."

August 31 While on defensive patrol, the carrier Saratoga is torpedoed by a Japanese submarine and put out of action for three months.

September 13-14 Japanese launch unsuccessful major offensive on Guadalcanal.

September 15 The American carrier Wasp, the battleship
   North Carolina, and the destroyer O'Brien are all hit by
   Japanese submarine torpedoes en route to the Solomons
   from Espiritu Santo. The damaged Wasp had later to be
   abandoned and sunk by her own escort while the partially
   repaired destroyer sank en route to a state-side shipyard.
October 11-12 The Americans win the Battle of Cape
   Esperance, sinking an enemy cruiser and destroyer while
   taking damage to a pair of cruisers and a destroyer in
   exchange.
October 13 U.S. Army units land on Guadalcanal as reinforcements for the Marines.
October 13-14 The Japanese battleships Kongo and Haruna
   bombard Henderson Field, destroying many American
   planes and putting the place temporarily out of commis-
   sion. Japanese units ashore prepare to launch a massive
   counterattack.
October 16 Admiral William F. Halsey replaces Admiral
   Robert Ghormley as the American theater commander.
October 23 The Japanese launch their counteroffensive on
   Guadalcanal.
October 25-26 The Japanese attack fails.
October 26 In the aerial Battle of the Santa Cruz Islands,
   the Japanese carriers Zuiho and Shokaku are damaged.
   The U.S. carrier Hornet is fatally injured; abandoned,
   she is later sunk by enemy destroyers. The American
   carrier Enterprise, also coming under heavy Japanese
   attack, is saved by a remarkable display of anti-aircraft
   fire from the new battleship South Dakota.
November 1 American forces on Guadalcanal launch their
   own offensive.
November 12 The Naval Battle of Guadalcanal opens when
   Rear Admiral Richmond K. Turner's transports are attacked by Japanese aircraft while offloading.
November 13 The American Landing Support Group under
   Rear Admiral Daniel J. Callaghan takes on the Japanese
   Raiding Group, including two battleships, sent to bombard
   Henderson Field. A devastating naval action, reminiscent
   of the days of close-in sailing ship encounters, takes place
   in the darkness of the evening. Heavy damage is inflicted
   on the U.S. group, including the loss of its commander,
   before the Japanese are driven off: in exchange for a light
   cruiser and four destroyers sunk, the Japanese battleship
   Hiei is so damaged that she proves an easy target for
   "Cactus Air Force" planes the next morning.
November 14 Japanese cruisers and destroyers engaged in
   a pre-dawn bombardment of Henderson Field are attacked

by U.S. PT-boats. Retiring after sunrise, the Japanese
force is attacked by planes from the carrier Enterprise
and by elements of the "Cactus Air Force." These planes
also take out seven enemy transports that afternoon.

November 14-15 Shortly before midnight, the American
battleship force of Rear Admiral Willis A. Lee meets and
turns back a large Japanese naval group in the climatic
phase of the battle. In exchange for damage to the South
Dakota, and the loss of three destroyers sunk, the Americans, especially those manning the 16-inch guns aboard
the U.S.S. Washington, destroy the Japanese battleship
Kirishima and the destroyer Ayanami.

November 30 Although thwarted in their effort to reinforce
Guadalcanal, the Japanese defeat Rear Admiral Carleton
H. Wright in the Battle of Tassafaronga. The Americans
lose a cruiser sunk and three damaged in exchange for
the sinking of one of Raizo Tanaka's destroyers.

December 31 Emperor Hirohito grants permission for the
evacuation of Guadalcanal.

1943

February 1-8 The "Tokyo Express" evacuates Guadalcanal.

February 9 Organized Japanese resistance ends on Guadalcanal.

April 18 Admiral Isoroku Yamamoto is killed when his plane
is shot down by Guadalcanal-based U.S.A.A.F. fighters.

June 30 The American launch "Operation Cartwheel" with
landings in New Guinea and more importantly to this
section, on Rendova and New Georgia in the Central Solomons.

July 5 Despite the loss of the cruiser Helena, Rear Admiral
W. L. Ainsworth's task group defeats the "Tokyo Express"
in its attempt to reinforce Kolombangara Island in the
Central Solomons. The Japanese lose two of their ten
destroyers in this Battle of Kula Gulf.

July 13 Ainsworth's group, fighting in the darkness off
Kolombangara, fails to prevent Japanese reinforcements
from being landed on the island. In this Battle of Kolombangara or Second Battle of Kula Gulf, the Americans lost
a destroyer sunk, and three cruisers and two destroyers
damaged in exchange for the sinking of one Japanese
cruiser.

August 5 After a dozen days of heavy fighting, Munda Airfield on New Georgia is taken by the Allies.

August 6 Four Japanese destroyers of the "Tokyo Express,"
attempting to bring in reinforcements to Kolombangara, are
surprised by six American destroyers under Commander

F. Moosbrugger. In this Battle of Vella Gulf, the Americans sink three of the enemy and damage the fourth suffer-
ing no damage in the process.
October 2 The Japanese successfully withdraw from Kolombangara.
October 6-7 In the Battle of Vella Lavella, American destroyers attempting to smash the evacuation of the Japanese
from Vella Lavella are beaten off by a superior enemy
squadron.
November 1 The Americans land on Bougainville, northern-
most of the Solomon Islands.
November 2 Rear Admiral A. S. Merrill's task force inter-
cepts after dark a Japanese force planning to attack the
Allied transports. In the Battle of Empress Augusta Bay,
the Yanks sink a Japanese light cruiser and destroyer and
turn the enemy back in exchange for damage to a pair of
light cruisers and three destroyers.
December 24 The Bougainville beachhead is secured.

1944

March 8 Japanese attack the perimeter around Bougainville's
airfields but are beaten off.
March 24 Organized Japanese resistance is broken on Bougainville and the Solomons campaign is completed.

4116 "Alexander A. Vandegrift. " CurrBio:IV:49-50.
        Notes on the American Marine general who led
        the troops ashore on Guadalcanal.

4117 "American Cruisers Sunk: Photographs of the Astoria,
        the Quincy, and the Vincennes. " Illustrated London
        News, CCI (October 17, 1942), 428.
        Lost in the August 9 Battle of Savo Island, along
        with the R. A. N. cruiser Canberra.

4118 "American Fighting Fronts on Guadalcanal. " Illustrated
        London News, CII (October 31, 1942), 242-245.

4119 Andrews, Ernest S. Close-Up on Guadalcanal. Well-
        ington, N. Z. : Progressive Publications Society,
        1944. 54p.

4120 Andrews, F. A. , jt. author. See Weems, George B. ,
        no. 4448.

4121 Armstrong, David M. "The Battle of Sealark Channel."

American History Illustrated, VIII (October 1973),
4-9, 44-49.
Destroyer action off Guadalcanal.

4122 Azine, Harold. "The Bougainville Landing." Harper's,
CLXXXVIII (March 1944), 289-299.

4123 Baglien, Samuel. "The Second Battle For Henderson
Field." Infantry Journal, LIV (May 1944), 24-29.

4124 Baldwin, Hanson W. "Solomons Action." Marine
Corps Gazette, XLIX (November 1965), 75-77.

4125 _____. "Solomons Action Develops Into Battle For
the South Pacific." Marine Corps Gazette, LVI
(August 1972), 42-44.
Reprinted from the November 1942 issue of
this journal.

4126 Barnett, B. J. "Blood and Wheat." Leatherneck,
XXV (December 1942), 16-17+.
Marines in action on Guadalcanal.

4127 Batten, L. W., 3rd. "Guadalcanal: Twenty Years
After." Yale Review, LII (March 1963), 418-426.

4128 "Battle Action in the Solomons." Life, XIII (October
5, 1942), 40-41.

4129 "The Battle for Mastery of the Pacific Looms Behind
the Solomons Crisis." Newsweek, XX (October 26,
1942), 21-26.

4130 "The Battle of Santa Cruz on October 25-26." Life,
XIII (December 14, 1942), 42-43.
During which the American carrier Hornet was
sunk.

4131 "The Battle of the Solomons." Current History, New
Series III (December 1942), 294-296.

4132 "The Battle of the Solomons." In: William H. Fet-
ridge, ed. The Navy Reader. Indianapolis: Bobbs-
Merrill, 1943. p. 299-303. Rpr. 1971.
Reprints five official U.S. Navy communiqués.

4133 "The Battle of the Solomons Approaches a Climax."
Scholastic, XLI (October 26, 1942), 5.

4134 "The Battle of the Solomons: Photographs." Illustrated
       London News, CCI (November 7, 1942), 507-510.

4135 "The Battle of Vella Gulf." All Hands, no. 586, (No-
       vember 1965), 56-60.
           The August 6, 1943 contest in which three
       Japanese destroyers were sunk.

4136 Bean, Lawrence L. "The Death of the Hornet." In:
       Norman Carlisle, ed. The Air Forces Reader.
       Indianapolis: Bobbs-Merrill, 1944. p. 326-330.
           A surgeon's report of the sinking as reprinted
       from the January 1943 issue of Douglas Airview.

4137 Blackman, R. V. B. 'New Battleship Proof Against
       Aircraft." Engineer, CLXXVII (February 4, 1944),
       87-88.
           The U.S.S. South Dakota (BB-57) in the October
       26, 1942, Battle of Santa Cruz.

4138 Blankfort, Michael. The Big Yankee: The Life of
       [Evans F.] Carlson of the Raiders. Boston: Little,
       Brown, 1947. 380p.
           Employing Commando tactics, Carlson's Marine
       Raider Battalion made a now-famous incursion into
       the Japanese lines and operated behind them in
       November 1942, causing alarm and disruption
       amongst the forces of Nippon.

4139 "Blood on the Shore." Time, XL (August 24, 1942),
       25.
           Concerns Japanese resistance on Tulagi, Gavutu,
       and Tanambogo (all near Guadalcanal) to American
       attempts to recapture them.

4140 "Bougainville Perimeter: The Fiery Battle of Cannon
       Ridge Repels a Jap Attempt at Attack." Newsweek,
       XXIII (March 27, 1944), 28-29.

4141 Bowers, Richard H. "Bougainville Rendezvous."
       USNIP, LXXVIII (1952), 762-767.

4142 Bowser, Alpha L., Jr. "End Run in the Solomons."
       Marine Corps Gazette, XXXI (November 1947), 24-
       32.

4143 Boyington, Gregory "Pappy." Baa Baa Black Sheep.

New York: Putnam, 1958. 384p.
An account of the Marine ace-author's Fighter
Squadron (VMF) 222, known as the "Black Sheep."

4144 Braun, Saul. The Struggle for Guadalcanal. American
Battles and Campaigns Series. New York: Putnam,
1969. 128p.

4145 Brown, Neville. "Guadalcanal." In: Cyril Falls, ed.
Great Military Battles. London and New York:
Spring Books, 1964. p. 270-278.
A pictorial essay.

4146 Burke, Donald. "Carlson of the Raiders." Life, XV
(September 20, 1943), 53-54+.

4147 Butterfield, Roger. "Al Schmid, Hero." Life, XIV
(March 22, 1943), 35-36.

4148 _____. Al Schmid, Marine. New York: W. W.
Norton, 1944. 142p.
The story of a Marine Navy Cross winner who
was blinded during the Battle of the Tenaru on
Guadalcanal, 21 August 1942.

4149 Cant, Gilbert. "Rescue in the Pacific: The Helena's
Survivors on the Japanese-Held Island of Vella
Lavella." Saturday Evening Post, CCXVI (January
29, 1944), 17-18+.
The American light cruiser Helena (CL-50) was
sunk during the July 1943 Battle of Kula Gulf; 165
of her crew managed to reach the island where
they hid out from the Japanese until rescued.

4150 Casey, John F., Jr. "An Artillery Forward Observer
on Guadalcanal." Field Artillery Journal, XXXIII
(August 1943), 563-568.

4151 _____. "A Firing Battery on Guadalcanal." Field
Artillery Journal, XXXIII (October 1943), 740-744.

4152 Cates, Clifton B. "Battle of the Tenaru." Marine
Corps Gazette, XXVII (October 1943), 5-6.
On Guadalcanal.

4153 Cave, Hugh B., et al. Long Were the Nights, the
Saga of PT Squadron "X" in the Solomons. New
York: Dodd, Mead, 1943. 220p.

4154 Claypool, James V. God on a Battlewagon. Philadelphia: John C. Winston, 1944. 110p.
The activities of the U.S.S. South Dakota (BB-
57), known in those days as "Battleship X" during
the Solomons campaign.

4155 Clemens, Martin. "A Coastwatcher's Diary." Un-
published paper, Files of the Historical Branch,
Research and Records Division, Headquarters, U.S.
Marine Corps, n. d.
Activities on Guadalcanal.

4156 Coggins, Jack. The Campaign for Guadalcanal. Garden City, N.Y.: Doubleday, 1972. 208p.
A fine illustrated volume with considerable data
on weapons, ships, and planes employed by both
sides during the operation.

4157 "The Conquest of Guadalcanal." USNIP, LXIX (1943),
736-743.
A Navy Department press release.

4158 Cook, Charles. The Battle of Cape Esperance:
Strategic Encounter at Guadalcanal. New York:
Crowell, 1968. 192p.

4159 Cooke, F. O. "He Tells the Big Shots." Leatherneck, XXVI (April 1943), 14+.

4160 _____. "Solomons Spearhead." Leatherneck, XXV
(October 1942), 13-18.

4161 Cronin, Francis D. Under the Southern Cross: The
Saga of the Americal Division. Washington: Combat Forces Press, 1951.
The U.S. Army outfit which fought alongside
the Marines on Guadalcanal. Interchangeable data.

4162 "Cruisers in Action." Engineering, CLIV (October 16,
1942), 311-312.
A discussion of American losses in the August
9 Battle of Savo Island.

4163 Cupp, James N. "Shot Down." In: Patrick O'Sheel
and Gene Cook, eds. Semper Fidelis: The U.S.
Marines in the Pacific, 1942-1945. New York:
William Sloane Associates, 1947. p. 109-113.

A Marine aviator shot down over Kolombangara
in the Solomons and rescued by a U.S. PT-Boat.

4164 Custer, Joseph J. Through the Perilous Night: The
Astoria's Last Battle. New York: Macmillan,
1944. 243p.
The American cruiser was sunk as a result of
damages received during the Battle of Savo Island.

4165 "Daniel J. Callaghan." CurrBio:IV:9.
In command of the heavy cruiser San Francisco,
the admiral, a former naval aide to President
Roosevelt, took his five cruisers and eight destroyers up against two Japanese battleships, four
cruisers, and ten destroyers in the first round of
the Naval Battle of Guadalcanal. The San Francisco, although heavily damaged, disabled several
vessels, including a battleship. Callaghan, who
was killed in the melee, saved Henderson Field
from a punishing bombardment designed for it by
the frustrated enemy fleet.

4166 Davis, Burke. Get Yamamoto! New York: Random
House, 1969. 231p.
On April 17, 1943, American intelligence picked
up a radio signal which indicated that the Japanese
admiral planned to make an inspection tour the
following day. Long-range P-38's were sent after
him, shot down his plane, and returned safely to
base. Given a state funeral, the scrappy little
Pearl Harbor architect was the only major military
leader of World War II to be successfully assassi-
nated.

4167 "The Death of the Wasp: An Interview With M.
Thrash." Flying, XXXV (September 1944), 46-47+.
Torpedoed on September 15, 1942 by a Japanese
submarine.

4168 DeChant, John A. "The Landing on Bougainville."
Marine Corps Gazette, XXVIII (January 1944),
passim.

4169 _____. "Milk Run to Munda." Leatherneck, XXVII
(July 1944), 20-23.
New Georgia.

4170 Del Valle, Pedro A. "Marine Field Artillery on Guad-
      alcanal. " Field Artillery Journal, XXXIII (October
      1943), 722-733.

4171 _____. "Dual Functions in the Solomons. " Coast
      Artillery Journal, LXXXVII (January-February
      1944), 4-8.
           U.S.M.C. artillery employed against both land
      and air targets.

4172 _____. "Marine Artillery in Guadalcanal. " Marine
      Corps Gazette, XXVII (November 1943), 9-13;
      XXVIII (January-February 1944), 27-30, 39-43.

4173 Devine, Frank. "How We Captured Cape Torokina. "
      Leatherneck, XXVII (April 1944), passim.
           On Bougainville.

4174 Dexter, Dwight H. "Guadalcanal Ferry. " Yachting,
      LXXIII (May 1943), 30.

4175 "The Doings of 'Sara': The U.S.S. Saratoga Tries
      to Draw Out the Jap Fleet. " Time, XLII (Decem-
      ber 27, 1943), 24-25.

4176 Donner, Christopher. "Guadalcanal Revisited. " Marine
      Corps Gazette, LI (August 1967), 32-38.

4177 Donovan, Robert J. PT-109: John F. Kennedy in
      World War II. New York: McGraw-Hill, 1961.
      247p.
           The basis for the movie version starring Cliff
      Robertson, this work was reprinted by the Green-
      wich, Conn., firm of Fawcett in 1970 under the
      title, One Hundred Nine.

4178 Dorris, Donald H. A Log of the Vincennes. Louis-
      ville, Ky.: Standard Printing Company, 1947.
      402p.
           The first Vincennes (CA-44) was lost in the
      Battle of Savo Island.

4179 "Douglas Albert Munro: Coast Guard Hero. " U.S.
      Coast Guard Academy Alumni Association Bulletin,
      IX (December 1942), 100.
           Munro won the Congressional Medal of Honor for
      his bravery on Guadalcanal.

4180   Duncan, David D.   "Fiji Patrol on Bougainville."
         National Geographic, LXXXVII (January 1945), 87-
         104.

4181   _____.   "The Greatest Jungle Fighters of All."   Satur-
         day Evening Post, CCXVII (March 24, 1945), 28-29+.

4182   Dupuy, R. Ernest.   "Biblolo Hill--and Beyond: A
         Report of the New Georgia Island Campaign."
         Infantry Journal, LIV (January 1944), 21-26.

4183   Durdin, F. Tillman.   "Life on Guadalcanal."   Time,
         XL (September 28, 1942), 37.

4184   _____.   "The Roughest and the Toughest: Carlson's
         Raiders."   New York Times Magazine, (November
         8, 1942), 13.
               This article, abridged, appeared in Science
         Digest, XIII (February 1943), 67-69, under the title,
         "Guerrilla Fighters of the Marines."

4185   "The Epic of Guadalcanal: Views." New York Times
         Magazine, (February 14, 1943), 6-7.

4186   "Evans F. Carlson."   CurrBio:IV:14-16.

4187   Falk, Stanley L.   "The Ambush of Admiral Yamamoto."
         Navy, VI (April 1963), 32-34.

4188   Falk, V. S., Jr.   "A Marine Dive Bomber Squadron
         at Guadalcanal, 1942." Journal of Aviation Medi-
         cine, XXIV (June 1953), 237-239.

4189   Falls, Cyril.   "The Battle of the Solomon Islands."
         Illustrated London News, CCI (August 22, 1942),
         208.

4190   Field, James.   "How O'Hare Downed Five Jap Planes
         in One Day." Life, XII (April 13, 1942), 12+.

4191   Field, John.   "Joe Foss: No. 1 Ace, What He Learned
         on a Dakota Farm Helped Him Down 26 Japs."
         Life, XIV (June 7, 1943), 88-94.

4192   "The First Marines in the South Pacific." Leatherneck,
         XXV (October 1942), 19+.

4193   "The First Offensive. " Time, XL (August 17, 1942),
           20-22.
               Guadalcanal.

4194   "The First Round Won. " Time, XL (August 31, 1942),
           26.
               Optimism over the Guadalcanal operation.

4195   Foss, Joseph, as Told to Walter Simmons.   Joe Foss,
           Flying Marine: The Story of His Flying Circus.
           New York: Books, Inc. , 1943. 160p.
               In Solomons action, October 1942-January 1943,
           the noted aviator of Marine Fighter Squadron (VMF)
           121 downed 26 enemy aircraft, thereby winning the
           Congressional Medal of Honor.

4196   Foster, John. Guadalcanal General: The Story of
           A. A. Vandegrift, U.S.M.C. New York: William
           Morrow, 1966. 224p.

4197   "Four Day's Solomons Battle: A Chart of Japanese
           and United States Losses and Aggregate Losses,
           December 1941-November 1942. " Illustrated Lon-
           don News, CCI (November 28, 1942), 609.

4198   Fraser, Robert B.   "Wing Talk: Combat in the Solo-
           mons Campaign in June 1943. " Collier's, CXII
           (November 13, 1943), 8+.
               Naval aviation at work!

4199   "Gains by Yards: The Tough Battle For Munda is
           Worth Its High Cost to Us. " Newsweek, XXII
           (September 9, 1943), 27-28.
               New Georgia.

4200   Gallant, T. Grady. On Valor's Side.   Garden City,
           N.Y. : Doubleday, 1963. 364p.
               Reminiscences of Marine Corps service on
           Guadalcanal.

4201   Gatch, Thomas L.   "A Battle Wagon Fights Back. "
           Saturday Evening Post, CCXIV (May 1-8, 1943),
           9-10+, 26+.

4202   _____. _____. In: William H. Fetridge, ed. The
           Second Navy Reader. Indianapolis: Bobbs-Merrill,
           1944. p. 116-143. Rpr. 1971.

The U.S.S. South Dakota, "Battleship X," in Solomons action.

4203 Gehring, Frederick P. A Child of Miracles. New York: Funk & Wagnalls, 1962. 305p.
      Concerns the orphan girl, Patty Ling, adopted by the U.S. Marines on Guadalcanal. The author was a priest serving as a Marine chaplain.

4204 "General Alexander A. Vandegrift: An Interview." Knickerbocker's Weekly, (February 8, 1943), 16-25.
      A lengthy discussion devoted primarily to the Guadalcanal operation.

4205 George, John B. Shots Fired in Anger: A Rifleman's-Eye View of the Activities on the Island of Guadalcanal in the Solomons, During the Elimination of the Japanese Forces There by the American Army Under General [Alexander] Patch, Whose Troops Included the 132nd Infantry of the Illinois National Guard, A Combat Unit of the Americal Division, in Which Organization the Author Served While Encountering the Experiences Described Herein. Platersville, S. C.: Small Arms Technical Publishing Company, 1947. 421p.

4206 Gildart, Robert C. "Guadalcanal's Artillery." Field Artillery Journal, XXXIII (October 1943), 734-739.

4207 Girardeau, Marvin D. Dragon's Peninsula. New York: Vantage Press, 1967. 141p.
      The New Georgia campaign.

4208 "Glory For a Tin Can, the Destroyer O'Bannon." Time, XLIII (April 17, 1944), 65.

4209 "Good to the Last Gun: The Epic of the U.S. Destroyer Laffey." Scholastic, XLII (February 1, 1943), 2.
      DD-459 was sunk in action during the Naval Battle of Guadalcanal in November 1942.

4210 Graham, Garrett. Banzai Noel! New York: Vanguard Press, 1944. 159p.
      One of the few detailed memoirs of experiences on a troop transport bound for the Pacific, the volume also recalls the author's service as a ground

officer with the 1st Marine Aircraft Wing on Guadalcanal.

4211 _____. "Our Number One Ace Comes Home: The
Story of Captain Joe Foss. " Saturday Evening
Post, CCXV (April 3, 1943), 22+.

4212 Grattan, C. H. "The Solomons, a Frontier. " Asia,
XLIII (January 1943), 51.

4213 Greenberg, J. A. "Twenty-Seven Minutes of Roaring
Glory. " In: William H. Fetridge, ed. The Navy
Reader. Indianapolis: Bobbs-Merrill, 1943.
p. 213-219. Rpr. 1971.
    Reprinted from a 1943 issue of Sea Power, this
is an account of the cruiser Boise in action off
Guadalcanal, October 11, 1942, in the Battle of
Cape Esperance.

4214 Griffin, Alexander R. A Ship to Remember: The
Saga of the Hornet. New York: Howell, Soskin,
1943. 288p.
    The carrier which launched Doolittle's Tokyo
Raid was sunk during the Battle of the Santa Cruz
Islands, October 26, 1942.

4215 Griffith, Samuel B. , 2nd. "Action at Enogai. " Marine
Corps Gazette, XXVIII (March 1944), 14-19.
New Georgia.

4216 _____. The Battle for Guadalcanal. Great Battles
of History Series. Philadelphia: Lippincott, 1963.
282p.
    The author was commander of the 1st Marine
Raider Battalion during the early days of the engagement.

4217 _____. "Corry's Boys. " Marine Corps Gazette,
XXXVI (March 1952), passim.
    Personal experiences of the commander of the
1st Marine Raider Battalion on New Georgia.

4218 "Guadalcanal. " Life, XIII (November 9, 1942), 32-39.
    Features a map for those readers unfamiliar
with the island's location--and there were millions.

4219 "Guadalcanal Awaits the Japanese Onslaught. " Scholastic,
XLI (November 2, 1942), 3.

4220 "Guadalcanal Fighting Stops as Japs Abandon the Island
       to the Americans. " Life, XIV (March 1, 1943),
       68-71.

4221 "Guadalcanal: Grassy Knoll Battle. " Life, XIV (Feb-
       ruary 1, 1943), 21-27.

4222 "Guadalcanal Shores. " Life, XIV (April 19, 1943),
       48-51.

4223 "Guadalcanal's Week. " Time, XL (October 27, 1942),
       30-31.

4224 Guenther, John C. "Artillery in the Bougainville
       Campaign. " Field Artillery Journal, XXXV (June
       1945), passim.

4225 _____. "The Second Battle of Bougainville. " Infantry
       Journal, LV (February 1945), passim.

4226 Gurney, Gene. "How They Got Yamamoto. " American
       Legion Magazine, LXVI (January 1959), 12-13+.

4227 Hailey, Foster B. "One Thousand Men and a Ship:
       The Saga of the Minneapolis. " New York Times
       Magazine, (March 12, 1944), 5-7+.
           CA-36 was active in the naval segments of the
       Guadalcanal operation.

4228 Haines, Howard F. "Three Months on Bougainville. "
       Field Artillery Journal, XXXIV (July 1944), passim.

4229 Harker, Jack S. Well Done Leander. London: Col-
       lins, 1971. 316p.
           H. M. N. Z. cruiser saw considerable action in
       the Solomons, where she was severely damaged in
       the July 12-13 1943 Battle of Kolombangara.

4230 Hart, Thomas C. "Amphibious War Against Japan. "
       USNIP, LXIX (1943), 267-272.

4231 _____. In: William H. Fetridge, ed. The
       Navy Reader. Indianapolis: Bobbs-Merrill, 1943.
       p. 281-291. Rpr. 1971.

4232 _____. Saturday Evening Post, CCXV (October
       10, 1942), 16-17+.

The first two citations above are reprintings of the third, which is subtitled, "An Analysis of the Most Difficult of All Forms of Warfare. "

4233 _____. "What Our Navy Learned in the Pacific. " Saturday Evening Post, CCXV (October 2, 1942), 9-10+.

4234 _____. _____. USNIP, LXIX (1943), 111-117.

4235 _____. _____. In: William H. Fetridge, ed. The Navy Reader. Indianapolis: Bobbs-Merrill, 1943. p. 269-281. Rpr. 1971.

4236 Hayashi, Saburo. "The Japanese Army in the Pacific War: Part I, Guadalcanal. " Marine Corps Gazette, XLII (November 1958), 8-14.

4237 Hayes, Robert C. "Return to the Islands--Guadalcanal." Leatherneck, XLIII (July 1960), 25-31+.

4238 _____. "Return to the Islands: Tulagi-Bougainville. " Leatherneck, XLIII (March 1960), 32-37.

4239 Hedlinger, Charles. Bless 'em All: A Cartoon History of the 1st Marine Raiders. Titusville, Pa.: Titusville Herald, 1943. Unpaged.

4240 Henderson, Frederick P. "Naval Gunfire in the Solomon Islands Campaign. " Unpublished paper, Files of the U.S. Marine Corps Historical Library, Headquarters, U.S. Marine Corps, 1954.
     Although we have and will cite many unpublished papers available from the U.S. Navy and Marine Corps departmental libraries, one who is interested in this type of source material should not fail to look into that held by other service institutions and educational facilities. Examples of these include the Air University Library, the National Archives, the Library of Congress, the New York Public Library, the U.S. Army Military History Research Collection, the U.S. Naval, Military, and Air Force Academy Libraries, the U.S. Naval War College Library, and such universities as Harvard, Notre Dame, University of Maine, Stanford University, etc.

4241 Henri, Raymond. "Guadalcanal Encampment." In:
      Patrick O'Sheel and Gene Cook, eds. Semper
      Fidelis: The U.S. Marines in the Pacific, 1942-
      1945. New York: William Sloane Associates,
      1947. p. 46.

4242 Hersey, John. "The Battle of the Matanikau River:
      A Typical Marine Engagement in the Mud and
      Jungle of Guadalcanal." Life, XIII (November 23,
      1942), 99-101+.
          The same article abridged appeared in the
      Reader's Digest, XLII (February 1943), 65-71.

4243 _____. "Guadalcanal: The Jap, With Paintings of
      the Solomons Campaign by Navy Lieut. David
      Shepler." Life, XV (December 27, 1943), 50-51.

4244 _____. Into the Valley: A Skirmish of the Marines.
      New York: Alfred A. Knopf, 1943. 138p.
          A vivid picture of the inland fighting on Guadal-
      canal.

4245 _____. "Marines on Guadalcanal." Life, XIII (Novem-
      ber 9, 1942), 36-39.

4246 _____. "A PT Squadron in the South Pacific." Life,
      XIV (May 10, 1943), 74-76+.

4247 _____. "Rendova: The Jungle, with Color Paintings
      of the First Landings in New Georgia." Life, XV
      (December 27, 1943), 72-77.

4248 _____. "Santa Cruz: The U.S.S. South Dakota in
      the Battle of the Santa Cruz Islands." Life, XV
      (December 27, 1943), 52-53.

4249 Heyn, Allen C. "One Who Survived: A Recorded War-
      time Interview With a Naval Interrogator." Ameri-
      can Heritage, VII (June 1956), 64-73.

4250 _____. _____. In: Robert G. Athearn. American
      Heritage New Illustrated History of the United
      States. 16 vols. New York: American Heritage,
      1963. XV, 1341-1349.
          Recollections of a Gunner's Mate 2nd Class,
      one of 10 survivors of the light cruiser Juneau
      during the Naval Battle of Guadalcanal in mid-No-
      vember 1942.

4251 "Hit Hard, Hit Fast, Hit Often. " Time, XL (November
        30, 1942), 28-31.
          Admiral William F. Halsey and the naval battles
        of the Solomons operation.

4252 Horan, James D.   "The Battle of Cibik's Ridge. "
        Saturday Evening Post, CCXVII (November 18,
        1944), 19+.
          Action on Bougainville in 1943.

4253 "The Hornet's Last Day: Tom Lea Paints the Death
        of a Great Carrier. " Life, XV (August 2, 1943),
        42-49.

4254 Horton, Dick C. Fire Over the Islands: The Coast
        Waters of the Solomons. Sydney, Australia: Reed,
        1970. 256p.

4255 "How the Marines Landed. " Newsweek, XX (September
        7, 1942), 20-23.
          On Guadalcanal.

4256 "How We Lost a Gallant Lady: The Final Hours Aboard
        the U.S. Aircraft Carrier Hornet, an Interview
        With C. P. Mason. " American Magazine, CXXXVI
        (November 1943), 32-33+.

4257 Hubbard, Lucien. "Colonel [Evans F.] Carlson and
        His Gung-Ho Raiders. " Reader's Digest, XLIII
        (December 1943), 63-68.

4258 Hubler, Richard G. "Limeade on Guadalcanal. "
        USNIP, LXX (1944), 1501.

4259 ____. "Wolf Pack: A Squadron of Marine Fighters
        Established a Record. " Flying, XXXIV (March-
        April 1944), 34+, 63+.

4260 Hunt, Richard C. D. "Bougainville. " USNIP, LXIX
        (1943), 1449-1450.

4261 "Isle of Nightmare: What Happened to the Marine
        Heroes of Guadalcanal. " Newsweek, XXI (May 24,
        1943), 88-89.

4262 Jackson, Reginald S.   "The Second Battle of Bougain-
        ville. " Military Review, XXV (April 1945), passim.

4263 "Jap Black Friday: A Big Battle and Heavy Losses
      Repulse a Convoy for the Solomons. " Newsweek,
      XX (November 23, 1942), 28-29.
          A study of the facts contained in standard naval
      histories should be reviewed in connection with
      most of the on-the-scene or contemporary maga-
      zine articles cited in this section.

4264 "Jap Bomber's Suicide Dive on the U.S. Aircraft
      Carrier Hornet. " Illustrated London News, CCII
      (January 23, 1943), 97.

4265 "Japanese Driven Out of the Solomons. " Illustrated
      London News, CCIII (September 4, 1943), 264.

4266 "Jungle War: Bougainville and New Caledonia. "
      National Geographic, LXXXV (April 1944), 417-432.

4267 "Jungle War--Comments from Fighting Men in the
      South Pacific. " Infantry Journal, LII (March 1943),
      8-15.

4268 Karig, Walter and Eric Purdon.   "The Battle of Em-
      press Augusta Bay. " USNIP, LXXII (1946), 1569-
      1575.
          Fought off Bougainville on the night of November
      1, 1943.

4269 Kent, Graeme. Guadalcanal: Island Ordeal.   Ballan-
      tine's Illustrated History of World War II.   New
      York: Ballantine Books, 1971.   160p.

4270 Kiralfy, Alexander.   "How to Stop Japan's Tinclads. "
      New Republic, CVI (February 9, 1942), 196-197.

4271 Kirkland, Thomas V.   "The Incredible Cactus Air
      Force. " Marine Corps Gazette, XLIII (May 1959),
      42-46.
          The joint U.S. Army, Navy, and Marine Corps
      aircraft group operating from Henderson Field
      during the Guadalcanal campaign.

4272 Lanphier, Thomas G. , Jr.   "I Shot Down Yamamoto. "
      Reader's Digest, LXXXIX (December 1966), 82-87.

4273 Lardner, John.   "Fulfillment on the Beaches of the
      Solomons. " Newsweek, XX (August 31, 1942), 24.

4274 Lea, Tom. "Aboard the U.S.S. Hornet." Life, XIV
      (March 22, 1943), 49-58.

4275 _____. "Sinking the Wasp." Life, XIV (April 5,
      1943), 48-49.

4276 Leckie, Robert. Challenge For the Pacific: Guadal-
      canal, the Turning Point of the War. Crossroads
      of World History Series. Garden City, N.Y.:
      Doubleday, 1965. 372p.

4277 _____. Helmet For My Pillow. New York: Random
      House, 1957. 312p.
          The author, a former enlisted Marine, recalls
      his training at Parris Island and service with the
      1st Marine Division in the Pacific, especially on
      Guadalcanal.

4278 "Life on Guadalcanal." Newsweek, XX (October 26,
      1942), 22-25.

4279 Love, Edmund G. War Is a Private Affair. New
      York: Harcourt, Brace, 1959. 192p.

4280 McKennan, William J. "The Battle of Bloody Hill:
      How Henderson Field was Saved." Saturday Even-
      ing Post, CCXV (February 20, 1943), 16-17+.

4281 _____. _____. In: Patrick O'Sheel and Gene Cook,
      eds. Semper Fidelis: The U.S. Marines in the
      Pacific, 1942-1945. New York: William Sloane
      Associates, 1947. p. 11-20.

4282 McMillan, George. "I've Served My Time in Hell."
      American Heritage, XVII (February 1966), 10-15.
          Guadalcanal.

4283 Maitland, Patrick. "Under Fire on Guadalcanal."
      Harper's, CLXXXVI (February 1943), 267-277.

4284 Mangrum, Richard C. "Guadalcanal Diary." American
      Magazine, CXXXV (February 1943), 15-20.
          Not to be confused with the Tregaskis work cited
      below.

4285 Marder, Murrey. "And They Sent Us Mortar Shells!"
      In: Patrick O'Sheel and Gene Cook, eds. Semper

Fidelis: The U.S. Marines in the Pacific, 1942-1945. New York: William Sloane Associates, 1947. p. 21-25.
The capture of Enogai in the Solomons.

4286   _____. "The Marines Against the Jungle." Ibid.,
        p. 311-316.
        Life on Guadalcanal.

4287   "Marine Aviation in the Munda Campaign." Marine Corps Gazette, XXVII (October 1943), passim.
        New Georgia.

4288   "Marine Corps Equipment in Use on Guadalcanal."
        Marine Corps Gazette, XXVII (March 1943), 15.

4289   "Marines Attack the Solomons." Life, XIII (August 24, 1942), 19-25.

4290   "Marines Still Busy in the Solomon Islands." Scholastic, XLI (October 19, 1942), 5.

4291   Marshall, Samuel L. A. Island Victory. Washington: Infantry Journal Press, 1944. 213p.
        Guadalcanal.

4292   Mathieu, Charles, Jr. "The Capture of Munda."
        Marine Corps Gazette, XXVIII (November 1943), passim.

4293   Mattiace, John M. "Joe Foss at Guadalcanal."
        Marine Corps Gazette, LVII (June 1973), 43-47.

4294   Merillat, Herbert L. "Guadalcanal." In: Patrick O'Sheel and Gene Cook, eds. Semper Fidelis: The U.S. Marines in the Pacific, 1942-1945. New York: William Sloane Associates, 1947. p. 278-282.

4295   _____. The Island: A History of the First Marine Division on Guadalcanal. Boston: Houghton, Mifflin, 1944. 283p.
        A step-by-step military description, void of human interest stories, for the period of August 7-December 9, 1942.

4296   Michel, Marshall. "To Kill an Admiral." Aerospace Historian, XIV (Spring 1966), 25-29.

The "getting" of Japanese Admiral Yamamoto.

4297 Miller, Hugh B., Jr.   "The Battle of Arundel Island:
      For 39 Days a Wounded, Shipwrecked Navy Lieu-
      tenant Was a One-Man Army Behind Jap Lines."
      Life, XV (November 8, 1943), 57-58+.
           Washed ashore after his destroyer, the U.S.S.
      Strong, was torpedoed, Miller ordered his three
      companions to leave him.   When well enough to
      travel, he began seeking his own lines and knock-
      ing off those Japanese who got in his way (a total
      of 23).   Eventually picked up by a Navy PBY, he
      received the Navy Cross from Mrs. Franklin D.
      Roosevelt.

4298 Miller, John, Jr. Guadalcanal, the First Offensive.
      United States Army in World War II--The War in
      the Pacific.   Washington: Office of the Chief of
      Military History, Department of the Army, 1949.
      413p.
           Contains appropriate attention to naval and Marine
      Corps operations as well.

4299 Miller, Robert C.   "Air Power in the Solomons."
      Marine Corps Gazette, XXVII (March-April 1943),
      45-50.

4300 Miller, Thomas G., Jr.   The Cactus Air Force.   New
      York: Harper and Row, 1969.   242p.
           Flying out of Henderson Field during the great
      battles on Guadalcanal and on the surrounding seas.

4301 Mitchell, Donald W.   "The Navy at Its Best: The Fifth
      Battle of the Solomons." Nation, CLV (December
      26, 1942), 716-717.

4302 Mitchell, Ralph J.   "Marine Airmen on Guadalcanal."
      Flying, XXXII (April 1943), 22-24.

4303 Monks, John, Jr.   A Ribbon and a Star: The Third
      Marines at Bougainville.   New York: Henry Holt,
      1945.   242p.

4304 Montgomery, Robert.   "Hell by the Clock: Outfoxing
      the Japs in the Raid on Kula Bay." American
      Magazine, CXXXVI (August 1943), 19+.

4305 Morison, Samuel E.   "Guadalcanal, 1942." Saturday

Evening Post, CCXXXV (July 28, 1962), 22-23+.

4306 Morris, C. G. "I Saw the Helena Go Down: A Cruiser
       Dies Nobly in the Kula Gulf, Taking Four Enemy
       Ships With Her." Saturday Evening Post, CCXVI
       (January 22, 1944), 20-21+.

4307 Morris, Frank D. "The First Lap on Tokyo: The
       Battle of the Solomons." Collier's, CX (October
       3-10, 1942), 16-17+, 17+.

4308 _____. "Mike Moran's Men: The U. S. S. Boise's
       Epic Battle off Guadalcanal." Collier's, CXI (Feb-
       ruary 6-13, 1943), 18-19+, 26+.

4309 _____. "Pick Up the Biggest": Mike Moran and the
       Men of the Boise. Boston: Houghton, Mifflin,
       1943. 131p.
            This and the citation above concern the activities
       of CL-47 in the Battle of Cape Esperance.

4310 "Munda Airfield: After a Month of Hard Fighting U. S.
       Troops Take an Important Base." Life, XV (Sep-
       tember 6, 1943), 36+.
            New Georgia.

4311 Murphy, Francis X. Fighting Admiral: The Story of
       Dan Callaghan. New York: Vantage Press, 1952.
       214p.

4312 Murphy, Mark. "Socked: Interviewing a Survivor of
       the Wasp." New Yorker, XVIII (February 6, 1943),
       42+.
            Reprinted in Scholastic, XLII (April 5, 1943),
       15-16.

4312a Myers, Robert. "Joe Foss, No. 1 Ace." Leatherneck,
       XXVI (June 1943), 60-61.

4313 "The Naval Career of John F. Kennedy." All Hands,
       no. 564, (January 1964), 2+.

4314 "Naval Victory in the Solomons." Life, XIII (November
       30, 1942), 29-33.
            The First and Second Naval Battles of Guadalcan-
       al.

4315 "The New Georgia Offensive." Life, XV (July 26,
      1943), 36-38.

4316 "New Landings and Fleet Action Speed War's Pace in
      the Pacific." Newsweek, XXII (November 15, 1943),
      30-31.
            Bougainville and the Battle of Empress Augusta
      Bay.

4317 Newcomb, Richard F. Savo: The Incredible Naval
      Debacle Off Guadalcanal. New York: Holt, Rine-
      hart and Winston, 1961. 278p.

4318 Nolan, John E., Jr. "Tactics and the Theory of
      Games: The Theory of Games Applied to the Bat-
      tle of Guadalcanal." Army, XI (August 1960), 77-
      81.

4319 Norton-Taylor, Duncan. I Went to See For Myself.
      London: Heinemann, 1945. 156p.
            An Englishman's impressions of early Pacific
      naval battles, with emphasis on the Battle of Kula
      Gulf to which he was a witness.

4320 _____. "Victory in Kula Gulf." Time, XLII (July 19,
      1943), 28-30.

4321 Ohmae, Toshikazu. "The Battle of Savo Island."
      Edited by Roger Pineau. USNIP, LXXXIII (1957),
      1263-1278.
            As seen from the Japanese viewpoint.

4322 _____. "Japanese Commentary on Guadalcanal."
      USNIP, LXXVII (1951), 56-59.

4323 Olszuk, Louis. "Tell It to the Marines." Future,
      (October 1942), 7-9.

4324 "The One-Ship Fleet: The Battered Cruiser Boise
      Comes Home." Scholastic, XLI (December 7,
      1942), 2.

4325 O'Sheel, Patrick. "Life on a Bull's Eye." Leather-
      neck, XXVII (June 1944), 15-19.

4326 _____. _____. In: Patrick O'Sheel and Gene Cook,
      eds. Semper Fidelis: The U.S. Marines in the

Pacific, 1942-1945. New York: William Sloane
Associates, 1947. p. 25-29.
Events on Puruata Island, some 1000 yards off
Cape Torokina on Bougainville.

4327 Pabuck, Stephen B. "The Battle for Guadalcanal, 7
Aug. 1942-7 Feb. 1943." Strategy and Tactics,
(July-August 1973), 23-38.

4328 "Pacific Gains: The Wewak Airfields Devastated and
Amphibians Attack in the Solomons." Newsweek,
XXII (August 30, 1943), 25-27.

4329 "Pacific Skirmishes." Newsweek, XX (August 31,
1942), 23-25.

4330 "Pappy Boyington Comes Home: The Skipper of the
Marine Black Sheep Fighter Squadron." Life, XIX
(October 1, 1945), 29-31.

4331 "Patch of Destiny." Time, XL (November 2, 1942),
28-32.
Guadalcanal.

4332 Penfold, John B. "'Lady Butch' of Kula Gulf." In:
William H. Fetridge, ed. The Second Navy Reader.
Indianapolis: Bobbs-Merrill, 1944. p. 45-52.
Rpr. 1971.
The activities of the ill-fated U.S.S. Helena.

4333 Pineau, Roger, ed. See Ohmae, Toshikazu, no. 4321.

4334 _____., jt. author. See Tanaka, Raizo, no. 4388.

4335 Potter, Elmer B. "Guadalcanal." In: his Sea Power:
A Naval History. Englewood Cliffs, N.J.: Prentice-Hall, 1960. p. 689-711.

4336 Powell, Paulus P. "Camp Crocodile." Unpublished
paper, Individual Personnel File, U.S. Navy Department, Naval History Division, Operational
Archives, 1950. 13p.
A character study of Vice Admiral Theodore S.
Wilkinson by his Chief-of-Staff, taking its title from
the Third Amphibious Force headquarters on Guadalcanal.

209

4337 Pratt, Fletcher. "Battleship Admiral: The Story of
Dan Callaghan." Harper's, CLXXXIX (September
1944), 343-355.

4338 _____. "The Campaign for the Solomons." Harper's,
CLXXXVIII (March-May 1944), 348-360, 467-480,
564-576.

4339 _____. "The Loss of the Wasp." USNIP, LXXII
(1946), 909-915.

4340 _____. "Memorial of the Wasp." Harper's, CLXXXVI
(May 1943), 545-555.

4341 _____. Night Work: The Story of Task Force 39.
New York: Holt, 1946. 267p.
The unit of Admiral A. Stanton Merrill composed
of destroyers and cruisers which won the November
2, 1943 Battle of Empress Augusta Bay off the
coast of Bougainville.

4342 _____. "Vandegrift of Guadalcanal." Infantry Journal,
LX (June 1947), 28-36; LXI (July 1947), 14-18.

4343 Pratt, William V. "Guadalcanal Finale: The Japanese
Tried Everything." Newsweek, XXI (March 1,
1943), 20.

4344 _____. "How the Japanese Attempted to Retake
Guadalcanal." Newsweek, XX (November 30,
1942), 21.

4345 _____. "The Strategy of the Solomons Attack." Newsweek, XX (August 24, 1942), 20.

4346 _____. "Why the Japanese Keep After the Solomons."
Newsweek, XX (September 14, 1942), 24.

4347 Purdon, Eric, jt. author. See Karig, Walter, no.
4268.

4348 Rawlings, Charles A. "In the Dark of the Solomons'
Moon." Saturday Evening Post, CCXVI (August 7,
1943), 12-13+.
The activities of and against the "Tokyo Express."

4349 _____. "The McFarland Comes Home: The Epic of

a U.S. Destroyer's Forty-Two Days of Peril."
Saturday Evening Post, CCXV (March 13, 1943),
9-11+.
    According to naval sources, McFarland was a
bogus name supplied to an unnamed vessel damaged
in action during the Solomons campaign.

4350 "The Reconquest of the Solomon Islands by U.S.
      Marines." Illustrated London News, CCI (Septem-
      ber 12, 1942), 296-297.

4351 Reinecke, Frank M. "Hellzapoppin Ridge, 8-18
      December 1943: The Bougainville Campaign, a
      Study of Offensive Principles." Unpublished paper,
      Senior Course, Amphibious Warfare School, Marine
      Corps Schools, Quantico, Va., 1947.

4352 Rentz, John N. Bougainville and the Northern Solomons.
      Washington: Historical Section, U.S. Marine Corps,
      1948. 166p.

4353 _____. Marines in the Central Solomons. Washing-
      ton: Historical Branch, U.S. Marine Corps, 1952.
      186p.

4354 Revels, W. O. Charles. "Bougainville Patrol." Marine
      Corps Gazette, XXVIII (January 1944), 77.

4355 Richmond, Herbert W. "War in the Pacific: The Im-
      portance Attached to the Solomon Islands." Fort-
      nightly, CLVIII (November 1942), 327-329.
      A British view.

4356 "Robert Schindler at Tulagi." U.S. Coast Guard Aca-
      demy Alumni Association Bulletin, V (April 1943),
      16.

4357 "Roy S. Geiger." CurrBio:VI:230-232.
      The Marine Corps commander of the Cactus Air
      Force on Guadalcanal who would play important
      roles in later Pacific campaigns.

4358 Rust, Kenneth C. "The Battle of Santa Cruz." RAF
      Flying Review, XVII (January 1962), 35-37+.

4359 "Savo and History." Time, XLVIII (August 19, 1946),
      24-25.

Thoughts on the August 8, 1942 naval battle off
Guadalcanal.

4360 Schmuck, Donald M. "The Battle of Piva Forks."
Marine Corps Gazette, XXVIII (June 1944), 5-13.
Action on Bougainville.

4361 Schwartz, Robert L. "The Big Bastard." In: Editors
of Yank. The Best From Yank, the Army Weekly.
New York: E. P. Dutton, 1945. p. 43-48.
The U. S. battleship Washington in the Naval
Battle of Guadalcanal.

4362 Seleo, Nicholas. "I Fought the Japs in the Jungle."
Science Digest, XVI (July 1944), 75-80.
Guadalcanal.

4363 "'Semper Fidelis': The Marines in the Solomons."
Time, XL (September 7, 1942), 34-36.

4364 Shalett, Sidney. Old Nameless: The Epic of a U.S.
Battlewagon. New York: D. Appleton-Century,
1943. 177p.
The U.S.S. South Dakota (BB-57) in the Solomons campaign.

4365 Shaw, James C. "Commanding a Mothballer." USNIP,
LXXVIII (1952), 160-167.

4366 _____. "The Japanese Guessed Wrong at New Georgia." Marine Corps Gazette, XXXIII (December
1949), 36-42.

4367 _____. "Jarvis (DD-393), the Destroyer That Van-
ished." USNIP, LXXVI (1950), 118-127.
She was bombed and sunk off Guadalcanal during
the time of the August 8, 1942 Battle of Savo Island.

4368 Shea, G. H. "The Lessons of Guadalcanal." Infantry
Journal, LIII (July 1943), 8-15.

4369 Shepard, Tazewell. J. F. K.: Man of the Sea. Wau-
kisha, Wisc.: Country Beautiful Foundation, 1965.
161p.
Contains some data on his PT-Boat adventures.

4370   Sherman, V. A.   "The Battle of Vella Gulf."   USNIP,
          LXXI (1945), 61-69.
              Admiral Samuel E. Morison, the distinguished
          naval historian, has called this one of the "neatest"
          U.S. victories of the Pacific war.

4371   "The Sinking of the Wasp."   Time, XL (November 2,
          1942), 28.

4372   Smith, Dale O.   "Who Shot Down Yamamoto?: An
          Editorial."   Aerospace Historian, XIV (Spring
          1967), 9.

4373   Smith, Edward L., 2nd.   "Marine, You Die!"   Harper's,
          CLXXXVII (September 1943), 314-323.
              A catchy Japanese phrase employed on Guadal-
          canal.

4374   Smith, Stanley E.   The Battle of Savo.   New York:
          Mcfadden-Bartell, 1962.   152p.

4375   _____.   The Navy at Guadalcanal.   New York: Lancer
          Books, 1963.   160p.

4376   "Solomon Islands--Now Mainly Taken from Japan by
          U.S. Forces."   Illustrated London News, CCI
          (August 22, 1942), 209.

4377   "Solomon Islands Spoils: The U.S. Marines Capture
          Japanese Camps and Equipment."   Life, XIII
          (September 14, 1942), 34-35.

4378   "Solomons Battle Back."   Leatherneck, XXV (Decem-
          ber 1942), 12-15.

4379   "Solomons Duel."   Newsweek, XX (November 9, 1942),
          17-19.
              Battle of the Santa Cruz Islands.

4380   "Solomons Ladder."   Newsweek, XXII (November 8,
          1943), 26.

4381   "Solomons Lowdown."   Newsweek, XX (October 5,
          1942), 24.

4382   "Solomons Spearhead."   Newsweek, XX (August 24,
          1942), 20-24.

The Guadalcanal landings and the Battle of Savo Island.

4383 Southerland, James J. "One of the Many Personal Adventures in the Solomons." USNIP, LXIX (1943), 539-547.

4384 Sternlicht, Sanford V. "We Want the Big Ones: Saga of a Tragic Victory." Navy, III (March 1960), 16-18.
        The Battle of Cape Esperance.

4385 Stonecliffe, D. W. "An Historical Study of the Initial Landing at Empress Augusta Bay, Bougainville, B.S.I., by the Third Marine Division on 1 November 1943." Unpublished paper, Senior Course, Amphibious Warfare School, Marine Corps Schools, Quantico, Va., 1947.

4386 Strope, Walmer E. "The Decisive Battle of the Pacific War." USNIP, LXXII (1946), 627-641.
        Guadalcanal.

4387 "Suspense in the Solomons." Newsweek, XX (September 28, 1942), 20-21.

4388 Tanaka, Raizo. "Japan's Losing Struggle For Guadalcanal." Edited by Roger Pineau. USNIP, LXXXII (1956), 687-699, 814-831.
        An important source for the Japanese viewpoint.

4389 Thacker, Joel D. "Wings of the Marine Corps." Marine Corps Gazette, XXVII (August 1943), 29-32.
        Deployment in the Solomons.

4390 "They, Too, Were Expendable: The Battered Boise Came Home." Time, XL (November 30, 1942), 19.

4391 "Thirty-Five Days on 'Guadal': A Single Navy Dive Bomber Squadron Attacked 94 Ships." Time, XLI (January 4, 1943), 72.

4392 Tregaskis, Richard W. Guadalcanal Diary. Garden City, N.Y.: Blue Ribbon Books, 1943. 263p. Rpr. 1955.

4393 _____. "Guadalcanal Diary: The First Few Weeks
      of an Historic American Campaign." Life, XIV
      (March 1, 1943), 72-74+.

4394 _____. John F. Kennedy: War Hero. New York:
      Dell, 1962. 223p.

4395 _____. "Tenaru Front." Infantry Journal, LII (Jan-
      uary 1943), 28-37.
            On Guadalcanal.

4396 _____. _____. Marine Corps Gazette, XXVII (January
      1945), 9.

4397 Trumbull, Robert. "All Out With Halsey!" New York
      Times Magazine, (December 6, 1942), 14+.

4398 Turner, Richmond K. "Speech to the Naval War Col-
      lege, February 23, 1951." Unpublished paper,
      Files of the Historical Division, U.S. Marine Corps,
      1951.

4399 "The U.S. Fights For the Solomons." Life, XIII
      (November 9, 1942), 29-39.

4400 "U.S. Marines and Japs Fight for Guadalcanal Airport."
      Life, XIII (October 27, 1942), 40-42.
            Henderson Field.

4401 United States. Marine Corps. "Final Report on the
      Guadalcanal Operation, Phase I." Unpublished
      paper, Files of the Historical Branch, Research
      and Records Division, Headquarters, U.S. Marine
      Corps, n.d.

4402 _____. _____. "Final Report on the Guadalcanal
      Operation, Phase II." Unpublished paper, Files of
      the Historical Branch, Research and Records Divi-
      sion, Headquarters, U.S. Marine Corps, n.d.

4403 _____. _____. "Final Report on the Guadalcanal
      Operation, Phase III." Unpublished paper, Files
      of the Historical Branch, Research and Records
      Division, Headquarters, U.S. Marine Corps, n.d.

4404 _____. _____. "Final Report on the Guadalcanal
      Operation, Phase IV." Unpublished paper, Files of

the Historical Branch, Research and Records Division, Headquarters, U.S. Marine Corps, n.d.

4405 _____. _____. "Final Report on the Guadalcanal Operation, Phase V." Unpublished paper, Files of the Historical Branch, Research and Records Division, Headquarters, U.S. Marine Corps, n.d.
The above five citations are samples of the voluminous amount of unpublished material available for study. Although additional titles from the Marines' files will be cited in this section, that will be discontinued in the following sections of Vol. II. Readers wishing this sort of material for other campaigns, say Iwo Jima, are urged to remember that it is available.

4406 _____. _____. The Guadalcanal Campaign, August 1942-February 1943. Washington: Historical Branch, U.S. Marine Corps, 1945. 96p.

4407 _____. _____. First Marine Amphibious Corps. "Bougainville Beachhead, Phase I." Unpublished paper, Files of the Historical Branch, Research and Records Division, Headquarters, U.S. Marine Corps, n.d. 45p.

4408 _____. _____. _____. "Bougainville Beachhead, Phase II." Unpublished paper, Files of the Historical Branch, Research and Records Division, Headquarters, U.S. Marine Corps, n.d. 84p.

4409 _____. _____. _____. "Bougainville Operation Report, Phase III." Unpublished paper, Files of the Historical Branch, Research and Records Division, Headquarters, U.S. Marine Corps, n.d. 96p.

4410 _____. _____. First Marine Division, Fifth Marines. "Record of Events, June 26-December 9, 1942." Unpublished paper, Files of the Historical Branch, Research and Records Division, Headquarters, U.S. Marine Corps, n.d.

4411 _____. _____. _____. "Report of Operations, January 4-February 19, 1943." Unpublished paper, Files of the Historical Branch, Research and Records Division, Headquarters, U.S. Marine Corps, n.d.

4412 _____. _____. _____, First Parachute Battalion.
"Report of Operations on Lunga Ridge, September
13-14, 1942." Unpublished paper, Files of the
Historical Branch, Research and Records Division,
Headquarters, U.S. Marine Corps, n.d.

4413 _____. _____. _____. "Report on Operations on
Gavutu Tanambogo, August 7-9, 1942." Unpublished
paper, Files of the Historical Branch, Research and
Records Division, Headquarters, U.S. Marine Corps,
n.d.

4414 _____. _____. _____. "Report on the Tasimboko
Raid, September 7-8, 1942." Unpublished paper,
Files of the Historical Branch, Research and
Records Division, Headquarters, U.S. Marines,
n.d.

4415 _____. _____. _____, First Raider Battalion. "Report of Operations, October 7-9, 1942." Unpublished paper, Files of the Historical Branch, Research and Records Division, Headquarters, U.S.
Marine Corps, n.d.

4416 _____. _____. _____, Seventh Marines, First Bat-
talion. "Summary of Operations on Guadalcanal."
Unpublished paper, Files of the Historical Branch,
Research and Records Division, Headquarters,
U.S. Marine Corps, n.d.

4417 _____. _____. _____, Seventh Marines, Third Battalion. "Notes on the Japanese Attack of September 20, 1942." Unpublished paper, Files of the
Historical Branch, Research and Records Division,
Headquarters, U.S. Marine Corps, n.d.
        These are only a few of the reports available
covering the activities of the First Marine Division
on Guadalcanal.

4418 _____. _____. Historical Branch. Marines in the
Central Solomons. Washington, 1952. 186p.

4419 _____. _____. _____. "The Bougainville Operation."
Unpublished paper, USMC File, U.S. Navy Department, Naval History Division, Operational Archives,
n.d. 44p.
        Based on official reports.

4420   _____. _____. Second Marine Division, Second Raider
Battalion. "Miscellaneous Reports. " Unpublished
paper, Files of the Historical Branch, Research
and Records Division, Headquarters, U.S. Marine
Corps, n. d.
    Includes Col. Evans F. Carleson's famous "long
patrol" behind the enemy lines on Guadalcanal.

4421   _____. _____. Third Marines. "Third Marines on
Bougainville. " Marine Corps Gazette, XXVIII
(May 1944), 4-15.

4422   _____. Naval War College. "The Battle of Savo
Island. " Unpublished paper, Battle Analysis Series,
Training Commands File, U.S. Navy Department,
Naval History Division, Operational Archives, 1950.
378p.
    A detailed tactical analysis of the August 8,
1942, Japanese victory, based on Allied and enemy
sources.

4423   _____. Navy Department. Amphibious Force South
Pacific. "Action Report, August 8-9, 1942. "
Unpublished paper, Forces File, U.S. Navy De-
partment, Naval History Division, Operational
Archives, n. d.
    Contains reports of individual ships on the Battle
of Savo Island. A copy is also available in the
Historical Branch, Research and Records Division,
Headquarters, U.S. Marine Corps.

4424   _____. _____. _____. "The Solomon Islands Operation. " Unpublished paper, Forces File, U.S.
Navy Department, Naval History Division, Operational Archives, n. d.
    Another set of individual ship reports. The
Marines also have a copy.

4425   _____. _____. Office of the Chief of Naval Operations,
Intelligence Division. "Combat Narrative: Anti-
Aircraft Action, April 7, 1943, Guadalcanal-Tulagi."
Unpublished paper, CNO-ONI File, U.S. Navy
Department, Naval History Division, Operational
Archives, 1943. 110p.

4426   _____. _____. _____. "Combat Narrative: Japanese
Attacks on Shipping in the Guadalcanal-Tulagi Area,

1943. " Unpublished paper, CNO-ONI File, U.S.
Navy Department, Naval History Division, Operational Archives, 1943.   85p.

4427 _____._____._____. "Combat Narrative: The
Movement of Supplies Into the Guadalcanal-Tulagi
Area. " Unpublished paper, CNO-ONI File, U.S.
Navy Department, Naval History Division, Opera-
tional Archives, n. d.   22p.

4428 _____._____._____. "Combat Narrative: The Solo-
mon Islands Campaign. " Unpublished paper, CNO-
ONI File, U.S. Navy Department, Naval History
Division, Operational Archives, 1942-1943.   1, 200p.
The thirteen chapters are: I. "The Landing in
the Solomons, 7-8 August 1942, " II. "The Battle of
Savo Island, 9 August 1942, " III. "The Battle of the
Eastern Solomons, 23-25 August 1942, " IV. "The
Battle of Cape Esperance, 11 October 1942, "
V. "The Battle of the Santa Cruz Islands, 26 Octo-
ber 1942, " VI. "The Battle of Guadalcanal, 11-15
November 1942, " VII. "The Battle of Tassafaronga,
30 November 1942, " VIII. "The Japanese Evacuation
of Guadalcanal, 29 January-8 February 1943, "
IX. "The Bombardments of Munda and Vila-Stan-
more, January-May 1943, " X. "Operations in the
New Guinea Area, 21 June-5 August 1943, " Tech-
nically not a part of this section. XI. "Kolombangara and Vella Lavella, 6 August-7 October
1943, " XII. "The Bougainville Landing and the
Battle of Empress Augusta Bay, 27 October-2 November 1943, " and XIII. "Bougainville Operations,
1943. "

4429 _____._____._____. Fighting on Guadalcanal.   Washington, 1943.   63p.
Now declassified.

4430 _____._____. Pacific Fleet and Pacific Ocean Area.
"Preliminary Report, Solomon Islands Operation. "
Unpublished paper, U.S. Navy Department, Naval
History Division, Operational Archives, 1942.

4431 _____._____._____. Observations of Marine Pilots
at Guadalcanal.   Cincpac-Cincpoa Bulletin 1-42.
N. p. , 1942.

4432 _____.____.____, Third Amphibious Force.
      "Seizure and Occupation of Northern Empress
      Augusta Bay, Bougainville, November 1-13, 1943."
      Unpublished paper, U.S. Navy Department, Naval
      History Division, Operational Archives, 1944.   18p.
         Another copy of Admiral Theodore Wilkinson's
      action report is available at the Historical Branch,
      Research and Records Division, Headquarters, U.S.
      Marine Corps.

4433 _____.____.____, Third Amphibious Force, Trans-
      port Group.   "Report of Landing Operations, North-
      ern Empress Augusta Bay Area, Bougainville Island,
      November 1-2, 1943." Unpublished paper, U.S.
      Navy Department, Naval History Division, Opera-
      tional Archives, 1943.   29p.
         The Marine Corps also has a copy of this study.

4434 _____. War Department. Fighting on Guadalcanal.
      Washington: U.S. Government Printing Office,
      1943.   69p.

4435 _____.____. Army Air Forces.   Pacific Counter-
      blow: The 11th Bombardment Group and the 67th
      Fighter Squadron in the Battle for Guadalcanal; An
      Interim Report.   Wings at War Series, no. 3.
      Washington: U.S. Government Printing Office,
      1945.   56p.

4436 _____.____. Southwest Pacific Headquarters, His-
      torical Section.   "The Bougainville Campaign."
      Unpublished paper, Noumea, 1945.

4437 "Upsetting Tokyo's Timetable."   Business Week,
      (August 15, 1942), 70-72.
         Guadalcanal.

4438 Vader, John.   New Georgia.   Ballantine's Illustrated
      History of World War II.   New York: Ballantine
      Books, 1971.   160p.

4439 Vandegrift, Alexander A.   "Letters From the U.S.
      Commander on Guadalcanal."   Life, XIII (November
      16, 1942), 83-84+.

4440 _____. Once A Marine: The Memoirs of General
      A. A. Vandegrift, U.S.M.C.   New York: W. W.

Norton, 1964. 338p. Rpr. 1969.

4441 Van Deurs, George. "The Segi Man." USNIP,
        LXXXIV (1958), 56-61.
           How Commander William Painter built an air-
        field on Guadalcanal.

4442 Van Orden, George O., author. See U.S. Marine
        Corps, Third Marines, no. 4421.

4443 Volcansek, Max J., Jr. "The Bougainville Beachhead
        'TA' Operation." Unpublished paper, Senior Course,
        Amphibious Warfare School, Marine Corps Schools,
        Quantico, Va., 1947.

4444 Waindel, Gerald A. "Incident on the Natamo." In:
        Patrick O'Sheel and Gene Cook, eds. Semper
        Fidelis: The Marines in the Pacific, 1942-1945.
        New York: William Sloane Associates, 1947. p.
        173-177.
           Fighting on Guadalcanal.

4445 Walker, Gordon. "The Art of War in a Jungle."
        Christian Science Monitor Magazine, (June 12,
        1943), 2+.

4446 Walker, Wayne T. "Operation Cactus." World War
        II Magazine, II (July 1973), 50-58.
           Guadalcanal air battles.

4447 "War Blazes Higher in the Pacific." Newsweek, XX
        (November 2, 1942), 19.

4448 Weems, George B. and F. A. Andrews. "Solo-
        mons Battle Log." USNIP, LXXXVIII (1962),
        80-91.

4449 Werstein, Irving. Guadalcanal. New York: Crowell,
        1963. 186p.

4450 Whipple, A. B. Chandler. Lt. John F. Kennedy--Ex-
        pendable! Envoy Books. New York: Universal
        Publishing Company, 1962. 160p.

4451 Whyte, William H., Jr. "Throw Away the Book?"
        Marine Corps Gazette, XXVIII (March 1944), 7-9.

Recalls an incident on the Matanikau River
front, Guadalcanal.

4452 Wible, John T. "The Yamamoto Mission." American
Aviation Historical Society Journal, XII (Fall 1967),
159-167.
Carried out by the Guadalcanal-based 339th
Fighter Squadron, U.S.A.A.F., on April 18, 1943--
a year to the day after the Doolittle raid on
Tokyo.

4453 Wilcox, Richard. "Captain [John L.] Smith and His
Fighting 223." Life, XIII (December 7, 1942),
120-122+.
Guadalcanal.

4454 "Willis A. Lee, Jr." CurrBio:VI:345.
The battleship admiral of the Naval Battle of
Guadalcanal.

4455 Wolfert, Ira. Battle for the Solomons. Boston:
Houghton, Mifflin, 1943. 199p.
Action off Guadalcanal in October and November
1942 recorded from eye-witness accounts.

4456 _____. "A Grandstand View of a Jap Naval Disaster."
Reader's Digest, XLII (February 1943), 11-16.

4457 _____. "The Japs Tried to Drive Us Crazy: The
Campaign on New Georgia One of the Grisliest in
American Military History." Collier's, CXII
(November 13, 1943), 18-19+.

4458 _____. "Talk on Guadalcanal." Nation, CLVI (January 23, 1943), 117-119.

4459 Worden, William L. "A Jap Remembers the First
Marines." Saturday Evening Post, CCXVIII (January 12, 1946), 28-29+.

4460 Wyman, Frank. "Douglas A. Munro, Coast Guard
Hero." Connecticut Circle, VI (August 1943), 12+.

4461 Zimmerman, John L. The Guadalcanal Campaign.
Washington: Historical Branch, U.S. Marine Corps,
1949. 189p. Rpr. 1971.

Further References: Readers are reminded that
additional data relative to this section will be found in sections
IIA and IIC-1 above, as well as in the general works cited in
Volume III, Part 1, and the appropriate sections of Part 2.

(6) BLOODY NEW GUINEA

Introduction. As we mentioned at the beginning of
the last section, the Japanese, who had landed on New Guinea
back in early March, were interested in completing their conquest of the huge island by taking Port Moresby--a move
which would endanger all U.S.-Australian sea communication.
It was the building of air facilities on islands of the nearby
Solomons that set off the Allied counteroffensive.
The Guadalcanal-Solomons operation was, in fact,
only one half of a two-pronged effort aimed at knocking out
the key Japanese base of Rabaul in New Britain. Consequently when the Joint Chiefs of Staff gave their July 2, 1942,
order to commence "Operation Watchtower," General Mac-
Arthur was given the green light to begin a second assault
on Rabaul via New Guinea. The campaign from the Central
Solomons and New Guinea would become known as the "Dual
Advance on Rabaul." Here is a chronology:

1942

July 22 The Japanese land at Gona and Buna, New Guinea,
   for an overland advance against Port Moresby.
August 25 Japanese commence attack on Milne Bay in an
   effort to outflank Port Moresby. The defenders hold.
September 4 The Japanese evacuate their Milne Bay Beach-
   head.
September 16 The advance on Port Moresby is halted; unable
   to continue, the Japanese troops are withdrawn toward
   Kokoda pending the outcome of the Guadalcanal campaign.
November 18 Pursued by a pair of Australian brigades, the
   Japanese, having recrossed the Owen Stanley Mountain
   Range in much poorer order than when they first entered
   it in July, returned to Gona and Buna on the eastern
   coast of the Papuan peninsula.
November 19 The Americans and Australians move against
   the entrenched Japanese.
December 9 Gona falls to the Australians.
December 14 Buna village falls to the Americans. Fighting
   continues.

1943

January 2 Buna government station falls to the Americans.
January 18 Japanese positions around Sanananda are over-
     run by the Australians.
January 22 The last Japanese resistance is over, signalled
     by their withdrawal. The six-month Papua campaign
     closes a few days before the Guadalcanal operation with
     Japan's southern drive blunted and the Australian-Ameri-
     can communication route intact.
March 2-4 U. S. A. A. F. bombers sink an entire Japanese
     convoy and half its escort en route to the Lae-Salamaua
     front in the Battle of the Bismarck Sea.
June 30 Timed to coincide with the other element of "Opera-
     tion Cartwheel, " the landing in the Central Solomons,
     General MacArthur begins his famous "leap-frog" or "is-
     land-hopping" operations in New Guinea, blessed with a
     touch of sea power from the likes of Rear Admiral Daniel
     Barbey and air power from General George Kenney.
     American forces land at Nassau Bay, 17 miles south of
     Japanese-held Salamaua.
August 17-18 U. S. Fifth Air Force strikes Japanese airfields
     at Wewak, destroying more than 200 warplanes.
September 4 The Australian Ninth Division makes an am-
     phibious landing near Lae.
September 5 U. S. airborne troops are dropped at Nadzab
     in the Mark River Balley above Lae.
September 6-7 The Australian Seventh Division is brought
     into Nadzab by troop-carrying aircraft and move out toward
     Lae.
September 12 U. S. and Australian forces capture Salamaua.
September 16 Lae is taken.
September 22 A brigade of the Australian Ninth Division is
     landed near Finschhafen.
October 2 Finschhafen is secured.
October 12 General Kenney's air force commences its heavy
     raids on Rabaul.
November 25 Captain Arleigh A. Burke's destroyer squadron
     defeats a Japanese tincan squadron of equal strength off
     New Ireland in the Battle of Cape St. George. The Ameri-
     can's emerge undamaged while their enemy loses three
     destroyers.
December 15 In a diversionary move, the U. S. 112th Caval-
     ry RCT is landed at Arawe on the southwest coast of New
     Britain.
December 26 The First Marine Division assaults Cape
     Gloucester, New Britain.
December 30 The First Marine Division secures Cape
     Gloucester's airfields.

1944

January 2   U.S. forces land at Saidor on the northwest coast
of the Juon Peninsula of New Guinea.

January 16   The Australian Ninth Division secures Sio, on
the northeast coast of New Guinea, while the First Marine
Division on New Britain completes the establishment of
their defensive perimeter.   Talesea, halfway to Rabaul,
falls to the Marines in March thereby insuring Allied
control of the Vitiaz and Dampier straits between New
Britain and New Guinea.   With the western part of New
Britain secured, and Allied communications through the
straits safeguarded, New Britain becomes a backwater.

February 29   American forces are landed on Los Negros
Island in the Admiralties.

March 5   Elements of the 32nd Infantry Division are landed
at Mindiri, west of Saidor, and during the next month a
pair of Australian infantry brigades move up the coast to
take Bogadjim, Madang, and Alexishafen.

March 9   The U.S. First Calvary secures Los Negros,
giving the Allies another base athwart the enemy's communication lines to Rabaul.

March 20   Allied forces land on Emirau Island, where as
after earlier assaults, an airfield was constructed.   This
was the last link in the encirclement of Rabaul, which
could now be left to "wither on the vine" without the
necessity of mounting a costly expedition for its reduction.

April 22   Having control of the Admiralty Islands, MacArthur
cancelled his plans for an assault on the Hansa Bay area
and instead ordered a "leap frog" invasion of the Hollandia
area of the Netherlands New Guinea.   On this day, the
U.S. 24th Infantry Division was landed at Tanahmerah
Bay and the 41st Infantry Division at Humboldt Bay, 25
miles to the east.   The attack was supported by carrier
planes from the U.S. Fifth Fleet, which also struck
Japanese air installations at Wakde and Sarmi to the
northwest.

April 24-26   The 24th and 41st secure Japanese air fields in
their area.   In the meantime, an invasion of Aitape in
Australian New Guinea, about 125 miles southeast of
Hollandia, is undertaken.

May 27   The 41st Infantry Division landed on Biak Island,
west of Hollandia.   The Japanese valiantly defended the
place, even managing to get some 1000 reinforcements
into the contest.

July-August   The Japanese 18th Army attacks Aitape, but
is driven off.   In the same month, the U.S. 6th Infantry
Division occupies the Sansapor-Mar area of the Vogelkop

Peninsula, thereby bringing the western tip of New Guinea
under Allied control.

August 20 Biak Island is secured. The entire northern
coast of New Guinea was now in Allied hands, except for
a few scattered pockets. Airfields were then quickly built
or reconditioned from which bombers would be able to
supply aid in MacArthur's drive against the Philippines.

November The Australian Sixth Division relieves U.S. Army
units at Aitape and begins a drive down the coast toward
Wewak.

May 10, 1945 Wewak is secured.

     The New Guinea campaign was a grand example of
combined operations, not only between the various armed
services, but between two great Allies, America and Australia. It was a bloody contest, often similar to that fought on
Guadalcanal. Its successful completion would allow its victors to commence operations towards the Philippines in one
prong of the dual advance which was begun earlier by Admiral Nimitz through the Central Pacific.

4462 "The Admiralties: Another Springboard. " Newsweek,
      XXIII (March 13, 1944), 29-30+.

4463 "Air Views Show the Great Battle Which Cost the Japs
      22 Ships and 15,000 Men. " Life, XIV (May 3,
      1943), 33-34+.
           The figures for this account of the Battle of the
      Bismarck Sea are a bit inflated!

4464 "The Allied Pacific Offensive: The Big Jap Base at
      Rabaul Appears to be the Ultimate Goal. " Life,
      XV (July 12, 1943), 34-35.

4465 "The Allies Advance in New Guinea. " Life, XVI (May
      22, 1944), 27-33.

4466 "American Planes Bomb a Big Jap Base. " Life, XIV
      (February 22, 1943), 28-29.
           Rabaul on New Britain.

4467 "Americans on New Guinea Close in on the Japs With
      Australian Allies. " Life, XIII (November 30,
      1942), 34-35.

4468 Australia. Army. Director of Public Relations.

The Jap Was Thrashed: An Official Story of the Australian Soldier, First Victor of the "Invincible" Jap, New Guinea, 1942-1943. Melbourne, [1944?] 128p.

4469 _____. _____. The Reconquest of New Guinea, September 1943-June 1944. Melbourne, [1944?] 160p.

4470 _____. _____. Salamawa Siege: An Official Publication. Sydney, Australia: A. H. Pettifer, 1944. 32p.

4471 _____. Department of Information. War in New Guinea, Official War Photographs. Sydney, Australia: F. H. Johnstone, 1943. 48p.

4472 Bamford, Hal. "Return to Rabaul." Airman, IV (January 1960), 12-13.

4473 Barbey, Daniel E. "MacArthur's Amphibious Navy." USNIP, XCV (1969), 88-99.

4474 _____. MacArthur's Amphibious Navy: Seventh Amphibious Force Operations, 1943-1945. Annapolis: U.S. Naval Institute, 1969. 375p.

4475 "The Battle for Buna." Time, XL (December 21, 1942), 28.

4476 "The Battle for New Guinea." Newsweek, XX (November 23, 1942), 29.

4477 "The Battle of Buna." Life, XIV (February 15, 1943), 17-29.

4478 Benson, James. Prisoner's Base and Home Again. London: Robert Hale, 1957.
    A look at the Japanese invasion of New Guinea.

4479 "Booty at Buna." Life, XIV (February 22, 1943), 81-87.

4480 Bordages, Asa C. "Suicide Creek." In: Patrick O'Sheel and Gene Cook, eds. Semper Fidelis: The U.S. Marines in the Pacific, 1942-1945. New York: William Sloane Associates, 1947. p. 36-46.

Action near a small river in the jungles of Cape
Gloucester.

4481 _____. "Suicide Creek: The Marines at Cape Gloucester." Collier's, CXV (May 26-June 2, 1945),
11-12+, 21+.

4482 Brett, George H. "The MacArthur I Knew." True,
XXI (October 1947), 141-147+.
In Australia and New Guinea.

4483 "Buna is Like This." Time, XLI (January 4, 1943),
31-32.

4484 "Buna Revisited: Postscript to a Bloody Pacific Campaign in Which 4000 Allies Were Killed." Life,
XV (November 1, 1943), 81-82+.

4485 "Buna Squeeze." Newsweek, XX (October 19, 1942),
22-23.

4486 Burns, Eugene. "We Avenge Pearl Harbor: Planes
From the Saratoga and a CVL Caught the Japs
Flatfooted at Rabaul." Saturday Evening Post,
CCXVII (July 22, 1944), 18-19+.

4487 "Cape Gloucester." Life, XVI (January 31, 1944),
33-34.

4488 "Cape Gloucester Prelude: A Day in MacArthur's
Command." Newsweek, XXIII (January 3, 1944),
22.

4489 Cheesman, L. E. "Japanese Operations in New
Guinea. Geographical Journal, (March 1943), 97-
110.
British view.

4490 Chudoba, Edward. "Victory in the Bismarck Sea."
In: Norman Carlisle, ed. The Air Forces Reader.
Indianapolis: Bobbs-Merrill, 1944. p. 130-139.
Reprinted from the January 1944 issue of Douglas
Airview.

4491 Cowie, Donald. "Prelude in Papua." 19th Century,
CXXXIII (January 1943), 38-43.

4492   Crown, John A. , jt. author. See Hough, Frank O. ,
       no. 4520.

4493   "Daniel E. Barbey. " CurrBio:VI:32-35.

4494   Darnton, Byron. "Jungle War Without Quarter. " New
       York Times Magazine, (October 25, 1942), 5+.
           This account of the New Guinea campaign was
       abridged in Reader's Digest, XIII (January 1943),
       52-56.

4495   Davenport, William. "The Jungle is Beaten: The
       Story of the American Men Who Fought in the New
       Guinea Jungle. " Collier's, CXVI (July 21, 1945),
       11+.

4496   Deacon, Kenneth J. "Arara Beachhead. " Military
       Engineer, LIX (March-April 1967), 120.
           New Guinea.

4497   _____. "Cave War on Biak Island, 1944. " Military
       Engineer, LIV (January-February 1962), 4-6.
           A look at the action on this small island, part
       of the Schouten Islands off the northwest coast of
       New Guinea, which was retaken by the Allies after
       hard fighting, May 27-June 20, 1944.

4498   _____. "Los Negros Island, 1944. " Military Engi-
       neer, LVIII (November-December 1966), 403+.

4499   _____. "Milne Bay, 1942. " Military Engineer, LIII
       (May-June 1961), 175.

4500   _____. "They Held the Beachhead. " Military Engi-
       neer, LII (November-December 1960), 467.
           The MacKechnie force at Nassau Bay, June 1943.

4501   Dexter, David. The New Guinea Offensives. Australia
       in the War of 1939-1945: Series 1. Canberra:
       Australian War Memorial, 1961. 851p.

4502   Dixon, Charles. "Southwest Pacific Springboard. "
       Canadian Geographic Journal, XXVII (December
       1943), 294-297.

4503   "Duckbilled Admiral. " Newsweek, XXIV (October 23,
       1944), 31-32.
           Daniel E. Barbey.

4504 Edmundson, Charles. "What We Learned in New
        Guinea." Fortune, XXVII (June 1943), 140-144+.

4505 Eichelberger, Robert L. Our Jungle Road to Tokyo.
        New York: Viking, 1950. 306p.
            The author was the victorious commander in the
        Buna offensive, serving throughout the New Guinea
        campaign. He was also in charge of the U.S.
        Eighth Army in the Philippines campaign (IIE-3) for
        which this reference should also be employed.

4506 Ellison, M. C. "Engineers in the Attack on Lorengau,
        Admiralty Islands." Military Engineer, (September
        1944), 290-292.

4507 Elrod, Bernard. "Beer Bottle Blitz: A Harassing
        Raid on Rabaul." Flying, XXXVI (February 1945),
        45+.

4508 "Enveloping Rabaul." Newsweek, XXIII (January 24,
        1944), 27-28.

4509 Falls, Cyril. "The Battle of the Bismarck Sea."
        Illustrated London News, CCII (March 13, 1943),
        281-282.

4510 Goodwin, Harold L. "Above Rabaul." In: Patrick
        O'Sheel and Gene Cook, eds. Semper Fidelis:
        The U.S. Marines in the Pacific, 1942-1945. New
        York: William Sloane Associates, 1947. p. 114-
        119.
            U.S. Marine airmen in the attack on the Japanese
        base.

4511 Graham, Burton. None Shall Survive; The Graphic
        Story of the Annihilation of the Japanese Armada
        in the Bismarck Sea Battle by the U.S. Fifth Air
        Force and the Royal Australian Air Force. Sydney,
        Australia: F. H. Johnston, 1946. 109p.

4512 Graham, W. J. "There's Only One Winner." Ameri-
        can Legion Magazine, LXII (February 1957), 22-23+.
            How a U.S. Navy search plane took on several
        Japanese fighters near Nufuketau on December 1,
        1943.

4513 Gufrin, Mark. "Saga of the U.S.S. England."

American History Illustrated, V (June 1970), 12-23.

How DE-635 set America's anti-submarine warfare record in May 1944 by sinking I-16, RO-106, RO-104, RO-116, RO-108, and RO-105. For this gallant action in the waters between Bougainville and New Guinea the ship won a Presidential Unit Citation.

4514   Harrison, J. W.   "The Australians in the South West Pacific. " Army Quarterly, (October 1944), 97-105.

4515   Hastings, H. T.   "No Survivors: A View of the Bismarck Sea Battle. " Saturday Evening Post, CCXV (May 22, 1943), 18-19+.

4516   Haugland, Vern.   Letter From New Guinea.   New York: Farrar, 1943.   148p.
The trials of an AP correspondent forced to bail out over the Owen Stanley Mountains.

4517   Hayes, Robert C.   "Return to the Islands: Rabaul. " Leatherneck, XLIII (May 1960), 38-41.

4518   Heath, Doris, trans.   See Yoshihara, Tsutomu, no. 4605.

4519   Hough, Frank O.   "The Cape Gloucester Campaign. Marine Corps Gazette, XXVIII (April 1944), 7-17.

4520   _____. and John A. Crown.   The Campaign on New Britain.   Washington: Historical Branch, U.S. Marine Corps, 1952.   220p.

4521   "How the Heroic Boys of Buna Drove the Japs Into the Sea. " Life, XIV (February 22, 1943), 24.

4522   Hunt, Frazier.   "Uncle Dan, the Amphibious Man. " Saturday Evening Post, CCXVII (July 1, 1944), 24+.
Admiral Barbey.

4523   James, D. Clayton.   The Years of MacArthur, 1880-1941.   Boston: Houghton, Mifflin, 1970.
The first of a multi-volume set.

4524   "Jap Trap: The Bastion of Lae on New Guinea. " Newsweek, XXII (September 20, 1943), 30-31.

4525 Johnston, George H. New Guinea Diary. London:
        Gollancz, 1944. 240p.
            First published in America the year before by
        the New York firm of Duell, Sloan and Pearce,
        under the title The Toughest Fighting in the World,
        this account of the Buna campaign was unsurpassed
        for many years. The most recent study, published
        just after this bibliography's cut-off date, is Lida
        Mayo's 210-page Bloody Buna issued by the Garden
        City, N.Y., firm of Doubleday in 1974, should also
        be consulted.

4526 _____. "Out There: Old-Fashioned War in the Steamy
        Jungles of New Guinea." Life, XIV (January 4,
        1943), 22-24.

4527 _____. "War in the Papuan Jungle." Time, XL
        (December 14, 1942), 40.

4528 Jones, Kenneth. Destroyer Squadron 23: The Combat
        Exploits of Arleigh Burke's Gallant Force. Phila-
        delphia: Chilton, 1959. 288p.
            Contains useful coverage of the November 25,
        1943 Battle of Cape St. George.

4529 Kahn, Ely J., Jr. "The Terrible Days of Company
        E: The March of the Big Rapids Boys Over the
        Owen Stanley Mountains to Help Win the Battle of
        Buna." Saturday Evening Post, CCXVI (January
        8-16, 1944), 9-11+, 22+.

4530 _____. "Somewhere in New Guinea." New Yorker,
        XVIII (December 5, 1942-January 30, 1943), 71-
        72+, 92, 36+, 38+; XIX (February 20-April 10,
        1943), 38+, 56-58, 62+.
            Readers should also consult the author's GI
        Jungle: An American Soldier in Australia and New
        Guinea cited in section IIB-8 above.

4531 Kluckhohn, Frank L. "Master of Amphibious Warfare:
        General [Walter] Kruger Has Led MacArthur's
        Ground Forces." New York Times Magazine,
        (December 31, 1944), 11+.
            Special emphasis on New Britain.

4532 Kruger, Walter. From Down Under to Nippon: The
        Story of the Sixth Army in World War II. Washing-
        ton: Combat Forces Press, 1953. 393p.

Also contains data relative to section IIE-3
below.

4533   Lardner, John. "From a Grandstand Seat at Port
       Moresby." Newsweek, XIX (May 4, 1942), 24.

4534   _____. "Moresby Salient." Newsweek, XX (August
       17, 1942), 24.

4535   _____. "This is Port Moresby." Saturday Evening
       Post, CCXV (October 17, 1942), 11+.

4536   Lawless, R. E. "The Biak Operation." Military
       Review, XXXIII (May-June 1953), 53-62, 48-62.

4537   Luckey, Robert B. "Cannon, Mud, and Japs." Marine
       Corps Gazette, XXVIII (October 1944), 50-54.
             U.S. Marine artillery in the Cape Gloucester
       campaign.

4538   "MacArthur's Leap-Frog Maneuver Traps the Japs
       Left on New Guinea." Newsweek, XXIII (May 1,
       1944), 21.

4539   McCarthy, Dudley. South-West Pacific Area--First
       Year: Kokoda to Wan. Australia in the War of
       1939-1945: Series 1. Canberra: Australian War
       Memorial, 1959. 656p.

4540   Manuel, Gordon. "70,000 to 1: An American Flier
       Plays the Game of Survival Against New Britain's
       Jungles and Japs." Collier's, CXVII (March 30-
       April 6, 1946), 11-12+, 19+.
             The author's exploits.

4541   Miller, John, Jr. Cartwheel: The Reduction of Rabaul.
       U.S. Army in World War II--The War in the Pacific.
       Washington: Office of the Chief of Military History,
       Department of the Army, 1959. 418p.

4542   _____. "MacArthur and the Admiralties." In: Kent
       R. Greenfield, ed. Command Decisions. Wash-
       ington: Office of the Chief of Military History,
       Department of the Army, 1960. p. 287-302.

4543   Milner, Samuel. "The Battle of Milne Bay." Military
       Review, XXX (April 1950), 18-29.

Reprinted in the Canadian Army Journal, IV
(May 1950), 42-50.

4544 _____. Victory in Papua. U.S. Army in World War
II--The War in the Pacific. Washington: Office of
the Chief of Military History, Department of the
Army, 1957. 409p.

4545 Murray, Mary. Hunted: A Coast Watcher's Story.
San Francisco, Calif.: Tri-Ocean Books, 1967.
240p.
Originally published in Australia, this work concerns the effort in New Guinea.

4546 "New Britain." Newsweek, XXII (December 20, 1943),
19-20.

4547 "New Britain Invader." Scholastic, XLIII (January 24,
1944), 9.
General Walter Kruger, U.S. Army.

4548 "The New Guinea War." Life, XIII (November 23,
1942), 51-52.

4549 "The Night Landing on New Britain." Life, XVII
(August 21, 1944), 48-56.
Includes paintings by D. Frendenthal.

4550 "Northern New Guinea." Newsweek, XXIII (April 3,
1944), 30-31.

4551 "The Old Soldier." Time, XLV (January 29, 1945),
29-30+.
General Kruger.

4552 "The Pacific Battleground: The Allied Tide Advances."
New York Times Magazine, (September 5, 1943),
4-7.
Also contains data relative to section IID-1 below.

4553 "Pacific Fury." Newsweek, XXII (July 19, 1943), 24-
25.
Also contains information relative to section
IID-1 below.

4554 "Pacific Toil: Stubborn Terrain and Enemy Slow Mac-
Arthur's Drive." Newsweek, XXII (July 26, 1943),
26-27.

4555 "Pacific Victory: The Conquest of Cape Gloucester."
      Newsweek, XXIII (January 10, 1944), 27-28.

4556 Palmer, R. K.   "There's Just More Bloody New
      Guinea." Newsweek, XXI (January 11, 1943), 24.

4557 "Papuan Mop-Up." Newsweek, XXI (February 1,
      1943), 23.

4558 Paull, Raymond. Retreat From Kokoda. Melbourne,
      Australia: Heinemann, 1958. 319p.
          The Aussies in the New Guinea campaign of
      1942.

4559 Pratt, William V.   "How Japan's Mistakes Gave
      MacArthur His Chance." Newsweek, XXIII (June
      12, 1944), 28.

4560 "The Rabaul Raid." Flying, XXXIV (February 1944),
      28-29.

4561 "Rabaul's Extinct Volcanoes Alive With Targets For
      the Allies." Newsweek, XXII (July 5, 1943), 29-
      30.

4562 Rawlings, Charles A.   "Pacific Thriller: The Savage
      Blow at the Jap's Wewak Base." Saturday Evening
      Post, CCXVI (January 8, 1944), 16-17+.

4563 _____. "The Strike on Rabaul." Saturday Evening
      Post, CCXVI (February 19, 1944), 24-25+.

4564 _____. "They Paved Their Way With Japs: MacAr-
      thur at Los Negros." Saturday Evening Post,
      CCXVII (October 7-14, 1944), 14-15+, 28-29+.

4565 Reading, Geoffrey. Papuan Story. Sydney and Lon-
      don: Angus and Robertson, 1946. 198p.
          Further details of the Australian effort in New
      Guinea.

4566 Reinhold, William J.   The Bulldog Road to Wan.
      Brisbane, Australia: University of Queensland
      Press, 1946. 53p.

4567 Riegelman, Harold. Caves of Biak: An American
      Officer's Experiences in the Southwest Pacific.

Prefatory Notes by Robert L. Eichelberger and Hu
Shih. New York: Dial Press, 1955. 278p.

4568 "The Right Guess and Great Tactics Won Us the Bismarck Sea Victory. " Newsweek, XXI (March 15,
1943), 17-18.

4569 "The Road Back: The New Guinea Offensive is the
First Long Step to the Philippines. " Newsweek,
XXII (October 18, 1943), 24+.

4570 "The Road Back to the Philippines: The Invasion of
Hollandia and Aitape. " Scholastic, XLIV (May 15,
1944), 11.

4571 Robinson, Patrick. The Fight For New Guinea:
General MacArthur's First Offensive. New York:
Random House, 1943. 183p.

4572 "The Rout at Rabaul: Air Triumph Marks the Turn
of the War in the Southwest Pacific. " Newsweek,
XXII (October 25, 1943), 26-27.

4573 Russell, William B. The Second Fourteenth Battalion:
A History of an Australian Infantry Battalion in the
Second World War. Sydney, Australia: Angus and
Robertson, 1948. 336p.

4574 Selby, David. Hell and High Fever. Sydney, Australia:
Currawong, 1956. 198p.
This account of the New Guinea campaign was
published in Sydney and London the following year
by the firm of Angus and Robertson.

4575 Serle, R. P. , ed. The Second Twenty-Fourth
Australian Infantry Battalion of the 9th Australian
Division: A History. Brisbane, Australia: Jaca-
randa Press, 1963. 378p.

4576 Shaplen, Robert. "Hollandia. " Yale Review, New
Series XXXIV (September 1944), 87-98.

4577 _____. "Hollandia Landing. " Newsweek, XXIII (May
8, 1944), 23-25.

4578 Shaw, Henry I. , Jr. , et al. Isolation of Rabaul. Vol.
II of History of U.S. Marine Corps Operations in

World War II.   Washington: Historical Branch,
U.S. Marine Corps, 1963.   632p.

4579   Shaw, James C.   "Papua: A Lesson in Sea Power."
USNIP, LXXVI (1950), 1204-1211.

4580   _____   "The Rise and Ruin of Rabaul."   USNIP,
LXXVII (1951), 624-629.

4581   Sims, Edward H.   "Chase Over New Guinea."   Airman,
II (February 1958), 25-31.
A mission flown by John D. Landers as excerpted
from the author's book, American Aces.

4582   "Stand Before Moresby."   Newsweek, XX (September
28, 1942), 19.

4583   Sufrin, Mark.   "'Take Buna or Don't Come Back
Alive.'"   American History Illustrated, V (July
1970), 4-10, 43-47.
So said MacArthur to General Robert Eichel-
berger concerning the latter's objective in northern
Papua in late 1942.

4584   "Tactics at Buna."   Newsweek, XX (December 28,
1942), 23-25.

4585   "The Third Landing: Saidor, a Tiny New Guinea Port."
Newsweek, XXIII (January 17, 1944), 25.

4586   Thursfield, Henry G.   "Convoy of the Bismarck Sea."
National Review, CXX (April 1943), 318-323.

4587   "Twelve Minutes of Hell: The Attack on the Harbor
of Rabaul, November 2, 1943."   Flying, XXXV
(December 1944), 34-43.

4588   "The U.S. Victory in the Bismarck Sea."   Life, XIV
(March 22, 1943), 27-28.

4589   United States.   Navy Department.   Office of the Chief
of Naval Operations, Intelligence Division.   "Com-
bat Narrative: Operations in New Guinea Waters."
Unpublished paper, CNO-ONI File, U.S. Navy
Department, Naval History Division, Operational
Archives, n.d.   147p.

4590   _____ . _____ .   Pacific Fleet and Pacific Ocean Area.

The North Coast of New Guinea and the Bismarck
Archipelago--Special Bulletin. Cincpac-Cincpoa
Bulletin 39-44. N. p. , 1944.

4591 _____. _____. _____, Motor Torpedo Boat Squadrons,
Philippine Sea Frontier. "Command History of
Motor Torpedo Boat Squadrons, Philippine Sea
Frontier, Formerly Motor Torpedo Boat Squadrons,
Seventh Fleet. " Unpublished paper, Type Commands
File, U. S. Navy Department, Naval History Divi-
sion, Operational Archives, 1945. 880p.
The organization and operations of those PT-Boat
units active in the New Guinea campaign.

4592 _____. Strategic Bombing Survey (Pacific), Naval
Analysis Division. The Allied Campaign Against
Rabaul. Washington: U. S. Government Printing
Office, 1946. 273p.

4593 _____. War Department. Historical Division. The
Admiralties, Operations of the 1st Cavalry Division
(29 February-18 May 1944). American Forces in
Action Series, no. 8. Washington: U. S. Government Printing Office, 1946. 151p.

4594 _____. _____. _____. Papuan Campaign, the Buna-
Sananande Operation (16 November 1942-23 January
1943). American Forces in Action Series, no. 2.
Washington: U. S. Government Printing Office,
1945. 107p.

4595 _____. _____. _____. Fifth Army Air Force. Rabaul, 2 November 1943. Washington: U. S. Government Printing Office, 1944. 12p.
Between October 12 and November 2, General
Kenney's planes attempted to knock out the Japanese
stronghold with eight massive raids of 54 to 349
planes each.

4596 Vader, John. New Guinea: The Tide is Stemmed.
Ballantine's Illustrated History of World War II.
New York: Ballantine Books, 1971. 160p.

4597 Walker, John. "Uncle Dan Barbey: An Amphibious
Admiral Moved MacArthur's Army. " Life, XVII
(November 20, 1944), 16-19.

4598 "Wau to Salamaua Is the World's Toughest Front. "

Newsweek, XXI (May 17, 1943), 25.

4599   White, Osmar E. D.   Green Armor.   Sydney and
       London: Angus and Robertson, 1945.   246p.
          This Australian view of the New Guinea cam-
       paign was published in America simultaneously by
       the New York firm of Norton.

4600   Widhelm, William J.   "Bombing Fools."   In: Norman
       Carlisle, ed.   The Air Forces Reader.   Indiana-
       polis: Bobbs-Merrill, 1944.   p. 268-279.
          An account of the Battle of the Bismarck Sea as
       reprinted from the May 1943 issue of Skyways.

4601   Wieneke, James.   6th Division Sketches, Aitape to
       Wewak: Being a Collection of Sketches, Drawings
       and Notes From the Sixth Australian Division's
       Last New Guinea Campaign Through Aitope, Maprik,
       and Wewak, 1944-1945.   Sydney, Australia, 1946.
       60p.

4602   "World War II's Greatest Sub Killer: U.S.S. England."
       Sea Classics, IV (July 1971), 41+.

4603   Wright, Malcolm.   If I Die: Coastwatching and Guer-
       rilla Warfare Behind the Japanese Lines.   Mel-
       bourne, Australia: Lansdowne Press, 1965.   192p.
          Operations in the Bismarcks.

4604   "Yanks in New Guinea."   Time, XL (August 3, 1942),
       44-45.

4605   Yoshihara, Tsutomu.   Southern Cross: An Account of
       the Eastern New Guinea Campaign.   Translated
       from the Japanese by Doris Heath.   Tokyo, 1955.
          The memoirs of the Japanese Lt. General in
       charge.

       Further References: Readers will find additional
information relative to this section in sections IIA and IIC-1
above, as well as in the general works cited in Volume III,
Part 1.

IID ISLAND HOPPING

(1) GENERAL WORKS

Introduction. With the tide of defeat stemmed and
the enemy largely contained, Allied forces in the Pacific
began to take the offensive. All of this followed a master
plan worked out at the Casablanca Conference and at a meeting in Washington.

The plan called for three steps. First, North
Pacific units would remove the Japanese from the waters off
Alaska. Second, General MacArthur's South Pacific and
Southwest Pacific command would concentrate on Rabaul and
New Guinea. Third, Admiral Chester Nimitz would open a
Central Pacific drive. Thus, although a dual drive on the
Philippines, the next big goal, was underway, it was this
push via the islands of the middle Pacific which seemed to
come to the fore. It is to this campaign that the references
are given in this section.

General MacArthur in his memoirs gives perhaps
the best definition of island hopping, or "leap-frogging."
His use of the such tactics in his own area was also employed by those advancing from Pearl Harbor. Basically, it
consisted of seeking out islands within groups, usually which
would serve as airfields, capturing them, and by bombing
and blockade reduce the enemy garrisons on surrounding
islands to impotence. The Japanese, powerless really to do
much about it, grew to hate these methods and recognize
their superiority in a war which depended so heavily on control of the sea and air.

The American sea forces by the spring of 1943 were
becoming well equipped to handle such campaigns. Fast
carrier task forces built around Essex-class heavy and
Independence-class light carriers were formed, the fleet
supply train could give great mobility, and the Marines were
well trained. Fighting would be fierce, but planning and
equipment would show that the proper combinations had been
made.

4606   "The Airman's Admiral."   Time, XLIX (February 10,
          1947), 24-25.
          Marc A. Mitscher.

4607   "America's Fight in the Pacific."   Asiatic Review,
          New Series XL (October 1944), 427-430.

4608   Anderson, Carroll R.   "Mission to Kavieng."   Ameri-
          can Aviation Historical Society Journal, X (Summer
          1965), 88-101.
               The February 15, 1944 flight was made by a
          number of planes, including several PBY's.

4609   "Big Assaults in the Pacific Show."   Newsweek, XXIII
          (February 28, 1944), 21-24.

4610   "Bomb Attack on an American Aircraft Carrier."
          Illustrated London News, CCII (January 9, 1943),
          33.

4611   Bryan, Joseph, 3rd.   Aircraft Carrier.   New York:
          Ballantine Books, 1954.   205p.
               The exploits of the second U.S.S. Lexington
          (CV-16).

4612   _____, and Philip G. Reed.   Mission Beyond Dark-
          ness.   New York: Duell, Sloan & Pearce, 1945.
          133p.
               Concerns the members of Air Group 16, U.S.S.
          Lexington.   Abridged in Reader's Digest, XLVI
          (May 1945), 109-128.

4613   Busch, Noel F.   "Admiral Chester Nimitz Commands
          History's Greatest Fleet and a Watery Theater of
          65,000,000 Square Miles."   Life, XVII (July 10,
          1944), 82-84+.

4614   _____.   "Task Force 58."   Life, XVII (July 17, 1944),
          17-20+.

4615   "A Carrier Ready Room Has an Anxious Moment."
          Life, XVII (September 11, 1944), 12-14.

4616   Cass, Bevan C., ed.   History of the Sixth Marine
          Division.   Washington: Infantry Journal Press,
          1948.   262p.
               Should be used in connection with sections IID-4
          and IIE-5.

4617   Crider, John H.   "Navy to Press the Hunt in the
          Pacific."   USNIP, LXX (1944), 725-726.

4618   Crowl, Philip A. and Edmund G. Love.   Seizure of
          the Gilberts and Marshalls.   United States Army in
          World War II--The War in the Pacific.   Washington:
          Office of the Chief of Military History, Department
          of the Army, 1955.   414p.
             Entered here because the volume overlaps sec-
          tions IID-2 and IID-3 below.   Contains appropriate
          comments on sea forces operations around and on
          Tarawa and Roi-Namur.

4619   Davis, Forrest.   "[Admiral] King's Way to Tokyo."
          Saturday Evening Post, CCXVII (December 9, 1944),
          9-11+.

4620   Driscoll, Joseph.   Pacific Victory, 1945.   Philadelphia:
          Lippincott, 1944.   297p.
             A prediction.

4621   Eliot, George F.   "Requirements of the War in the
          Pacific."   Academy of Political Science Proceed-
          ings, XXI (May 1944), 41-49.

4622   Field, John.   "With the Task Force."   Life, XIV
          (May 3, 1943), 90-91+.

4623   "Flying Leathernecks Spearhead Allied Drives in the
          South Pacific."   Aviation News, I (January 10,
          1944), 16.
             Details activities in the Central Pacific as well.

4624   Fooks, H. E.   "The War in the Pacific: Guadalcanal
          to Leyte Gulf."   Journal of the Royal United
          Service Institute, XCV (1950), passim.

4625   "Forward in the Pacific."   New York Times Magazine,
          (April 23, 1944), 6-7.

4626   Friedman, William S.   "The Avenger Scores Again."
          Popular Science, CXLIV (January 1944), 92-93.
             The use of this torpedo-bomber in the Pacific
          drives.

4627   Garand, George W. and Truman R. Strobridge.   West-
          ern Pacific Operations.   Vol. IV of History of U.S.

Marine Corps Operations in World War II. Washington: Historical Branch, U.S. Marine Corps, 1971. 900p.

4628 Hailey, Foster. "Our Fleet Seeks a Showdown with Japan." New York Times Magazine, (November 28, 1943), 5-7+.

4629 _____. "Over the Side and God Go With You: The ABC's of an Assault on a Pacific Island." New York Times Magazine, (February 13, 1944), 5-7+.

4630 Halsey, William F. "We Cannot Be Halted." American Magazine, CXXXVII (February 1944), 95.

4631 Hemphill, William E., editor. See Moody, Donald, no. 4656.

4632 Hole, Theodore. "The War Against Japan." National Review, CXXII (February 1944), 130-135.

4633 Horne, George F. "War on History's Grandest Scale: The Panorama of the Battles in the Pacific." New York Times Magazine, (July 2, 1944), 8-9+.

4634 "In the Air, As by Land and Sea, the Marines Live Up to Tradition." Scholastic, XLIII (January 10, 1944), 28.

4635 "In the Pacific, As in Europe, the Allies Shape Their Victory Pattern." Newsweek, XXIII (February 7, 1944), 21.

4636 "The Japs Hard Hit and Strategy Upset, but They're Far from Licked." Newsweek, XXIII (March 6, 1944), 30-32.

4637 "The Job Before Us: The Approaches to Tokyo." Fortune, XXVIII (December 1943), 121-135.

4638 Kennedy, Paul. Pacific Victory. Ballantine's Illustrated History of World War II. New York: Ballantine Books, 1973. 160p.
       Sequel to the author's Pacific Onslaught.

4639 Kenney, George C. "Airpower in the Southwest Pacific War." Aero Digest, XLVI (July 15, 1944), 51-53+.

4640 Kiralfy, Alexander. "Exploratory Strategy in the
        Pacific." Far Eastern Survey, XII (August 11,
        1943), 159-160.

4641 _____. "Island Skipping in the Pacific." Asia, XLIII
        (June 1943), 348-351.

4642 _____. "The New Pacific Strategy." Asia, XLIII
        (March 1943), 172-175.

4643 _____. "Why Japan's Fleet Avoids Action." Foreign
        Affairs, XXII (October 1943), 45-58.

4644 Kluckhohn, Frank L. "Zero Hour on a South Sea Is-
        land." New York Times Magazine, (January 2,
        1944), 6-7+.

4645 "Life Goes to an Aircraft Carrier Party." Life, XVII
        (July 3, 1944), 82-85.

4646 Love, Edmund G., jt. author. See Crowl, Philip A.,
        no. 4618.

4647 Lucas, W. E. "Pacific Tide Turns." Christian
        Science Monitor Magazine, (February 26, 1944),
        10-11.

4648 Luke, Harry. "The Western Pacific and the War."
        United Empire, (January-February 1943), 3-6.

4649 "MacArthur-Nimitz Conference Hints at a New Blow in
        the Pacific." Newsweek, XXIII (May 8, 1944),
        21-25.

4650 McCain, John S. "The Blitzkrieg Goes to Sea." In:
        Norman Carlisle, ed. The Air Forces Reader.
        Indianapolis: Bobbs-Merrill, 1944. p. 36-43.
          Carrier warfare, reprinted from the July 1944
        issue of Aviation.

4651 _____. "Blitzkreig Goes to Sea: Carrier-Based
        Aviation in the Pacific." Aviation, XLIII (July
        1944), 112-115+.

4652 "Marines: Navy-Trained and Equipped Mariner Flyers
        are Leading Pacific Thrusts." Flying, XXXV
        (October 1944), 106-108+.

4653 Menken, J. "Progress in the Pacific." National Review, CXXII (June 1944), 478-484.

4654 Miller, John, Jr. "The Casablanca Conference and Pacific Strategy." Military Affairs, XIII (Winter 1949), passim.
Setting up island hopping and the dual advance.

4655 Mitchell, Donald W. "Counter Strategies in the Pacific." Current History, New Series VII (July 1944), 13-18.

4656 [Moody, Donald.] Aerial Gunner from Virginia, the Letters of Don Moody to His Family During 1944. Edited by William E. Hemphill. Richmond, Va.: State Library, 1950. 366p.
Moody was a member of the 307th Heavy bombardment group, U.S.A.A.F., Southwest Pacific.

4657 Morehouse, Clifford P. "Seaways to Tokyo." Marine Corps Gazette, XXVIII (June 1944), 17-24.

4658 Morris, Frank D. "Debut in Battle: Aboard a New Carrier When Its Fighters and Bombers Plaster a Japanese Island Air Base." Collier's, CXII (November 20, 1943), 11-12+.

4659 _____. "Don't Pray So Hard, Padre: A. A. Gunners on Carrier X Weren't Getting Half Enough Target Practice." Collier's, CXIII (January 29, 1944), 12-13+.

4660 _____. "Our Sunsung Admiral: Raymond A. Spruance, Chief of the New Central Pacific Command." Collier's, CXIII (January 1, 1944), 17+.

4661 _____. "Overnight Guest: How Wildcat Pilot Wells Cheated Death Twice." Collier's, CXIV (September 2, 1944), 53.

4662 _____. "Ralph Hank's Day: Carrier Pilot." Collier's, CXIII (June 10, 1944), 24.

4663 _____. "Short Cut: How to Get a Big Navy Airplane Carrier Through the Locks of the Panama Canal." Collier's, CXII (November 27, 1943), 30+.

4664 _____. "Surprise Party." In: William H. Fetridge,
       ed. The Second Navy Reader. Indianapolis:
       Bobbs-Merrill, 1944. p. 71-77. Rpr. 1971.

4665 _____. "Surprise Party." Collier's, CXII (October
       30, 1943), 14+.
            The Marcus Island Raid.

4666 Morton, Louis. "Crisis in the Pacific." Military
       Review, XLVI (April 1966), 12-21.
            Facing the revised Japanese strategy beginning
       in September 1943.

4667 "Naval Task Force Movements Speeded Up by Plane
       Carriers." Aviation News, I (February 21, 1944),
       17-18.

4668 "Navy Wings Over the Pacific: Color Photographs."
       National Geographic, LXXXVI (August 1944), 241-
       249.

4669 "New Landings and Fleet Action Speed the War's Pace
       in the Pacific." Newsweek, XXII (November 15,
       1943), 30-31.

4670 "New Style Sea War." U.S. News, (December 22,
       1944), 19-21.
            Pacific amphibious assaults.

4671 "New U.S. Thrusts in the Pacific Aim at a Showdown
       with the Japs." Newsweek, XXII (November 22,
       1943), 21-23.

4672 Norris, John G. "Air Assault on Japan: A New
       Carrier Armada Prepares to Spearhead an All-Out
       Attack by Air, Sea, and Land." Flying, XXXIII
       (November 1943), 21-23+.

4673 "Oliver Jensen." CurrBio:VI:302-304.
            Active duty naval lieutenant in the Pacific and
       author of citations in this volume.

4674 "Our War Against Japan." Life, XVII (July 10, 1944),
       74-81.

4675 "Pacific Thrust Sets the Pattern and Problems of Attacks
       Ahead." Newsweek, XXII (July 12, 1943), 17-20.

4676 Polk, George. "Climb into the Cockpit with a Scout
      Pilot on Night Recon." Popular Science, CXLIV
      (March 1944), 49-51.

4677 Potter, Elmer B. "Beginning the Central Pacific
      Drive." In: his Sea Power: A Naval History.
      Englewood Cliffs, N. J.: Prentice-Hall, 1960.
      p. 734-757.

4678 Prat., William V. "Clues to the Strategy in the South
      Pacific." Newsweek, XXIII (January 3, 1944), 23.

4679 _____. "Dictator of the Route to the Philippines:
      Geography." Newsweek, XXIV (August 14, 1944),
      35.

4680 _____. "Lines of Our Pacific Strategy." Newsweek,
      XXII (October 18, 1943), 22.

4681 _____. "The Longest Front in the World: Our
      Pacific Operations." Newsweek, XXIV (July 10,
      1944), 34.

4682 _____. "MacArthur and Pacific Strategy." Newsweek,
      XXII (October 4, 1943), 24.

4683 _____. "Opening the Pacific Seas." Newsweek,
      XXIII (March 27, 1944), 28-29.

4684 _____. "Our Tactics in the Pacific." Newsweek,
      XXIII (May 15, 1944), 27.

4685 _____. "The Pacific: Mindanao a Logical Invasion
      Target." Newsweek, XXIV (July 31, 1944), 45.

4686 _____. "What Have We Got to Gain by Occupying
      Japan's Island Bases?" Newsweek, XXIII (June 5,
      1944), 27.

4687 Price, William. "The Case for Island Hopping."
      Asia, XLIV (February 1944), 63-67.

4688 _____. "Fear: Navy Ace Escapes Jap Fighters."
      Saturday Evening Post, CCXVII (August 12, 1944),
      11+.

4689 "The Raid on Wake." Flying, XXXIV (January 1944),
      28-29.

4690 "The Rapidly Expanding U.S. Navy Moves in Toward
        the Jap Homeland. " Newsweek, XXII (September
        13, 1943), 28-29.

4691 Reed, Philip G. , jt. author. See Bryan, Joseph,
        3rd, no. 4612.

4692 Roosevelt, Franklin D.   "Removing the Menace of
        Japan: Report on Pacific Trip, August 12, 1944. "
        Vital Speeches, X (September 1, 1944), 678-681.

4693 Rosenfarb, Joseph. "Strategy in the Pacific War."
        Antioch Review, III (June 1943), 283-297.

4694 Sciutti, W. J.   "The First Air Commando Group,
        August 1943-May 1944. " American Aviation His-
        torical Society Journal, XIII (Fall 1968), 178-185.

4695 Shaw, Henry I. , Jr. , et al. Central Pacific Drive.
        Vol. III of History of U.S. Marine Corps Opera-
        tions in World War II. Washington: Historical
        Branch, U.S. Marine Corps, 1966. 685p.

4696 "The Slow Way to Tokyo. " Time, XLII (November 8,
        1943), 24-25.

4697 Smith, Robert R.   The Approach to the Philippines.
        United States Army in World War II--The War
        in the Pacific. Washington: Office of the Chief
        of Military History, Department of the Army, 1953.
        623p.

4698 "Spearheading the Pacific Drive: The Marine Corps
        on the March. " U.S. News, (December 10, 1943),
        20-21.

4699 Strobridge, Truman R. , jt. author. See Garand,
        George W. , no. 4627.

4700 "Task Force, the Pick of the Fleet. " Popular Me-
        chanics, LXXX (December 1943), 56-59.

4701 Tinsley, Frank. "How the First Sea-Air Rescue was
        Made. " Popular Mechanics, LXXXII (July 1944),
        114-115.

4702 _____. "Tell What to the Marines?" Popular
        Science, CXLIV (May 1944), 96-97.

4703   Tolbert, Frank X. "Tarawa A Year Later." Leather-
       neck, XXVII (November 1944), 26-29.

4704   _____. "The War's Toughest Job: Overseas Opera-
       tions." Leatherneck, XXVI (April 1943), 18-19.

4705   _____. "Water Buffaloes." Leatherneck, XXVI (June
       1943), 15-17.

4706   "Twelve Months of Marine History." Leatherneck,
       XXVII (November 1944), 15-17.
       Those of 1943-1944.

4707   United States. Navy Department. Pacific Fleet and
       Pacific Ocean Area. Allied Minefields, Central
       Pacific. Cincpac-Cincpoa Bulletin 203-45. N. p.,
       1945.

4708   _____. _____. _____. Central Pacific, Western
       Section--Special Bulletin. Cincpac-Cincpoa Bulle-
       tin 37-44. N. p., 1944.
       An intelligence report.

4709   _____. _____. _____. Combat Regulations for Japa-
       nese Garrison Units. Cincpac-Cincpoa Bulletin
       115-44. N. p., 1944.

4710   _____. _____. _____. Data on Japanese Naval Air
       Groups. Special Translation No. 20. N. p., ca.
       1944.

4711   _____. _____. _____. Data on [Japanese] Special
       Naval Landing Forces. Special Translation No. 10.
       N. p., ca. 1944.

4712   _____. _____. _____. Enemy Air Facilities--Ap-
       proaches to Japan. Cincpac-Cincpoa Bulletin 54-
       44. N. p., 1944.
       An intelligence report.

4713   _____. _____. _____. Guide to Pacific Islands.
       Cincpac-Cincpoa Bulletin 48-43. N. p., 1943.

4714   _____. _____. _____. Enemy Positions--The Kuriles.
       Cincpac-Cincpoa Bulletin 38-43. N. p., 1943.
       An intelligence report.

4715 _____. _____. _____. Japanese Military Installations.
Cincpac-Cincpoa Bulletin 71-44.   N. p. , 1944.

4716 _____. _____. _____. Japanese Striking Force Tactics.   Know Your Enemy Series.   N. p. , 1944.
Supplement to Cincpac-Cincpoa Weekly Intelligence, Vol. I, no. 10.

4717 _____. _____. _____. Marcus Island Information Bulletin.   Cincpac-Cincpoa Bulletin 75-44.   N. p. ,
1944.

4718 _____. _____. _____. Marcus Target Analysis.
Cincpac-Cincpoa Bulletin 113-44.   N. p. , 1944.

4719 _____. _____. _____. Tables--Carolines and Marianas.   Cincpac-Cincpoa Bulletin 31-44.   N. p. ,
1944.
Part I   Tides
Part II   Daylight and darkness.

4720 _____. _____. _____. Tables: Marianas, Western
Carolines, and Certain of the Philippines.   Cinc-
pac-Cincpoa Bulletin 114-44.   N. p. , 1944.
Part I   Tides and Currents.
Part II   Daylight and dark.

4721 _____. _____. _____. Wake--Target Survey.   Cincpac-Cincpoa Bulletin 80-44.   N. p. , 1944.

4722 _____. _____. _____. "Preliminary Arrangements
for the Surrender of Japanese-Held Island of Yap,
Sorol, and Fauripik. " Unpublished paper, Naval
Forces File, U. S. Navy Department, Naval History
Division, Operational Archives, 1945.   11p.
These islands were by-passed when U. S. forces
took the Carolines.

4723 "Wake Island: Air Base Attacked by U. S. Navy. "
Illustrated London News, CCIII (November 20,
1943), 563.

4724 "War in the Pacific: Photographs. " Illustrated London News, CCIV (March 4, 18, 1944), 270-271,
328.

4725 Wolfert, Ira.   "From a South Pacific Notebook. "

American Mercury, LVIII (February 1944), 165-171.

4726 Yarnell, Harry E. "The War in the Western Pacific."
      Annals of the American Academy, CCXXVI (March
      1943), 62-72.

        Further References: Readers are reminded that
additional information relative to this section will be found
in sections IIA and IID-1 above, as well as in the general
works cited in Volume III, Part 1.

(2) ASSAULT ON THE GILBERTS

        Introduction. The Gilbert Islands, formerly part
of the British Gilbert and Ellice Islands Colony, lie northeast of the Solomons and south southwest of the Marshalls.
Composed of 16 atolls, this group was the first target of the
new American Central Pacific drive, it being impossible in
1943 to step directly from southern victories to the Marshalls.
For the purposes of invasion, the three most important islets,
north to south, were Makin, Tarawa, and Abemama.
        Before moving on here, it should be recalled that
American naval and air forces, often months before an
assault, were usually busy raiding. In this connection, one
of the most famous U.S. attacks of the war took place on
Makin in early August 1942--at the time of the Guadalcanal
landings. The two large submarines Nautilus and Argonaut
landed two companies of Marine Commandos, under Colonel
Evans F. Carlson, on August 16. Their plans to create a
massive diversion away from the Solomons soon ran afoul of
relatively attentive Japanese and the Marines were evacuated.
Although this raid gave the Allies a needed morale boost,
the Japanese set to work constructing formidable defenses in
the Gilberts, especially on Tarawa, which would take a heavy
toll later on. Another important raid was the September 18-
19, 1943, carrier raid on Marcus Island, which destroyed
many enemy planes and installations and served as on-the-
job training for the pilots of new carrier air groups then
joining the Pacific Fleet. All of these activities, especially
of 1943, left the Japanese a bit uncertain as to where exactly the next American assault would take place.
        It was first thought in some quarters that the in-
vasion of the Gilberts, known as "Operation Galvanic," would
not prove overly difficult. Unfortunately, the landings of

November 20-21, 1943, undertaken less than a month after
the start of the Bougainville campaign, would prove most
shocking. In many respects, this would be the American
Dieppe.
          Most of the interest in the Gilberts operation has
been focused on the bloody battle for Tarawa, or more
exactly, Betio Island. This little dot, less than one square
mile in size, was manned by 4500 Japanese defenders.
          Despite what many experts considered "shattering"
naval and air pre-landing bombardments, the 2nd Marine
Division found the going tough. Faulty intelligence saw the
troops going ashore when the tide was wrong, often across
great distances which the available landing craft could not
cover. Mines and beach obstacles, which in later campaigns
would be cleared by frogmen, presented considerable diffi-
culty. Communications were often broken. Amphibious
tractors did have success; however, the three battalions
which went ashore in the first wave found the Japanese pillboxes a deadly headache. Despite heavy casualties, Tarawa
was in American hands by November 24.
          The capture of Makin took almost a week. Here
poor training showed its ugly head as small pockets of
Japanese resistance were often able to halt or slow the
soldiers of the U.S. 27th Infantry Division. Despite a number of mishaps, the Yanks, who outnumbered their opponents
23-1, succeeded in securing the atol by November 23.
          Abemama, defended by 25 Japanese, was captured
by a small group of U.S. Marine scouts put ashore from the
submarine Nautilus--without the formality of pre-invasion
bombardment or even a regulation assault.
          Despite rather heavy casualties (3772 American),
the Gilberts taught the Allies many important lessons and
proved a training school as much as any installation in the
States. Learning from these mistakes, the Navy and ground
forces would make such changes as to have greater success
in later operations.

4727 "Amphibious Operation: The Story of Tarawa. "
          Leatherneck, XXVII (February 1944), 23-33.

4728 "The Attack on Tarawa. " Marine Corps Gazette,
          XXVIII (January 1944), 7-14.

4729 Bailey, S. Thomas. Tarawa. Derby, Conn.: Monarch
          Books, 1962. 155p.

4730 Baldwin, Hanson W. "The Bloody Epic that was
          Tarawa." New York Times Magazine, (November
          16-23, 1958), 19-21+, 19+.

4731 "The Battle of Tarawa." Newsweek, XXII (December
          6, 1943), 22-23.

4732 "The Battle of Tarawa Atoll." Illustrated London News,
          CCIV (January 8, 1944), 44-45.

4733 Burns, Eugene. "Butch O'Hare's Last Fight." Satur-
          day Evening Post, CCXVI (March 11, 1944), 19+.
          The famed navy carrier pilot and Medal of
          Honor winner was shot down over Tarawa.

4734 _____. _____. In: Norman Carlisle, ed. The Air
          Forces Reader. Indianapolis: Bobbs-Merrill,
          1944. p. 251-259.
          Reprinted from the Saturday Evening Post article
          cited above.

4735 "Dagger Thrust at Marcus." Time, XLII (September
          13, 1943), 31.
          As a warm-up for the Gilbert Islands invasion,
          a three-carrier task force hit the little place in
          early September.

4736 Emmons, Roger M. "Tarawa Bombardment."
          Marine Corps Gazette, XXXII (March 1948), 42-47.
          How naval vessels offshore supported the Marines
          in their landing.

4737 "The Fight for Tarawa." Life, XV (December 13,
          1943), 27-35.

4738 Graham, Garrett. "Tarawa." Marine Corps Gazette,
          XXVIII (April 1944), 29-33.

4739 Hale, Willis H. "U.S. Planes Bomb Nauru: Phos-
          phate Plant Destruction." Life, XV (July 5, 1943),
          120-122+.
          A target in the Gilberts hit on March 25, 1943.

4740 Hannah, Richard. Tarawa: The Toughest Battle in
          Marine Corps History. New York: Duell, Sloan
          and Pearce, 1944. 126p.
          Written by a combat correspondent and eyewit-
          ness.

4741 Johnston, Richard W. "Tarawa." In: Louis L.
      Snyder, ed. Masterpieces of War Reporting. New
      York: Julian Messner, 1962. p. 310-314.
      Reprinting of an account by an AP correspondent.

4742 Jonas, Carl. "My First Day on Tarawa." Saturday
      Evening Post, CCXVI (March 4, 1944), 22-23+.

4743 Jones, Edgar L. "Marooned on the Rock: What Has
      Happened to the Mechanics, Seabees, and Ground
      Force Left Behind [on Tarawa]." Atlantic Monthly,
      CLXXV (April 1945), 48-54.

4744 Karig, Walter. "The Makin Island Raid." USNIP,
      LXXII (1946), 1277-1282.

4745 Keys, Henry. "Conquest of Tarawa." USNIP, LXX
      (1944), 85-88.

4746 Leary, R. T. "Semper Paratus." USNIP, LXX
      (1944), 405-413.
      The capture of Tarawa.

4747 LeFrancois, Wilfred S. "We Mopped up Makin Island."
      Saturday Evening Post, CCXVI (December 4-11,
      1943), 20-21+, 28-29+.
      The adventures of the Second Marine Raider
      Battalion under Evans F. Carlson.

4748 Lucas, Jim G. "The Beach." In: Patrick O'Sheel
      and Gene Cook, eds. Semper Fidelis: The U.S.
      Marines in the Pacific, 1942-1945. New York:
      William Sloane Associates, 1947. p. 30-36.
      The naval bombardment and landing on Tarawa.

4749 McKiernan, Patrick. "Tarawa, the Tide That Failed."
      USNIP, LXXXVIII (1962), 38-50.

4750 "Makin Atoll." Infantry Journal, LIV (February 1944),
      19-21.

4751 Marlowe, W. H. "Taking Makin." Infantry Journal,
      LIV (June 1944), 28-30.

4752 Marshall, Samuel L. A. "Fight on Saki Night: An
      Episode in the Conquest of Makin." Infantry
      Journal, LIV (April 1944), 8-15.

4753   "The Men of Tarawa." New York Times Magazine,
            (December 12, 1943), 18-19.

4754   Metcalf, Clyde H.   "This was Tarawa." Marine
            Corps Gazette, XXVIII (May 1944), 45-48.

4755   Moore, Robert W.   "The Gilbert Islands in the Wake
            of Battle." National Geographic, LXXXVII (Febru-
            ary 1945), 129-162.

4756   _____. "Round About Grim Tarawa." National Geo-
            graphic, LXXVII (February 1945), 137-166.

4757   Nalty, Bernard C.   The United States Marines in the
            Gilberts Campaign.   Marine Corps Historical Ref-
            erence Series, no. 28.   Washington: Historical
            Branch, U.S. Marine Corps, 1961. 9p.

4758   "No Fun for the Airedales, Navy Airmen." Time,
            XLII (Sep'ember 20, 1943), 38.
            The Marcus Island Raid.

4759   Pest, Wendell H., jt. author. See Rixey, Presley M.,
            no. 4765.

4760   Pratt, William V.   "Lessons of the Tarawa Fighting."
            Newsweek, XXII (December 13, 1943), 37.

4761   _____. "The Significance of Our Seizure of the Gil-
            berts." Newsweek, XXII (December 6, 1943), 24.

4762   "Pulverizing Marcus: How Navy Fliers Accomplished
            It." Newsweek, XXII (September 20, 1943), 29-30.

4763   "Researched at Tarawa." Time, XLIII (February 14,
            1944), 26-28.

4764   Richardson, William. The Epic of Tarawa. London:
            Odhams Press, 1945. 96p.

4765   Rixey, Presley M. and Wendell H. Pest. "Artillery
            at Tarawa." Marine Corps Gazette, XXVIII
            (November 1944), 32-37.
                The performance of Marine cannoneers. Reprint-
            ed in Field Artillery Journal, XXXV (January 1945),
            3-6.

4766   "Scene of Epic Struggle of U.S. Marines with the

Japanese." Illustrated London News, CCIII (December 11, 1943), 658-659.
Tarawa.

4767 Shaw, Henry I., Jr. Tarawa: A Legend Is Born.
Ballantine's Illustrated History of World War II.
New York: Ballantine, 1970. 160p.

4768 Sherrod, Robert. "Report on Tarawa." Time, XLII
(December 6, 1943), 24-25.

4769 _____. "76 Frightful Hours of Tarawa." Saturday
Evening Post, CCXXVI (November 28, 1953), 24-
25+.

4770 _____. "Tarawa, the Second Day." Marine Corps
Gazette, LVII (November 1973), 38-47.

4771 _____. Tarawa: The Story of a Battle. New York:
Duell, Sloan, and Pearce, 1944. 183p.
Written from notes jotted down while assaulting
the beaches.

4772 Smith, Julian C. "Tarawa." USNIP, LXXIX (1953),
1163-1175.

4773 Stockman, James R. The Battle for Tarawa. Washington: Historical Section, Division of Public Information, U.S. Marine Corps, 1947. 86p.

4774 "Tarawa: The Marines Win New Glory in the Gilberts
and Prove There is no Cheap Way to Victory."
Life, XV (December 6, 1943), 36.

4775 "This Was Tarawa." Time, XLII (December 13, 1943),
24-25, 36.

4776 United States. Navy Department. Office of the Chief
of Naval Operations, Intelligence Division. "Combat Narrative: The Capture of the Gilberts." Unpublished paper, CNO-ONI File, U.S. Navy Department, Naval History Division, Operational Archives,
n.d. 75p.

4777 _____. _____. Pacific Fleet and Pacific Ocean Area.
Enemy Positions, Gilbert Islands, Ocean Island,
and Nauru. Cincpac-Cincpoa Bulletin 42-43. N.p.,
1943.

An intelligence report.

4778 ___. ___. ___. Enemy Positions, Gilbert-Mar-
shall Area. Cincpac-Cincpoa Bulletin 30-43. N. p.,
1943.
An intelligence report.

4779 ___. ___. ___. Japanese Forces in the Gilbert
Islands. Cincpac-Cincpoa Bulletin 8-44. N. p.,
1944.
An intelligence report.

4780 ___. ___. ___. A Photographic Analysis of
Beach and Reef Conditions, Makin Atoll. Cincpac-
Cincpoa Bulletin 18-44. N. p., 1944.

4781 ___. ___. ___. Standard Japanese Field Fortifications (Tarawa and Makin). Cincpac-Cincpoa
Miscellaneous Publications. N. p., n. d.

4782 ___. ___. ___. Study of Japanese Installations
on Butaritari Island, Makin Atoll. Cincpac-Cincpoa Bulletin 4-44. N. p., 1944.

4783 ___. ___. ___. A Study of the Japanese Defense of Betio Island, Tarawa Atoll. Cincpac-Cincpoa Miscellaneous Publications. N. p., n. d.

4784 ___. ___. ___. Tables: Funafuti, Nukufetan,
Tarawa, January 15, 1944. Cincpac-Cincpoa Bul-
letin 6-44. N. p., 1944.
Part I   Tides.
Part II   Daylight and darkness.

4785 ___. War Department. Historical Division. The
Capture of Makin (20-24 November 1943). Ameri-
can Forces in Action Series, no. 10. Washington:
U. S. Government Printing Office, 1946. 136p.

4786 Werstein, Irving. Tarawa: A Battle Report. New
York: Crowell, 1965. 146p.

4787 Wertenbaker, Green P. "Appointment in Tarawa."
New Yorker, XIX (February 12, 1944), 52+.

4788 "Where U. S. Marines Won a Great Victory." Illustrated London News, CCIII (December 18, 1943), 676.
Tarawa.

4789   Wilson, Earl J., et al.   Betio Beachhead: The U.S.
       Marines' Own Story of the Battle for Tarawa.
       New York: Putnam, 1945.   160p.

       Further References: Readers are reminded that
additional information relative to this section will be found
in sections IIA and IID-1 above, as well as in the general
works cited in Volume III, Part 1.

                (3) TAKING THE MARSHALLS

       Introduction.   The Marshall Islands, a group of 32
atolls and hundreds of reefs, lies north northwest of the Gilberts and east of the Carolines.   Plans for conquering this
territory, "Operation Flintlock," were in the hopper even
before the invasion of the Gilberts.
       Also included within this section are details on
certain operations in the Caroline Islands, that group east of
the Philippines, which were "hopped" by the Americans.
The huge Japanese naval base at Truk, seen as a large road-
block, was taken out by massive raids from American carrier planes on February 16 and 17, 1944.   Fortunately for
the Japanese, they had moved most of their fleet out of the
40-mile-long lagoon anchorage a few days earlier.   Other
air raids were also aimed at the base and by late spring it
was no longer a problem to the Allies.   The U.S. Navy
established a large base of its own at nearby Ulithi and Yap,
another atoll in the chain, was also heavily bombed.   The
Palaus, which some consider part of this group, were invaded by the Yanks, which action is presented in section
IID-5 below.
       From mid-November 1943, American air forces
kept up rather constant raiding on the islands of the Marshalls,
especially Maloelap and Wotje.   But when it was time to go,
they elected to by-pass those heavily fortified areas and in a
classic of island-hopping, concentrated on Kwajalein, the
world's largest coral atoll, and Eniwetok.
       Heeding the lessons learned in the Gilberts, Gener-
al Holland M. Smith's invaders, the 5th Marine Corps, was
given better pre-landing bombardment and additional landing
craft, especially the tractor variety, so that more men could
be put ashore initially.   On January 29, the naval bombardment let fly every shell available and planes bombed constant-
ly.   On January 31, 1944, after two days of this, the U.S.

7th Division landed in the southern section of the atoll while
the northern islands, Roi-Namur, were assaulted by the 4th
Marine Division.

Despite some confusion, the Marines had Roi-Namur in hand within 27 hours. On Kwajalein the landings had
gone almost flawlessly. Resistance there continued through
the first week of February. A report on the action made
to General George Marshall comments that the island was
the scene of great devastation: "With the exception of rubble
left by concrete structures, there were no buildings standing." Majuro anchorage was also seized on January 31.
Smith's people had learned their lessons well.

Pushing on ahead of schedule, the 22nd Regiment,
U.S.M.C., and a combat team from the 27th Infantry Division were landed on Eniwetok, following a two-day naval and
air bombardment. It too came firmly into American hands
by February 22.

The heavily fortified Japanese bases at Wotje,
Maloelap, Mili, and Jaluit were not invaded, but rather left
to "wither on the vine." Cut-off from reinforcement, they
soon were left in a backwater, important only as practice
targets for newly arrived American aviators.

4790 "Action in the Marshalls." Time, XXXIX (February
        23, 1942), 21-22.

4791 "The Battle of Kwajalein." Newsweek, XXIII (Febru-
        ary 14, 1944), 22-26.

4792 "Battle of the Pacific." Time, XLIII (February 7,
        1944), 18-19.
        The Marshall Islands campaign.

4793 Bishop, John. "The Battle of the Drains: Roi and
        Namur Islands." Saturday Evening Post, CCXVI
        (June 8, 1944), 20-21+.
        Outposts in the Marshall Islands.

4794 Crown, John A., jt. author. See Heinl, Robert D.,
        Jr., no. 4797.

4795 "Four Coast Guardsmen Capture Nine Japs." U.S.
        Coast Guard Academy Alumni Association Bulletin,
        VI (April 1944), 17.
        During the invasion of Roi-Namur, near Kwaja-
        lein.

4796 Germano, Peter B.   "Behind the Lines." In: Patrick
      O'Sheel and Gene Cook, eds. Semper Fidelis:
      The U.S. Marines in the Pacific, 1942-1945. New
      York: William Sloane Associates, 1945. p. 119-
      121.
      Marine aviation in the Marshall Islands campaign.

4797 Heinl, Robert D., Jr. and John A. Crown. The Mar-
      shalls: Increasing the Tempo. Washington: His-
      torical Branch, U.S. Marine Corps, 1954. 188p.

4798 Jones, George E.   "Airpower and Gunnery: The Bat-
      tle of Truk." Harper's Magazine, CLXXXIX (June
      1944), 36-43.

4799 "The Lesson of Kwajalein." Newsweek, XXIII (Feb-
      ruary 21, 1944), 26-28.

4800 McMillan, I. E. "Naval Gunfire at Roi-Namur."
      Marine Corps Gazette, XXXII (July 1948), 50-55.

4801 Marshall, Samuel L. A.   "The After-Action Interview--
      the Kwajalein Experience." Army, XVI (Septem-
      ber 1966), 58-61.

4802 _____. Island Victory: The Battle of Kwajalein
      Atoll. Washington: Infantry Journal Press, 1945.
      117p.
      Based on interviews with American participants
      in the battle, primarily those in the Army's 7th
      Division.

4803 "Marshall Islands Invaded." USNIP, LXX (1944), 346-
      347.
      Reprinted from the February 2-3, 1944 issues
      of the New York Herald Tribune.

4804 Nalty, Bernard C. The United States Marines in the
      Marshalls Campaign. Marine Corps Historical
      Reference Series, no. 31. Washington: Historical
      Branch, U.S. Marine Corps, 1962. 9p.

4805 Nimitz, Chester W.   "Attack on Truk Island." USNIP,
      LXX (1944), 462-463.

4806 "Pacific War: The Successful Raid on Truk, Japan's
      Naval Base." Illustrated London News, CCIV
      (April 1, 1944), 381.

4807 "Pacific War: The U.S. Conquest of the Marshall
       Islands and the Successful Raid on Truk." Illustrat-
       ed London News, CCIV (April 1, 1944), 380-381.

4808 "Softening the Marshalls: 160 Sq. Miles of Sand,
       Coral, and Coconut Palms." Time, XLII (Decem-
       ber 27, 1943), 25-27.

4809 "Truk Severely Bombed." Illustrated London News,
       CCIV (February 26, 1944), 235.

4810 United States. Navy Department. Office of the Chief
       of Naval Operations, Intelligence Division. "Com-
       bat Narrative: The Assault on Kwajalein and Ma-
       juro." Unpublished paper, CNO-ONI File, U.S.
       Navy Department, Naval History Division, Opera-
       tional Archives, 1943. 92p.

4811 _____. _____. Pacific Fleet and Pacific Ocean Area.
       Dublon-Eten Islands--Information Bulletin. Cincpac-
       Cincpoa Bulletin 47-44. N.p., 1944.
           An intelligence report on two islands in the Truk
       group of the Central Carolines raided but bypassed
       by the advancing Americans.

4812 _____. _____. _____. Enemy Positions, Caroline
       Islands. Cincpac-Cincpoa Bulletin 33-43. N.p.,
       1943.
           An intelligence report.

4813 _____. _____. _____. Enemy Positions, Marshall
       Islands. Cincpac-Cincpoa Bulletin 43-43. N.p.,
       1943.
           An intelligence report.

4814 _____. _____. _____. Eniwetok Information Bulletin.
       Cincpac-Cincpoa Bulletin 3-44. N.p., 1944.
           An intelligence report on one of the Marshall
       Islands captured by the Americans, February 17-22,
       1944 and made into a naval base.

4815 _____. _____. _____. Information Bulletin on Moen,
       Param Tol, and Minor Islands. Cincpac-Cincpoa
       Bulletin 51-44. N.p., 1944.
           An intelligence report on islands in the Carolines.

4816 _____. _____. _____. Information Bulletin on the

Minor Carolines.   Cincpac-Cincpoa Bulletin 53-44.
N. p. ,   1944.

4817 _____ . _____ . _____ .   Information Bulletin-Truk.
Cincpac-Cincpoa Bulletin 22-44.   N. p. ,   1944.
An intelligence report on the important Japanese
base in the central Carolines which was often
bombed but not attacked by the "island-hopping"
Americans.

4818 _____ . _____ . _____ .   Information Bulletin--Yap.
Cincpac-Cincpoa Bulletin 65-44.   N. p. ,   1944.
An intelligence report on an island in the west-
ern Carolines.

4819 _____ . _____ . _____ .   Jaluit Information Bulletin.
Cincpac-Cincpoa Bulletin 56-43.   N. p. ,   1943.
An intelligence report on the largest of the
Marshall Islands, which was subsequently "hopped"
in favor of the invasion of Kwajalein.

4820 _____ . _____ . _____ .   The Japanese Defense of
Eniwetok.   Cincpac-Cincpoa Bulletin 89-44.   N. p. ,
1944.

4821 _____ . _____ . _____ .   Japanese Defenses--Kwajalein
Atoll.   Cincpac-Cincpoa Bulletin 48-44.   N. p. ,
1944.

4822 _____ . _____ . _____ .   Kusaie Information Bulletin.
Cincpac-Cincpoa Bulletin 60-43.   N. p. ,   1943.
An intelligence report on one of the "hopped"
Caroline Islands.

4823 _____ . _____ . _____ .   Kwajalein Information Bulletin.
Cincpac-Cincpoa Bulletin 53-43.   N. p. ,   1943.
An intelligence report.

4824 _____ . _____ . _____ .   Lesser Marshalls Information
Bulletin.   Cincpac-Cincpoa Bulletin 58-43.   N. p. ,
1943.
An intelligence report.

4825 _____ . _____ . _____ .   Maloelap Information Bulletin.
Cincpac-Cincpoa Bulletin 52-43.   N. p. ,   1943.
One of five Japanese air bases in the eastern
Marshalls which was raided by the U. S. fleet,

1942-1943, but bypassed in the advance towards Japan.

4826   .   .   .   Mille Information Bulletin.
Cincpac-Cincpoa Bulletin 50-43. N. p. , 1943.
An intelligence report on Mili Atoll, one of the Marshall Islands.

4827   .   .   .   Nomoi Information Bulletin.
Cincpac-Cincpoa Bulletin 5-44. N. p. , 1944.
An intelligence report on an atoll group in the southern Carolines.

4828   .   .   .   Ponape Information Bulletin.
Cincpac-Cincpoa Bulletin 27-44. N. p. , 1944.
An intelligence report on an island in the eastern Carolines originally known as Ascension Island.
Its garrison of 10, 000 Japanese troops was bypassed and cut-off by the advancing Americans.

4829   .   .   .   Special Bulletin--Truk, February 3, 1944. Cincpac-Cincpoa Bulletin 11-44.
N. p. , 1944.

4830   .   .   .   Tides and Currents, Major Marshalls. Cincpac-Cincpoa Bulletin 69-43. N. p. , 1943.

4831   .   .   .   Truk Informational Bulletin.
Cincpac-Cincpoa Bulletin 41-44. N. p. , 1944.

4832   .   .   .   Ujelang Information Bulletin, Feb. 3, 1944. Cincpac-Cincpoa Bulletin 10-44.
Intelligence report on an atoll in the Marshall Islands.

4833   .   .   .   Woleai Information Bulletin.
Cincpac-Cincpoa Bulletin 36-44. N. p. , 1944.
An intelligence report on an atoll in the western Carolines which was attacked by a U. S. task force on March 31, 1944 with heavy destruction of Japanese shipping.

4834   .   .   .   Wotje Information Bulletin.
Cincpac-Cincpoa Bulletin 57-43. N. p. , 1943.
An intelligence report on another of the Marshall Islands bypassed by the advancing Americans.

4835 ___.   ___.   ___.   Yap Information Bulletin.
         Cincpac-Cincpoa Bulletin 123-44.   N. p. , 1944.

4836 ___.   ___.   ___.   Yap--Place Names.   Cincpac-
         Cincpoa Bulletin 137-44.   N. p. , 1944.

4837 "Victory in the Marshalls. "   Infantry Journal, LIV
         (April 1944), 26-29.

4838 Wead, Frank W.   "We Plaster the Japs. "   American
         Magazine, CXXXVIII (September 1944), 40-41+.
         The Battle of Truk.

4839 Wilcox, Richard.   "The Battle of Eniwetok Atoll. "
         Life, XVI (March 13, 1944), 21-25.

4840 ___.   "Kwajalein. "   Life, XVI (February 21, 1944),
         34-37.

4841 Yeowart, Robert.   "Truk Reconnaissance. "   Flying,
         XXXIV (May 1944), 50+.

Further References: Readers are reminded
that additional data relative to this section will be found in
sections IIA and IID-1 above, as well as in the general works
cited in Volume III, Part 1.

(4) ACTION IN THE MARIANAS

Introduction.   The 700-mile advance to the Mar-
shalls, plus the 400-mile hop to Eniwetok, would be followed
by an even more ambitious leap of some 1200 miles to the
Marianas Islands.   This group lies about 1500 miles east of
the Philippines and start an almost continuous chain stretch-
ing up through the Bonin and Volcano Islands to Japan.
Branching off, one could travel via the Palau group to the
Philippines.   Foremost on the agenda for this "Operation
Forager" would be the recapture of Guam and the seizure of
Saipan and Tinian.   Once in hand, the Marianas would be
bulldozed into air bases from which the new B-29's could
bomb Japan.
         The Marianas campaign was the largest thus far
seen in the Central Pacific; the Gilberts and Marshalls were
mere warm-ups by comparison.   Over 600 U. S. Navy vessels

under Admirals Spruance and Turner brought over 300,000
naval, marine, and army personnel in for the fight.   Well
over 50,000 Japanese defenders were present on the three
islands mentioned above.

As in the other campaigns so far discussed, the
islands of the Marianas were subject to massive-pre-invasion
raids and bombardments.   Beginning in early June, U.S.A.A.F.
bombers raided deep into that area and the Carolines, as
did the fast battleships and carriers of Vice Admiral Marc
Mitscher's Fifth Fleet.   On June 11, a week after the Nor-
mandy invasion, carrier planes opened the assault by destroying over 100 planes off Saipan and sinking large parts
of two Japanese convoys.

Four days later on June 15, following a powerful
bombardment, General Holland Smith's Marines and GI's
stormed ashore on Saipan.   From that day through the official announcement of victory on July 9, the Americans
fought a doggedly determined enemy on both level and
mountainous land studded with dangerous defenses and caves.
In many instances, the Japanese let themselves be killed by
flamethrowers rather than fall back or surrender.   The capture of Mt. Tapotchan was one of the most difficult objectives
of the operation and later led to bitter controversy in American circles as to whether U.S. Army forces involved had
been overly cautious.

Japanese propaganda as to the results to be expected from an American victory led to one of the sadder episodes of the war.   On Marpi, Saipan's northern point, whole
families drowned themselves or killed themselves with gre-
nades.   Infants were thrown from high cliffs and little child-
ren obeyed orders to blow themselves up with explosives.
Over 800 of these native civilians were thus uselessly elimi-
nated.

After the fall of Mt. Tapotchan and the capture of
the capital city of Garapan, the desperate situation of the
defenders led to one last banzai or hurrah charge on July 7.
Over 3000 suicide-minded enemy soldiers were annihilated.
Overall American casualties in the Saipan conquest were over
3300 killed; the Japanese lost over 40,000 men.

Meanwhile the Imperial Navy, determined to prevent their opponent from gaining further advantage, sent
forth a large part of its remaining carrier fleet to open the
Battle of the Philippine Sea on June 19.   In the two-day
fight, the second most important naval engagement of the
Pacific war after Midway, Japan lost over 400 planes ("The
Great Marianas Turkey Shoot"), two carriers, a pair of
destroyers, and a tanker sunk plus a number of other ships

damaged.   This engagement marked the effective finish of
Japanese naval aviation.   Following this great battle, American forces, acting to prevent further reinforcement, carried
out a number of raids in late June and early July on targets
in the Bonins and Volcano Islands.

After the Saipan win, American forces were loosed
on Guam.   Following air raids which delivered up complete
control of the air, Major General Roy S. Geiger's Marines
and Infantry went ashore on July 21.   As these troops went
inland they here too ran into ferocious resistance.   Taking
heavy losses, the Yanks captured Apra harbor, the Orote
Peninsula, and Agana, the capital city.   Able to obtain more
supplies via these secure areas, the ground forces pushed
across the island to the east coast and thence northward to
the tip of the island.   Organized resistance ceased on August
10.   Few of the 18,500 Japanese defenders survived while
nearly 2000 American Marines and soldiers paid the full
price.

After 13 days of rest, the 2nd and 4th Marine
Divisions from Saipan crossed the four-mile channel to
Tinian on July 24.   Surprised, the Japanese attempted to
evacuate the island by small boat, but were turned back by
American warships.   Surrounded on all sides, the enemy
then dug in and made another last ditch stand.   It lasted
for nine days before the victors, at the cost of 416 killed,
were able to overcome it.

The loss of the Marianas was a severe blow to
Tokyo; in fact, the Tojo regime was forced out of office.
Communications were to a large extent cut with the so-called
Southern Resources Area and the Emperor himself could see
the handwriting on the wall.   The Imperial Navy, while still
quite powerful in surface vessels, was no longer much of a
threat in the air--if one thinks in terms of conventional warfare and not kamikazes--and the Americans had gained those
new bomber bases from which to begin a strategic bombing
campaign.

Perhaps unseen in some quarters, Japan served
notice as best she could via the last ditch stands in the
Marianas that from here on out the fighting in this theater
would become utterly savage.   Unwilling to surrender, her
leaders would sacrifice thousands upon thousands of lives
yet in a desperate attempt to stave off defeat.

4842   Adamson, Hane C., jt. author.   See Lockwood,
          Charles A., no. 4867.

4842a Bemis, John A., jt. author. See Del Valle, Pedro
      A., no. 4849.

4842b "The Big Blow--Philippine Sea, 1944." All Hands,
      no. 542, (March 1962), 59-63.

4843 "Bloody Saipan." Newsweek, XXIV (July 24, 1944),
      37.

4843a Burns, Eugene. "We Avenge Pearl Harbor." Satur-
      day Evening Post, CCXVII (July 22, 1944), 18-19+.

4843b Clark, Joseph. "The Marianas Turkey Shoot." Amer-
      ican Heritage, XVIII (October 1967), 26-29+.
         This excerpt from the author's memoirs recalls
      the First Battle of the Philippine Sea.

4844 Crossley, R. P. "Damn the Submarines! Turn on
      the Lights." Popular Mechanics, CXXXI (June
      1969), 111-115+.
         The decision to light up American carriers for
      the benefit of flyers returning from the Battle of
      the Philippine Sea.

4844a Crowl, Philip A. Campaign in the Marianas. United
      States Army in World War II--The War in the
      Pacific. Washington: Office of the Chief of Mili-
      tary History, U.S. Army, 1960. 505p.
         Action on Saipan, Tinian, and Guam with appro-
      priate data on cooperation with the Navy and
      Marines.

4844b Danton, J. Periam. "The Battle of the Philippine
      Sea." USNIP, LXXI (1945), 1023-1027.

4845 Daying, George. "Thirty Days on the Line." Leather-
      neck, XXVII (December 1944), 18-20.

4845a _____. "War on Japan's Doorstep: The Battle for
      Saipan." Leatherneck, XXVII (September 1944),
      15-19.

4846 "Deadlier than Volcanoes: The Battle for Saipan Is-
      land." Newsweek, XXIV (July 10, 1944), 38.

4847 Dempsey, David. "Green Troops on a Blue Beach."
      In: Patrick O'Sheel and Gene Cook, eds. Semper

Fidelis: The U.S. Marines in the Pacific, 1942-
1945. New York: William Sloane Associates,
1947. p. 46-53.
   Originally published in the Antioch Review, this
piece concerns the invasion of Saipan.

4848 De Valle, Pedro A.   "Massed Fire on the Island of
      Guam." Marine Corps Gazette, XXVIII (December
      1944), 19.

4849 _____, and John A. Bemis.   "Sea Island Serenade:
      The Recapture of Guam." Field Artillery Journal,
      XXXIV (December 1944), 803-806.

4850 Doying, George.   "The Buck Rogers Men." Leather-
      neck, XXVIII (April 1945), 27-29.
         The use of rocket launchers on Saipan and
      Tinian.

4851 Draper, William F.   "Victory's Portrait in the
      Marianas." National Geographic, LXXXVIII (No-
      vember 1945), 599-616.
         Written by a naval reserve lieutenant.

4852 Frances, Anthony A.   "The Battle For Banzai Ridge."
      Marine Corps Gazette, XXIX (June 1945), passim.
         Guam.

4853 Goe, William. Is War Hell? Los Angeles, 1947.
         Privately printed memoirs of a Marine chaplain
      who saw action on Saipan.

4854 "Guam and Tinian: The Pre-landing Bombardment."
      Newsweek, XXIV (July 31, 1944), 40-41.

4855 Haffert, William A.   "This was Saipan." U.S. Coast
      Magazine, XVIII (December 1944), 38.

4856 Hammer, D. Harry.   "Lion Six." USNIP, LXXIII
      (1947), 273-277.
         The taking of Guam.

4857 Hilton, Robert M.   "We Landed at Saipan." U.S.
      Coast Guard Academy Alumni Association Bulletin,
      VI (October 1944), 143.

4858 Hockmuth, Bruno A.   "Observations on Saipan."

Marine Corps Gazette, XXIX (September 1945),
passim.

4859 Hoffman, Carl W. Saipan: The Beginning of the End.
Washington: Historical Division, U.S. Marine
Corps, 1950. 286p.

4860 _____. The Seizure of Tinian. Washington: Historical Division, U.S. Marine Corps, 1951. 169p.

4861 Josephy, Alvin M., Jr. "Master Gunnery Sergeant."
In: Patrick O'Sheel and Gene Cook, eds. Semper
Fidelis: The U.S. Marines in the Pacific, 1942-
1945. New York: William Sloane Associates,
1947. p. 188-190.
Israel Margolis in the battle for the reconquest
of Guam.

4862 _____. "Routine Mission." In: Patrick O'Sheel and
Gene Cook, eds. Semper Fidelis: The U.S.
Marines in the Pacific, 1942-1945. New York:
William Sloane Associates, 1947. p. 56-62.
Action during the American recapture of Guam.

4863 _____. "Some Japs Surrendered." In: Patrick
O'Sheel and Gene Cook, eds. Semper Fidelis:
The U.S. Marines in the Pacific, 1942-1945. New
York: William Sloane Associates, 1947. p. 227-
239.
Fighting on Guam.

4864 _____. "They Lived Through Hell." In: Patrick
O'Sheel and Gene Cook, eds. Semper Fidelis:
The U.S. Marines in the Pacific, 1942-1945. New
York: William Sloane Associates, 1947. p. 62-74.
Further action during the battle for Guam.

4865 Kaufman, Millard. "The Attack on Guam." Marine
Corps Gazette, XXIX (April 1945), passim.

4866 Land, William G. and Adrian O. Van Wyen. "Naval
Air Operations in the Marianas." Unpublished
paper, Individual Personnel File, U.S. Navy Department, Naval History Division, Operational
Archives, 1945. 165p.

4867 Lockwood, Charles A. and Hans C. Adamson. Battles

of the Philippine Sea. New York: Crowell, 1967.
229p.
     Readers should note the new article by Command-
er T. B. Buell, "The Battle of the Philippine Sea,"
in USNIP, C (1974), 64-84, which is based on his
1974 The Quiet Warrior: A Biography of Admiral
Raymond A. Spruance, published by the Boston
firm of Little, Brown.

4868 Lodge, O. R. The Recapture of Guam. Washington:
      Historical Branch, U.S. Marine Corps, 1954.
      214p.

4869 Love, Edmund G. "The 27th's Battle for Saipan."
      Infantry Journal, LIX (September 1946), 8-17.

4870 Lucas, Jim G. "After the Battle." In: Patrick
      O'Sheel and Gene Cook, eds. Semper Fidelis:
      The U.S. Marines in the Pacific, 1942-1945. New
      York: William Sloane Associates, 1947. p. 53-56.
      An account of action on Saipan which was
      originally published in the American Magazine.

4871 McMillan, George E. "One Step Short of Tokyo:
      Guam." Popular Mechanics, LXXXIV (November
      1945), 43-46+.

4872 McMillan, I. E. "Naval Gunfire at Guam." Marine
      Corps Gazette, XXXII (September 1948), 52-56.

4873 Metzger, Louis, jt. author. See Umezawa, Haruo, no.
      4897.

4874 Miller, Thomas G., Jr. "Anatomy of an Air Battle."
      American Aviation Historical Society Journal, XV
      (Summer 1970), 115-120.
      The battle for the Marianas. First presented
      in a paper before the 5th Annual Northeast Aero
      Historians Meeting, Old Rhineback Airport, on
      October 10, 1969.

4875 Moore, W. Robert. "South from Saipan." National
      Geographic, LXXXVII (April 1945), 441-474.

4876 Morris, Frank D. "The Battle at Saipan." Collier's,
      CXIV (August 13, 1944), 16+.

4877 Morton, Louis. "The Marianas." Military Review,
      XLVII (July 1967), 71-82.

4878 "The Most Ambitious Amphibious Operation Yet At-
      tempted in the Pacific." Illustrated London News,
      CCV (July 15, 1944), 76-77.
      Saipan.

4879 Pratt, William V. "Out From Hiding: Jap Strategy
      at Saipan." Newsweek, XXIV (July 3, 1944), 26.

4880 _____. "Prize of the Marianas: Guam Important to
      Our Strategy." Newsweek, XXIV (July 24, 1944),
      34.

4881 Price, Willard D. "Springboard to Tokyo." National
      Geographic, LXXXVI (October 1944), 385-407.
      The Marianas.

4882 "Return to Guam." Time, XLIV (July 31, 1944), 25.

4883 Rowcliff, Gilbert J. "Guam." USNIP, LXXI (1945),
      781-793.

4884 Rust, Kenneth C. "They [Japanese planes] Fell Like
      Flies." RAF Flying Review, XVI (July 1961),
      30-32.

4885 Schmidt, R. K. "The Tinian Operation: A Study in
      Planning For an Amphibious Operation." Unpub-
      lished paper, Senior Course, Amphibious Warfare
      School, Marine Corps Schools, Quantico, Va., 1949.

4886 Sherrod, Robert. "Battalion on Saipan." Marine
      Corps Gazette, XXVIII (October 1944), 10.

4887 _____. "Beachhead in the Marianas." Time,
      XLIV (July 3, 1944), 32.
      Saipan.

4888 _____. "Saipan: An Eyewitness Tells of the Island
      Fight." Life, XVII (August 28, 1944), 75-83.

4889 Smith, H. E. "I Saw the Morning Break." USNIP,
      LXXII (1946), 403-415.
      The 1944 battle for Guam.

4890   "Stewed and Blued: The Jap Fleet Spurns the Bait Off
       Saipan." Newsweek, XXIV (July 3, 1944), 24-26.

4891   Stockman, James R.   "The Taking of Mt. Tapotchau."
       Marine Corps Gazette, XXX (July 1947), 15+.
       Saipan.

4892   Stott, Frederic A. Saipan Under Fire. Andover,
       Mass., 1945. 13p.
       Concerns the First Battalion, 24th Marines of
       the Fourth Marine Division during the campaign,
       June 15-July 12, 1944.

4893   "Task Force 58: The U.S. Navy's Great Cruise to
       Break the Japanese Power in the Marianas." Life,
       XVII (July 17, 1944), 17-24+.

4894   Thomason, John W., 3rd.   "The Fourth Marine Divi-
       sion at Tinian." Marine Corps Gazette, XXIX
       (January 1945), passim.

4895   "To the Victor: The Bases." Time, XLIV (July 17,
       1944), 28-29.
       The Battles for the Marianas.

4896   Turner, Gordon B.   "The Amphibious Complex: A
       Study of Operations at Saipan." Unpublished PhD
       Dissertation, Princeton University, 1950.

4897   Umezawa, Haruo and Louis Metzger.   "The Defense of
       Guam." Marine Corps Gazette, XLVIII (August
       1964), 36-43.

4898   United States. Navy Department. Office of the Chief
       of Naval Operations. "The Invasion of the Marianas,
       June to August 1944." Unpublished paper P-007,
       CNO File, U.S. Navy Department, Naval History
       Division, Operational Archives, 1944.
       A useful synthesis of action reports on the
       Saipan, Tinian, and Guam operations.

4899   _____.   _____.   _____. Intelligence Division.   "Combat
       Narrative: The Conquest of Saipan." Unpublished
       paper, U.S. Navy Department, Naval History Divi-
       sion, Operational Archives, n.d.   65p.

4900   _____.   _____.   Pacific Fleet and Pacific Ocean Area.

AA Defense of Saipan. Special Translation No. 39.
N. p. , ca. 1944.

4901 _____. _____. _____. Information Bulletin, Marianas,
January 25, 1944. Cincpac-Cincpoa Bulletin 7-44.
N. p. , 1944.

4902 _____. _____. _____. Information Bulletin on Guam.
Cincpac-Cincpoa Bulletin 52-44. N. p. , 1944.

4903 _____. _____. _____. Marianas, less Saipan, Infor-
mation Bulletin. Cincpac-Cincpoa Bulletin 42-44.
N. p. , 1944.
An intelligence report.

4904 _____. _____. _____. Saipan, Tinian and Rota Infor-
mation Bulletin. Cincpac-Cincpoa Bulletin 34-44.
N. p. , 1944.
An intelligence report.

4905 _____. _____. _____. Saipan, Tinian, Rota Informa-
tion Bulletin. Cincpac-Cincpoa Bulletin 73-44.
N. p. , 1944.
An intelligence report.

4906 _____. _____. _____. Saipan Shipping Schedule for
1943. Special Translation No. 6. N. p. , ca.
1943.

4907 _____. _____. _____. Saipan Target Analysis Bulletin. Cincpac-Cincpoa Bulletin 66-44. N. p. , 1944.

4908 _____. _____. _____. Special Bulletin--Guam, Yap,
Ulithi, Saipan, and Tinian, February 28, 1944.
Cincpac-Cincpoa Bulletin 30-44. N. p. , 1944.
An intelligence report.

4909 [No entry.]

4910 _____. _____. _____. Tinian--Target Analysis Bulletin. Cincpac-Cincpoa Bulletin 67-44. N. p. ,
1944.

4911 _____. _____. _____. Commander Fifth Fleet.
"Final Report on the Operation to Capture the
Marianas Islands. " Unpublished paper, U.S. Navy
Department, Naval History Division, Operational
Archives, August 30, 1944.

A copy of this study is also available in the
files of the Historical Division, U.S. Marine Corps.

4912 _____. War Department. Historical Division. Guam:
Operations of the 27th Division (21 July-10 August
1944). American Forces in Action Series, no. 9.
Washington: U.S. Government Printing Office,
1946. 136p.

4913 Van Wyen, Adrian O. "The Battle of the Philippine
Sea." USNIP, LXXVII (1951), 156-159.

4914 _____., jt. author. See Land, William G., no. 4866.

4915 Williams, J. A. "Guam." All Hands, no. 513,
(October 1959), 49.

4916 Winston, Robert A. "How Our Navy Outfoxed the
Japs at Saipan." Saturday Evening Post, CCXVII
(September 23, 1944), 19+.

4917 "Worth the Price?" Strategic Saipan a Tough Nut for
the U.S. Navy Pushing East. Newsweek, XXIII
(June 26, 1944), 38.

4918 Zimmerman, Sherwood R. "Operation Forager."
USNIP, XC (August 1964), 78-90.
Comment on this account of the Battle of the
Philippine Sea was prepared by RAdm. Charles J.
Moore, USN (Ret.) and Joseph D. Harrington and
appeared in the same journal, p. 113-114.

4919 Zurlinden, Cyril P. "Prelude to Saipan: 15 June,
1944." USNIP, LXXIII (1947), 581-584.

Further References: Readers will find additional
information relative to this section in sections IIA and IID-1
above, as well as in the general works cited in Volume III,
Part 1.

(5) THE PALAUS

Introduction. Following the capture of the Marianas,
two options were open to the advancing Americans in the

Central Pacific: they could move via the Volcano Islands and the Bonins straight north towards Japan or they could swing west-southwest to the Palaus and having secured them, join MacArthur's drive on the Philippines coming up from the New Guinea area.   The latter was elected.

The invasion of the Palau Islands, western outposts in the Carolines, and of the Molucca Islands can be viewed as both the concluding steps in the "dual advance to the Philippines" and as preliminaries to the actual assault on the Filipino republic.   No matter how one looks at these operations one thing was clear: when the Allies came to the Philippines, the Palaus would be useful for protection of the left flank of any invasion.

The Palau Islands consist of 7 large and 20 little islands.   To take them was assigned Admiral William F. Halsey's Third Fleet of over 800 vessels (when Admiral Halsey commanded the Central Pacific Fleet, it was known as the Third Fleet; when he retired for planning and exercises, Admiral Spruance took over and the unit's name was changed to the Fifth Fleet).   Many of these ships and smaller craft were newly commissioned from mainland shipyards.   The Third Fleet transported over 30,000 Marines and GI's under Major General Julian C. Smith, U.S.M.C.   Prior to the actual landings, Marc Mitscher's carrier pilots conducted numerous raids to knock out any Japanese planes in the area.   From August 31 through September 2, 1944, these swooped down on Chichi Jima, Haha Jima, and Iwo Jima, destroying 46 planes and six ships.   Yap was hit on September 7 and 8.   The actual pre-invasion air campaign for the Palaus began on September 6 and lasted through September 15; targets included Mindanao Island in the southern Philippines, the Visayas, the Celebes, and Talaud.

The landings on Peleliu and Morotai took place on September 15 with an attack on Anguar, six miles south of Peleliu, coming off two days later.

Following extensive pre-invasion bombardments, American forces from MacArthur's Seventh Amphibious Force, which had linked up with Central Pacific forces in a loose fashion, hit Morotai Island.   The attack was a surprise to the Japanese, who retired inland.   Most of the island was secured within two days; however, the surviving defenders conducted numerous raids on Yankee positions after the victory proclamation.   These were finally rooted out in a difficult campaign conducted by GI's from New Guinea during the period December 26, 1944 to January 14, 1945.

The conquest of little Peleliu, 500 miles to the northeast, was much tougher.   Bypassing heavily defended

Babelthuap, largest of the Palaus, the 25,000 men of the
First Marine Division went ashore expecting to find about
8000 Japanese--there were actually 10,500. Even before
the beachhead was secured, these defenders staged vicious
counterattacks from the cover of the dense tropical vegetation.
On D-day plus 1, the island's airfield was captured along
with much of the southern interior. Thereafter the going was
slow.

      The Japanese, employing automatic weapons, were
able to take advantage of their natural surroundings, especially Bloody Nose Ridge, to put up a stiff resistance. Their
plan of defense was also superior to that previously encountered. Even when U.S. Army soldiers from Anguar became
available, the battle was difficult. On September 26, the
Japanese were finally trapped on the ridge, but they continued
their last-ditch stand until October 12. To overcome this
stubborn delay, Americans suffered the highest casualty
rate--nearly 40 per cent--of any amphibious attack in their
history bar none.

      The 10,000 men of the 81st Infantry Division went
ashore on Anguar on September 17. Here the Japanese were
rather weak and except for one spot of high ground, the GI's
had control of the island inside three days. On September
26, troops from Peleliu landed on Ngesebus Island to the
north. Konguran and Ulithi, other islands in the group, were
seized later.

      The invasion of the Palaus has proven quite con-
troversial. The enemy put into motion all the ferocity un-
veiled in the Marianas as well as a defensive ingenuity
which would be quite familiar before V-J Day. U.S. forces
would have much to think about and plan against as they
moved closer to Japan.

4920 Blackford, C. M. "They Were All Giants at Peleliu."
      USNIP, LXXVI (1950), 1114-1117.
      Readers might also want to consult Stanley
      Falk's Bloodiest Victory: The Palaus. Ballantine
      Illustrated History of World War II (New York:
      Ballantine Books, 1974. 160p.).

4921 Boyd, Robert W. "1st Battalion, 5th Marines, 1st
      Marine Division in the Palau Operations: A Sum-
      mary of Offensive Action." Unpublished paper,
      Senior Course, Amphibious Warfare School, Marine
      Corps Schools, Quantico, Va., 1949.

4922 Boyer, Kimber H. "The 3rd Armored Amphibian
      Battalion, Palau Operation--15 September to 20
      October 1944." Unpublished paper, Senior Course,
      Amphibious Warfare School, Marine Corps Schools,
      Quantico, Va., 1949.

4923 Clark, R. William. "Monster Seven-Seven." USNIP,
      XCV (1969), 114-147.
         LCI(G)-77 at Peleliu.

4924 Conway, Walter F. "Peleliu Spa." In: Patrick
      O'Sheel and Gene Cook, eds. Semper Fidelis:
      The U.S. Marines in the Pacific, 1942-1945. New
      York: William Sloane Associates, 1947. p. 74-80.
         Life during the Peleliu invasion.

4925 The 81st Wildcat Division in World War II. Washing-
      ton: Infantry Journal Press, 1948. 201p.
         This outfit served on Peleliu as part of the 3rd
      Amphibious Corps under Marine general Roy S.
      Geiger.

4926 Evans, Richard A. "'Infantillery' on Peleliu." Marine
      Corps Gazette, XXIX (January 1945), 50-55.
         Short range fire by a Marine 155mm howitzer
      battalion which then served as infantry.

4927 _____. "Artillery on 'Nothing Atoll.'" Field Artillery
      Journal, XXXV (January 1945), 6-10.
         A rewording of the same story cited above.

4928 Finan, James. "The Valley at Night." In: Patrick
      O'Sheel and Gene Cook, eds. Semper Fidelis:
      The U.S. Marines in the Pacific, 1942-1945. New
      York: William Sloane Associates, 1947. p. 80-82.
         Further Marine adventures during the Peleliu
      invasion.

4929 Hipple, William. "The Navy's Raids on Palau and
      Yap." Newsweek, XXIII (April 17, 1944), 31-34.

4930 Hough, Frank O. The Assault on Peleliu. Washington:
      Historical Division, U.S. Marine Corps, 1950.
      209p.

4931 Hunt, George P. Coral Comes High. New York:
      Harper, 1946. 147p.

Memoirs of a Marine Corps captain, one of only
22 survivors of Company K, Third Battalion, First
Marines, who won the Navy Cross as a result of
his unit's action on the right flank during the
Peleliu invasion.

4932 _____. "Point Secured. " Marine Corps Gazette,
XXIX (January 1945), passim.

4933 Lea, Tom. The Peleliu Landing.   El Paso, Texas:
C. Hertzog, 1945.   34p.

4934 O'Leary, Jeremiah. "Hell in the Umurbrogol. "   True
Magazine, XVII (October 1945), passim.

4935 "Palau: A Huge U.S. Task Force Sails to Pound the
Japanese Base. "   Life, XVI (April 24, 1944), 34-
35.

4936 "Philippine Thrust: The Attacks on the Palaus and
Halmahera Presage a Big Drive Against the Japs. "
Newsweek, XXIV (September 18, 1944), 32-34.

4937 Schmuck, David M. "The Battle For Peleliu. "   Marine
Corps Gazette, XXVIII (December 1944), passim.

4938 Stauffer, Donald A. "Marine Aviation at Peleliu. "
Marine Corps Gazette, XXIX (February 1945), 17-
19.
In support of dirt Marines.

4939 United States. Navy Department.   Pacific Fleet and
Pacific Ocean Area.   Japanese Military Caves on
Peleliu.   Cincpac-Cincpoa Bulletin 173-45.   N. p. ,
1945.

4940 _____._____._____. Northern Palau--Information
Bulletin.   Cincpac-Cincpoa Bulletin 136-44.   N. p. ,
1944.

4941 _____._____._____. Palau Gazetteer.   Cincpac-Cincpoa Bulletin, 159-44.   N. p. , 1944.   44p.

4942 _____._____._____. Palau Information Bulletin.
Cincpac-Cincpoa Bulletin 17-44.   N. p. , 1944.
An intelligence report.

4943 _____ . _____ . _____ . Palau Information Bulletin.
     Cincpac-Cincpoa Bulletin 87-44. N.p. , 1944.
     An intelligence report.

4944 _____ . _____ . _____ . Potential Airfield Sites of
     Palau. Cincpac-Cincpoa Bulletin 32-44. N.p. ,
     1944.
     An intelligence report.

4945 _____ . _____ . _____ . Southern Palau Information
     Bulletin. Cincpac-Cincpoa Bulletin 124-44. N.p. ,
     1944.

4946 _____ . _____ . _____ . Third Amphibious Corps.
     "Operational Report, Palau Operation. " Unpublished
     paper, U.S. Navy Department, Naval History Divi-
     sion, Operational Archives, October 24, 1944.

4947 Wood, Noah P. "Field Artillery Support of the 1st
     Marine Division, Peleliu, 15 September to 20
     October 1944: A Study of Artillery Support of a
     Marine Division in an Amphibious Attack. " Un-
     published paper, Senior Course, Amphibious War-
     fare School, Marine Corps Schools, Quantico, Va. ,
     1949.

4948 Worth, John. "Jap Barges at Peleliu. " Coast Artil-
     lery Journal, LXXXVIII (March-April 1945), 29-30.

          Further References: Readers are reminded that
     additional information relative to this section will be found
     in sections IIA and IID-1 above, as well as in the general
     histories cited in Volume III, Part 1.

          (6) SUBMARINE OPERATIONS, 1941-1945

          Introduction. This section of Volume II is con-
     cluded with an examination of Japanese and American sub-
     marine operations in the Pacific Theater throughout the war.
     To avoid the problems which often occur when a topic is split-
     up, most references to underseas activities of the Pacific
     war have been assembled here regardless of the time or
     campaign involved.
          Despite a large submarine fleet, Japanese submarine

activities during the war were not successful. Hamstrung
by a narrow-minded high command and poor doctrine, these
brave sailors largely wasted their time carrying supplies to
isolated islands or mounting rather meaningless attacks on
the U.S. west coast. Despite attempts at cooperation with
German U-boats, the Japanese never seemed to understand,
despite the evidence provided by their German allies or
their U.S.-British opponents, that submarines could play
an effective role, especially in commerce raiding.

The Americans, on the other hand, never lacked
for aggressiveness in this arm of their sea service. Admiral Nimitz, an old submarine hand, raised his flag of command on the U.S.S. Grayling on December 31, 1941.

Throughout the war, the "silent service" ranged
far and wide throughout the Pacific attacking Japanese naval
and merchant shipping wherever possible. Despite a string
of poor shooting caused by faulty torpedoes, U.S. "pigboats"
played a vital role in nearly every campaign through the
Allied victory. In addition to scouting and "life-guard" duty,
they sent to the bottom over 5, 300, 000 tons of Japanese
merchant shipping, almost single-handedly ruining that service. Another 577, 626 tons of important naval shipping, from
battleships and carriers down through auxiliaries, was also
sunk. Only 52 American submarines were lost, all but
seven in action.

The Navy's UDT teams, popularly known as "frogmen, " as in Europe played an effective part in making invasions safer by removing dangerous obstacles in the waters
off and beaches of target areas. British forces, regular and
mini-sub, made an important contribution, especially in the
areas of the South and Southwest Pacific.

On November 24, 1945, in a tribute to the submarine arm, Admiral Nimitz again stood on the deck of a
United States submarine and turned over his command of the
Pacific fleet to Admiral Spruance. The job had been well
done.

4949 Adams, Henry H. "Submarines in the Pacific. " In:
        Elmer B. Potter, ed. Sea Power: A Naval His-
        tory. Englewood Cliffs, N.J.: Prentice-Hall,
        1960. p. 796-813.

4950 Adams, William H. "Tin Fish Away. " In: William
        H. Fetridge, ed. The Second Navy Reader. Indi-
        anapolis: Bobbs-Merrill, 1944. p. 224-231.
        Rpr. 1971.

4951 Adamson, Hans C., jt. author. See Lockwood,
      Charles A., nos. 5015-5016.

4952 Alden, John D. "'Away the Boarding Party.'" USNIP,
      XCI (1965), 68-75.
          U.S. submarines vs. Japanese small craft in
      the final months of the Pacific war.

4953 Allbury, A. G. Bamboo and Bushido. London: Hale,
      1955. 192p.
          How a British POW was picked up by an Ameri-
      can submarine after the latter had sunk the Japanese
      POW ship transporting the author.

4954 "American 'Wolf Pack' Tactics." USNIP, LXXII
      (1946), 462-465.
          Yankee submarine operations against Japan
      modeled on German operations against the Allies.

4955 "America's Silent Service." Popular Mechanics, LXXX
      (September 1943), 18-25.
          The submarine force, Pacific.

4956 Anscomb, Charles. Submarine. London: W. Kimber,
      1957. 208p.

4957 Baldwin, Hanson W. "They Dive at Dawn." New York
      Times Magazine, (February 14, 1943), 14-15.
          The Navy's submariners.

4958 Baugh, Barney. "Heroes in Action Under the Sea."
      All Hands, no. 470, (April 1956), 16-21.

4959 Beach, Edward L. Submarine. New York: Holt,
      1952. 301p.
          U.S.S. Trigger.

4960 _____. "Unlucky in June: Hiyo Meets Trigger."
      USNIP, LXXXIII (1957), 376-385.
          The former was sunk by the latter.

4961 Benitez, Rafael C. "Battle Stations Submerged."
      USNIP, LXXIV (1948), 25-35.
          Submarine action in the Battle of Leyte Gulf.

4962 Benton, Thomas. The Silent Service: In Memory of
      U.S.S. Dorado. North Chicago, Ill.: Abbott
      Laboratories, n.d. 24p.

4963   Bowers, Richard H.   "Bougainville Rendezvous. "
       USNIP, LXXVIII (1952), 762-767.
          Submarine navigation, 1943.

4964   Brown, Cecil.   "'Take 'er Down!': The Diary of
       Heroic Submarine Commander Lieut. Wreford Goss
       Chapple. " Collier's, CIX (May 16, 1942), 12-13+.
          Abridged in Reader's Digest, XLI (August 1942),
       101-105, this piece concerns Allied submarine
       operations in the Philippines during the early days
       of the war.

4965   Brown, Paul, pseud. See Hazlett, Edward E. , no.
       5000.

4966   Burns, R. C.   "Palawan Rescue. " USNIP, LXXVI
       (1950), 577-578.
          Concerns an exploit of the submarine Redfish.

4967   "By Sub from Corregidor. " Leatherneck, XXV (Sep-
       tember 1942), 11-13+.

4968   "California Attack by a U-boat Brings War Home to
       the U.S. " Newsweek, XIX (March 2, 1942), 13.

4969   Carmer, Carl L.   The Jesse James of the Java Sea.
       New York: Farrar & Rinehart, 1945.   119p.
          The U.S. submarine Sturgeon, SS-187.

4970   Casey, Robert J.   Battle Below: The War of the
       Submarine. Indianapolis: Bobbs-Merrill, 1945.
       380p.

4971   _____.   "A Sub, a Carrier, and Two Tin Fish: The
       Story of an American Submarine Attack on Tokyo
       Bay. " Scholastic, XLI (September 28, 1942), 2.

4972   Chamblis, William C.   The Silent Service.   New York:
       New American Library, 1959.   158p.
          The operations of U.S. submarines in the Pacific
       during World War II.

4973   Dissette, Edward.   Guerrilla Submarines.   New York:
       Ballantine, 1972.   236p.
          Filipino guerrillas and support given them by
       American submarines.

4974   Down Went Shinano. " Time, L (July 14, 1947), 18.

4975 Drake, Hal. "'Attack the U.S. With a 5-inch Gun.'"
       Navy, XI (June 1968), 30-31+.
          When a Japanese submarine shelled the Cali-
       fornia coast.

4976 Dugan, James. "The Aqua Lung." USNIP, LXXXIII
       (1957), 779.
          Concerns the Japanese cruiser Takao.

4977 Eliot, George F. "The Submarine War." Foreign
       Affairs, XXI (April 1943), 385-400.
          An abridged version appeared in Science Digest,
       XIII (June 1943), 63-67, under the title, "Sub War
       Key to Quick Victory."

4978 Fane, Francis D. and Donald Moore. The Naked War-
       riors. Foreword by Richmond K. Turner. New
       York: Appleton-Century-Crofts, 1956. 308p.
          This account of frogmen was published by the
       London firm of Wingate in 1957.

4979 _____. "The Naked Warriors." USNIP, LXXXII
       (1956), 913-922.
          UDT's in the Pacific war.

4980 Felsen, Henry G. He's in Submarines Now. New
       York: McBride, 1942. 175p.

4981 _____. Submarine Sailor. New York: E. P. Dutton,
       1943. 208p.

4982 Field, John. "A Submarine Trip to Japanese Waters:
       An Interview with Lieutenant Commander [Willard
       A.] Saunders." Life, XII (June 29, 1942), 14+.

4983 _____. "West to Japan: U.S. Sub Sinks 70,000 Tons
       of Jap Shipping." Life, XIV (March 15, 1943),
       84-86.

4984 Frank, Gerold, et al. U.S.S. Seawolf: Submarine
       Raider of the Pacific. New York: Putnam, 1945.
       197p.

4985 Fraser, Ian. "The Attack on Takao." In: John
       Winton, ed. The War at Sea: The British Navy
       in World War II. New York: William Morrow,
       1967. p. 379-390.

As told by the commander of the British mini-
sub XE-3, who sank her in the shallow waters of
Johore Straits, off Singapore, on July 31, 1945.

4986 _____. Frogmen V.C. London: Angus and Robertson, 1957. 224p.

4987 "Frog Men." Popular Science, CXLVII (December
1945), 121-124.

4988 Furnas, Joseph C. "The Catfish Navy." Saturday
Evening Post, CCXV (August 22, 1942), 10-11+.
American submarine operations.

4989 Gervasi, Frank. "What Our Submarines are Doing."
Collier's, CXI (April 3, 1943), 16-18.
Very limited data on the "Silent Service."

4990 _____. "What Our Submarines are Doing." In:
William H. Fetridge, ed. The Second Navy Reader. Indianapolis: Bobbs-Merrill, 1944. p. 143-
151.

4991 Gibson, John F. Dark Seas Above. London: Blackwood, 1947. 286p.
Firsthand account of British Pacific submarine
operations to the Japanese surrender of Hong Kong.

4992 _____. "From a Submariner's Notebook: East Indies
Patrol." Blackwood's, CCLX (August-September
1946), 112-119, 204-216.
British submarine operations in the Pacific.

4993 Goldingham, C. S. "United States Submarines in the
Blockade of Japan in the 1939-1945 War." Journal
of the Royal United Service Institute, XCVII (Feb-
ruary-May 1952), 87-98, 212-222.

4994 "The Grand Slam in Subs." Popular Mechanics,
LXXXIV (October 1945), 12-16+.

4995 Grider, George W. Warfish. As Told to Lydel Sims.
Boston: Little, Brown, 1958. 282p. Rpr. 1961.
The skipper's memoirs of the war cruises of
U. S. S. Flasher.

4996 Hashimoto, Mochitsura. Sunk: The Story of the

Japanese Submarine Fleet, 1942-1945. Translated
by E. H. M. Colegrave. London: Cassell, 1954.
218p.

4997 Hasrato, Stanley. "Heros Rising from the Sea."
Collier's, CXVI (July 28, 1945), 14-15+.
U.S. submarine operations in the Aleutians.

4998 Hawkins, Maxwell. "Rescue in the Night: How a
Crew of Submariners Struggled to Take Some
Brothers-in-Arms off a Jap-Infested Island."
Saturday Evening Post, CCXVI (July 17, 1943),
14-15+.

4999 _____. Torpedoes Away, Sir!: Our Submarine Navy
in the Pacific. New York: Holt, Rinehart &
Winston, 1946. 268p.

5000 Hazlett, Edward E. He's Jake: The Story of a Submarine Dog. By Paul Brown, pseud. New York:
Dodd, Mead, 1947. 154p.

5001 _____. Rig for Depth Charges!: The Career of a
Young Naval Officer on Submarine Duty. Career
Books. New York: Dodd, Mead, 1945. 269p.

5002 Hersey, John. "Submarine Warfare, with Color Paintings by Peter Sample." Life, XV (December 27,
1943), 54-59.

5003 Herzog, James H. "Oil to Japan." Military Review,
XLV (October 1965), 68-76.
Cut by American submarine action.

5004 Higgins, Edward T., with Dean Phillips. Webfooted
Warriors: The Story of a "Frogman" in the Navy
During World War II. Banner Books. New York:
Exposition Press, 1955. 172p.
Reminiscences of the Pacific war.

5005 Holmes, Wilfred J. Undersea Victory: The Influence
of Submarine Operations on the War in the Pacific.
Garden City, N.Y.: Doubleday, 1966. 505p.
Contains a number of charts drawn by Dorothy
DeFontaine.

5006 Horie, Y. "The Failure of the Japanese Convoy Escort." USNIP, LXXXII (1956), 1072-1081.

5007 Hubbell, John G. "The Great Manila Bay Silver Opera-
      tion." Reader's Digest, LXXIV (April 1959), 123-
      132.
             Precious ore removed by American submarine.

5008 "Iron Men for the Iron Sharks." Time, XLII (July 5,
      1943), 55-56.
             Submarines.

5009 Krec, Ted. "Enemy Off Ellwood." Westways, XLVIII
      (February 1956), 6-7.
             The shelling of the Ellwood, California, oil field
      by a Japanese submarine in February 1942.

5010 Lockwood, Charles A. Down to the Sea in Subs: My
      Life in the U.S. Navy. New York: W. W. Norton,
      1967. 276p.

5011 _____. "Our Pacific Sub Commander Tells How We
      Gave the Japs a Licking Underseas." Saturday
      Evening Post, CCXXII (July 16-30, 1949), passim.

5012 _____. Sink 'em All: Submarine Warfare in the
      Pacific. New York: Dutton, 1951. 416p.

5013 _____. Submarine Operations in the Pacific. Navy
      Day Speech at Cleveland, Ohio, Oct. 27, 1945.
      N.p., 1945. 25p.

5014 _____. Through Hell and Deep Water: The Stirring
      Story of the Navy's Deadly Submarine, The U.S.S.
      Harder, Under the Command of Sam Dealy, De-
      stroyer Killer! New York: Greenburg, 1956.
      317p.

5015 _____, and Hans Christian Adamson. Hellcats of the
      Sea. New York: Greenberg, 1955. 335p.
             U.S. submarine operations in World War II.

5016 _____, _____. Zoomies, Subs, and Zeros. New
      York: Greenberg, 1956. 301p.
             American submarine search and rescue opera-
      tions.

5017 Long, E. John. "Airplanes Under the Sea." Ships
      and the Sea, III (October 1953), 10-13, 47-48.
             How Japanese submarines transported aircraft

aboard during the Big War with details on their
abortive attack on the Panama Canal.

5018 Martin, Harold H. "Kazuyuki Sugai Comes Home in
       a Box." In: Patrick O'Sheel and Gene Cook, eds.
       Semper Fidelis: The U.S. Marines in the Pacific,
       1942-1945. New York: William Sloane Associates,
       1947. p. 241-246.
            What happened to the remains (ashes) of 500
       dead Japanese soldiers of Truk when the submarine
       I-14 was taken by American naval forces.

5019 Martin, William T. "Tokyo Bound: Life on an Ameri-
       can Submarine." Saturday Evening Post, CCXVI
       (July 3-July 10, 1943), 9-11+, 26-27+.

5020 _____. "Twenty Thousand Headaches Under the Sea."
       Saturday Evening Post, CCXVII (June 16-23, 1945),
       9-11, 20+.
            American submarine operations.

5021 Master, David. "Dodging Death in a Submarine."
       Science Digest, XIV (September 1943), 77-80.

5022 Mayers, Colin. "Submarines--a Key to Victory."
       USNIP, LXVIII (1942), 1775-1777.

5023 Moore, Donald, jt. author. See Fane, Francis D.,
       nos. 4978-4979.

5023a Moore, Lynn L. "Shinano: The Jinx Carrier."
       USNIP, LXXIX (1953), 142-149.

5024 "'Must be Presumed...': The Loss of the Wahoo."
       Time, XLII (December 13, 1943), 68.

5025 Oi, Atsushi. "Why Japan's Anti-Submarine Warfare
       Failed." USNIP, LXXVIII (1952), 587-601.

5026 "Our Submarine Victory in the Pacific." USNIP,
       LXXIV (1948), 1147-1155.

5027 Parker, Thomas C. "Thirteen Women in a Subma-
       rine." USNIP, LXXVI (1950), 716-721.
            Their escape from Corregidor in early 1942.

5028 Parrish, Thomas D. Victory at Sea: The Submarine.

A Rutledge Book. New York: Published for
Scholastic Book Services by Ridge Press, 1959.
60p.

5029 Pratt, Fletcher. "Submarines Pacific: Americans in
      Battle. " Harper's Magazine, CLXXXVII (October
      1943), 385-396.

5030 Pratt, William V. "Scouts in the Pacific: The Work
      of the Scouting Submarine. " Newsweek, XXIV
      (August 21, 1944), 36.

5031 ____. "Submarines: Shock Troops That Hammer at
      Supply Lines. " Newsweek, XXII (October 25, 1943),
      28.

5032 Reynolds, Clark G. "Submarine Attacks on the Pacific
      Coast, 1942. " Pacific Historical Review, XXXIII
      (1964), 183-193.

5033 Reynolds, Quentin. "Take 'er Down. " Collier's, CXIV
      (November 4, 1944), 16-19+.
      American submarine operations.

5034 Roscoe, Theodore. United States Submarine Operations
      in World War II. Annapolis: U.S. Naval Institute,
      1949. 577p.
      An abridgement, entitled Pigboats, was published
      by Bantam Books in 1958.

5035 Ruhe, William J. "The Gamesmen's Game. " USNIP,
      LXXXIII (1957), 292-299.
      American submarine operations.

5036 ____. "He Gave His Name to the U.S.S. Dealey. "
      USNIP, LXXXIII (1956), 205-206.
      Samuel D. Dealey, U.S.N., skipper of the sub-
      marine Harder in World War II.

5037 ____. "Hot Fish in Tube 4. " American Legion
      Magazine, LIX (September 1955), 16-17.

5038 ____. "A Submarine's Cable Cutting Preparations
      in 1945. " USNIP, LXXXV (1959), 99-100.

5039 Rush, Charles W., Jr. "Deep Battleground. " USNIP,
      LXXXIV (March 1958), 73-76.
      Submarine operations.

5040 Russell, E. W. "Gold Ballast: War Patrol of the
      U.S.S. Trout." USNIP, LXXXVI (1960), 94-96.

5041 "Saga on the Tang: Submarine Rescues 22 Pacific
      Aviators." Newsweek, XXIII (May 29, 1944), 28.

5042 "Salmon: The One That Got Away." All Hands, no.
      483, (April 1957), 43-47.
            The story of SS-182 in the Pacific war.

5043 Saville, Allison W. "German Submarines in the Far
      East." USNIP, LXXXVII (1961), 80-92.

5044 Say, Harold B. "They Hit the Beach in Swim Trunks:
      The Navy's Human Secret Weapon." Saturday
      Evening Post, CCXVIII (October 13, 1945), 14-15+.
            Frogmen in World War II.

5045 Sayre, Elisabeth E. "A Submarine from Corregidor."
      Atlantic Monthly, CLXX (August-September 1942),
      22-28, 40-46.

5046 Sheridan, Martin. Overdue and Presumed Lost: The
      Story of the U.S.S. Bullhead [SS-332]. Frances-
      town, N.H.: Marshall Jones, 1947. 143p. Rpr.
      1959.

5047 _____. "With the Terrorists of the High Seas."
      Travel, LXXIX (October 1942), 4-8.
            Relatively limited operational data on the "Si-
      lent Service."

5048 [No entry.]

5049 Shrader, Grahame F. The Phantom War in the North-
      west. Edmonds, Wash., 1969. 59p.
            Japanese submarine attacks on the U.S. coast
      and countermeasures.

5050 Sterling, Forest J. Wake of the Wahoo. Philadelphia:
      Chilton Books, 1960. 210p.

5051 "Submarines in the Battle of Leyte Gulf." Military
      Review XXX (December 1950), 102-108.

5052 "TNT Divers." Popular Mechanics, LXXXIV (Novem-
      ber 1945), 72-73.
            Navy UDTs.

5053 Torisu, Kennosuke. "Japanese Submarine Tactics."
      USNIP, LXXXVII (1961), 78-83.

5054 Truxton-Decatur Naval Museum. United States Sub-
      marines in Action, 1900-1952. Washington, 1952.
      20p.

5055 Underbrink, Robert L. Destination Corregidor.
      Annapolis: U.S. Naval Institute, 1971. 240p.
      The attempt to supply Bataan and Corregidor
      before their fall to the Japanese.

5056 _____. "Your Island is Moving at 20 Knots." USNIP,
      XCV (1969), 81-88.
      The U.S. submarine Archerfish vs. the Japanese
      carrier Shinano.

5057 "U.S. Subs at Work: The Destruction Done to Jap
      Ships." Life, XIV (February 8, 1943), 26-27.

5058 "U.S. Submarines Sank 5,320,094 Tons of Japanese
      Shipping in World War II." Army and Navy Journal,
      LXXXIX (March 15, 1952), 874.

5059 United States. Navy Department. Office of the Chief
      of Naval Operations, Intelligence Division. "Combat
      Narrative: Submarine Encounters, 31 August-15
      September 1942." Unpublished paper, CNO-ONI
      File, U.S. Navy Department, Naval History Divi-
      sion, Operational Archives, 1942. 20p.

5060 _____. _____. Pacific Fleet and Pacific Ocean Area.
      Japanese Aerial Anti-Sub Tactics. Special Trans-
      lation No. 18. N.p., ca. 1944.

5061 _____. _____. _____. Amphibious Forces, Underwater
      Demolition Teams. "Histories." Unpublished
      papers, 21 vols., Shore Establishment File, U.S.
      Navy Department, Naval History Division, Opera-
      tional Archives, 1945.
      Brief accounts of UDT units 1-30 averaging
      2-20 pages in length.

5062 _____. _____. _____. _____. "History of Commander
      UDT and UDF, Amphibious Forces, Pacific Fleet."
      Unpublished paper, Shore Establishment File, U.S.
      Navy Department, Naval History Division, Opera-
      tional Archives, n.d. 6p.

5063 _____. _____. _____. Seventh Fleet Intelligence
      Center. "Submarine Activities Connected with
      Guerrilla Organizations." Unpublished paper, Type
      Commands File, U.S. Navy Department, Naval
      History Division, Operational Archives, 1945.
      42p.
           Relates primarily to aid extended "friendlies"
      in the Philippines, January 1943-January 1945.

5064 _____. _____. _____. Submarine Force. "The His-
      tory of Submarine Warfare in the Pacific." Un-
      published paper, Type Commands File, U.S. Navy
      Department, Naval History Division, Operational
      Archives, n.d. 275p.
           A narrative of selected patrols based on the
      reports of various submarines ending with Novem-
      ber 1943.

5065 _____. _____. _____. _____. "Submarine Operational
      History World War II." Unpublished paper, 4 vols.,
      Type Commands File, U.S. Navy Department, Naval
      History Division, Operational Archives, 1947.
           A massive account based on 1500 war patrol
      reports which forms the basic source for Theodore
      Roscoe's history of U.S. submarine operations
      cited above.

5066 Walker, Gordon. "Saga of the Pacific Periscope."
      Christian Science Monitor Magazine, (August 18,
      1945), 4.
           U.S. submarine operations.

5067 Wheeler, Stanley A. "The Lost Merchant Fleet of
      Japan." USNIP, LXXXII (1956), 1295-1299.
           Much of it sunk by American submarines.

5068 Whitehouse, Arthur G. J. "Arch." "How to Win the
      D.S.O." Saturday Evening Post, CCXVII (April
      21, 1945), 6+.

5069 Widder, Arthur. Action in Submarines. New York:
      Harper & Row, 1967. 213p.

5070 Wolfert, Ira. "Silent, Invisible War Under the Sea:
      Secret Weapons and Secret Tactics and the Hidden
      Deeds of Heroes." Reader's Digest, XLVII (No-
      vember 1945), 116-128.

5071   Worden, William L.   "Boarders From the Tyrant
          Fish." Saturday Evening Post, CCXVIII (Decem-
          ber 1, 1945), 34+.
              U.S. submarine searches of Japanese coastal
          vessels.

5072   Wright, Bruce S.   The Frogmen of Burma.   London:
          Irwin, 1968.   152p.

5073   Zimmerman, Sherwood R.   "Operation Forager."
          USNIP, XC (1964), 78-89.
              American submarines in the Marianas campaign.

          Further References: Readers will find further
data relative to this section in section IIA above, as well as
in the general works cited in Volume III, Part 1.

IIE THE ALLIES TRIUMPHANT

(1) GENERAL WORKS

Introduction. The completion of the Marianas and Palaus operations saw the combination of the dual advance on the Philippines into a single coordinated effort. MacArthur, as we shall see, was able to redeem his pledge, "I shall return." Once the southern islands of that chain were secured and the Japanese were defeated in the greatest of history's naval battles, that in Leyte Gulf, the forces of the Southwest Pacific command finished up the war recapturing all of the Philippines and operating with British support in Borneo.

The forces of the Allies in the Central Pacific, reinforced by men and material coming out from the European Theater, including a part of the Royal Navy, turned north to obtain additional bases for the giant B-29's. By the early part of July 1945, Japan was completely surrounded by sea and air blockade and was being severely bombarded.

This is not to say that the Japanese were in a rush to surrender. As the Allies knew from bitter experience, the invasion of the home islands, still able to put forth thousands of dedicated soldiers, supplied with hundreds of thousands of tons of ammunition, and equipped with over 5000 kamikaze planes, if forced would be the biggest blood bath in history. Not until Hirohito himself, moved by the two atomic blasts and the Russian invasion of Manchuria, personally saw to the surrender did the war lords capitulate.

The war in the Pacific was, as opposed to the European Theater, primarily a naval war. This section contains citations to the general events which closed out the campaign; specific operations will be referenced in the subsections that follow.

5074 Ahilin, Alan I. "To Wantan and Beyond." Marine
Corps Gazette, XXIX (July 1945), 12-18.

293					IIE Allies Triumphant 1

5075	Allred, Gordon T., jt. author. See Kuwahara, Yasuo, no. 5124.

5076	Armagnec, Alden P. "I Cruised on the Iowa." Popular Science, CXLVI (January 1945), 80-83+.

5077	Baldwin, Hanson W. "America at War: And Now Japan." Foreign Affairs, XXIII (July 1945), 539-542.

5078	Barker, A. J. Suicide Weapon: Japanese Kamikaze Forces in World War II. Ballantine Illustrated History of World War II. New York: Ballantine Books, 1961. 160p.
	Not "officially" organized until late 1944, the "Divine Wind" would play an important and deadly role in the final struggles.

5079	Bauer, K. Jack. "Olympic vs. Ketsu-Go." Marine Corps Gazette, XLIX (August 1965), 32-44.
	A study of Allied plans for the assault on Kyushu in the fall of 1945 and Japanese preparations to resist.

5080	Bishop, John. "Sniper Ship: On the Seaway to Tokyo." Saturday Evening Post, CCXVII (November 4-11, 1944), 24-25+, 20+.

5081	Blackton, Charles S. "Surrender of the Fortress of Truk." Pacific Historical Review, XV (December 1946), 400-408.

5082	Caidin, Martin. A Torch to the Enemy. New York: Ballantine Books, 1960.
	The air war in the Pacific and the kamikazes.

5083	Cant, Gilbert. "The Pacific Revisited." Time, XLV (June 4, 1945), 32.

5084	"The Captain Stands Accused: The Indianapolis Lost." Time, XLVI (December 10, 1945), 23-24.
	She was sunk by a Japanese submarine late in the conflict.

5085	Carrison, Daniel J. "Death Rode the Division Wind (the Kamikaze)." Marine Corps Gazette, XXXIX (July 1955), 40-46.

5086 Chapelle, Dixie. What's a Woman Doing Here? A
         Reporter's Report on Herself. New York: William
         Morrow, 1961. 200p.
              The author, killed during the Vietnam conflict,
         served as a combat correspondent during the Iwo
         Jima and Okinawa operations.

5087 "Combing the Sea for Lost Flyers." Popular Mechan-
         ics, LXXXIII (March 1945), 33-37.
              The rescue service set up for saving downed
         B-29 pilots and crews.

5088 Coox, Alvin. Japan--The Final Agony. Ballatine's
         Illustrated History of World War II. New York:
         Ballantine Books, 1970. 160p.
              Relates in photos and text the final year of the
         Pacific war.

5089 Corey, Herbert. "Manila to Tokyo--Rough Seas
         Ahead." Free World, IX (March 1945), 27-30.

5090 _____. "Pacific War--Closing in for the Kill." Free
         World, IX (June 1945), 55-58.

5091 Courtenay, William. "The Pacific Theater of Opera-
         tions." Geographic Journal, CV (March 1945),
         112-120.

5092 _____. "War in the Pacific." Journal of the Royal
         United Service Institute, CI (February 1945), 13-20.

5093 _____. _____. United Empire, (March 1945), 61-63.

5094 DeValle, Pedro A. "Cave Warfare." Marine Corps
         Gazette, XXIX (July 1945), 58-59.

5095 "The End of the Indianapolis Case." Time, XLVII
         (March 4, 1946), 24.

5096 Eyre, James K., Jr. "Shattering the Myth of Japa-
         nese Invincibility." USNIP, LXXI (1945), 977-987.

5097 "The Fleet Opens the Battle of Japan With Great Air
         Blows at Tokyo." Newsweek, XXV (February 26,
         1945), 27-28.

5098 "Fleet Under Two Flags." Popular Mechanics,

LXXXIV (October 1945), 82-87.
The British Pacific Fleet in the last months of
the war.

5099 Ford, Walter C. "High Spot of the Pacific. " USNIP,
LXXI (1945), 551-553.

5100 Francis, Devon. "The Pattern For Pacific Victory. "
Popular Science, CXLV (October 1944), 67-71.

5101 Frank, Bemis M. and Henry I. Shaw, Jr. Victory
and Occupation. Vol. V of History of U.S. Marine
Corps Operations in World War II. Washington:
Historical Branch, U.S. Marine Corps, 1968.
945p.

5102 Fromm, Joseph. "England and the Pacific War. "
Nation, CLX (April 14, 1945), 409-410.

5103 Grant, Benjamin J. "Air Mastery in the Far East. "
Infantry Journal, LVII (August 1945), 49-52.

5104 "H.M. Fleet: The American Plan. " Newsweek, XXV
(April 9, 1945), 35.
For its deployment.

5105 Hailey, Foster. "With a Task Force in the Pacific. "
New York Times Magazine, (November 5, 1944),
8+.

5106 Halsey, William F. "The Plan For Japan. " Collier's,
CXV (April 28, 1945), 18-19+.

5107 "Halsey Goes Hunting. " Life, XVIII (March 19, 1945),
110-112.

5108 "Hara-Kiri on Wings. " Infantry Journal, LVII (September 1945), 34-35.
Kamikazes.

5109 Haugland, Vern. "Bombing Tokyo Difficult. " USNIP,
LXXI (1945), 247-248.
Reprinted from the January 8, 1945 issue of the
New York Herald-Tribune.

5110 Haynes, Lewis L. "U.S.S. Indianapolis. " In: Saturday Evening Post, Editors of. True Stories of

Courage and Survival. Cleveland: World, 1963.
p. 141-154. Rpr. 1966.
Memoirs of a navy doctor on the sinking of the
cruiser.

5111 _____. "We Prayed While 883 Died: The Sinking of
the Indianapolis." Saturday Evening Post, CCXXVIII
(August 6, 1955), 28-29+.

5112 Helm, Thomas. Ordeal by Sea: The Tragedy of the
U.S.S. Indianapolis. New York: Dodd, Mead,
1963. 243p.

5113 Henry, Frederick. "Japan's Pearl Harbor, Ogasawara
Jima." USNIP, LXIX (1943), 1459-1460.
One of the Bonin Islands bombed by American
carrier planes.

5114 Hipple, William. "New Year's Report on the Pacific."
Newsweek, XXV (January 1, 1945), 28-29.

5115 Inoguchi, Rikihel. The Divine Wind: Japan's Kamikaze Force in World War II. Written with the
assistance of Tadashi Nakajima and Roger Pineau.
Annapolis: U.S. Naval Institute, 1958. 240p.
Rpr. 1972.

5116 _____, and Tadashi Nakajima. "The Kamikaze Attack
Corps." USNIP, LXXIX (1953), 932-945.

5117 "Japanese Fighter Pilots' Suicide Tactics Against
Allied Warships." Illustrated London News, CCVI
(June 30, 1945), 694-695.

5118 Jones, George E. "Brain Center of the Pacific War:
Nimitz Headquarters, Guam." New York Times
Magazine, (April 8, 1945), 10-11+.

5119 "The Kamikaze Attack Corps." Military Review,
XXXIII (January 1954), 71-80.

5120 Kearney, Paul W. "Pete Mitscher, Boss of Task Force
58." Reader's Digest, XLVII (July 1945), 33-36.

5121 "Kinkaid: Master of Sea War." New York Times
Magazine, (November 5, 1944), 8-9+.

5122   "Kinkaid of the Seventh Fleet." Newsweek, XXIV
        (November 6, 1944), 32.
            Both of the above articles concern Admiral
        Thomas C. Kinkaid.

5123   Kluckhohn, Frank L.   "The Total Fury of Amphibious
        War." New York Times Magazine, (January 7,
        1945), 9+.

5124   Kuwahara, Yasuo and Gordon T. Allred.   Kamikaze.
        New York: Ballantine Books, 1957.   187p.

5125   Larteguy, Jean, ed.   The Sun Goes Down: Last
        Letters from Japanese Suicide Pilots and Soldiers.
        Translated from the French by Nora Wydenbruck.
        London: Kimber, 1956.   183p.

5126   Lott, Arnold S.   "Japan's Nightmare--Mine Blockade."
        USNIP, LXXXV (1959), 39-41.
            A largely unheralded part of the final American
        squeeze.

5127   McCain, John S.   "So We Hit Them in the Belly: The
        Sortie of Carrier Task Force, Third Fleet, Into
        the South China Sea." Saturday Evening Post,
        CCXVII (July 14-21, 1945), 12-14+, 22-23+.

5128   McGovern, John B.   "Transport Squadron Sixteen."
        Unpublished paper, Individual Personnel File, U.S.
        Navy Department, Naval History Division, Opera-
        tional Archives, 1945.   28p.
            An administrative, staff, and operational history
        of the author's unit during the Iwo Jima and Okina-
        wa operations.

5129   McVay, Charles B., 3rd, defendant.   Charges and
        Specifications in the Case of Capt. Charles B.
        McVay, 3rd, U.S.N., in the Sinking of the U.S.S.
        Indianapolis by a Japanese Submarine.   Washington:
        Navy Department, 1946.   13p.
            McVay was the cruiser's skipper.

5130   "Men Against the Sea: The Indianapolis Explosion."
        Time, XLVI (August 27, 1945), 25.

5131   Menken, J.   "Notes on the Eastern War." National
        Review, CXXV (July 1945), 58-64.

5132 Millot, Bernard. Divine Thunder: The Life and Death
      of the Kamikazes. New York: McCall Publishing
      Co., 1971. 243p.

5133 Mitchell, Donald W. "Japan Is Doomed! American
      Forces Rule the Pacific." Current History, New
      Series VII (November 1944), 361-366.

5134 "A Mitscher Shampoo." Time, XLV (February 26,
      1945), 25.
          Navy air raids on Japan.

5135 Myers, Leo M. "The Almost Forgotten Emergency
      Rescue Squadrons." Aero Album, III (1970), 2-7.
          Catalinas out of New Guinea and the Philippines
      during 1944-1945.

5136 Nakajima, Tadashi, jt. author. See Inoguchi, Rikihei,
      no. 5115.

5137 Newcomb, Richard F. Abandon Ship! Death of the
      U.S.S. Indianapolis. New York: Holt, 1958.
      305p.

5138 Nimitz, Chester W. "The Latest Moves in the Pacif-
      ic." Vital Speeches, X (October 1, 1944), 744-
      746.
          Does not give too much away!

5139 "Nobody Looked: The Cruiser Indianapolis." News-
      week, XXVI (July 27, 1945), 26.

5140 O'Neill, Herbert C. "Deployment in the Pacific."
      By "Strategicus," pseud. Spectator, CLXXIV
      (June 22, 1945), 565.

5141 "Pacific War: Damaged Warships." Illustrated Lon-
      don News, CCVII (July 7, 1945), 11.

5142 Packard, Vance. "Closing in on Japan." American
      Magazine, CXXXIX (February 1945), 34-36.

5143 Peck, J. L. H. "Why Japan Fears Our Flattops."
      Air Trails Pictorial, (September 1945), 24-26+.

5144 "Piloted Flying Bombs: The Latest Japanese Suicide
      Tactics." Illustrated London News, CCVII (July
      28, 1945), 88-89.

5145   Pineau, Roger. "Spirit of the Divine Wind."   USNIP,
       LXXXIV (1958), 23-29.
       The origin and history of the kamikazes.

5146   Potter, Elmer B.   "The Defeat of Japan." In: his
       Sea Power: A Naval History.   Englewood Cliffs,
       N. J.:   Prentice-Hall, 1960.   p. 813-842.

5147   _____.   "The Dual Advance to the Philippines."
       Ibid., p. 757-777.

5148   Pratt, Fletcher.   "The Big Pacific Push."   Harper's,
       CXC (May-June 1945), 541-555, 635-645.

5149   Pratt, William V.   "Blockade: Its Comeback in the
       Pacific." Newsweek, XXV (March 26, 1945), 42.

5150   _____.   "Can Our War of Attrition Starve Out the
       Japs?" Newsweek, XXV (May 28, 1945), 42.

5151   _____.   "Forward by the Amphibious Trail."   News-
       week, XXV (March 19, 1945), 38.

5152   _____.   "Selecting the Final Steppingstones."   News-
       week, XXIV (December 18, 1944), 36.

5153   Rawlings, Charles A.   "The 'Big-E' and the Divine
       Wind." Saturday Evening Post, CCXVIII (September
       1, 1945), 9-11+.
       The carrier Enterprise (CV-6) received a bomb
       and two kamikaze hits during her support of the
       Okinawa invasion.

5154   Raymond, Arthur.   "Jap Suicide Killers: The Kami-
       kaze Corps." Popular Science, CXLVI (June 1945),
       65-67.

5155   "Return of the Samurai: A War Reunion of One of the
       Kamikaze Special Attack Corps." Time, LXXXVIII
       (August 19, 1965), 34.

5156   Shaw, Henry I., Jr., jt. author. See Frank, Bemis
       M., no. 5101.

5157   "Sir Bernard H. Rawlings." CurrBio:VI:486-488.
       Commander of the British Pacific Fleet in
       1945.

5158 Smith, Peter C. Task Force 57: The British Pacific
      Fleet, 1944-1945. London: Kimber, 1969. 206p.

5159 Smith, Robert R. The Approach to the Philippines.
      U.S. Army in World War II--The War in the Pacif-
      ic. Washington: Office of the Chief of Military
      History, Department of the Army, 1953. 623p.

5160 Steele, Theodore M. A Pictorial Record of the Com-
      bat Duty of Patrol Bombing Squadron 109 in the
      Western Pacific, 20 April 1945 to 15 August 1945.
      New York: General Offset, 1946. Unpaged.
      The unit's "cruise book."

5161 "Strategicus," pseud. See O'Neill, Herbert C., no.
      5140.

5162 Sudo, Hajime. "I Flew in Japan's Secret Air Corps."
      R.A.F. Flying Review, XVI (November 1959),
      36-38.

5163 Thursfield, Henry G. "Strategy in the Pacific."
      National Review, CXXIV (March 1945), 208-213.
      A British view.

5164 Tregaskis, Richard. "The Road to Japan." Saturday
      Evening Post, CCXVIII (August 18-October 27,
      1945), 17+, 20+, 20+, 22+, 20+, 20+, 20+, 20+,
      18+, 20+.

5165 Trumbull, Robert. "The Spirit of Nelson Joins Us
      in the Pacific: Life Aboard a British Battleship."
      New York Times Magazine, (May 27, 1945), 10-
      11+.

5166 United States. Marine Corps. Fifth Marine Division,
      G-2. "Special Study of the Enemy Situation."
      Unpublished paper, USMC File, U.S. Navy Depart-
      ment, Naval History Division, Operational Archives,
      1944. 19p.
      A summary of Japanese strength in the Bonins in
      late 1944.

5167 _____. Navy Department. Pacific Fleet and Pacific
      Ocean Area. Airways Data. Special Translation
      No. 96-45. Cincpac-Cincpoa Bulletin 96-45. N.p.,
      1945.

5168 _____. _____. _____. Climatology and Oceanography of Operational Areas of the Western Pacific. Cincpac-Cincpoa Bulletin 4-45. 2 vols. N. p., 1945.

5169 _____. _____. _____. Evasive Action Against Enemy Aircraft. Cincpac-Cincpoa Bulletin 42-45. N. p., 1945.

5170 _____. _____. _____. Guide to the Western Pacific. Cincpac-Cincpoa Bulletin 126-44. N. p., 1944.

5171 _____. _____. _____. Japanese Aerial Tactics. Special Translation No. 57. Cincpac-Cincpoa Bulletin 87-45. N. p., 1945.

5172 _____. _____. _____. Japanese Army Order of Battle. Special Translation No. 75. Cincpac-Cincpoa Bulletin 163-45. N. p., 1945.

5173 _____. _____. _____. Japanese Field Artillery Gunnery Methods. Cincpac-Cincpoa Bulletin 69-45. N. p., 1945.

5174 _____. _____. _____. Japanese Fortifications and Emplacements. Special Translation No. 58. Cincpac-Cincpoa Bulletin 94-45. N. p., 1945.

5175 _____. _____. _____. Japanese Heavy DP Gun Emplacements. Special Translation No. 59. Cincpac-Cincpoa Bulletin 97-45. N. p., 1945.

5176 _____. _____. _____. [Japanese] Suicide Force Combat Methods. Special Translation No. 67. Cincpac-Cincpoa Bulletin 129-45. N. p., 1945.

5177 _____. _____. _____. The Kurile Islands. Cincpac-Cincpoa Bulletin 70-44. N. p., 1944.
An intelligence report.

5178 _____. _____. _____. POW Camps in Japanese-Occupied Areas--Preliminary Report. Cincpac-Cincpoa Bulletin 36-45. N. p., 1945.

5179 _____. _____. _____. Searching Caves. Cincpac-Cincpoa Bulletin 189-45. N. p., 1945.
Or, how not to get killed in the process!

5180 _____. _____. _____. Shore Defenses--Anguar Island.
Cincpac-Cincpoa Bulletin 51-45. N. p. , 1945.
An intelligence report.

5181 _____. _____. _____. Suicide Bombing Attacks--Pacific Fleet Confidential Letter. Cincpac-Cincpoa
Miscellaneous Publications. N. p. , n. d.

5182 Vogel, Bertram. "The Great Strangling of Japan. "
USNIP, LXXIII (1947), 1304-1309.
By minefields.

5183 _____. "Who Were the Kamikaze?" USNIP, LXXIII
(1947), 832-837.

5184 Walker, Wayne T. "The Fate of the Indianapolis. "
World War II Magazine, II (December 1972), 53-58.

5185 "Watchdog of H. M. Navy, Now Britain's Jap-Hunting
Admiral. " Newsweek, XXIV (August 14, 1944), 30.
Sir Bernard H. Rawlings.

5186 Williams, Dwight M. B. "Suicide Tactics. " USNIP,
LXXXVI (1960), 104-106.
Japanese kamikazes.

5187 Winton, John. The Forgotten Fleet: The British Navy
in the Pacific, 1944-1945. New York: Crown,
1969. 433p.
Serving well with and apart from the American
Navy.

5188 Woodward, Clark H. "Landing Raids Bring Pacific
into Spotlight. " USNIP, LXXI (1945), 123-124.
Reprinted from the December 17, 1944 issue of
the Washington Star.

5189 Wydenbruck, Nora, trans. See Larteguy, Jean, no.
5125.

    Further References: Readers will find additional
information relative to this section in section IIA above, as
well as in the general works cited in Volume III, Part 1.

(2) THE GREATEST NAVAL BATTLE: LEYTE GULF

      Introduction. The Battle of Leyte Gulf, often
known as The Second Battle of the Philippine Sea, was
intimately tied to the invasion of the Philippines (section
IIE-3) and would prove to be the Imperial Navy's last big
banzai.
      From the Japanese viewpoint, Leyte Gulf was one
of the best planned of their naval engagements with the Americans. Had things gone according to schedule, as they almost
did in several instances, it would have proved a glorious
victory. Instead, the outcome left the one-time invincible
fleet a negligible factor, beaten beyond recovery.
      As the Allies moved into their Philippine invasion,
the Japanese fleet launched their complicated operation which
was designed to lure away Halsey's Third Fleet and allow for
the destruction of MacArthur's troopships and landing vessels.
To do this, a Japanese force of carriers and hybrid carrier-
battleships would move down from the area north of Luzon
making as if to engage the Third Fleet. After establishing
contact, these vessels would move off, taking the pursuing
Americans out of Leyte Gulf. Meanwhile a second Japanese
fleet, composed mostly of big-gun ships, would split into two
forces. One would penetrate Leyte Gulf from the north and
the other from the south catching the U.S. invasion fleet in
a pinchers movement and thereby annihilating it. Once this
part of the plan, called Sho-Go, was complete, the reunited
force would attack Halsey from the rear.
      (Despite relatively few references in this section in
comparison to some others in this volume, I have elected to
pay this battle the tribute it is worth with a rather lengthy
introduction. It is hoped that this will contribute in some
small measure to a better understanding of the engagement
and stimulate further research on it.)
      The Japanese hoped that their plan would not be
uncovered too early, but they were unfortunate in this. On
the morning of October 23, 1944, the American submarines
Darter and Dace, on offensive patrol in the South China Sea,
spotted a huge Japanese surface fleet. Two heavy cruisers
therein were torpedoed, recon reports were made, and the
submarines continued to shadow the enemy.
      Early the next morning, Third Fleet search planes
spotted the Japanese southern and central fleet, which contained no carriers. Knowing by now that something big was
afoot, Halsey deduced that an enemy carrier force must be
about. That afternoon his guess was proved correct when

the Japanese northern force was sighted moving south in the vicinity of Cape Engano, the northern tip of Luzon. Planes from Luzon attacked the American task force in the north and although some 100 Japanese planes were downed, the light carrier Princeton was so damaged that she had to be abandoned--the first U.S. carrier lost in almost two years.

The Americans, planning quickly, reeled off three task groups to contact the Japanese that afternoon. One under Admiral Frederick Sherman would attack the enemy to the north. A second under Admiral Gerald Bogan would divide its attention between supporting Sherman and fighting the Japanese central group. The third established contact with the Japanese southern force closing in on Surigao Strait, but failed to bring about conclusive results. To take care of this, Admiral Kinkaid, the invasion commander, appointed Rear Admiral Jesse Oldendorf to remedy this threat with a surface fleet of six old battleships, nine cruisers, and smaller vessels, including PT boats.

Meanwhile early that morning (October 24), the Japanese central force, heading for San Bernardino Strait and the east coast of Samar on Leyte Gulf, came under attack from Third Fleet aircraft. In an intensive action, the giant battleship Musashi, sister to the Yamato, was sunk along with a cruiser and a destroyer. Expecting no further difficulties in that area, Halsey then threw all of his fast carriers and battleships into the pursuit of the Japanese northern force, leaving none behind to guard against an enemy surprise from the south. This action was later severely criticized.

While Halsey was moving north, the Japanese did indeed move in. The Leyte beachhead was guarded only by a handful of escort carriers and destroyers. One of these task units, "Taffey Three," composed of six jeep carriers, three destroyers, and four destroyer escorts would now become involved in one of the strangest and wildest chases in naval history, the little battle off Samar.

Admiral Kurita's central force, despite the loss of Musashi, was not destroyed. On the morning of October 25, it suddenly reappeared behind Rear Admiral Cliffton A. F. Sprague's "Taffey Three." By any measure, the Americans, up against 14-inch guns and completely outclassed as to speed, should have been massacred. The escort carriers were not armored and their planes lacked fuel, and were low on bombs and torpedoes. The Yanks, nevertheless, fought gallantly. As the American carriers sped away at their top speed, their escorting destroyers attacked. Overwhelmed and sunk, the destroyers Hoel and Johnston and the

DE Roberts paid the full price, but allowed the carriers, whose planes also made valiant attacks, for the most part to survive. In the roughly one and a quarter hours of the unequal contest, only the Gambier Bay was sunk, although several other "jeeps" were badly damaged. With victory almost in hand and certainly within reach, the Japanese admiral, supposing he was facing a larger foe and fearing that Halsey might descend upon him at any time, broke off the action and withdrew. His losses were one cruiser and one destroyer sunk.

Sprague and others had sent out many distress calls, but no one was close enough to help. "Taffey Three" survived because of its own guts and should be credited today, as it was then, with one of the bravest fights in all naval history.

On the afternoon of October 25, Admiral Halsey's forces came to grips with the Japanese northern force off Cape Engano. All of the enemy carriers, which were offered as bait, were hit and sunk with heavy damage to the remaining elements of the Imperial fleet. Crippled ships were attacked later by U.S. cruisers and destroyers.

When Halsey learned of Strague's plight, he sent several units to help, but when these arrived they found that all of the enemy's central force, except one damaged cruiser, had gone. Later in the evening, the Japanese southern force entered Surigao Strait and in the last battleship encounter, Oldendorf's gunners caught them in the classic maneuver of "crossing the T," i.e., all of the American's broadside guns could be brought against only the enemy's forward turrets. Two enemy battlewagons and three destroyers were sunk almost before they could open fire. A number of Japanese units were able to escape, but most were later picked off by air attack. Not a single Imperial shell hit the invasion fleet off Leyte and the only American casualty was the destroyer Grant, which suffered heavy damage.

The following day the survivors of the Japanese central force which nearly did in "Taffey Three" were located by American carrier aircraft. The Yamato, of whom we will hear more during the Okinawa operation, was damaged. Another battleship was hit and later the next month was finished off near the China coast by the submarine Sealion.

The grand Japanese scheme to regain the upper hand at sea ended in total failure. The alertness of the Americans, despite some mistakes, outclassed the confused and disunited Imperial Navy. Perhaps not so important strategically as Midway or the First Battle of the Philippine Sea, Leyte Gulf was without a doubt the most spectacular naval battle.

5189a Baldwin, Hanson W.   "The Battle of Leyte Gulf."
       In: Don Congdon, ed. Combat: Pacific Theater.
       New York: Dell, 1958. p. 327+.
            Reprinted from the author's Sea Fights and
       Ship Wrecks, this useful account is enhanced by
       remarks from Admirals Halsey and Kinkaid.

5190   _____. "The Most Dramatic Sea Battle in History."
       New York Times Magazine (October 25-November
       7, 1954), 14-15+, 4+.
            Leyte Gulf, 1944.

5191   "The Battle for the Philippines." Fortune, XXXI
       (June 1945), 156-164.
            Leyte Gulf.

5192   "Battle of the Philippines." Illustrated London News,
       CCV (November 4, 1944), 518-519.
            Leyte Gulf.

5193   "The Battle That Won the Pacific: The Second Battle
       of the Philippine Sea Last October." Popular
       Mechanics, LXXXIII (February 1945), 17-25.
            Battle of Leyte Gulf.

5194   "Battleship-Carrier Fleet Task Force Proves Efficacy
       in the Philippines." Aviation News, II (November
       6, 1944), 28.

5195   Bean, P. W. "Prisoners Pay Off." Infantry Journal,
       LVIII (April 1946), 41-43.
            With regard to the Battle of Leyte Gulf.

5196   Brodie, Bernard. "Trafalgar for Japan." Nation,
       CLIX (November 11, 1944), 580-583.
            Leyte Gulf.

5197   Buracker, William H.   "The Saga of the Carrier
       Princeton." National Geographic, LXXXVIII (August
       1945), 189-218.

5198   Cant, Gilbert. "Bull's Run: Was Halsey Right at
       Leyte Gulf?" Life, XXIII (November 24, 1947),
       73-76+.
            According to Admiral Morison, Halsey was
       never called "Bull"; rather, the title was a cor-
       ruption of his nickname "Bill" devised by newsmen
       to foster fighting spirit.

5199   "Color Story: The Navy Communique on the Second
       Battle of the Philippine Sea. " Newsweek, XXIV
       (November 27, 1944), 34.

5200   Coward, Jesse G.   "The Battle of Surigao Strait."
       USNIP, LXXV (19 59), 103.

5201   Cullinane, Leo.   "Detailed Story of Victory in the
       Philippines. " USNIP, LXXI (1945), 101-102.
       Reprinted from the November 18, 1944 issue of
       the New York Herald Tribune.

5202   Deac, Wilfred P.   "The Battle off Samar. " American
       Heritage, XVIII (December 1966), 20-23+.

5203   "End Run, Touchdown. " Time, XLIV (December 18,
       1944), 26-27.
       Battle of Leyte Gulf.

5204   Falk, Stanley L. Decision at Leyte. New York:
       W. W. Norton, 1966.   330p.   Rpr. 1967.

5205   Falls, Cyril.   "Naval Battle of the Philippines. "
       Illustrated London News, CCXII (March 27, 1948),
       346.

5206   _____. "Sea Battle in the Philippines. " Illustrated
       London News, CCV (November 4, 1944), 520.
       Leyte Gulf.

5207   Field, James A. The Japanese at Leyte Gulf: The
       Sho Operation.   Princeton, N. J. : Princeton Uni-
       versity Press, 1947.   162p.

5208   Fletcher, Leon.   "The Attack on Taffy Three. " Sea
       Classics, V (November 1972), 54-62.
       The loss of the U. S. S. Gambier Bay (CVE-73),
       during the October 1944 Battle of Leyte Gulf.

5209   Forester, Cecil S.   "The Great Naval Battle of the
       Philippines. " Saturday Evening Post, CCXVII
       (January 20, 1945), 18-19+.
       Battle of Leyte Gulf.

5210   Golinkin, J. W.   "Landscape of War: Excerpts from a
       Letter Written by a Naval Officer in the Pacific. "
       New York Times Magazine, (December 3, 1944),
       47.

5211 "The Greatest and Last Battle of a Naval Era." Time,
      LXXIV (November 26, 1959), 16-18.
          Leyte Gulf.

5212 "The Greatest Sea and Air Victory of the Pacific War:
      Photographs." Illustrated London News, CCVI
      (January 6, 1945), 20-21.
          Leyte Gulf.

5213 Hagen, Robert C. "We Asked for the Jap Fleet, and
      Got It: The Story of the Last Battle of the U.S.S.
      Johnston." Saturday Evening Post, CCXVII (May
      26, 1945), 9-10+.
          Sunk defending U.S. jeep carriers during the
      Battle of Leyte Gulf.

5214 Half Moon, U.S.S. "The Half Moon (AVP-26) Views
      a Naval Battle: An Eyewitness Account." Unpub-
      lished paper, Ships File, U.S. Navy Department,
      Naval History Division, Operational Archives,
      1962. 11p.
          The first part of the paper recounts "a view
      of a major naval engagement from the 50-yard
      line" at Surigao Straits in October 1944, while the
      second part constitutes a chronology of support
      operations to December 1944.

5215 Halsey, William F. "The Battle for Leyte Gulf."
      USNIP, LXXVIII (1952), 486-495.

5216 Hamilton, Andrew. "Where is Task Force 34?"
      USNIP, LXXXVI (1960), 76-80.
          On October 25, 1944, a garbled message from
      Admiral Nimitz to Admiral Halsey resulted in a
      loss of opportunity for the American fleet.

5217 Harris, Russell L., jt. author. See Karig, Walter,
      nos. 5222-5223.

5218 Hathaway, Amos T. "The Battle [of Leyte Gulf] as
      I Saw It." American Magazine, CXXXIX (April
      1945), 41+.

5219 Hoyt, Edwin P. The Battle of Leyte Gulf. New
      York: Weybright and Talley, 1972. 314p. Rpr.
      1973.

5220 Hurt, Samuel H.   "Battle for Leyte Gulf."   Unpublished
      paper, Individual Personnel File, U.S. Navy Depart-
      ment, Naval History Division, Operational Archives,
      1945.   39p.
      A May 23, 1945 lecture before students at the
      Naval War College.

5221 Ito, Masanori.   The End of the Imperial Japanese
      Navy.   Translated by Andrew Y. Kuroda and Roger
      Pineau.   New York: Norton, 1962.   240p.

5222 Karig, Walter, Russell Harris, and Frank A. Mason.
      "Battleship Banzai!" USNIP, LXXV (1949), 1150-
      1157.

5223 _____. "Jeeps Versus Giants." USNIP, LXXIII
      (1947), 1444-1453.
      U.S. escort carriers and DEs vs Japanese bat-
      tleships and cruisers in the Battle of Samar.

5224 Koyanagi, Tomiji. "With [Takeo] Kurita in the Battle
      of Leyte Gulf." Translated by Toshikazu Ohmae
      and edited by Roger Pineau. USNIP, LXXIX (1953),
      118-133.
      Reminiscences of the Japanese admiral's Chief-
      of-Staff.

5225 Kuroda, Andrew Y., jt. trans. See Ito, Masanori,
      no. 5221.

5226 Lane, Richard. "The Battle of Leyte Gulf." USNIP,
      LXXXV (1959), 101-103.

5227 Levert, Lee J. "The Battle of Leyte Gulf." Forum,
      CX (December 1948), 328-334.

5228 Macintyre, Donald. Leyte Gulf: Armada in the Pacif-
      ic. Ballantine's Illustrated History of World War
      II. New York: Ballantine, 1973. 160p.

5229 McManes, K. M. "The Battle For Leyte Gulf."
      Journal of the Royal United Service Institute, CI
      (November 1945), 492-502.

5230 Manson, Frank A., jt. author. See Karig, Walter,
      nos. 5222-5223.

5231 "Mastery in the Pacific: The Prize of the Showdown
      Battle off Leyte." Newsweek, XXIV (November 6,
      1944), 29-33.

5232 Morison, Samuel E.   "The Battle of Surigao Strait."
      USNIP, LXXXIV (1958), 31-36.

5233 Moskow, Shirley.   "The Battle for Leyte Gulf." Sea
      Classics, V (September 1972), 20-26, 63-66.
      A heavily-illustrated account.

5234 "The Navy Helps MacArthur." New Republic, CXI
      (December 18, 1944), 821.
      Battle of Leyte Gulf.

5235 Ohmae, Toshikazu, trans. See Koyanagi, Tomiji,
      no. 5224.

5236 Oldendorf, Jesse B.   "Comments on the Battle of
      Surigao Strait." USNIP, LXXXV (1959), 104-107.

5237 Pineau, Roger, ed. See Koyanagi, Tomiji, no. 5224.

5238 _____, jt. trans. See Ito, Masanori, no. 5221.

5239 Pope, Quentin.   "Sidelights on the Second Battle of the
      Philippines." USNIP, LXXII (1946), 308-310.
      An account of the Leyte Gulf battle reprinted
      from the December 17, 1945 issue of the Chicago
      Tribune.

5240 Potter, Elmer B.   "The Battle of Leyte Gulf." In:
      his Sea Power: A Naval History. Englewood
      Cliffs, N.J.: Prentice-Hall, 1960. p. 777-796.

5241 Pratt, Fletcher.   "The Great Victory of Leyte Gulf."
      Harper's Magazine, CXCI (November-December
      1945), 431-444, 537-552.

5242 Reynolds, Quentin, et al.   "America's Greatest Naval
      Battle: The Second Battle of the Philippines."
      Collier's, CXV (January 13-27, 1945), 11-13+,
      18-19+, 18+.
      The Battle of Leyte Gulf.

5243 Roupe, R. H.   "Halsey's Famous Signals." USNIP,
      LXXVII (1951), 828-829.

5244 Ruddock, T. D. "The Battle of Surigao Strait."
      USNIP, LXXXV (1959), 102.

5245 "The Sea Epic of the Philippines: Photographs." New
      York Time Magazine, (December 17, 1944), 6-7.

5246 See (periodical). Second Battle of the Philippines:
      Official Story of the Navy's Victorious Fight to
      Protect Gen. MacArthur's Invasion Forces and
      Supply Lines. A See Magazine Fotobook. New
      York: McGraw-Hill, 1945. 40p.

5247 "Showdown at Leyte." Newsweek, XXIV (November
      20, 1944), 50.

5248 Sprague, Cliffton A. F. "The Japs Had Us on the
      Ropes: Leyte." American Magazine, CXXX
      (April 1945), 40-41+.

5249 "The Story of Victory: The Second Battle of the
      Philippine Sea." Time, XLIV (November 27, 1944),
      29.
      Battle of Leyte Gulf.

5250 "Types of Japanese Warships Defeated in the Battle of
      the Philippines." Illustrated London News, CCV
      (November 4, 1944), 521.

5251 United States. Naval War College. "The Battle for
      Leyte Gulf, October 1944." Unpublished paper,
      Battle Analysis Series, Training Commands File,
      U.S. Navy Department, Naval History Division,
      Operational Archives, 1953-1958. 2, 643p.
      Perhaps the most detailed tactical analysis
      available based on both Allied and Japanese sources.
      Covers the period 17-25 October 1944.

5252 _____. Navy Department. Pacific Fleet and Pacific
      Ocean Areas. Operations in the Pacific Ocean
      Areas During the Month of October 1944. Washing-
      ton, 1945.

5153 Warner, Oliver. "Leyte Gulf." In: his Great Sea
      Battles. London: Spring Books, 1963. p. 292-
      298.

5254 "Wing Talk: Heroic Flying in the Second Battle of the

Philippines." Collier's, CXV (May 26, 1945), 8.
Battle of Leyte Gulf.

5255 Woodward, Comer V. The Battle for Leyte Gulf. New
York: Macmillan, 1947. 244p.

Further References: Readers are reminded that
additional data relative to this section will be found in sections IIA and IIE-1 above, as well as in the general works
cited in Volume III, Part 1.

(3) RECAPTURE OF THE PHILIPPINES

Introduction. General Douglas MacArthur's plans
for the Philippines originally called for a landing on Mindanao, a southern island, on December 20, 1944. While his
thinking was moving in relation to that date, the Joint Chiefs
of Staff, meeting at Quebec in a conference called Octagon,
received a copy of a message from Halsey to Admiral Chester W. Nimitz which suggested an earlier time. His sug-
gestion also included a note that the invasion be centered on
Leyte, rather than Mindanao. The JCS requested the general's reaction to the admiral's idea. MacArthur replied that,
yes, he was willing to change his plans and advance his
timetable. Both he and Nimitz were then ordered to cooper-
ate and move their schedules back to October 20. From
that date to February 1945, most of the Pacific Fleet would
be involved in the Philippine campaign. The Central Pacific
drive was halted and no operations were undertaken during
that time in a northerly direction.
While the invasion forces were assembling, U.S.A.-
A.F. and carrier planes concentrated on isolating Leyte.
Attacks, mainly from carriers, were made on airfields
throughout the Philippines. These destroyed many planes
and installations, but did not do a thorough job. In early
October, Admiral Halsey's pilots bore down as far afield as
Okinawa and Formosa seeking enemy planes. In the air off
Formosa more than 300 Japanese planes were downed on
October 12-13.
The first of the American invasion fleet hove to in
Leyte Gulf on October 17, followed three days later by the
main fleet from New Guinea and the Admiralties. The Americans landed and met with little opposition. Initial objectives
were secured on schedule and MacArthur went ashore to
broadcast, "I Have Returned."

From here on out, the operations ashore, although
backed up by Navy and Marine aircraft, became primarily an
Army campaign (and thus are covered here only as incidental
to the sea forces' action).
    The remaining Japanese air force in the Philippines
recovered rather quickly and began attacking the invasion
fleet. It was during this campaign that a new group, the
Kamikaze Special Attack Corps, made its first appearance
in strength. Designed to crash with suicidal intent upon
American ships, the various planes of this "Divine Wind"
were stripped of their armor and loaded down with high explosives. They were, in fact, human-flown bombs. Among
Allied ships damaged offshore in the opening stages of the
Leyte invasion by these planes were the cruisers U.S.S.
Honolulu and H.M.A.S. Australia. Kamikazes would be employed throughout the Philippine campaign, but are especially
remembered for their role in the Okinawa operation (IIE-5).
The Essex-class fleet carriers of the Americans came in for
heavy punishment from Japanese regular and kamikaze aircraft. Examples include the Essex herself, hit by a kamikaze on November 25, 1944; the Intrepid, hit by a kamikaze
off Luzon the same day; the Franklin, hit by kamikazes off
Luzon on October 15 and 30, 1944 (for purposes of this compilation, all references to the trials of this particular ship
are entered in this section); and the Ticonderoga, which was
severely damaged by kamikazes off Formosa on January 21,
1945. Lesser carriers and other American warships suffered
in proportion.
    Following Leyte, MacArthur next moved on Mindoro.
Pre-landing air and naval attacks were made on surrounding
islands, netting a number of planes and ships. The December 15 main event came off easily with little resistance encountered. Two days later a violent typhoon occurred which
did more damage to American landing craft than enemy aircraft. Three destroyers, the Hull, Spence, and Monaghan,
were lost. The day after Christmas a Japanese naval force,
including a battleship, attempted to raid the Mindoro area
but was quickly driven off by air attack.
    A number of amphibious attacks were made on
islands throughout the Philippine chain. For purposes of
completion, it should be noted that Corregidor was retaken
in late February to early March of 1945. Meanwhile, as
the new year dawned, the Third Fleet struck once more at
Formosa and in heavy raids there, over Luzon, and off
Okinawa accounted for several hundred more Japanese aircraft. The Americans even entered the South China Seas,
Japan's private lake, and carried off large-scale attacks on

fields near Saigon, Cam-ranh, Quinhon, Conton, Hongkong, Hainan, and Swatow. During its 3800 mile voyage, few enemy aircraft came closer than 20 miles from the avenging American fleet.

Despite pockets of enemy resistance, the Philippine campaign was over by March 1945. A pledge was fulfilled and a brave people liberated.

5256 "Air Blows Soften Jap Defenses as the Philippine Campaign Unfolds." Newsweek, XXIV (October 23, 1944), 29-32.

5257 "American Return to the Philippines Opens Drive to Split Jap Power." Newsweek, XXIV (October 30, 1944), 29-31.

5258 "The Battle Begins For Luzon." Life, XVIII (January 22, 1945), 19-25.

5259 "Battle for the Philippines." Fortune, XXXI (June 1945), 156-164+.
       A summing up.

5260 Beaufort, John D. "The Marines Land: The Pacific Front." Christian Science Monitor Magazine, (December 16, 1944), 7.

5261 "Big Ben Still Ticks: The American Essex-Class Carrier Franklin." Newsweek, XXV (May 28, 1945), 42+.
       CV-13 was caught by an enemy bomb while supporting the Philippine reconquest and lost a huge portion of her crew before she was saved.

5262 Blackmore, Armand N. "Live Torpedo!" Air Classics, VIII (February 1972), 42-49, 65.
       Reminiscences of life aboard the escort carrier U.S.S. Nehenta Bay (CVE-74), particularly that time during the Philippine invasion when a badly damaged Avenger launched its live torpedo right on the flight deck!

5263 Boggs, Charles W., Jr. Marine Aviation in the Philippines. Washington: Historical Division, U.S. Marine Corps, 1951. 166p.

5264   Cannon, M. Hamlin. <u>Leyte: The Return to the Philip-</u>
       <u>pines.</u> U.S. Army in World War II--The War in
       the Pacific. Washington: Office of the Chief of
       Military History, 1954. 420p.

5265   "The Carrier <u>Franklin</u> Refuses to Go Down." <u>Life</u>,
       XVIII (May 28, 1945), 36-37.

5266   Christoffersen, Lee A.   "The Employment of Marine
       Dive Bombers in Support of the Sixth Army on
       Luzon." Unpublished paper, Senior Course, Am-
       phibious Warfare School, U.S. Marine Corps
       Schools, 1950.

5267   "Combined Sea and Air Attacks Test the Defenses of
       the Philippines." <u>Newsweek</u>, XXIII (April 10,
       1944), 19.
            Attacks undertaken during the period of our
       section IID.

5268   Conlin, Paul A. , jt. author. <u>See</u> Moses, Frank B.,
       no. 5298.

5269   Conner, John. "Guns Before Ormoc." <u>Leatherneck</u>,
       XXVIII (May 1945), 25-27.
            Amphibious Corps V artillery in the Leyte cam-
       paign.

5270   Connor, Karl. "Amphibious Operations on Navigable
       Rivers: Exploitation of Rivers in the Mindanao
       Campaign." <u>Military Review</u>, XXXI (September
       1951), 15-25.

5271   Craw, Clarence F. "Corregidor Again Changes
       Hands." <u>Coast Artillery Journal</u>, XC (November-
       December 1947), 25-29.

5272   "Cruiser's Death: Manila Harbor Receives Another
       Jap Ship." <u>Life</u>, XVII (December 11, 1944), 37-
       38+.

5273   Deacon, Kenneth J. "LCM's at Ormoc Bay, 1944."
       <u>Military Engineer</u>, LVIII (March-April 1966), 83.

5274   _____. "Mine Warfare in Manila, 1945." <u>Military</u>
       <u>Engineer</u>, LVII (September-October 1965), 348.

5275 Dean, John M. , Jr. "History of Group One, Fleet
      Air Wing Seventeen. " Unpublished paper, Type
      Commands File, U.S. Navy Department, Naval
      History Division, Operational Archives, 1945.
      81p.
      Covering the period from January-August 1945,
      this study relates the missions of AG-1 in patrol-
      ling west of Mindoro, its base, and over those
      parts of Southeast Asia controlled by the enemy.

5276 "Decision in the Philippines. " Life, XVII (November
      13, 1944), 25-31.

5277 Falk, Stanley L. Liberation of the Philippines. Bal-
      lantine's Illustrated History of World War II. New
      York: Ballantine, 1971. 160p.

5278 "Fireworks on Leyte. " Time, XLIV (November 13,
      1944), 31-32.

5279 Forester, Cecil S. "Part of a Battle: The Destroyer
      Irwin Saves Men of the Flaming Carrier Princeton.
      Saturday Evening Post, CCXVII (May 5, 1945), 9-
      10+.

5280 Frazer, Fred J. "Close Air Support in the Luzon
      Campaign. " Unpublished paper, Senior Course,
      Amphibious Warfare School, U.S. Marine Corps
      Schools, 1950.

5281 Gehres, Leslie E. "Before the Colors Fade: Captain
      of the Franklin. " American Heritage, XX (April
      1969), 60-63+.

5282 Gunnison, Royal A. "The Burning of Manila. " Col-
      lier's, CXV (April 7, 1945), 21+.

5283 _____. "Close Call at Leyte. " Collier's, CXIV
      (December 9, 1944), 11+.

5284 _____. "The Flag Goes Up Again. " Collier's, CXIV
      (December 2, 1944), 15+.

5285 _____. "Japan's Failure in the Philippines. " Col-
      lier's, CXV (February 24, 1945), 20-21+.

5286 Hipple, William. "Riding the Bombs: A Torpedo-

Bomber Ride to Manila on October 29." Newsweek,
XXIV (December 11, 1944), 32-34.

5287 Hubbard, Lucien. "Scrub-Team at Tacloban: Courage
and Ingenuity Got Us Past a Critical Moment in the
Invasion of the Philippines." Reader's Digest,
XLVI (February 1945), 8-11.

5288 Kenney, George C. "Far Eastern Air Forces, Leyte."
Unpublished paper, Files of the Air University
Library, Maxwell Air Force Base, Alabama, n. d.

5289 Kluckhohn, Francis L. "MacArthur of the Philippines."
New York Times Magazine, (October 29, 1944),
8-9+.

5290 Koury, Philip. "The Pacific Pay Wagon: 80, 000
Navy-Employed Civilians in the Philippines."
Saturday Evening Post, CCXVII (April 7, 1945), 6.

5291 Lippard, John B. "Return to 'the Rock.'" Leatherneck, XLI (November 1958), 22-27.
Corregidor.

5292 MacArthur, Douglas. "I'm a Little Late, But We
Came." Life, LVII (July 17, 1964), 82-83+.
The liberation of the Philippines and the Battle
of Leyte Gulf.

5293 _____. "They Died Hard, Those Rugged Men." Life,
LVII (July 10, 1964), 72-74+.
This excerpt from the author's memoirs recalls
the reconquest of the Philippines.

5294 McCutcheon, Keith B. "Close Air Support on Luzon."
Marine Corps Gazette, XXIX (September 1945), 38-
39.
MAG-24's support of the Army's 1st Cavalry
Division.

5295 _____. "Close Air Support SOP." Marine Corps
Gazette, XXIX (August 1945), 48-50.
What was effective use of aircraft in ground
support? Some answers.

5296 McMahon, Perry R. "Retaking the Harbor Defenses
of Manila and Subic Bay." Coast Artillery Journal,
LXXXVIII (July-August 1945), 4-19.

5297 Mayer, Arnold R. "The First to Go In." Yachting,
         LXXVII (March 1945), 56+.
              The Coast Guard in the American invasion of
         the Philippines.

5298 Moses, Frank B. and Paul A. Conlin. "'I Have Re-
         turned.'" Coast Artillery Journal, LXXXVIII (March-
         April 1945), 10-16.

5299 Nash, David. "Those Wonderful Naval Aviators."
         USNIP, LXXXVII (May 1961), 84-87.
              A POW's account of American air attacks on
         Japanese positions in the Philippines, 1944-1945.

5300 O'Callahan, Joseph T. I Was Chaplain on the Frank-
         lin. New York: Macmillan, 1956. 158p.

5301 _____. _____. USNIP, LXXXIII (1957), 451+.

5302 Paine, Ralph D., Jr. "Carrier Notebook." Fortune,
         XXXII (July 1945), 151-153+.
              Concerns U.S.S. Franklin.

5302a Petillo, James T. "The Japanese Air Defense of the
         Philippine Islands." Unpublished research paper,
         U.S. Naval Academy, 1966.

5303 "Philippine Lightning." Time, XLV (March 12, 1945),
         34.

5304 "Philippine Strategy." Scholastic, XLVI (February 5,
         1945), 2.

5305 "The Philippines Are Invaded." Life, XVII (October
         30, 1944), 26-27.

5306 Pratt, William V. "The Campaign for the Recapture
         of the Philippines." Newsweek, XXIV (October 2,
         1944), 32.

5307 _____. "Lingayen Gulf: A Model Amphibious Attack."
         Newsweek, XXV (January 22, 1945), 30.

5308 _____. "Why Leyte Was Chosen for the Landing."
         Newsweek, XXIV (October 30, 1944), 33.

5309 "Promise Fulfilled." Time, XLIV (October 30, 1944),
         19-22.

5310 Reilly, Henry J. "Battle For the Philippines." Fly-
      ing, XXXVI (February 1945), 23-25+.

5311 "Rescued by the Valour of Her Crew: U.S.S. Frank-
      lin Set on Fire by Japanese Bombs Brought Home
      to New York." Illustrated London News, CCVI
      (June 2, 1945), 595.

5312 Reynolds, George A. "Flying, Floating, and Fighting
      Angels." Aerospace Historian, XVIII (Fall 1971),
      202-204.
          Catelina rescues out of the Philippines in 1944.

5313 Reynolds, Quentin. "Chaplain Courageous: U.S.S.
      Franklin." Collier's, CXV (June 23-30, 1945),
      11-13+, 15+.
          This article referring to Father Joseph O'Calla-
      han was abridged in Reader's Digest, XLVII (Sep-
      tember 1945), 13-18.

5314 Romulo, Carlos P. "The Lesson of Leyte." Rotarian,
      LXVI (February 1945), 6-7.

5315 St. John, Joseph F. Leyte Calling. New York: Van-
      guard Press, 1945. 222p.

5316 "The Ship That Wouldn't Be Sunk: Story of the U.S.S.
      Franklin." All Hands, no. 574, (November 1964),
      54-62.

5317 Smith, Robert F. "Luzon Versus Formosa." In:
      Kent R. Greenfield, ed. Command Decisions.
      Washington: Office of the Chief of Military History,
      U.S. Army, 1960. p. 461-477.

5318 _____. Triumph in the Philippines. United States
      Army in World War II--The War in the Pacific.
      Washington: Office of the Chief of Military History,
      Department of the Army, 1963. 765p.

5319 Templeman, Harold. The Return to Corregidor. New
      York: Strand Press, 1945. 35p.

5320 United States. Marine Corps. Division of Aviation,
      Intelligence Section. "Marine Dive Bombers in the
      Philippines." Unpublished paper, USMC File,
      U.S. Navy Department Naval History Division,
      Operational Archives, 1945. 15p.

5321 _____.   _____.   _____.   _____.   "Marine Fighter Squad-
     rons in the Philippines." Unpublished paper,
     USMC File, U.S. Navy Department, Naval History
     Division, Operational Archives, 1945.   15p.
     February-April, 1945.

5322 _____.   Navy Department.   Pacific Fleet and Pacific
     Ocean Area.   Amphibious Operations, Invasion of
     the Philippines, October 1944 to January 1945.
     COMINCH P-008.   Unpublished paper, Files of the
     Department of Records Branch, Adjutant Generals
     Office, Department of the Army, 1945.

5323 _____.   _____.   _____.   Information Bulletin-Leyte.
     Cincpac-Cincpoa Bulletin 144-44.   N. p. , 1944.

5324 _____.   _____.   _____.   Information Bulletin--Philip-
     pines and Halmahera.   Cincpac-Cincpoa Bulletin
     125-44.   N. p. , 1944.

5325 _____.   _____.   _____.   Luzon and Mindoro Air Informa-
     tion Summary.   Cincpac-Cincpoa Bulletin 166-44.
     N. p. , 1944.

5326 _____.   _____.   _____.   Preliminary Information Bulle-
     tin--Philippines and Halmahera.   Cincpac-Cincpoa
     Bulletin 110-44.   N. p. , 1944.

5327 _____.   _____.   _____.   Special Memorandum on Leyte.
     Cincpac-Cincpoa Bulletin 148-44.   N. p. , 1944.

5328 _____.   _____.   _____.   LSM Group Five.   "The His-
     tory of LSM Group Five Aboard the U.S.S. LSM-26."
     Unpublished paper, Type Commands File, U.S.
     Navy Department, Naval History Division, Opera-
     tional Archives, 1945.   18p.
     Primarily concerned with its operation during
     the reconquest of the Philippines.

5329 _____.   War Department.   Army Air Forces.   Air
     Force Evaluation Board, Pacific Ocean Area.
     "Report Number III, the Occupation of Leyte,
     Philippine Islands." Unpublished paper, Air Force
     File, U.S. Navy Department, Naval History Division,
     Operational Archives, 1944.   76p.
     A report on the effectiveness of naval close air
     support during the amphibious invasion of Leyte by

two U.S.A.A.F. officers sent to observe the operation.

5330 "War Comes Back to the Philippines. " Life, XVII
(October 23, 1944), 21-27.

5331 "Warrior's Ordeal: The Carrier Franklin. " Time,
XLV (May 28, 1945), 26-27.

Further References: Readers will find additional
information relative to this section in sections IIA and IIE-1
above, as well as in the general works cited in Volume III,
Part 1.

(4) IWO JIMA

Introduction. Following their defeat in the Marianas
in the summer of 1944, the Japanese came to expect that
eventually the Americans would attempt the capture of one of
the islands in the Bonin-Volcano group. Inspecting that area,
it was decided that the most likely target would be Iwo Jima,
which could readily accommodate the huge enemy American
superfortresses. Accordingly, they set out to make this
little eight-mile ash heap the most heavily defended spot in
the entire Pacific. In his final Official Report, Fleet Admiral Ernest J. King bore testimony to the efficiency of the
enemy's preparations: "The defensive organization of Iwo
Jima was the most complete and effective yet encountered.
The beaches were flanked by high terrain favorable to the
defenders. Artillery, mortars, and rocket launchers were
well concealed, yet could register on any point of the island.
Observation was possible both from Mount Suribachi at the
south and from a number of commanding hills rising above
the northern plateau. The rugged volcanic crags, severe
escarpments and steep defiles sloping to the sea from all
sides of the central Motoyama tableland afforded excellent
natural cover and concealment, and lent themselves readily
to the construction of subterranean positions to which the
Japanese are addicted. "
As mentioned, United States forces regularly bombed Iwo beginning at least seven months before the invasion,
which was pushed back to February 1945 due to delays in the
Philippines. American surface warships also brought their
heavy guns to play on supposed Japanese defenses.

Admiral Raymond A. Spruance, commander of the U.S. Fifth Fleet, was in over-all command of the operation, with Vice Admiral Richmond K. Turner in charge of the amphibious forces, and the expeditionary forces under General Holland M. Smith. Following a massive softening-up bombardment, almost 60,000 Marines were sent ashore on February 19 to wrest the islet from its approximately 20,000 Japanese defenders.

Storming ashore, the Americans almost immediately ran into intense heavy artillery, mortar, and rocket fire from some of the newest ordnance in the Japanese arsenal. Interlocking caves, pillboxes, and blockhouses had to be assaulted and carried against what was becoming the standard form of fanatical resistance. On February 23, the flag was raised over Mount Suribachi and by March 2, the three major airfields were in U.S. hands.

Iwo Jima was captured after some 26 days of actual fighting. The toll on both sides was heavy; most of the Japanese were killed as were 4300 Americans. Of the valor shown by the Marines, Admiral King wrote: "American history offers no finer example of courage, ardor, and efficiency." Naval forces off shore also suffered; kamikazes sank the escort carrier Bismarck Sea on February 21 and damaged two others. Despite these losses, the Americans had moved another 725 miles or about half the remaining distance to Japan. Only one more campaign was left before the home islands were reached and that would be the most horrible: Okinawa.

5332 "Banzai on Iwo." Newsweek, XXV (March 19, 1945), 37.

5333 Bartley, Whitman S. Iwo Jima: Amphibious Epic. Washington: Historical Branch, U.S. Marine Corps, 1954. 253p.

5334 "The Battlefield of Iwo." Life, XVIII (April 9, 1945), 93-101.

5335 Books, Walter Y. "Engineers on Iwo." Marine Corps Gazette, XXIX (October 1945), 48-52.

5336 Cant, Gilbert. "Home to Chichi Jima." Life, XX (June 24, 1946), 17-19.

5337 Cates, C. B. "Iwo Jima." Marine Corps Gazette, XLIX (February 1965), 28-31.

5338   Chapin, John C.   "The Fifth Marine Division in World
       War II. " Unpublished paper, USMC File, U.S.
       Navy Department, Naval History Division, Opera-
       tional Archives, 1945.   17p.
       Contains command and staff personnel and or-
       ganizational tables as well as battle accounts of the
       Iwo Jima Campaign.

5339   Clayton, K. "Iwo Never was a Push Over. " Flying,
       XXXVI (June 1945), 48-49+.

5340   Cline, David. "Iwo Jima Twenty Years Ago. " AF
       Times, XXV (March 3, 1965), M1.

5341   Cockrel, Francis W.   "How It Was on Iwo. " In:
       Patrick O'Sheel and Gene Cook, eds. Semper
       Fidelis: The U.S. Marines in the Pacific, 1942-
       1945. New York: William Sloane Associates,
       1947. p. 100-106.

5342   Conner, Howard M.   The Spearhead: The World War
       II History of the 5th Marine Division. Washington:
       Infantry Journal Press, 1950. 325p.
       Action on Iwo Jima.

5343   "Costly Iwo Jima. " U.S. News, (March 2, 1945), 13.

5344   Davenport, Walter.   "Men and Guns at Iwo Jima. "
       Collier's, CXV (March 31, 1945), 16-17+.

5345   Decker, Duane. "Iwo--D Plus 180. " Leatherneck,
       XXVIII (September 1945), 33-35.

5346   Dunnagan, C. G. "Iwo Jima. " Marine Corps Gazette,
       XLIX (February 1965), 28-31.

5347   Emmons, R. M. "Narrative of Iwo Jima. " Marine
       Corps Gazette, XXXIV (June 1950), 25-27.

5348   Gallant, T. Grady. The Friendly Dead. Garden City,
       N.Y.: Doubleday, 1964. 198p.
       The Marines on Iwo Jima.

5349   Garretson, Frank E. "Operations of the 2nd Btn. ,
       24th Marines on Iwo Jima, Volcano Islands, 19th
       February to 18th March 1945. " Unpublished paper,
       Advanced Officers Course, the Infantry School,
       Ft. Benning, Ga. , 1947.

5350 "H Hour on Iwo Jima." Newsweek, XXV (February 26, 1945), 29.

5351 Haynes, F. E. "Left Flank at Iwo." Marine Corps Gazette, XXXVII (March 1953), 48-53.

5352 Heinl, Robert D., Jr. "Dark Horse on Iwo." Marine Corps Gazette, XXIX (August 1945), passim.

5353 _____. "Target: Iwo." USNIP, LXXXIX (1963), 70-82.
A study of the Army/Navy dispute over the duration of the Navy's pre-invasion bombardment. A comment on the article was offered by Captain L. R. Flore in the same journal, pp. 102-103.

5354 "Hell's Acre." Time, XLV (February 26, 1945), 25-27.
Iwo Jima.

5355 Henri, Raymond H. Iwo Jima, Springboard to Final Victory. Cleveland: World, 1945. 96p.
A U.S. Camera Book featuring photographs by combat cameramen.

5356 _____, James G. Lucas, and Alvin M. Josephy, Jr. The U.S. Marines on Iwo Jima. New York: Dial Press, 1945. 294p.

5357 Hill, Arthur N. "Battalion on Iwo." Marine Corps Gazette, XXIX (November 1945), 27-30.

5358 Hindsman, C. Earl. The Iwo Jima Story. Washington, 1955. 48p.

5359 Hipple, William. "This Is Iwo." Newsweek, XXV (March 5, 1945), 38.

5360 Horie, Y. "The Japanese Defense of Iwo Jima." Marine Corps Gazette, XXXVI (February 1952), 18-27.

5361 _____. "The Japanese Plan for Chichi Jima." Marine Corps Gazette, XXXVII (July 1953), 36-40.

5362 Hunt, R. D. "Target: Iwo." USNIP, LXXXIX (1963), 70-82.

5363   "The Inevitable Island."   Time, XLV (March 5, 1945), 25-27.
       Iwo Jima.

5364   "The Invasion of Iwo Jima."   Illustrated London News, CCVI (March 10, 1945), 271.

5365   Isely, Jeter A.   'Iwo Jima, Acme of Amphibious Assault."   USNIP, LXXVII (1951), 1-13.

5366   "Iwo, Bloody Inches."   Newsweek, XXV (March 12, 1945), 34-35.

5367   "Iwo Jima."   Life, XVIII (March 5, 1945), 36-38.

5368   Jones, Edgar L.   "To the Finish: A Letter from Iwo Jima."   Atlantic Monthly, CLXXV (June 1945), 50-53.

5369   Josephy, Alvin M., Jr.   "Iwo Transport."   In: Patrick O'Sheel and Gene Cook, eds.   Semper Fidelis: The U.S. Marines in the Pacific, 1942-1945.   New York: William Sloane Associates, 1947.   p. 340-344.
       Marine life aboard a transport headed for the invasion of Iwo Jima.

5370   _____.   "Jungle of Stone."   Infantry Journal, LVII (September 1945), 10-17.
       Iwo Jima.

5371   _____, jt. author.   See Henri, Raymond H., no. 5356.

5372   Lardner, John.   "D-day, Iwo Jima."   New Yorker, XXI (March 17, 1945), 48+.

5373   _____.   "This Is Iwo: The Story of the Battle."   Newsweek, XXV (March 5, 1945), 38-39.

5374   Lucas, James G., jt. author.   See Henri, Raymond H., no. 5356.

5375   McCandless, Bruce.   "Incident in the Nanpo Shoto."   USNIP, XCIX (1973), 67-77.
       U.S.S. Gregory rescues three downed airmen from the carrier Enterprise near Iwo Jima in 1945.

5376 "Marines Win the Bloody, Barren Sands of Iwo." Life,
       XVIII (March 12, 1945), 34-37.

5377 Marquand, John P. "Iwo Jima Before H-Hour."
       Harper's Magazine, CXC (May 1945), 492-499.

5378 Matthews, Allen R. The Assault. New York: Simon
       and Schuster, 1947. 216p. Rpr. 1958.
       A vivid eyewitness account of the Marines in
       the battle for Iwo Jima.

5379 _____. "The Landing." In: Patrick O'Sheel and
       Gene Cook, eds. Semper Fidelis: The U.S.
       Marines in the Pacific, 1942-1945. New York:
       William Sloane Associates, 1947. p. 82-88.
       On Iwo Jima.

5380 Nalty, Bernard C. The United States Marines on Iwo
       Jima: The Battle and the Flag Raising. Marine
       Corps Historical Reference Pamphlets. Washington:
       Historical Division, U.S. Marine Corps, 1970.
       29p.

5381 Newcomb, Richard F. Iwo Jima. New York: Holt,
       Rinehart and Winston, 1965. 338p.

5382 Patrick, John M. "Iwo Jima--Sulphur Island."
       USNIP, LXXVI (1950), 1028-1029.

5383 "Picture that Thrilled a Nation: The Flag Raising on
       Iwo Jima." Reader's Digest, LXVI (February
       1955), 85-87.

5384 Popham, John N. "Ie Shima." In: Patrick O'Sheel
       and Gene Cook, eds. Semper Fidelis: The U.S.
       Marines in the Pacific, 1942-1945. New York:
       William Sloane Associates, 1947. p. 196-199.
       The death of correspondent Ernie Pyle recorded
       by a marine combat correspondent serving with him.

5385 Pratt, William W. V. "What Makes Iwo Worth the
       Price." Newsweek, XXV (April 2, 1945), 36.

5386 Rodabaugh, Delmer. "The Seebee Library on Iwo
       Jima." Wilson Library Bulletin, XX (April 1946),
       600-602.
       Brought ashore after the invasion.

5387 Rosenthal, Joseph. "A Picture That Will Live For-
         ever: The Flag Raising on Iwo Jima." Collier's,
         CXXXV (February 18, 1955), 62-67.

5388 Sherrod, Robert. "Account of the Battle of Iwo."
         Time, XLV (March 5, 1945), 25-27.

5389 _____ . "The First Three Days: Courageous Marines
         Attack the World's Best Defended Island." Life,
         XVIII (March 5, 1945), 41-42+.
         Iwo Jima.

5390 Shershun, Carroll S. "The World's Most Costly Air-
         strip." Aerospace Historian, XIV (Winter 1967),
         239-244.
         Iwo Jima.

5391 Stebbins, Owen T. "Rifle Company vs. Fortress."
         Marine Corps Gazette, LVII (April 1973), 36-42.
         Operations against Sugar Loaf Hill on Okinawa.

5392 "Telling It to the Marines: San Francisco Examiner
         Editorial." Time, XLV (March 19, 1945), 60.

5393 [No entry.]

5394 Trumbull, Robert. "The Road to Tokyo: The Red
         Epic of Iwo." New York Times Magazine, (March
         4, 1945), 8-9+.

5395 Turton, Howard J. "A Division Pre-Dawn Attack."
         Unpublished paper, Senior Course, Amphibious War-
         fare School, Marine Corps Schools, Quantico, Va.,
         1947.

5396 Tyree, William F. "Iwo Jima." In: Louis L. Snyder,
         ed. Masterpieces of War Reporting. New York:
         Julian Messner, 1962. p. 402-404.
         Reprinted from the February 19, 1945 issue of
         the Chicago Daily News.

5397 United States. Navy Department. Office of the Chief
         of Naval Operations. "Report of Amphibious Opera-
         tions to Capture Iwo Jima." Unpublished paper
         P-0012, CNO File, U.S. Navy Department, Naval
         History Division, Operational Archives, July 17,
         1945.

5398 _____._____. Pacific Fleet and Pacific Ocean Area.
Defense Installations on Iwo Jima. Cincpac-Cincpoa
Bulletin 136-45. N. p., 1945.

5399 _____._____._____. Information Bulletin--Nanpo
Shoto. Cincpac-Cincpoa Bulletin 122-44. N. p.,
1944.
An intelligence report.

5400 _____._____._____. Information Bulletin on Iwo
Jima. Cincpac-Cincpoa Bulletin 145-44. N. p.,
1944.

5401 _____._____._____. Information on Iwo Jima:
Supplement to 122-44. Cincpac-Cincpoa Bulletin
9-45. N. p., 1945.

5402 _____._____._____. Progressive Construction and
Camouflage of [Japanese] Defense Installations on
Iwo Jima. Cincpac-Cincpoa Bulletin 137-45.
N. p., 1945.

5403 _____._____._____. Southern Nanpo Shoto "Bonin
and Kazan Islands." Cincpac-Cincpoa Bulletin 15-
44. N. p., 1944.

5404 _____._____._____, Commander Amphibious Forces.
"Report on the Capture of Iwo Jima." Unpublished
paper, U.S. Navy Department, Naval History
Division, Operational Archives, May 19, 1945.

5405 Ward, J. F. "Radioman Tells Iwo Jima Experience."
Science News Letter, XLVIII (September 22, 1945),
181.

5406 Wheeler, Joseph. "The First Flag Raising on Iwo
Jima." American Heritage, XV (April 1964), 54-
60, 102-105.

5407 Wheeler, Keith. We Are the Wounded. New York:
E. P. Dutton, 1945. 224p.
How the author was wounded on Iwo Jima.

5408 Wheeler, Richard. The Bloody Battle for Suribachi.
New York: Thomas Y. Crowell, 1965. 148p.
Story of the famous flag-raising incident.

5409 Williams, Robert H. "Up the Rock on Iwo the Hard
     Way." Marine Corps Gazette, XXIX (August
     1945), passim.

5410 Zurlinden, Cyril P., Jr., et al. "Iwo: The Red-hot
     Rock." In: Patrick O'Sheel and Gene Cook, eds.
     Semper Fidelis: The U.S. Marines in the Pacific,
     1942-1945. New York: William Sloane Associates,
     1947. p. 88-100.
     Also published in Collier's, CXV (April 14,
     1945), 16-17+.

Further References: Readers are reminded that
additional citations relative to this section will be found in
sections IIA and IIE-1 above, as well as in the general works
cited in Volume III, Part 1.

(5) OKINAWA AND THE DIVINE WIND

Introduction. The Ryukyu Islands extend in a
chain southward from Kyushu, southernmost of the home
islands, towards Formosa. Okinawa, the largest of the
group at 67 miles in length, is only some 350 miles from
Kyushu. If the Americans could obtain that spot, they
would be able to further isolate the homeland by cutting communications from Tokyo to Korea, Indo-China, and China,
would have excellent close airfields for bombers and fighters,
and most importantly be in a position to build up a large
base for the invasion of Japan proper.
     Okinawa physically is a tough nut. Divided by an
isthmus into almost equal northern and southern halfs, the
northern end is wooded, rugged and mountainous while the
southern area is generally rolling but often broken by steep
slopes and ravines. The capital city of Naha and the island's
airfields were in the southern half.
     Following operations in support of the Iwo Jima
campaign, Mitscher's fast carriers began raiding the Ryukyus
in early March. Japanese planes were destroyed by the
hundred, but American planes and carriers were also damaged. Here the carrier Franklin was severely bombed for
the second time in only a few months; only this second
tragedy was much worse than the first (Franklin citations
are in section IIE-3). These preliminary air raids, for
the most part, prevented the Japanese from countering with

their own aircraft until almost a week after the start of the Okinawa fight.

Prior to the actual landings on Okinawa, several offshore islands, including part of the Kerama Retto group and Keise Shima, was seized rather easily. These were captured so as to provide the invaders with supply and seaplane bases as well as long-range artillery platforms. On March 24, 1945, minesweepers and frogmen cleared paths to the main landing beaches on Okinawa itself.

Admiral Spruance was again in over-all command of this campaign. Turner controlled the joint amphibious force, or those people engaged directly in the landing, while Lt. Gen. Simon Bolivar Buckner, U.S.A., commanded the expeditionary or ground forces once ashore. Mitscher continued to oversee the fast carrier covering force, with Vice Admiral Henry B. Rawlings in charge of the British Carrier Force newly readied for participation. The Anglo-American force (navy, marines, army) consisted of 548,000 men, 318 combat ships and 1139 auxiliary vessels. Against them, the Japanese would pit 120,000 defenders, including Okinawan draftees, under Lt. Gen. Ushijima employing an inland defense.

For seven days preceding the invasion, Okinawa was subjected to an intense bombardment. On Easter Sunday-- April 1, 1945--the landings were made by the 24th Army Corps and the 3rd Marine Corps on the Hagushi beaches on the southwest coast. A demonstration, designed to confuse the enemy, was also carried out near the southeast coast. By nightfall the Americans had over 50,000 men ashore, had captured the local airfields, and had driven across the island to the east, meeting little resistance.

It was not until the invaders began moving north that they ran into Ushijima's defenders. Employing the natural ruggedness of the island's upper end, the Japanese had built or employed pillboxes, blockhouses, and caves, studding them with mines, artillery, and double-apron barbed wire. Space does not permit a detailed examination of what came next, although it can be said with no exaggeration that the fight was carried out not by miles but by yards for well over a month. Almost all of the Japanese defending the island were dead by the time victory was declared 82 days after the landing. American casualties, in killed, wounded, and missing, came to over 79,000, including naval losses.

The fighting offshore was just as savage as in the hills of the island. Japanese kamikazes here made the supreme effort and secured much success for their heavy losses. American radar-picket destroyers, stationed out to sea to give warning of attack, suffered the heaviest losses.

Mitscher's carriers were in constant trouble and the Hancock,
Intrepid, Bunker Hill, and Enterprise all sustained serious
damage. Interestingly enough, the British carriers, whose
decks--unlike the Americans--were armored, took a number
of hits but were barely scratched. A typhoon in early June
did heavy damage to the covering fleet, preventing scheduled
raids on Kyushu and support to the GI's and Marines on
Okinawa.
        One should not leave Okinawa without mentioning
the banzai charge of the Yamato. Hoping to do trouble to
the invasion fleet, the Imperial Navy sent its superbattleship,
with destroyer/cruiser cover only, on a one-way run in
early April. It was a stupid attempt which resulted in the
loss of the battlewagon, the cruiser Yahagi, and four destroyers, to say nothing of thousands of lives.
        For purposes of chronology, Okinawa was the last
major battle of the Pacific war. It was also the single most
costly engagement of the entire theater. This terrifying
campaign, on land and sea, was only a preview of what
might be expected in an amphibious invasion of Japan itself.

5411 Adams, Phelps. "Kamikazes." In: Louis L. Snyder,
        ed. Masterpieces of War Reporting. New York:
        Julian Messner, 1962. p. 487-492.
            Reprinted from the May 28, 1945 issue of the
        Baltimore Sun, this piece describes the attack on
        the carrier Bunker Hill off Okinawa.

5412 Adamson, Hans C. and George F. Kosco. Halsey's
        Typhoons, a Firsthand Account of How 2 Typhoons,
        More Powerful Than the Japanese, Dealt Death
        and Destruction to Admiral Halsey's Third Fleet.
        New York: Crown, 1967. 206p.

5413 Ahilin, Alan I. "The 6th Marine Division in Southern
        Okinawa." Marine Corps Gazette, XXIX (Septem-
        ber 1945), 23-27.

5414 Appleman, Roy E., et al. Okinawa: The Last Battle.
        U.S. Army in World War II--The War in the Pa-
        cific. Washington: Office of the Chief of Military
        History, U.S. Army, 1948. 529p.

5415 Baldwin, Hanson W. "Okinawa: Victory at the
        Threshold." Marine Corps Gazette, XXXIV (De-
        cember 1950), 40-47; XXXV (January 1951), 42-49.

5416 Beaufort, John D. "A Flattop Rides It Out." Christian
      Science Monitor Magazine, (February 17, 1945), 4.

5417 "Becton's Word: The Destroyer Laffey's Two Hour
      Battle, April 16, 1945." Time, XLV (June 4,
      1945), 32-34.
      Against Kamikazes.

5418 Belote, James H. and William M. Typhoon of Steel:
      The Battle of Okinawa. New York: Harper and
      Row, 1970. 368p.

5419 "The Bloodiest of All." Newsweek, XXV (June 18,
      1945), 39-40.

5420 Borning, Bernard C. "Artillery on Offshore Islands."
      Marine Corps Gazette, XXX (May 1946), 45-46.
      The support of amphibious landings by Marine
      artillery based on offshore islands, e. g., Okinawa.

5421 Braman, Don. "Cannonball Support." Leatherneck,
      XXVIII (October 1945), 30-32.
      Air support in the Okinawa campaign.

5422 Brown, David T., Jr. Marine from Virgina: Letters,
      1941-45 of David Tucker Brown, Jr., United States
      Marine Corps Reserve, Killed in Action on Okinawa,
      Shima, Ryuku Islands, 9 May 1916-14 May 1945.
      Chapel Hill: University of North Carolina Press,
      1947. 105p.
      As the title indicates, the author was only 29
      when killed.

5423 "The Bunker Hill, Victim of Jap Suicide Planes, Comes
      Home for Repairs." Life, XIX (July 9, 1945),
      28-29.

5423a Burton, Thomas M. "Okinawa in Review." Marine
      Corps Gazette, XLII (September 1958), 28-30.

5424 Cant, Gilbert. "Jap Superships." Life, XXII (Janu-
      ary 20, 1947), 19-20+.
      Abridged in the Reader's Digest, L (April 1947),
      109-110, under the title, "The Secret of Japan's
      Super-Battleships."

5425 Carleton, Phillips D. The Conquest of Okinawa: An

Account of the Sixth Marine Division. Washington:
Historical Division, U.S. Marine Corps, 1946.
133p.

5426 De Valle, Pedro A. "Old Glory on Shuri." Marine
Corps Gazette, XXIX (August 1945), passim.

5427 _____. "Southward from Shuri." Marine Corps Gazette, XXIX (October 1945), 39-43.

5428 Duncan, David. "Okinawa: Threshold to Japan."
National Geographic, LXXXVII (October 1945), 411-
428.

5429 Elliott, Allen W. "Ships Against the Sea: Three
U.S. Destroyers and a Number of Smaller Craft
Lost in Philippine Typhoon." Popular Mechanics,
LXXXIV (July 1945), 18-25.

5430 "Epic of the Bunker Hill." Illustrated London News,
CCVII (July 7, 1945), 2-5.
Concerns the highly damaging kamikaze attack
on CV-17 while she was supporting the Okinawa
invasion, May 11, 1945.

5431 Florida, University of. Department of Geography.
Ryuku Islands Project. Research and Information
Papers, no. 19. Gainesville, Fla., 1972.
Contains a useful article on the battle for Oki-
nawa.

5432 Fooks, H. E. "Okinawa." Journal of the Royal
United Service Institute, XCVIII (August 1953),
389-400.

5433 Frank, Bemis M. Okinawa: Capstone to Victory.
Ballantine's Illustrated History of World War II.
New York: Ballantine, 1971. 160p.

5435 Fraser, Bruce A. "The Contribution of the British
Pacific Fleet to the Assault on Okinawa, 1945,
Operation 'Iceberg'." Supplement 38308, London
Gazette, June 2, 1948.
Reprinting of a despatch from C-in-C, British
Pacific Fleet, originally dated June 7, 1945.

5436 Hersey, John. "Kamikaze." Life, XIX (July 30,
1945), 68-75.

5437 "Holiday Inn: Japanese Bombs Turned the Bunker Hill
      into a Floating Inferno. " Time, XLVI (July 2,
      1945), 26-28.

5438 "How Effective is 2%?: The Kamikaze Victims. " Time,
      XLVI (July 16, 1945), 21-22.

5439 Hunt, Richard C. D. "Typhoons of the North Pacific. "
      USNIP, LXXII (1946), 657-659.

5440 Inoguchi, Rikihei. "Eyewitness Story of the Kamikaze
      Suicide Missions. " Reader's Digest, LXIII (Decem-
      ber 1953), 137-140.

5441 "Islands of Fear. " Time, XLV (April 9, 1945), 26-27.
      Okinawa and the other Ryukyu Islands.

5442 Japan. Hikiage Engochō, Fukuinkyoku, Dai 2 Fukuin-
      kyoku Zammu Shoribu. Okinawa Area Naval Opera-
      tions, Jan. -June 1945. Compiled by the Welfare
      Ministry Demobilization Bureau, 2nd Demobilization
      Bureau, Liquidation Department. Tokyo: Allied
      Translator and Interpreter Section, General Staff,
      Military Intelligence Section, General Headquarters,
      Far East Command, 1948. Unpaged.

5443 Kosco, George F. , jt. author. See Adamson, Hans
      C. , no. 5412.

5444 Kublin, Hyman. "Okinawa: A Key to the Western
      Pacific. " USNIP, LXXX (1954), 1358-1365.

5445 Lardner, John. "Jap Sure Death Corps Sure Flops at
      Okinawa. " Newsweek, XXV (April 23, 1945), 56-
      58.

5446 _____. "Japs in Flying Caskets Go V-Bombs One
      Better. " Newsweek, XXV (May 7, 1945), 46-47.
      The Kamikazes at Okinawa.

5447 _____. "A Reporter on Okinawa." New Yorker, XXI
      (May 19-26, 1945), 32-36+, 46+.

5448 Lewis, Murray. "Okinawa: Nightmare of Rain and
      Death. " In: Patrick O'Sheel and Gene Cook, eds.
      Semper Fidelis: The U.S. Marines in the Pacific,
      1942-1945. New York: William Sloane Associates,
      1947. p. 106-108.

5449 Lott, Arnold S. Brave Ship, Brave Men. Indianapolis:
      Bobbs-Merrill, 1964. 272p.
      The fight between the Japanese kamikazes and
      the picket destroyer Aaron Ward off Okinawa.

5450 McMillian, Ira E. "The U.S.S. Newcomb (DD-586)--
      Victim of the Kamikazes." USNIP, LXXIV (1948),
      683-689.

5451 Manson, Frank A. "Seventy-nine Minutes on the Picket
      Line." USNIP, LXXV (1949), 996-1003, 1412-1413.
      American destroyers vs. Japanese Kamikazes.

5452 Martin, Harold H. "Close Support Bombing." In:
      Patrick O'Sheel and Gene Cook, eds. Semper
      Fidelis: The U.S. Marines in the Pacific, 1942-
      1945. New York: William Sloane Associates,
      1947. p. 122-126.
      Marine aviation in the Okinawa campaign.

5453 Martin, Paul W. "Kamikaze!" USNIP, LXXII (1946),
      1055-1057, 1589-1591; LXXIII (1947), 329-332.

5454 Mason, Arthur T. "The Battle of Wana Draw."
      Marine Corps Gazette, XXIX (October 1945), 25-30.
      Action on Okinawa.

5455 Morris, Frank D. "The Flying Coffin Corps: Japanese
      Suicide-Plane Pilots." Collier's, CXV (June 9,
      1945), 18+.

5456 _____. Okinawa: A Tiger by the Tail. New York:
      Hawthorn, 1968. 238p.

5457 Nichols, Charles S., Jr. and Henry I. Shaw, Jr.
      Okinawa: Victory in the Pacific. Washington:
      Historical Branch, G-3 Division, U.S. Marine
      Corps, 1955. 332p.

5458 Nimitz, Chester W. "Lessons of Damage in the
      Typhoon: Letter to Pacific Fleet and Naval Shore
      Activities, Pacific Areas, February 18, 1945."
      USNIP, LXXXII (1956), 82-88.

5459 _____. "Reports from Okinawa, Released by Admiral
      Chester W. Nimitz, U.S.N." USNIP, LXXI (1945),
      852-853.

5460 "Now the Ryukyus: The Navy is Prepared for Toughest
      Show by Hammering the Japanese Fleet. " News-
      week, XXV (April 2, 1945), 35.

5461 "The Okinawa Blow: Key to the Ryukyus. " Newsweek,
      XXV (April 9, 1945), 31-33.

5462 Olds, Robert, jt. author. See Gault, Owen, no. 5435.

5463 Paro, Eugene E. "The Okinawa Operation. " USNIP,
      LXXII (1946), 61-67.

5464 Pratt, William V. "Reply to the Okinawa Critics. "
      Newsweek, XXVI (July 2, 1945), 36.

5465 Pyle, Ernest T. Last Chapter. New York: Holt,
      1946. 150p.
      The famed correspondent's last report based
      on his landing with the Marines on Okinawa.

5466 Rew, R. E. , Jr. "Typhoon off Okinawa. " Reader's
      Digest, XLVIII (January 1946), 67-72.

5467 Sarokin, Paul. "Okinawa. " Leatherneck, XLI (April
      1959), 22-27.

5468 Scott, J. Davis. "No Hiding Place--Off Okinawa. "
      USNIP, LXXXIII (1957), 1208-1213.
      From the kamikazes.

5469 _____. "The Ship that Haunted Mitscher: Japan's
      Battleship, the Yamato. " Saturday Evening Post,
      CCXVIII (October 20, 1945), 27+.

5470 Shaw, Henry I. , Jr. , jt. author. See Nichols, Charles
      S. , Jr. , no. 5457.

5471 Shepherd, Lemuel C. , Jr. "The Battle for Motobu
      Peninsula. " Marine Corps Gazette, XXIX (August
      1945), passim.
      Okinawa.

5472 "Shock and Flame: The Kamikazes Strike. " New
      York Times Magazine, (July 1, 1945), 5+.

5473 Skuse, Margaret. Okinawan Briefs. Rutland, Vt. :
      C. E. Tuttle, 1954. 48p.

5474 Stockman, James R. The First Marine Division on
      Okinawa, 1 April-30 June, 1945. Washington:
      Historical Branch, U.S. Marine Corps, 1946. 62p.

5475 _____. "Night Operations on Okinawa." Marine
      Corps Gazette, XXX (September 1946), passim.

5476 Tashman, N. W., Jr. "Typhoon: The Ordeal of a
      Ship." New York Times Magazine, (April 22,
      1945), 12+.

5477 Tennis, Melvin H., Jr. "LCT's in a Typhoon."
      USNIP, LXXXIV (1958), 48-51.
      Off Okinawa in 1945.

5478 Tomlinson, L. A., Jr. "Tank-Artillery on Okinawa."
      Marine Corps Gazette, XXIX (November 1945), 37.

5479 United States. Defense Department. Armed Forces
      Staff College. "The Ryukyus Operation." Unpub-
      lished paper, Type Commands File, U.S. Navy
      Department, Naval History Division, Operational
      Archives, 1948. 69p.
      A recounting useful for placing the Okinawa cam-
      paign into the "Big Picture."

5480 _____. Marine Corps. Division of Aviation, Intelli-
      gence Section. "Marine Air Intelligence Bulletin,
      August-September 1945." Unpublished paper,
      USMC File, U.S. Navy Department, Naval History
      Division, Operational Archives, 1945. 28p.
      Relates particularly to Marine aviation during
      the Okinawa campaign.

5481 _____. _____. Sixth Marine Division, Intelligence
      Section. "The Sixth Marine Division on Okinawa
      Shima." Unpublished paper, USMC File, U.S.
      Navy Department, Naval History Division, Opera-
      tional Archives, 1945. 64p.

5482 _____. Navy Department. Office of the Chief of
      Naval Operations. Amphibious Operations--The
      Capture of Okinawa, 27 March to 21 June 1945.
      Unpublished paper, P-0700, U.S. Navy Department,
      Naval History Division, Operational Archives, 1946.

5483 _____. _____. Pacific Fleet and Pacific Ocean Area.

Information Bulletin--Amami Gunto. Cincpac-Cincpoa Bulletin 163-44. N. p., 1944.

5484   .   .   . Information Bulletin--Amami
Gunto. Cincpac-Cincpoa Bulletin 63-45. N. p.,
1945.
Supplement to Bulletin 163-44.

5485   .   .   . Information Bulletin--Nansei
Shoto. Cincpac-Cincpoa Bulletin 63-44. N. p.,
1944.
An intelligence report on part of the Ryukyu
Islands.

5486   .   .   . Information Bulletin--Okinawa
Gunto. Cincpac-Cincpoa Bulletin 161-44. N. p.,
1944.

5487   .   .   . Information Bulletin--Sakishima
Gunto. Cincpac-Cincpoa Bulletin 162-44. N. p.,
1944.

5488   .   .   . Information Bulletin--Sakishima
Gunto. Cincpac-Cincpoa Bulletin 62-45. N. p.,
1945.
Supplement to Bulletin 162-44.

5489   .   .   . Land Mines and Mine Fields
on Okinawa. Cincpac-Cincpoa Bulletin 193-45.
N. p., 1945.

5490   .   .   . Osumi and Tokara Guntos
Information Bulletin. Cincpac-Cincpoa Bulletin 78-
45. N. p., 1945.

5491   .   ., Amphibious Force. Gazetteer
to Maps of Okinawa Gunto. N. p., U. S. S. Eldorado,
1945. 41p.

5492   . War Department. Army Forces, Pacific
Ocean Areas. Participation in the Okinawa Operations. Unpublished paper, 2 vols. Washington,
1946.

5493 Van Deurs, George. "Two Block Fox." USNIP,
LXXXI (1955), 301-305.
Memoirs of the Okinawa Campaign by the skipper
of the escort carrier Chenango.

5494 Walker, Wayne T. "The Last Sea Battle." World
        War II Magazine, II (December 1972), 50-53.
        Sinking the Yamato.

5495 Worden, William L. "Kamikaze: Aerial Banzai
        Charge." Saturday Evening Post, CCXVII (June
        23, 1945), 17+.

5496 ____. "Rugged Bachelors of Okinawa." Saturday
        Evening Post, CCXXIX (March 30, 1952), 26-27.

5497 Yoshida, Mitsuri. "The End of the Yamato." USNIP,
        LXXVII (1952), 116-129.

        Further References: Readers will find additional
information relative to this section in sections IIA and IIE-1
above, as well as in the general works cited in Volume III,
Part 1.

        (6) ACTION ON THE ASIAN FRINGES

        Introduction. Although most of the war in the
Pacific might be considered as having been fought on the
fringes of Asia, for purposes of this work, and this section,
it is Asia--especially just off the Chinese Mainland--and the
islands of the Dutch East Indies that constitute the "fringes."
The purpose of locating this section after Okinawa, the last
major Pacific battle, is more or less, as was the Allied
aim, to tie up the loose ends of the reconquests in the area.
Many of the references herein cover the entire period of the
Allied advance.

5498 Adamson, Iain. The Forgotten Men: Commandos in
        Wartime China. London: Bell, 1965. 195p.

5499 Arnold, Elliott and Donald Hough. Big Distance.
        New York: Duell, Sloan & Pearce, 1945.
        U.S.A.A.F. raids on the Japanese oil refineries
        at Balikpapan, Borneo, in late 1944.

5500 Balev, B. "The Seaborne Landing at Novorossiisk."
        Soviet Military Review, VII (July 1972), 40-42.

5501 Blake, Alfred E. Convoy to India. By Ethelred

Blackeley, pseud. Brooklyn, N.Y.: Trilon Press, 1953. 214p.

5502 "Britain's Powerful Battleship Fleet in the Indian Ocean." Illustrated London News, CCI (October 31, 1942), 489.

5503 Brown, Frederick A. "U.S. Naval Weather Stations in Siberia." USNIP, LXXXVIII (1962), 76-83.
On a pair of unsuccessful units which had as much hinderance as help from their Soviet hosts.

5504 Caldwell, Oliver J. A Secret War: Americans in China, 1944-1945. Carbondale: Southern Illinois University Press, 1972. 218p.

5505 Calnan, Denis. "'It Was Quite Simple: We Were to Sink Her.'" In: John Winton, ed. The War at Sea: The British Navy in World War II. New York: William Morrow, 1967. p. 372-378.
The attack by Captain Manley Power's 26th Destroyer Flotilla which sank the IJN cruiser Haguro in the Malacca Straits on the night of May 15-16, 1945, as recorded by the captain's secretary.

5506 _____. "The Saumarez and the Haguro." USNIP, XCIV (1968), 147-150.
How the Royal Navy took out a Japanese cruiser in the Indian Ocean late in the Pacific war.

5507 Clark, R. W. An End to Tears. Sydney, Australia: Huston, 1946. 180p.
An account by an Aussie war correspondent who entered Hong Kong with the British surrender fleet in 1945.

5508 Connell, Brian. Return of the Tiger: An Account of Ivan Lynn's Surprise World War II Raid on Japanese Shipping in Singapore. London: Evans, 1960. 282p.
Published simultaneously in Canada by the Toronto firm of Doubleday.

5509 Evans-Lombe, E. M. "The Royal Navy in the Pacific." Journal of the Royal United Service Institute, XCII (August 1947), 333-347.

5510 Fellows-Gordon, Ian. The Magic War: The Battle for
      North Burma. New York: Scribner's, 1972. 180p.

5511 Fitzgerald, Oscar P. "Naval Group China: A Study of
      Guerrilla Warfare During World War II. " Unpub-
      lished paper, Individual Personnel File, U.S. Navy
      Department, Naval History Division, Operational
      Archives, 1968. 119p.
         Originally presented as an M.A. thesis, the
      work covers the group commanded by Captain Milton
      E. Miles which advised and trained Nationalist
      Chinese irregulars.

5512 Frank, W. F. "The Soviet Landing at Novorossiisk. "
      Military Review, XXXIX (March 1960), 12-16.

5513 Garthoff, Raymond L. "Soviet [Naval and Amphibious]
      Operations in the War with Japan, August 1945. "
      USNIP, XCII (1966), 50-63.

5514 Goodwin, Hal. "Marine Over Formosa. "   Leatherneck,
      XXVIII (September 1945), 20-21.
         Aviation.

5515 Goodwin, Ralph B. Hong Kong Escape.   London:
      Arthur Barker, 1953. 223p.
         Memoirs of a Royal New Zealand Navy Volunteer
      Reserve officer who was also present when the
      Japanese surrendered the island at the end of the
      war.

5516 Hauser, E. O. "Hong Kong Homecoming: Blowing
      Up a Big Oil Installation. " Saturday Evening Post,
      CCXVI (November 20, 1943), 22+.

5517 Hay, R. C. "Palenbang. " In: John Winton, ed.
      The War at Sea: The British Navy in World War
      II. New York: William Morrow, 1967. p. 364-
      369.
         The assault by aircraft from British Pacific
      Fleet carriers on these oil refineries in southern
      Sumatra on January 24, 1945, as reported by the
      Air Co-ordinator.

5518 Horan, James E. "Sinking the Haguro. " USNIP,
      LXXXVI (1960), 39-44.
         Five British destroyers nailed her in the Indian
      Ocean on May 15, 1945.

5519 Hough, Donald, jt. author. See Arnold, Elliott, no.
      5499.

5520 Kengle, W. A. "Mission in Tuntsin." Marine Corps
      Gazette, XXVIII (October 1944), 57.

5521 Kimmins, Anthony. "The Surrender of Hong Kong."
      In: John Winton, ed. The War at Sea: The
      British Navy in World War II. New York: William
      Morrow, 1967. p. 390-392.

5522 Kittredge, George W. "Stalking the Takao in Singapore
      Harbor." USNIP, LXXXIII (1957), 392-395.
      The Takao was a Japanese cruiser.

5523 McKie, Ronald C. H. The Heroes. Sydney and Lon-
      don: Angus and Robertson, 1960. 285p. Rpr.
      1961.
      Concerns 1943 raids on shipping in Singapore
      harbor.

5524 Mansfield, Walter R. "Ambush in China. Ma-
      rine Corps Gazette, XXX (March 1946), 12-16,
      39-42.
      The author, a Marine and O.S.S. agent, served
      with Chinese guerrillas against the Japanese, 1944-
      1945.

5525 Meister, J. "Soviet Seapower, Amphibious Assault."
      Military Review, XXXVIII (December 1958), 107-
      109.

5526 Miles, Milton E. A Different Kind of War: The
      Little-Known Story of the Combined Guerrilla
      Forces Created in China by the U. S. Navy and the
      Chinese During World War II. Garden City, N. Y.:
      Doubleday, 1967. 629p.

5527 _____. "U. S. Naval Group, China." USNIP, LXXII
      (1946), 921-931.
      Guerrilla warfare in China, 1943-1945.

5528 Miller, J. G. "The Mad Monks." Marine Corps
      Gazette, LII (November 1968), 45-48.
      Sino-Marine co-operation.

5529 Moore, James A. "X-Craft." USNIP, LXXXIII (1957),
      663.

The Japanese cruiser <u>Takao</u>.

5530 Mountbatten, Lord Louis. <u>South-East Asia, 1943-1945:</u>
      <u>Report to the Combined Chiefs of Staff by the Su-</u>
      <u>preme Allied Commander.</u> London: H. M. Station-
      ery Office, 1951. 218p.
      Little effort has been made to cover the CBI
      theater in this work as most of the operational
      history was conducted primarily on land.

5531 _____. "The Strategy of the South-East Asia Cam-
      paign. " <u>Journal of the Royal United Service Insti-</u>
      <u>tute</u>, XCIV (November 1946), 469+.

5532 Myers, Richard T. "The Saigon Raid. " Unpublished
      paper, Individual Personnel File, U. S. Navy De-
      partment, Naval History Division, Operational
      Archives, 1947. 4p.
      A brief account of the January 12, 1945 bombing
      attack written by an ex-British POW who witnessed
      it from the ground.

5533 "The Naval Surprise Attack at Sabang in Sumatra, April
      19. " <u>Illustrated London News</u>, CCIV (May 20,
      1944), 578.

5534 Noonan, William. <u>The Surprising Battalion: Australian</u>
      <u>Commandos in China.</u> Sydney, Australia: Book-
      stall Co. , 1945. 194p.

5535 Powell, J. B. "Today on the China Coast. " <u>National</u>
      <u>Geographic</u>, LXXXVII (February 1945), 217-238.

5536 Pratt, William V. "The Burma Campaign and the
      Way Back to Singapore. " <u>Newsweek</u>, XXIII (Jan-
      uary 31, 1944), 26.

5537 Pratt, W. V. "How Sets the Wind for Singapore?"
      <u>Newsweek</u>, XXIV (November 20, 1944), 42.

5538 _____. "Keys to the China Sea. " <u>Newsweek</u>, XXIV
      (September 25, 1944), 35.
      Formosa.

5539 _____. "Stalin's Strategy and Ours in the Pacific. "
      <u>Newsweek</u>, XXIII (April 24, 1944), 23.

5540 Reynolds, Clark G. "'Sara' in the East. " <u>USNIP</u>,

LXXXVII (1961), 75-83.
The American carrier <u>Saratoga</u> which was attached
to the British Pacific Fleet from March-May 1944.

5541   Sherrod, Robert. "Captain Dixie and the 'Ti'." <u>Time</u>,
XLVI (July 23, 1945), 30-31.
U.S. carrier <u>Ticonderoga</u>, CV-14, hit by kami-
kazes following a January 1945 raid on Formosa.

5542   Somerville, James F. "Report of a Gallant Action
by H. M. I. S. <u>Bengal</u> and <u>M. V.</u> Onida With Two
Japanese Raiders. " Supplement 38349, <u>London</u>
<u>Gazette</u>, July 12, 1948.
Reprinting of a despatch from the C-in-C,
Eastern Fleet, originally dated January 8, 1943.

5543   Stratton, Roy O. "Navy Guerrillas. " <u>USNIP</u>, LXXXIX
(1963), 83-87.
In China.

5544   _____. <u>SACO, the Rice Paddy Navy</u>. Pleasantville,
N. Y. : C. S. Palmer Publishing Company, 1950.
408p.
American-Chinese naval co-operation in World
War II.

5545   United States. Navy Department. Pacific Fleet and
Pacific Ocean Area. <u>Air Information Summary--</u>
<u>Formosa and the Pescadores.</u> Cincpac-Cincpoa
Bulletin 150-44. N. p. , 1944.

5546   _____._____._____. <u>Allied Airfields--China.</u> Cincpac-Cincpoa Bulletin 134-45. N. p. , 1945.

5547   _____._____._____. <u>China Coast--Air Information</u>
<u>Summary.</u> Cincpac-Cincpoa Bulletin 165-44. N. p. ,
1944.

5548   _____._____._____. <u>China Coast Air Information</u>
<u>Summary.</u> Cincpac-Cincpoa Bulletin 47-45. N. p. ,
1945.

5549   _____._____._____. <u>The China Seas.</u> Cincpac-
Cincpoa Bulletin 9-44. N. p. , 1944.

5550   _____._____._____. <u>China Sense; or, Rice-Paddy</u>
<u>Tales.</u> Cincpac-Cincpoa Miscellaneous Publications.
N. p. , n. d.

5551 ___.___.___ Chou-Shan, Yin-Hsien Area
Information Bulletin. Cincpac-Cincpoa Bulletin 128-
45. N. p., 1945.
An intelligence report on areas of the Chinese
coast.

5552 ___.___.___ Enemy Airfields--China. Cincpac-Cincpoa Bulletin 133-45. N. p., 1945.

5553 ___.___.___ Formosa Air Information Summary. Cincpac-Cincpoa Bulletin 29-45. N. p.,
1945.

5554 ___.___.___ Formosa Guide. Cincpac-Cincpoa Bulletin 40-45. N. p., 1945.
A manual.

5555 ___.___.___ Formosa (Taiwan) Information
Bulletin. Cincpac-Cincpoa Bulletin 49-44. N. p.,
1944.
An intelligence report.

5556 ___.___.___ A Gazetteer of the China
Coast. Cincpac-Cincpoa Bulletin 74-45. N. p.,
1945.

5557 ___.___.___ India-Burma-China Coast from
Shanghai to Swatow. Cincpac-Cincpoa Bulletin 128-
44. N. p., 1944.

5558 ___.___.___ Information Bulletin--Formosa.
Cincpac-Cincpoa Bulletin 119-44. N. p., 1944.

5559 ___.___.___ Information Bulletin--Northern
Formosa and the Pescadores. Cincpac-Cincpoa
Bulletin 146-44. N. p., 1944.

5560 ___.___.___ Information Bulletin--Prelimi-
nary Survey, Amoy Sector, China Coast (Ningpo
to Swatow). Cincpac-Cincpoa Bulletin 99-44. N. p.,
1944.

5561 ___.___.___ Information Bulletin--Shantung
Peninsula. Cincpac-Cincpoa Bulletin 119-45. N. p.,
1945.

5562 ___.___.___ Shanghai-Ninpo Information

Bulletin. Cincpac-Cincpoa Bulletin 30-45. N. p.,
1945.

5563 _____ . _____ . _____ . South China Sea--Air Information Summary. Cincpac-Cincpoa Bulletin 170-44.
N. p. , 1944.

5564 _____ . _____ . _____ . Special Report--Shanghai-
Ningpo Area. Cincpac-Cincpoa Bulletin 164-44.
N. p. , 1944.

5565 _____ . _____ . _____ . Special Report--Yellow Sea
Area. Cincpac-Cincpoa Bulletin 157-44. N. p. ,
1944.

5566 _____ . _____ . _____ . Target Information--China,
Hong Kong, Canton. Cincpac-Cincpoa Bulletin 142-
44. N. p. , 1944.

5567 _____ . _____ . _____ . U. S. S. Franklin. Cincpac-
Cincpoa Bulletin 98-45. N. p. , 1945.
Originally classified "secret. "

5568 _____ . _____ . _____ . Yellow Sea Information Bulletin.
Cincpac-Cincpoa Bulletin 48-45. N. p. , 1945.

5569 Wheeler, C. Julian. "We Had the British Where We
Needed Them. " USNIP, LXXII (1946), 1583-1585.
Also useful in connection with IIE-5 above.

Further References: Readers will find additional
information relative to this section in sections IIA, IID-6,
and IIE-1 above, as well as in the general works cited in
Volume III, Part 1.

(7) HITTING THE JAPANESE HOMELAND

Introduction. It was not necessary, as nearly
everyone knows, for the Allies to invade the Japanese home
islands. A number of events contributed to the enemy's
decision to surrender, including the A-bombs, Russian inter-
vention (IIE-6), and the continued bombing and bombardment
by Allied naval and air forces. The purpose of this final
section is to examine in some detail, especially by citing
official documents, the final stages of the Pacific war.

5570 Baldwin, Hanson W. "America at War: Victory in the
        Pacific. " Foreign Affairs, XXIV (October 1945),
        26-39.

5571 Brumby, F. H. , Jr. "When the Navy Landed in Ja-
        pan. " USNIP, LXXIX (1953), 1120-1121.
        For occupation duty following the surrender.

5572 Butow, Robert J. C. Japan's Decision to Surrender.
        Stanford, Calif. : Stanford University Press, 1954.
        259p.

5573 _____. "The Surrender of Japan. " USNIP, LXXXI
        (1956), 853-865.
        Aboard the battleship Missouri.

5574 Casari, Robert. "Thoughts on Japan's Naval Defeat. "
        USNIP, LXXXVII (1961), 109-110.

5575 Cochrane, Robert B. "Tokyo Bay. " In: Louis L.
        Snyder, ed. Masterpieces of War Reporting. New
        York: Julian Messner, 1962. p. 520-526.
        The surrender aboard the battleship Missouri as
        described in the September 3, 1945 issue of the
        Baltimore Sun.

5576 Feis, Herbert. Japan Subdued: The Atomic Bomb
        and the End of the War in the Pacific. Princeton,
        N. J. : Princeton University Press, 1961. 199p.

5577 Gozawa, Sadaichi, defendant. Trial of Sadaichi Gozawa
        and Nine Others. Edited by Colin Sleeman. London:
        Hodge, 1948. 245p.
        For war crimes in connection with the ship
        Thames Maru.

5578 Hailey, Foster B. "The War Converges on Japan. "
        Yale Review, New Series XXXIV (June 1945), 587-
        600.

5579 Halliwell, Martin. "The Projected Invasion of Japan. "
        Journal of the Royal United Service Institute, XCII
        (August 1947), 348-351.

5580 Ingram, M. D. "The United States Navy in Japan,
        1945-1950. " USNIP, LXXVIII (1952), 378-388.

5581 Kalisch, Bertram. "Photographing the Surrender

Aboard the U.S.S. Missouri. " USNIP, LXXXI
(1955), 866-874.

5582 Mitscher, Marc A. "Mass Suicide Can't Stop Us. "
American Magazine, CXL (September 1945), 24+.

5583 Morison, Samuel E. "Why Japan Surrendered. " Atlantic, CCVI (October 1960), 41-47.

5584 "Naval Bombardment of Jap Soil Warns the Foe the
Final Blow Is Near. " Newsweek, XXVI (July 23,
1945), 34-35.

5585 Nimitz, Chester W. "The Surrender of Japan. " Vital
Speeches, XI (September 15, 1945), 708-709.

5586 "133 Ships Hit Japan in Final Operations. " USNIP,
LXXI (1945), 1242-1243.
Reprinted from the August 17, 1945 issue of
the Chicago Daily Tribune.

5587 "Personalities Present at the Historic Scene on board
U.S.S. Missouri. " Illustrated London News, CCVII
(September 8, 1945), 264.
The Japanese surrender.

5588 Pratt, William V. "Can Air Power Bring Tokyo to
Terms?" Newsweek, XXV (June 4, 1945), 48.

5589 _____. "Sea Blockade by Air. " Newsweek, XXV
(April 16, 1945), 34.

5590 _____. "War Tides. " Newsweek, XXVI (July 16,
1945), 39.

5591 Shaw, Henry I. , Jr. The United States Marines in the
Occupation of Japan. Marine Corps Historical
Reference Pamphlets. Washington: Historical
Branch, U.S. Marine Corps, 1969. 29p.

5592 Sleeman, Colin, editor. See Gozawa, Sadaichi, no.
5577.

5593 Tavis, Frederick R. "Finale at Yokuska. " Marine
Corps Gazette, XXIX (December 1945), 19-22.

5594 United States. National Archives. The End of the

War in the Pacific: Surrender Documents in Fac-
simile. National Archives Publication, no. 46-6.
Washington, 1945. 24p.

5595   _____. Navy Department. Pacific Fleet and Pacific
Ocean Area. Air Information Summary and Target
Analysis Tokyo Bay Area. Cincpac-Cincpoa Bulle-
tin 169-44. N. p., 1944.

5596   _____. _____. _____. Air Information Summary,
Kyushu and Kure-Okayama. Cincpac-Cincpoa Bulletin 8-45. N. p., 1945.

5597   _____. _____. _____. First Supplement to Air Information Summary, Kyushu and Kure-Okayama (Cincpac-Cincpoa Bulletin 8-45). Cincpac-Cincpoa Bulletin 34-45. N. p., 1945.

5598   _____. _____. _____. Second Supplement to Air In-
formation Summary--Kyushu and Kure-Okayama
(Cincpac-Cincpoa Bulletin 8-45). Cincpac-Cincpoa
Bulletin 39-45. N. p., 1945.

5599   _____. _____. _____. Air Information Summary,
Nagoya and Osaka-Kobe. Cincpac-Cincpoa Bulletin
1-45. N. p., 1945.

5600   _____. _____. _____. First Supplement to Air Information Summary, Nagoya and Osaka-Kobe (Cincpac-Cincpoa Bulletin 1-45). Cincpac-Cincpoa Bulletin 33-45. N. p., 1945.

5601   _____. _____. _____. Air Information Summary on
North Honshu and Hokkaido. Cincpac-Cincpoa Bulletin 59-45. N. p., 1945.

5602   _____. _____. _____. Air Information Summary--
Southwest Honshu and Kyushu. Cincpac-Cincpoa
Bulletin 156-44. N. p., 1944.

5603   _____. _____. _____. Air Information Summary--
Tokyo Bay Area. Cincpac-Cincpoa Bulletin 61-45.
N. p., 1945.
Supplement to Bulletin 169-44.

5604   _____. _____. _____. Air Objective Folder--Aircraft
Engine and Assembly Plants in Japan. Cincpac-
Cincpoa Bulletin 112-44. N. p., 1944.

5605 . . . Airways Data Chosen Chiho. Special Translation No. 35. Cincpac-Cincpoa Bulletin 80-45. N. p. , 1945.

5606 . . . Airways Data: Chugoku and Shikoku Chiho Emergency Landing Fields. Special Translation, No. 33. Cincpac-Cincpoa Bulletin 37-45. N. p. , 1945.

5607 . . . Airways Data Kanto C. Special Translation No. 28. Cincpac-Cincpoa Bulletin 57-45. N. p. , 1945.

5608 . . . Airways Data Kinki A. Special Translation No. 31. Cincpac-Cincpoa Bulletin 58-45. N. p. , 1945.

5609 . . . Airways Data on Chiho. Special Translation No. 34. Cincpac-Cincpoa Bulletin 50-45. N. p. , 1945.

5610 . . . Bomb Damage Repairs Motoyama A/F No. 1--Nanpo Shoto Air Group Record for Jan. 1945. Special Translation No. 50. Cincpac-Cincpoa Bulletin 84-45. N. p. , 1945.

5611 . . . Daito Shoto Information Bulletin. Cincpac-Cincpoa Bulletin 77-45. N. p. , 1945. An intelligence report.

5612 . . . Gazetteer of Approaches to Southern Japan. Cincpac-Cincpoa Bulletin 168-44. N. p. , 1944. 48p.

5613 . . . Guide to Japan. Cincpac-Cincpoa Bulletin 209-45. N. p. , 1945.

5614 . . . Coastal Survey of Paramushiro and Shimushu. Special Translation No. 12. N. p. , ca. 1944.

5615 . . . Enemy Mine Fields. Cincpac-Cincpoa Bulletin 208-45. N. p. , 1945.

5616 . . . Enemy Minefields--Yellow Sea and East China Sea. Cincpac-Cincpoa Bulletin

168-45. N. p. , 1945.
An intelligence report originally classified as
"Top Secret. "

5617 _____ . _____ . _____ Experiences Against Japanese
Radar. Cincpac-Cincpoa Bulletin 191-45. N. p. ,
1945.

5618 [No entry.]

5619 _____ . _____ . _____ Hypothetical Defense of Kyushu.
Special Translation No. 72. Cincpac-Cincpoa Bulletin 158-45. N. p. , 1945.

5620 _____ . _____ . _____ Important Installations in the
Tokyo Area. Cincpac-Cincpoa Bulletin 175-45.
N. p. , 1945.

5621 _____ . _____ . _____ Industrial Targets, Northern
Kyushu. Cincpac-Cincpoa Bulletin 132A-45. N. p. ,
1945.

5622 _____ . _____ . _____ Information Bulletin--Kurile
Islands. Cincpac-Cincpoa Bulletin 60-45. N. p. ,
1945.

5623 _____ . _____ . _____ Information Bulletin--Southern
Kyushu. Cincpac-Cincpoa Bulletin 81-45. N. p. ,
1945.

5624 _____ . _____ . _____ Information Bulletin--Tokyo
Bay Area. Cincpac-Cincpoa Bulletin 147-44. N. p. ,
1944.

5625 _____ . _____ . _____ Izu Shichito Information Bulletin. Cincpac-Cincpoa Bulletin 154-45. N. p. , 1945.

5626 _____ . _____ . _____ The Japan Sea. Cincpac-
Cincpoa Bulletin 92-44. N. p. , 1944.

5627 _____ . _____ . _____ Kagoshima Defense Battle
Plan. Special Translation No. 90. Cincpac-Cincpoa Bulletin 205-45. N. p. , 1945.

5628 _____ . _____ . _____ Kobe-Osaka-Kyoto. Cincpac-
Cincpoa Bulletin 211-45. N. p. , 1945.

5629   .   .   . Koshiki Retto Information Bulletin. Cincpac-Cincpoa Bulletin 153-45. N. p., 1945.

5630   .   .   . La Perouse Straits Information Bulletin. Cincpac-Cincpoa Bulletin 131-45. N. p., 1945.
An intelligence report on the Soya Strait, a channel about 25 miles wide between northwestern Hokkaido Island and the southern tip of Sakhalin Island (Japan).

5631   .   .   . Niigate Harbor Facilities. Special Translation No. 68. Cincpac-Cincpoa Bulletin 138-45. N. p., 1945.
An intelligence report on the seaport located on the northwest coast of Honshu Island, Japan.

5632   .   .   . Northern Kyushu Information Bulletin. Cincpac-Cincpoa Bulletin 132-45. N. p., 1945.

5633   .   .   . The Pacific Coast of Japan. Cincpac-Cincpoa Bulletin 38-44. N. p., 1944.

5634   .   .   . Selected Coastal Targets, Eastern Coast of Japan (North of Muroto Zaki). Cincpac-Cincpoa Bulletin 114-45. N. p., 1945.

5635   .   .   . Tokyo Area Information Bulletin. Cincpac-Cincpoa Bulletin 155-45. N. p., 1945.

5636   .   .   . Tokyo Fire Tests. Special Translation No. 45. Cincpac-Cincpoa Bulletin 38-45. N. p., 1945.

5637   .   .   . Tsu Shima Information Bulletin. Cincpac-Cincpoa Bulletin 130-45. N. p., 1945.

5638   .   .   . Underwater Sound Wave Transmission Conditions in Japanese Waters. Special Translation No. 87. Cincpac-Cincpoa Bulletin 197-45. N. p., 1945.

5639   .   .   . Yokosuka Airfield and Air Group and Vicinity: Supplement #1 to 169-44.

Cincpac-Cincpoa Bulletin 19-45.   N. p. ,   1945.

5640 _____. _____. _____. Yokosuka--Special Study.
Cincpac-Cincpoa Bulletin 207-45.   N. p. ,   1945.

5641 _____. War Department.   Army Air Forces.   Mission Accomplished: Interrogations of Japanese
Industrial, Military and Civil Leaders of World War
II.   Washington: U. S. Government Printing Office,
1946.   110p.

        Further References: Readers will note further
citations relative to this section in sections IIA and IIE-1
through 6 above, as well as in the general works cited in
Volume III, Part 1.

APPENDIX

THE JAPANESE MONOGRAPHS

Introduction. In October 1945, barely a month
after V-J Day, General Headquarters of the U.S. Army Far
East Command ordered the Japanese government to prepare
a complete history of the Pacific War. The volumes which
appeared in connection with this dictate were written by
former officers of the Imperial Army and Navy, with little
assistance or supervision from American personnel. They
became known as the Japanese Monographs.

These studies vary widely in value and coverage.
Some were done by officers with a considerable historical
bent, while others were very poorly organized and written.
Some contained quite a bit of information based on diaries,
orders, and directives, while a number were composed entirely from memory. All have been translated, although
many of the translators were not familiar with either U.S.
or Japanese military terminology.

When the U.S. Army began the preparation of its
massive official history in 1951, the Chief of Military History
requested that copies of these works be sent to Washington.
Upon review, it was discovered that many of the works contained errors. Consequently, the Far East Command established the Japanese Research Division to verify and edit the
monographs anew. Led by an American editor with former
Japanese military and naval personnel in consulting roles,
the group functioned under a number of commands until the
time of its inactivation on April 15, 1960. In many instances,
the Japanese Research Division completely rewrote the exist-
ing translations, adding greatly to their value. Some of the
originals were combined into a single study in an effort to
eliminate duplication and allow for a more complete study of
the operation under consideration. Others were left to stand
as originally compiled.

Collectively, the Japanese Monographs must stand
as the single most important "enemy" source on the Pacific
Theater. While many are being supplemented by the various

354

official histories either finished or in process, none will be
entirely supplanted.   The fact that all have been translated
into English adds greatly to their value as sources for
students employing this bibliography.
        Unfortunately, these studies are not commonly
available.   Those wishing to consult them will find at least
microfilm copies available at the following locations: U.S.
Naval Academy; Library of Congress; Office of the Chief of
Military History, Department of the Army; Operational
Archives, Naval History Division, U.S. Navy Department;
Research and Records Division, Headquarters, U.S. Marine
Corps.   Additionally, a number will be had at the U.S. Army
Military History Research Collection, Carlisle Barracks, Pa.
For more information on the works, to borrow or loan or
purchase copies, one should consult these agencies, especially
LC, directly.
        The following list is not in alphabetical or chrono-
logical order.   Rather it follows the pattern of the monographs
as issued.   Each entry will be preceeded by the letters JM
(Japanese Monograph) and the Arabic numeral of sequence.
This code will then give the branch of service, e.g., Army,
and the type of operation involved, e.g., Defense Preparation.   All will be fully annotated.   In passing, it should be
noted that much of the material contained here comes from
the following: U.S. Department of the Army, Office of the
Chief of Military History, Guide to Japanese Monographs and
Japanese Studies on Manchuria, 1945-1960 (Washington, 1960),
282p.   In order that this might be a complete list, references
are included to some topics not touched upon to any great
extent earlier in this primarily "sea forces" compilation.
An example of this is the Burma Campaign.   About a third
of the following citations relate directly to the Imperial
Japanese Navy.

5642   JM-1.   Army: Invasion Operation. Philippines Opera-
        tions Record, Phase I: (6 November 1941-30 June
        1942).   Unedited translation, 243p.
            The Japanese invasion of the Philippines is herein
        described from the viewpoint of the 14th Army
        Headquarters.   The Luzon landings and southern
        drive, including the taking of Manila, Bataan, and
        Corregidor, are covered while landings on other
        islands in the Philippine group receive light treat-
        ment.

5643   JM-2.   Army: Invasion Operation. Philippines

Operations Record, Phase I: (1 December 1941-10
April 1942).   Unedited translation, 109p.
Outlines General Homma's personal estimate of
the Bataan situation in February 1942 with a résumé
of American defenses on Luzon, Bataan, and Corregidor.   Contains some information on "The Rock"
and other Manila Bay fortifications and installations, with detailed data on the missions, employment, and firing data of Japanese artillery.

5644   JM-3.   Army: Defense Preparation.   Philippines
Operations Record, Phse II: (December 1942-June
1944).   Unedited translation, 56p.
Primarily a record of the Japanese effort to
pacify the area with some discussion of the islands
as a logistical base for their Southern Theater of
Operations.

5645   JM-4.   Army: Defense Preparation.   Philippines
Operations Record, Phase III: (July-November
1944).   Unedited translation, 50p.
A look at the 14th Army's plans and preparations
for the over-all defense of the area against the invasion known to be coming.   Covers construction
of fortifications, mobilization, and training of re-
placements as well as the Army-Navy agreement
for joint defense operations.   Includes a little information on the beginning of the Leyte Defense
Operation.

5646   JM-5.   Army: Defense Operations.   Philippines Operations Record, Phase III: (July-December 1944).
Unedited translation, 18p.
Apparently written from memory, this brief
study goes into the 14th Army's defense against
MacArthur's landings on Leyte.   Few dates or
strength and casualty figures are provided.

5647   JM-6.   Army: Defense Operations.   Philippines Operations Record, Phase III: (June 1944-August 1945).
Unedited translation, 171p.
An account of the 35th Army's defense of the
Southern Philippines, with full coverage of the defense of Leyte from the level of Army headquarters.
Describes the withdrawal of the 35th to Cebu and
provides some coverage of the defense of Mindanao
and other islands.   Many maps and charts are
featured.

5648   JM-7.   Army: Defense Operations.   <u>Philippines Opera-</u>
       <u>tions Record, Phase III: (January-August 1945).</u>
       Unedited translation, 222p.
       An account of the 14th Army's defense of Luzon,
       with a large portion written in daily journal format
       from the level of Area Army Headquarters.   A
       very complete look at unit locations and over-all
       coverage, backed up by a large number of maps and
       charts.

5649   JM-8.   Army: Defense Operations.   <u>Philippines Oper-</u>
       <u>ations Record, Phase III: (December 1944-August</u>
       <u>1945).</u>   Unedited translation, 36p.
       Provides information on the defense plans, prepa-
       rations, and operations of the Shimbu Group in
       Southern Luzon.   A limited amount of coverage is
       given the defense of Manila.

5650   JM-9.   Army: Defense Operations.   <u>Philippines Oper-</u>
       <u>ations Record, Phase III: (December 1944-August</u>
       <u>1945).</u>   Unedited translation, 31p.
       An examination of the plans, preparations, and
       operations of the Shimbu Group in the defense of the
       Clark Field area.   Written in outline form and
       lacks cohesion.

5651   JM-10.   Army: Defense Operations.   <u>Philippines Oper-</u>
       <u>ations Record, Phase III: (November 1944-April</u>
       <u>1945).</u>   Unedited translation, 9p.
       A vague account of the activities of two provision-
       al companies that garrisoned Mindoro and Lubang
       Islands.   At one point, this monograph was rec-
       ommended for deletion from the series.   Should be
       used with No. 137 below.

5652   JM-11.   Army Air Force: Invasion Operations.
       <u>Philippines Air Operations Record, Phase I: (De-</u>
       <u>cember 1941-May 1942).</u>   Edited translation, 71p.
       An operational history of the 5th Air Group
       which flew in support of the initial invasion, includ-
       ing the Bataan battles and the reduction of Corregi-
       dor.   Amounts to a record of sorties executed and
       results, often inaccurate, reported.

5653   JM-12.   Army Air Force: Defense Operations.
       <u>Philippines Operations Record, Phase III: (August</u>
       <u>1944-February 1945).</u>   Unedited translation, 119p.

A look at the 4th Air Army and its defense of
Leyte and Luzon, with some coverage of its operations over Mindoro. Gives much space to plans
and unit listings.

5654 JM-13. Army: Defense Operations. North of Australia Operations Record (1943-1945). Unedited
translation, 108p.
Provides coverage of the operations of the
Second Area Army in the defense of Biak, Noemfoor, and Halmahera areas near New Guinea. The
primary thrust of this study is logistical, with
emphasis on interisland transportation.

5655 JM-14. Army: Defense Operations. Second Area
Army Operations in the Western New Guinea Area
(May 1944-January 1945). Unedited translation,
18p.
Recommended for deletion from the series, this
account provides an indefinite study of the operations of the 35th and 36th Divisions in northwestern
New Guinea, Biak, and Noemfoor. Some data on
guerrilla activities conducted by those units after
they were cut off.

5656 JM-15. Army: Defense Operations. Outline of the
Battle for Morotai (15 September-13 May 1945).
Unedited translation, 19p.
Written in journal format, this monograph covers
the efforts of the 32nd Division to send reinforcements and supplies to Morotai. Some data on small
raiding units.

5657 JM-16. Army: Invasion Operations. Ambon (Ambonia)
and Timor Invasion Operations (January-February
1942). Edited translation, 23p.
A simple description of two easy operations conducted by the Eastern Detachment.

5658 JM-17. Army: Defense Preparations. Homeland
Operations Record (1941-1945). Rewritten trans-
lation, 246p.
A look at the defense preparations in the Japanese
Home Islands, with the exception of Hokkaido. In-
cludes the establishment of the General and Area
Armies and the separate air command. Provides
information on the organization of forces, the

building of defenses, mobilization, and the disposi-
tion of units. Sketches of typical defense positions
are provided.

5659 JM-18. Army: Defense Preparations. Homeland
Operations Record, Vol. II.
Deleted and combined with JM-17.

5660 JM-19. Army: Defense Preparations. Homeland
Operations Record, Supplement to Volume III.
Deleted and combined with JM-17.

5661 JM-20. Army: Defense Preparations. Homeland
Operations Record, Supplement to Volume III.
Deleted and combined with JM-17.

5662 JM-21. Army: Defense Preparations. Homeland
Operations Record, Vol. IV: Fifth Area Army
(Late 1943-1945). Edited translation, 50p.
The defense plans and preparations for Hokkaido
and the Kurile Islands not covered in JM-17 above.
The defense of Attu and the withdrawal from Kiska
in the Aleutians is given light treatment. Some
data on the Soviet move into Sakhalin, with details
on the subsequent surrender and demobilization of
Japanese forces on that island.

5663 JM-22. Army: Plans and Preparations. Seventeenth
Area Army Operations (1941-1945). Rewritten
translation, 46p.
Plans and preparations for the defense of Korea
are covered with some information on this group's
co-operation with the Kwantung Army in China.

5664 JM-23. Army Air Force: Defense Operations. Air
Defense of the Homeland (1944-1945). Rewritten
translation, 91p.
An account of preparations for air operations to
be undertaken in the event of an invasion of Japan.
Primarily concerned with organization, personnel,
and logistical problems, together with last-minute
efforts to establish an efficient intelligence network.
The whole is seen from the advantage of Headquarters, Air General Army.

5665 JM-24. Army: Over-All Southern Area Operations.
History of the Southern Army (1941-1945). Rewritten translation, 159p.

A general review of the entire Southern Army's theater of operations. Examines high-level strategy and planning, as well as, troop movements, assignments for units, and offensive and defensive operations.

5666 JM-25. Army: General Coverage. French Indo-China Area Operations Record (1940-1945). Edited translation, 40p.

A brief description of the entry of Japanese forces into Indo-China for the purpose of disrupting Chungking's supply lines during the China Incident. The latter part of this study covers preparations for defense against a possible Allied invasion and Japanese operations against the French Indo-China Army.

5667 JM-26. Army: General Coverage. Borneo Operations (1941-1945). Rewritten translation, 98p.

A study of the plans, preparations, and invasion operations conducted by the Japanese in Sarawak and British North Borneo. Includes a brief description of the occupation activities of the Borneo Garrison Army and preparations for defense of the area by the 37th Army. An appendix provides excerpts from Australian Army reports on the recapture of Borneo in 1945.

5668 JM-27. Army: Invasion Operations. Jolo Island Invasion Operations Record (December 1941). Edited translation, 3p.

A brief look at the virtually unopposed two-day occupation of Jolo Island by the battalion strength Matsumoto Detachment.

5669 JM-28. Army: Invasion Operations. Tarakan Invasion Operations Record (January 1942). Edited translation, 6p.

A skimpy examination of the three-day operation by the Sakaguchi Detachment in the seizing of Tarakan Island.

5670 JM-29. Army: Invasion Operations. Balikpapan Invasion Operations Record (January 1942). Edited translation, 8p.

Describes the capture of Balikpapan by elements of the Sakaguchi Detachment from Tarakan Island

and the subsequent mopping up of the surrounding
area.

5671 JM-30. Army: Invasion Operation. Bandjermasin
      Invasion Operations Record (February 1942).
      Edited translation, 7p.
          A brief study of the combination overland and
      amphibious operation conducted by elements of the
      Sakaguchi Detachment, moving from Balikpapan to
      assault and capture Bandjermasin.

5672 JM-31. Army Air Force: General Coverage. Southern
      Area Air Operations Record (1941-1945). Unedited
      translation, 37p.
          Little combat operational coverage is provided
      herein as this work is primarily devoted to record-
      ing the organization and activities of air headquar-
      ters units, together with the transfers and attach-
      ments of subordinate units.

5673 JM-32. Army Air Force: Defense Preparations.
      Southeast Area Air Operations (November 1942-April
      1944). Unedited translation, 39p.
          An account of the plans, preparations, and or-
      ganization of the 4th Air Army for defensive opera-
      tions in Eastern New Guinea and the Solomon Islands.
      Written in expanded outline form, this record un-
      fortunately contains little material on combat opera-
      tions.

5674 JM-33. Army: Invasion Operations. Southeast Area
      Operations Record, Part I: South Seas Detachment
      Operations (3 January-30 May 1942). Unedited
      translation, 15p.
          A brief outline of the operations of the South Seas
      Detachment of the 55th Division, and the 4th Fleet
      in the capture of Rabaul, the invasion of Lae and
      Salamauna, and the unsuccessful move against Port
      Moresby. Recommended for deletion in favor of
      JM-143.

5675 JM-34. Army: Counteroffensive. Southeast Area
      Operations Record, Volume I: (May 1942-January
      1943). Unedited translation, 162p.
          A description of the efforts of the 17th Army to
      cut the lines of communication between the United
      States and Australia by establishing bases in the

Solomon Islands and at Port Moresby. Contains
information on plans and preparations for amphibious
and land operations against the latter, but has little
on actual combat operations. Discusses Japanese
attempts to dislodge the Americans from Guadalcanal,
including the co-operation given the Army by the
Naval Air Arm and the naval bombardment of shore
installations. Some data is presented on the supply
and troop movement accomplished by the Imperial
Navy and nicknamed by the Yanks, "The Tokyo
Express. "

5676 JM-35. Army: Defense Operations. Southeast Area
      Operations Record, Volume II: (February 1943-
      August 1945). Unedited translation, 172p.
         A continuation of JM-34 covering the withdrawal
      of the 2nd and 3rd Divisions of the Japanese Army
      from Guadalcanal and the defense of the central
      and northern Solomons plus the Bismarck Archi-
      pelago.

5677 JM-36. Army: Defense Operations. Southeast Area
      Operations Record: Map Supplement.
         Deleted and combined with JM-34 and JM-35.

5678 JM-37. Army: Invasion Operations. Southeast Area
      Operations Record: 18th Army Operations, Volume
      I, (January 1942-June 1943). Rewritten translation,
      195p.
         Covering the invasion of Eastern New Guinea and
      Rabaul by the South Seas Detachment, this work
      contains useful information on the move against
      Port Moresby as well as the defense of Buna and
      Giruwa.

5679 JM-38. Army: Defense Operations. Southeast Area
      Operations Record: 18th Army Operations, Volume
      II, (June 1943-February 1944). Unedited translation,
      212p.
         Presented in expanded outline form, this account
      follows the operations of the 20th and 51st Divisions
      in the Salamaua, Lae, and Finchhafen areas, includ-
      ing their withdrawal to Madang. Included herein
      one will find much material on minor engagements,
      supply problems, food shortages, and transportation
      difficulties.

5680   JM-39. Army: Defense Operations. <u>Southeast Area
       Operations Record: 18th Army Operations, Volume
       III, (March 1944-August 1944)</u>. Unedited transla-
       tion, 191p.
              Another study presented in expanded outline form,
       this one covers the defense of northeast New Guinea
       by the 20th, 41st, and 51st Divisions under the
       18th Army and the Second and Eighth Area Armies.
       Details on the unsuccessful defenses of Aitape,
       Hollandia, and Wewak are included, plus information
       on supply and transportation problems on top of
       food shortages.

5681   JM-40. Army: Defense Operations. <u>Southeast Area
       Operations Record: 18th Army Operations, Volume
       IV, (September 1944-June 1945)</u>. Unedited trans-
       lation, 321p.
              This study is almost entirely devoted to orders
       from the 18th Army to the 20th, 41st, and 51st
       Divisions in their last-ditch defense of the north-
       east New Guinea coast in the vicinity of Wewak.
       It covers in some detail the efforts of the 18th
       Army to attain self-sufficiency by producing its own
       food and other supplies.

5682   JM-41. Army: Defense Operations. <u>Southeast Area
       Operations Record: 18th Army Operations, Volume
       V, (June 1945-March 1946)</u>. Unedited translation,
       236p.
              A look at the final operations of the 18th Army
       with the 20th, 41st, and 51st Divisions in the Prince
       Alexander Mountain Range, south of Wewak.   Due
       to excessive casualties, operations had shrunk to
       large-scale guerrilla raids.   Much of this last
       volume is devoted to the surrender, internment,
       and repatriation of the Japanese forces.

5683   JM-42. Army. <u>Southeast Area Operations Record
       Chart Supplement, (1943-1945)</u>.   29 charts re-
       drawn from Japanese originals.
              A series of charts and graphs illustrating the
       logistical and strength aspects of 18th Army opera-
       tions as covered in JM-37-JM-41.   An appendix
       contains the Japanese policy on defensive concepts
       for New Guinea.

5684   JM-43. Army. <u>Southeast Area Operations Record:
       Map Supplement (1941-1945)</u>.

Deleted and combined with JM-37 through JM-41.

5685 JM-44. Army: Defense Operations. History of the
Eighth Area Army (November 1942-August 1945).
Unedited translation, 114p.
A study of the plans and orders of this group
for the defense of Eastern New Guinea, the Bismarck, Solomon, and Admiralty Islands. Contains
little material on actual combat operations, but is
very strong on organization, troop movement,
logistics, etc. Recommended for deletion in favor
of JM-127, but having some data not contained in
that latter study, it was retained.

5686 JM-45. Army: Over-All Operations. History of Imperial General Headquarters, Army Section (1941-
1945). Rewritten translation, 382p.
Covers the establishment of the Imperial General
Headquarters and the problems encountered by the
Army Section in the prosecution of the Greater
East Asia War. Contains brief references to political and diplomatic aspects, showing the relation of
the IGHQ to other branches of the Japanese government. Gives an over-all review of the Pacific War,
including the preparations and decision to enter war
with America, Britain, and the Netherlands. Appendices contain Army orders and an explanation
of unit designations.

5687 JM-46. Army: Invasion and Defense Operations.
Aleutians Operations Record (June 1942-July 1943).
Unedited translation, 181p.
A detailed study of the landings on Kiska and
Attu, plans and preparations for the defense of the
western Aleutians, the defense of Attu, and the
evacuation of Kiska. Although rather poorly organized, it provides quite a bit more material than
other Japanese works on the subject, translated or
not.

5688 JM-47. Army: Defense Operations. Northern Area
Monthly Combat Reports (January-May 1943). Unedited translation, 80p.
This is not actually a "monograph" in the strict
sense of the word, but rather a collection of in-
complete reports on conditions in the Aleutians and
the activities of the Kiska and Attu garrisons.

5689   JM-48. Army: Invasion and Defense Operations.
       Central Pacific Operations Record, Volume I,
       (December 1941-August 1945). Unedited translation,
       48p.
          A vague account of the operations of the South
       Seas Detachment in the capture of Guam. Moves on
       to provide some data on defense preparations on
       various islands in the Central Pacific area, with
       brief coverage of the defense of Guam, Saipan,
       and Tinian against the advancing Americans. Con-
       cludes with considerable information on the Japanese
       defense of Iwo Jima.

5690   JM-49. Army: Defense Operations. Central Pacific
       Operations Record, Volume II, (April-November
          1944). Unedited translation, 204p.
          Supposedly an account of the 31st Army and the
       14th Division in the defense of the Palau Island
       group and Yap, this study wanders far afield to
       give a lengthy resume of the general situation in
       the entire Pacific area and devotes much space to
       estimates of the American situation, both naval
       and air. Written in expanded journal format, the
       work gives a nice coverage to the Palau operation.

5691   JM-50. Army Air Force: Defense Operations. Cen-
       tral Pacific Air Operations Record (1944-1945).
       Edited translation, 14p.
          A brief and extremely loose-knit account of the
       efforts made to organize the outer islands of the
       Central Pacific for the air defense of Japan. Covers
       raids on U.S. bases on Saipan and Tinian and de-
       scribes some aspects of the Sho-Go Operations.
       Some data is contained on Army-Navy co-operation
       for the defense of the home islands. Most of this
       material is duplicated in JM-23.

5692   JM-51. Army Air Force: Defense Operations. Iwo
       Jima and Ryukyu Island Air Operations (February-
       June 1945). Unedited translation, 52p.
          A description of the operations of the 6th Air
       Army, under the control of the Combined Fleet, in
       the Iwo Jima and Okinawa defensive operations.
       Written partly in journal format, this study gives
       day-to-day reports of sorties flown and results,
       often inflated, reported.

5693 JM-52. Army: Defense Operations. Formosa Area
      Operations Record (1943-1945). Unedited transla-
      tion, 142p.
          A look at the efforts of the 10th Area Army to
      prepare for the anticipated invasion of Taiwan, to
      assist in the defense of Okinawa, and to serve as
      a logistical base for the 14th Area Army in the
      Philippines.

5694 JM-53. Army: Defense Operations. 32nd Army
      Operations in Okinawa (March-June 1945). Unedited
      translation, 27p.
          A brief outline of the defense of Okinawa which,
      although recommended for deletion in favor of
      JM-135, was retained because it contained some
      material the other study did not.

5695 JM-54. Army: Invasion Operations. Malay Operations
      Record (November 1941-March 1942). Unedited
      translation, 104p.
          A detailed description of the invasion by the 25th
      Army, along with the 5th, 18th, and Imperial
      Guards Division. Gives a day-by-day account of
      the movements of various Japanese units and dis-
      cusses the British surrender.

5696 JM-55. Army Air Force: Invasion Operations. South-
      west Air Operations Record, Phase I: (November
      1941-February 1942). Unedited translation, 113p.
          Operations of the 3rd Air Force, later the 3rd
      Air Army, in support of the advance of the 15th
      Army into Burma and the movement of the 25th
      Army down the Malay Peninsula.

5697 JM-56. Army Air Force: Offensive Operations.
      Southwest Area Air Operations Record, Phase II:
      (July 1942-June 1944). Unedited translation, 44p.
          A view of the operations of the 3rd Air Army
      in the areas of Borneo, Burma, Malaya, South
      China, and French Indo-China. Provides little
      material on combat operations being more of a
      unit listing.

5698 JM-57. Army: Invasion Operations. Burma Opera-
      tions Record, Phase I: (November 1941-December
      1942). Unedited translation, 86p.
          Covers preparations for the invasion of Burma

by the Southern Army, the movement through
Thailand and the actual assault on Burma by the
15th Army.   Records movement to, and the capture
of, Rangoon and the Japanese expansion into the
northern part of Burma.   With a minimum of
coverage on actual combat operations, this study is
primarily a record of movement with some information on the organization of the 15th Army.

5699   JM-58. Army: Offensive Operations.   Burma Operations Record, Phase II (1943-1944).   Unedited
translation, 76p.
       An examination of the operations undertaken by
the Japanese to secure Burma and push into India
and China.   Special emphasis is given to the
Imphal Operation.   Written from the level of Hqd.,
Burma Area Army, this study gives an over-all
description of the operations of the 15th, 28th, and
33 Armies.   Should be used in connection with
JM-132, JM-134, and JM-148.

5700   JM-59a. Army: Defense Operations.   Burma Operations Record, Phase III (1944-1945).   Unedited
translation, 26p.
       A very general account of the attempts of the
15th Army to defend northern Burma, hold along
the Irrawaddy River, and to recapture Meiktila.
The work also describes the withdrawal of the 15th
and 33rd Armies to the south and east following
the collapse of this northern defense.   As so much
of the material covered is duplicated in JM-148,
it was recommended that this monograph be deleted
in favor of JM-59b.

5701   JM-59b. Army: Defense Operations.   Burma Operations Record, Phase III: (April 1944-August 1945).
Unedited translation, 126p.
       An account of the over-all operations of the
Japanese in Burma from the failure at Imphal to
the final surrender.   Written from the level of
Hqd., Burma Area Army, this study is primarily
concerned with orders and movements of armies
and divisions.   It covers the same information as
JM-59a, though in greater detail.   One should also
consult JM-132, JM-134, and JM-148.

5702   JM-60. Army: Invasion Operations.   Burma Operations Record: Map Supplement.

Deleted and combined with JM-57.

5703 JM-60a. Army: Offensive Operations. Burma Opera-
      tions Record: Map Supplement.
      Deleted and combined with JM-58.

5704 JM-61. Army: Defense Operations. Burma Operations
      Record, Supplement No. 1: (October-November
      1943). Unedited translation, 7p.
         A brief account of the operations of the 18th and
      56th Divisions, under the 15th Army, against the
      36th and 108th Divisions of the Nationalist Chinese
      Army.

5705 JM-62. Army: Defense Operations. Burma Opera-
      tions Record, Supplement No. 2: (April 1944-Janu-
      ary 1945). Unedited translation, 97p.
         A look at the defense of northeastern Burma by
      the 56th Division which when examined turns out to
      be primarily a description of the individual defense
      operations of a number of garrison units established
      for the purpose of cutting the India-China overland
      route, holding the Ledo Road, and protecting the
      rear of the 15th Army against the advancing Chinese
      Yunnan Expeditionary Force. Much of the material
      contained herein is covered in greater detail in
      JM-148.

5706 JM-63. Army: Defense Operations. Burma Opera-
      tions Record: Map Supplement.
      Deleted and combined with JM-62.

5707 JM-64. Army Air Force: Over-All Operations.
      Burma Air Operations Record (January 1942-August
      1945). Unedited translation, 114p.
         A description of the 5th Air Division's success
      in driving American and British air units out of
      Burma in 1942. Covers support of ground units
      in later operations and gives an account of the
      final defense operations with those Japanese air
      units relocated to Thailand and French Indo-China.

5708 JM-65. Army Air Force: Defense Operations. South-
      west Area Air Operations Record, Phase III (July
      1944-August 1945). Unedited translation, 52p.
         Provides skimpy coverage of the 3rd Air Army
      in the final defense of the Southwest Area, but does

give considerable data on transfers, reorganization
of units, logistical problems, and attempts by the
Japanese to convert their outmoded aircraft so as
to make them competitive with the late model
planes of the Allies.

5709   JM-66.   Army: Invasion Operations.   The Invasion of
the Netherlands East Indies (November 1941-March
1942).   Rewritten translation, 59p.
A condensed version of the operations of the 16th
Army in its approach to Java via Borneo and Sumatra, including the taking of Java.   Combat operations
in these areas were light and mostly unopposed.

5710   JM-67.   Army: Invasion Operations.   Palembang and
Bangka Islands Operations Record (January-February
1942).   Rewritten translation, 16p.
A brief description of the virtually unopposed
move of the Japanese 38th Division against these
two spots, together with some information on the
airdrop of the 1st Parachute Brigade on Palembang
Airfield.

5711   JM-68.   Army.   Report on Installations and Captured
Weapons, Java and Singapore, 1942.   Rewritten
translation, 112p.
A report by an inspection team which surveyed
captured weapons, ammunition, and fortifications
in Java and Singapore, together with their evaluation
and recommendations for future use.

5712   JM-69.   Army Air Force: Invasion Operations.   Java-
Sumatra Area Air Operations Record (December
1941-March 1942).   Unedited translation, 107p.
An examination of the operations of the 3rd Air
Force, later 3rd Air Army, in support of the 16th
Army in the invasions of Java and Sumatra.   Con-
tains details of the airborne operations of the 1st
Parachute Brigade in the first Japanese airdrop
of the war.

5713   JM-70.   Army: Invasion Operations.   China Area
Operations Record Revised (July 1937-November
1941).   Rewritten translation, 85p.
A brief study of the outbreak of the China Incident and the subsequent punitive operations of the
Japanese Army.   Contains some discussion of that
organization's move into French Indo-China.

5714 JM-71. Army: Offensive Operations. <u>Army Opera-
      tions in China (December 1941-December 1943).</u>
      Rewritten translation, 170p.
          Describes the capture of Hong Kong by units of
      the 23rd Army as well as the efforts of the China
      Expeditionary Army, with the 11th and 12th Armies,
      to consolidate positions and eliminate Chinese op-
      position in Central China. Some effort is made to
      relate the attempts to destroy American air bases
      in China.

5715 JM-72. Army: Offensive Operations. <u>Army Opera-
      tions in China (January 1944-August 1945).</u> Re-
      written translation, 225p.
          A study of the efforts of the China Expeditionary
      Army, using the North China Area Army and the
      6th Area Army, to destroy U.S. and Chinese air-
      fields, secure transportation facilities, and over-
      throw the Chungking Government (Ichi-Go Opera-
      tion).

5716 JM-73. Army: Offensive Operations. <u>Combat in the
      Tao-Erh-Chuang Area (February-June 1938).</u> Edited
      translation, 12p.
          A vague account of the operations of the Japanese
      2nd Army in attempting to contain the China Incident
      by subduing the 1st, 3rd, and 5th Chinese War
      Sector Armies in the Tiensin-Kaifeng-Tsingtao tri-
      angle of northeast China.

5717 JM-74. Army: Offensive Operations. <u>Operations in
      the Kun-Lun-Kuan Area (November 1939-February
      1940).</u> Edited translation, 13p.
          A brief study of the efforts of the 21st Army to
      retain control of that part of southern China through
      which the French Indo-China to Chungking supply
      routes ran.

5718 JM-75. Army: Invasion Operations. <u>Operations at
      Changsha.</u>
          Deleted and combined with JM-70.

5719 JM-76. Army Air Force: Over-All Coverage. <u>Air
      Operations in the China Area (July 1937-August
      1945).</u> Rewritten translation, 211p.
          Includes a look at the following: air operations
      in support of ground forces in the China Incident,

the Ichi-Go Operation in which attempts were made
to eliminate U.S. air bases in China and to inter-
cept American planes en route to bomb Japan, the
final efforts to build up strength to protect coastal
installations against the anticipated Allied invasion
of China.

5720   JM-77.   Army: Plans and Preparations. Japanese
Preparations for Operations in Manchuria (1931-
1942). Edited translation, 64p.
A review of the background of the Kwantung
Army and a description of its build-up and subsequent weakening through transfer of some of its
units to the South Pacific theater. The appendix
contains a thorough record of units and listings of
transfers in and out of the Kwangtung Army.

5721   JM-78.   Army: Plans and Preparations. The Kwan-
tung Army in the Manchurian Campaign (1941-1945).
Unedited translation, 45p.
Virtually all of the information contained herein
is also found in JM-77, JM-138, JM-154, and
JM-155.

5722   JM-79.   Navy: Invasion Operations. Burma and
Andaman Invasion Naval Operations (March-April
1942). Edited translation, 12p.
A brief summary of the invasion of the Andaman
Islands by one battalion of the 18th Division and
elements of two naval base forces, escorted by the
1st Escort Force. The Burma operation mentioned
in the title was not actually an assault but merely
a large-scale troop escort operation in which the
56th Division was landed in the already secure port
of Rangoon by the 2nd Escort Force.

5723   JM-80.   Navy: Invasion Operations. Sumatra Invasion
and Southwest Area Naval Mopping-Up Operations
(January-May 1942). Edited translation, 3p.
A quick look at naval assistance to the Japanese
Army in its occupation of northern Sumatra, Christmas Island, and the Netherland's owned section of
New Guinea. Some coverage is given to naval operations in the Lesser Sunda Islands. None of this
includes any actual combat coverage; however, the
whole contains helpful organizational charts and
situation maps.

5724 JM-81. Naval Air Force: Invasion Operations.
Operational Situation of the Japanese Navy in the
Philippines Invasion Operations (December 1941).
Unedited translation, 18p.
A short chronicle of the attacks by the 11th Air
Fleet which preceeded the landing of Japanese Army
invasion forces on Luzon, Mindanao, and Jolo Is-
lands. Some data is presented on escort of troop
convoys and landing operations

5725 JM-82. Naval Air Forces: Defense Preparations.
Philippines Area Naval Operations, Part I: (Jan-
uary-September 1944). Unedited translation, 22p.
Originally titled Naval Air Operations in the
Philippines, this study covers Japanese naval plans
and preparations for the air defense of the Philippines. Contains some information on American
air attacks and Japanese countermeasures in September 1944.

5726 JM-83. Naval Air Force: Defense Operations. Okinawa Area Naval Operations (January-June 1945).
Unedited translation, 177p.
A description of naval, air, and land operations.
in defense of Okinawa which boils down to an account of the 3rd, 5th, and 10th Air Fleets and
their efforts to support the Japanese Army defense
of the island by destroying the U.S. invasion fleet.
Covers the ill-fated attack of the 1st Diversionary
Attack Force and actions of land-based naval forces.

5727 JM-84. Navy: Defense Operations. Philippines Area
Naval Operations, Part II: (October-December
1944). Unedited translation, 115p.
An examination of naval air operations prior to
the American invasion of Leyte and the surface
force operations of the Imperial Navy in the Battle
of Leyte Gulf. Contains some coverage on the
Formosa naval engagement which preceded the
Philippines operations.

5728 JM-85. Navy: Plans and Preparations. Preparations
for Operations in Defense of the Homeland (July
1944-July 1945). Unedited translation, 59p.
A view of naval plans for the defense of Japan
proper including details of joint Army-Navy defenses
against any invasion. Contains an estimate of the

of the general situation in July 1944 together with
charts showing the strength and planned employment
of the naval air arm.

5729 JM-86. Naval Air Force: Defense Operations. 5th
Air Fleet Operations (February-August 1945). Unedited translation, 144p.
      A daily record of the 5th Air Fleet's operations
in defense of Japan. Contains description of reconnaissance missions and attacks on U.S. and
British task forces, including operations in defense
of Okinawa. Briefly examines the plans and preparations for the final defense of Japan known as Operation Ketsu-Go.

5730 JM-87. Navy: Defense Operations. Western New
Guinea and North of Australia Area Naval Operations (April-September 1944). Unedited translation,
21p.
      An incoherent account of air and surface opera-
tions by the Southwest Area Fleet and the 4th Southern Expeditionary Fleet in defense of northwest
New Guinea and the Netherlands East Indies. Includes air operations in defense of Biak and surface
force attempts to land reinforcements for the defending ground troops.

5731 JM-88. Navy: Offensive Operations. Aleutian Naval
Operations (March 1942-February 1943). Edited
translation, 85p.
      This is primarily an account of the plans and
preparations for Japanese naval operations in support of the occupation of the western Aleutians.
Discusses the bombing of Dutch Harbor and times
the entire campaign into the Midway Invasion Operation, showing the strategic importance of the Aleutians and Midway to Tokyo. Provides limited
coverage of the withdrawal from Kiska.

5732 JM-89. Navy: Defense Operations. Northern Area
Naval Operations (February 1943-August 1945).
Unedited translation, 72p.
      An account of the Northern Area Force (5th
Fleet and 12 Air Force) in its mission of protect-
ing, reinforcing, and supplying Attu and Kiska.
Provides coverage of the loss of Attu and evacuation
of Kiska, as well as information on the establishment

of the Northeast Area Force (naval) and its preparations for the defense of Hokkaido and the Kuril
Islands.

5733 JM-90. Navy: Defense Operations. The "A-Go"
      Operations (May-June 1944). Unedited translation,
      63p.
         A description of the reorganization and con-
      centration of the Combined Fleet and all available
      naval air power in the Central and South Pacific in
      an all-out effort to deal the American navy a
      decisive blow. Includes a brief discussion of the
      KON Operations, a joint Japanese Army-Navy at-
      tempt to reinforce Biak.

5734 JM-91. Navy: Defense Operations. The "A-Go"
      Operations Log, Supplement (May-June 1944). Un-
      edited translation, 25p.
         Covers the same data as JM-90, only in daily
      journal format.

5735 JM-92. Navy: Consolidation. Southwest Area Naval
      Operations (April 1942-April 1944). Unedited trans-
      lation, 31p.
         A look at the Japanese Army and Navy agree-
      ments for occupation duties in Burma, Java, Malaya,
      Sumatra, and the Indian Ocean. Gives us some
      information on the establishment and maintenance
      of air bases in the Netherlands East Indies and
      western New Guinea, with subsequent air attacks
      on northern Australia.

5736 JM-93. Navy: Offensive Operations. Midway Opera-
      tions (May-June 1942). Unedited translation, 91p.
         An outline of the Imperial Navy's plans and
      preparations for the invasion of Midway and the
      Aleutians, together with details of the great Battle
      of Midway. Attempts to demonstrate the relation-
      ship between the Midway and Aleutians operations.
      Repeats some of the data provided in JM-88, how-
      ever, the information here on fleet composition and
      organization is well covered.

5737 JM-94. Naval Air Force: Defense Operations. Iwo
      Jima Operation (February-March 1945). Unedited
      translation, 24p.
         A brief account of the defense of Iwo Jima by

Army and Navy units, with particular reference to
the 3rd Air Fleet. Although written from the level
of the Navy General Command, few operational details are supplied.

5738 JM-95. Navy: Defense Operations. Submarine Operations in the Philippines Area (September 1944-March
1945). Unedited translation, 30p.
A detailed narrative of operations in the Philippines during the Battle of Leyte Gulf. Also a narrative is provided of silent service activities in
the Caroline and Molucca Islands as well as Iwo
Jima. When boiled down, it comes out as an account of missions, assignments, bases, and estimate
of damage inflicted.

5739 JM-96. Navy: Invasion Operation. Eastern New
Guinea Invasion Operations (March-September 1942).
Edited translation, 13p.
A quick examination of Japanese Army and Navy
co-operation in the assaults on Lae, Salamaua, and
Buna. Contains some coverage of the Milne Bay
Operation.

5740 JM-97. Navy: Offensive Operations. Pearl Harbor
Operations: General Outline of Orders and Plans
(5 November-2 December 1941). Edited translation,
31p.
This monograph consists primarily of a series
of thirteen orders and directives issued by the
Naval General Staff, the Combined Fleet, and the
Carrier Striking Force concerning the Hawaii raid.
The appendix contains Japanese general instructions
for operations and actions after hostilities were
commenced.

5741 JM-98. Navy: Defense Operations. Southeast Area
Naval Operations, Part I: (May 1942-February
1943). Unedited translation, 680.
The Japanese version of naval operations in the
Solomon Islands, including Admiral Tanaka's efforts
to land reinforcements and supplies ("The Tokyo
Express") on Guadalcanal and to aid the Army with
gunfire and air support. Also contains coverage
of the Japanese withdrawal from Guadalcanal and
the assistance rendered the troops by the Imperial
Navy. Some coverage is given concerning Army

operations in Eastern New Guinea, Port Moresby,
Lae, Salamaua, and Buna.

5742 JM-99. Navy: Defense Operations. Southeast Area
Naval Operations, Part II: (February-October 1943).
Unedited translation, 73p.

A description of the joint Japanese Army-Navy
operations undertaken in defense of the Central
Solomons area and the Lae-Salamaua-Finschhafen
areas of Eastern New Guinea. Includes details on
the unsuccessful air offensive launched in an effort
to neutralize American air power in the Southeast
Area plus a partially successful effort to reinforce
and supply Army and Navy ground units in the
Solomons.

5743 JM-100. Naval Air Force: Defense Operations.
Southwest Area Naval Operations, Part III: (October 1943-February 1944). Unedited translation,
67p.

A badly organized account of naval air operations
in Eastern New Guinea, the Solomon Islands, and
Admiralty Islands. Description is provided of plans
and preparations for the defense of these areas and
the Navy's transfer of troops. Air operations are
presented in daily journal format, with combat
results given for each period.

5744 JM-101. Navy: Invasion Operations. Naval Operations
in the Invasion of the Netherlands East Indies (December 1941-March 1942). Unedited translation,
40p.

A look at the Navy's escort and air support
furnished the Army in the taking of Borneo, the
Celebes, Java, and Sumatra as well as naval amphibious operations and surface force encounters
with A.B.D.A. forces.

5745 JM-102. Navy: Offensive Operations. Submarine
Operations (December 1941-April 1942). Edited
translation, 57p.

Coverage here is provided for the attack on
Pearl Harbor and subsequent operations in U.S.
coastal waters, including the use of mini-subs.
Also we find brief information on the 6th Fleet
(Submarine) operations in the Central Pacific,
Netherlands East Indies, Malaya, the Philippines,

and the Indian Ocean. Charts are included showing
submarine types and specifications.

5746 JM-103. Army: Consolidation. Outline of Adminis-
      tration in Occupied Areas (1941-1945). Unedited
      translation, 86p.
          A generalized description of military administra-
      tion in Malaya, Java, Sumatra, Borneo, Burma,
      the Philippines, and Hong Kong.

5747 JM-104. Army. Sources of Materials Used in the
      Preparation of Japanese Monographs (Army). Un-
      edited translation, unpaged.

5748 JM-105. Navy: Offensive Operations. General Sum-
      mary of Naval Operations, Southern Force (Novem-
      ber 1941-April 1942). Edited translation, 12p.
          A synopsis of naval plans and preparations for
      Japanese operations in the South Pacific Area
      drawn up before the outbreak of war. Includes
      some data on the initial invasions showing the Navy's
      roles.

5749 JM-106. Navy: Plans and Preparations. Naval Opera-
      tions Against the Soviet Union (1941-1945). Edited
      translation, 23p.
          In spite of the title, this chronicle is simply
      an account of Japanese contingency plans drawn up
      for use in the event Russia entered the war while
      Japan was fighting on other fronts. Contains a
      limited amount of information on Soviet attacks after
      August 9, 1945.

5750 JM-107. Navy: Invasion Operations. Malaya Invasion
      Naval Operations (Revised), (December 1941-Febru-
      ary 1942). Edited translation, 62p.
          Chronicles the invasion of Malaya from the Im-
      perial Navy viewpoint with brief accounts of am-
      phibious landings and naval support of same. Re-
      cords the sinking of H. M. ships Repulse and Prince
      of Wales.

5751 JM-108. Navy: Offensive Operations. Submarine
      Operations in First Phase Operations, (December
      1941-April 1942). Unedited translation, 5p.
          An extremely general look at underseas opera-
      tions in the Pacific and Indian Oceans.

5752   JM-109. Navy: Plans and Preparations. Homeland
       Defense Naval Operations, Part I: (December
       1941-March 1943). Edited translation, 24p.
            This account contains little on operational as-
       pects but much on organization. It does however
       give a view of the Doolittle Raid.

5753   JM-110. Navy: Offensive Operations. Submarine
       Operations in Second Phase Operations, Part I:
       (April-August 1942). Edited translation, 48p.
            The work of Japan's silent service in the Aleu-
       tians, South Pacific, Indian Ocean and at Midway.
       Includes some information on the reorganization
       of the 6th Fleet (Submarines) and the agreement
       with Nazi Germany regarding submarine operations
       in the Indian Ocean.

5754   JM-111. Navy: Defense Operations. Submarine
       Operations in Second Phase of Operations, Part II:
       (August 1942-March 1943). Unedited translation,
       59p.
            Covers virtually all areas of the Pacific, al-
       though the main thrust of this account is aimed at
       operations in Guadalcanal waters. Gives a good
       look at that arm's efforts to prevent American
       reinforcement while supplying the troops of Nippon
       and later helping with their withdrawal.

5755   JM-112. Navy: Defense Operations. Southeast Area
       Naval Operations, Part IV: (February-April 1944).
       Unedited translation, 19p.
            Although listed as a naval study, an examination
       shows this to be in fact primarily devoted to the
       problems of the Japanese Army in the Solomons,
       New Britain, and Northeast New Guinea.

5756   JM-113. Naval Air Force: Offensive Operations.
       Task Force Operations (November 1941-April 1942).
       Unedited translation, 90p.
            An account of naval air attacks and task force
       operations against Pearl Harbor, Darwin and north-
       ern Australia, the Netherlands East Indies, and
       British shipping, warships, and bases in the Indian
       Ocean. Written in expanded outline form, it gives
       little detailed information on actual combat opera-
       tions, but rather simply lists engagements with
       results. Numberous organizational charts show the

composition of Japan's various task forces during the period.

5757 JM-114. Navy: Defense Operations. Philippine Area Naval Operations, Part IV: (January-August 1945). Edited translation, 39p.
A description of the activities of naval land forces in the defense of Luzon, Manila, Corregidor, and Clark Field. No naval engagements are reported--mainly because none occurred.

5758 JM-115. Navy: Defense Operations. Borneo Area Naval Operation (February-July 1945). Edited translation, 7p.
A quick look at the reorganization of the remainder of the naval forces of Japan remaining in the South Pacific after the Battle of Leyte Gulf. Describes the defense and loss of Tarakan and Balikpapan by the 23rd Naval Base Force.

5759 JM-116. Navy. The Imperial Japanese Navy in World War II (1941-1945). Edited translation, 279p.
One of the most valuable unpublished reference works on the Pacific War seen during the compilation of this volume. Tables of organization--and reorganization--throughout the war are accompanied by a list naming every Japanese combatant and noncombatant vessel sunk or damaged, including the location of each incident and the cause. Deserves wider dissemination.

5760 JM-117. Navy: Defense Operations. Outline of Third Phase Operations (February 1943-August 1945). Unedited translations, 44p.
Although few combat details are provided this study is a good general review of the Japanese naval situation from the Guadalcanal withdrawal to the final surrender. Quite comprehensive on defense plans, preparations, and operations.

5761 JM-118. Navy. Operational History of Naval Communications (December 1941-August 1945). Edited translation, 407p.
A massive technical discussion of the development, improvement, and use of communication facilities with coverage of experiments and research, codes and cryptography, and radar development.

Some data is provided on ship-to-ship and ship-to-shore visual and radio communications, VLF (Very Low Frequency) submarine communication systems, and special communications plans for various operations and actions.

5762 JM-119. Navy: Surrender. Outline of Operations Prior to the Termination of War and Activities Connected with the Cessation of Hostilities (July-August 1945). Edited translation, 31p.
A general look at the Navy's last weeks of the war as it, together with the Army, prepared for invasion. Covers the acceptance of the Potsdam Declaration and the decision to surrender.

5763 JM-120. Naval Air Force: Invasion Operations. Outline of Southeast Area Naval Air Operations, Part I: (December 1941-August 1942). Unedited translation, 55p.
A record of naval air operations in the Bismarck Archipelago, the Solomon Islands, and the Eastern New Guinea invasions, with information on patrol activity and the assaults on Port Moresby. Daily operational charts give details of sorties flown by the 15th Air Flotilla (later the 5th Air Attack Group).

5764 JM-121. Naval Air Force: Offensive Operations. Outline of Southeast Area Naval Air Operations, Part II: (August-October 1942). Unedited translation, 45p.
A sketch of air operations, including patrol activities, of naval air units over Guadalcanal, Eastern New Guinea, Rabi, and Port Moresby. Written in daily journal format.

5765 JM-122. Naval Air Force: Defense Operations. Outline of Southeast Area Naval Air Operations, Part III: (November 1942-June 1943). Unedited translation, 63p.
Outlines Japanese naval air operations and patrol activities undertaken in an effort to assist the Army units on Guadalcanal by attacking U.S. installations and covering the withdrawals. Some coverage is given of the attacks on Milne Bay, Rabi, Port Moresby, and other areas of Eastern New Guinea. Presented in daily journal format.

5766 JM-123. Navy: Defense Operations. Homeland De-
      fense Naval Operations, Part II: (March 1943-
      August 1945). Unedited translation, 138p.
      An account of the plans, preparations, and
      operations of the Imperial Navy to defend Japan
      proper, on both the mainland and by attacking
      American bases and task forces. Little on combat
      operations, but strong on orders, plans, and di-
      rectives of and to naval units.

5767 JM-124. Naval Air Force: Defense Operations.
      Homeland Defense Naval Operations, Part III (June
      1944-August 1945). Unedited translation, 58p.
      An account of the naval air defense of Japan
      against raids by American land-based and carrier-
      borne aircraft with coverage of air and submarine
      raids against enemy bases. Written partly in
      daily journal format, this study provides information
      on losses and estimated results of air combat oper-
      ations.

5768 JM-125. Navy: Over-All Operations. Surface Escort
      Operations (December 1941-August 1945). Unedited
      translation, 16p.
      A discussion of Japanese efforts to provide naval
      escorts for troop and freight convoys. Written from
      the Shipping Command Hqd. level, it provides little
      information on actual escort experiences, but is
      primarily concerned with organizations and plans.

5769 JM-126. Borneo Operations Record, Volume II.
      Deleted and combined with JM-26.

5770 JM-127. Army: Defense Operations. Southeast Area
      Operations Record, Part IV: (November 1942-Au-
      gust 1945). Unedited translation, 200p.
      Written from the level of the area Army Hqd.
      (8th), this record covers plans and preparations
      for the defense of Eastern New Guinea, the Solo-
      mon, Bismarck, and Admiralty Islands. Supply
      operations, reassignments, and movements of sub-
      ordinate units of the 17th and 18th Armies are also
      given space. Duplicates much of the material in
      JM-34 through JM-41.

5771 JM-128. Army: Defense Operations. Southeast Area
      Operations Record, Supplement, Part IV (September
      1943-April 1944). Unedited translation, 41p.

A vague account of the operations of the 17th
Division, including its movement to and defense of
western New Britain and its subsequent withdrawal
to Rabaul.

5772 JM-129. Army: Offensive Operations. China Area
Operations Record, Command of the China Expeditionary Army (August 1943-August 1945). Rewritten
translation, 201p.
Examines the prosecution of the three-pronged
Ichi-Go Operation, which had as its objective: (1)
the destruction of U.S. employed airbases; (2) the
reopening and maintenance of rail communications
between north and south China; and (3) the destruction of the Chungking regime. The latter part of
this study is devoted to an account of the fortifi-
cation of key defense areas on the China coast to
forestall the anticipated establishment of invasion
bases by the United States.

5773 JM-130. Army: Offensive Operations. China Area
Operations Record, Sixth Area Army Operations
(July 1944-August 1945). Edited translation, 126p.
An account of the activities of the Sixth Area
Army in connection with the Ichi-Go Operation noted
in JM-129. Primarily concerned with the 11th and
25th Armies' operational and logistical problems,
with a late section on the units' withdrawal from
interior areas to reinforce coastal defenses.

5774 JM-131. Army: Defense Operations. Burma Operations Record, Operations in the Hukawng Area (August 1943-July 1944). Unedited translation, 68p.
An account of the efforts of the 18th Division to
hold northern Burma and protect the rear areas of
the 15th Army at Imphal and the 56th Division on
the Yunnan Front. Some duplication of the coverage provided in JM-134 and JM-148.

5775 JM-132. Army: Defense Operations. Burma Opera-
tions Record, 28th Army Operations in the Akyab
Area (Revised), (November 1943-September 1945).
Rewritten translation, 212p.
A look at Japanese operations in southwestern
Burma, from the Irrawaddy River west to the Bay
of Bengal and from India south to Rangoon. Efforts
of the 28th Army to hold against the British south-

ward advance from India. Describes Northern
Arakan, Kaladan, Mai, and Kan Operations as well
as the withdrawal of the 28th from the coastal area
to the Sittang River.

5776   JM-133. Army: Logistics Operations. Burma Opera-
       tions Record, Outline of the Burma Area Line of
       Communications (1941-1945). Edited translation,
       41p.
              A general review of Japanese supply and trans-
       portation problems encountered in the initial in-
       vasion as well as in subsequent operations.

5777   JM-134. Army: Over-All Operations. Burma Opera-
       tions Record, 15th Army Operating in the Imphal
       Area and Withdrawal to Northern Burma (Revised),
       (January 1943-January 1945). Rewritten translation,
       191p.
              Covers the defense of northern Burma, including
       plans to strengthen the Japanese defense line by
       capturing Imphal. Describes the Imphal operation,
       its failure, and the subsequent withdrawal of the
       15th Army to the Irrawaddy River. Some informa-
       tion on the Mukawng Valley and Saleen River Opera-
       tions plus the Wingate airborne invasion.

5778   JM-135. Army: Defense Operations. Okinawa Opera-
       tions Record (March-June 1945). Unedited trans-
       lation, 265p.
              A detailed account of the plans, preparations,
       and operations of the 32nd Army in the defense of
       Okinawa. Much of this study is written in daily
       journal format, giving a day-by-day account of
       movements and actions. Some information is also
       contained on operations conducted by the 8th Air
       Division.

5779   JM-136. Army: Defense Operations. North of
       Australia Operations Record (January 1944-August
       1945). Unedited translation, 84p.
              A chronicle of the 36th Division in defense of the
       Wakde-Maffin Bay area, Sarmi, and Biak. Cites
       supply difficulties and gives details of Japanese
       efforts to achieve a degree of self-sustenance by
       establishing farms, etc. Includes a look at the
       efforts of the 2nd Area Army to reinforce Biak with
       the 2nd Amphibious Brigade. Written in expanded
       journal format.

5780   JM-137. Army: Defense Operations. Philippines
       Operations Record, Phase III, Volume IV, General
       Outline of Mindoro Operations (September 1944-Au-
       gust 1945). Edited translation, 10p.
          A brief description of two infantry companies of
       the 8th Japanese Division which were wiped out
       defending Mindoro and Lubang Islands.

5781   JM-138. Army: Plans and Preparations. Japanese
       Preparations for Operations in Manchuria (January
       1943-August 1945). Edited translation, 190p.
          Primarily an account of Japanese attempts to
       build the Kwantung Army and to prepare defenses
       against the U.S.S.R. in the face of tremendous
       troop levies being made to bolster defenses in other
       areas.

5782   JM-139. Navy: Invasion Operations. Outline of
       South Seas Naval Force Operations and General
       Situation (December 1941-March 1943). Unedited
       translation, 23p.
          A general description of naval operations, both
       surface and air, in support of the invasions of
       Guam, Lae, and Salamaua. Few details of combat.

5783   JM-140. Naval Air Force: Offensive Operations.
       Outline of Southeast Area Naval Air Operations,
       Part IV: (July-November 1943). Unedited trans-
       lation, 84p.
          A look at air operations principally in the Solo-
       mon Islands, with some additional information on
       missions flown in the Bismarck Archipelago and
       Eastern New Guinea. Written in daily journal for-
       mat, this study records reconnaissance and opera-
       tional flights showing the number of planes involved,
       losses, and estimated results of sorties. Little
       actual combat description.

5784   JM-141. Okinawa Area Naval Operations, Supplement,
       (January-August 1945).
          Deleted and combined with JM-33.

5785   JM-142. Naval Air Force: Defense Operations. Out-
       line of Southeast Area Naval Air Operations, Part
       V: (December 1943-May 1944). Unedited trans-
       lation, 63p.
          A general review of operations in the entire

Southeast Area, ending with the conversion of the
air force to ground units after all aircraft had
either been expended or transferred. The appendix contains a review and critique of Japanese air
operations in the Southeast Area by Capt. N.
Miyazaki of the 25th Air Flotilla staff.

5786 JM-143. Army: Invasion Operations. Southeast Area
Operations Record, Part I: (January-May 1942).
Unedited translation, 19p.
An account of the organization of the South Seas
Detachment and its operations in connection with the
capture of Rabaul and the occupation of New Britain,
as well as the invasion of Lae and Salamaua. Preparations for movement against Port Moresby are
included.

5787 JM-144. Political Strategy Prior to the Outbreak of
War, Part I: (September 1931-January 1940).
Edited translation, 98p.
Although written by ex-naval personnel and previously listed as naval monographs, only one of the
series of five Political Strategy monographs has
any appreciable connection with naval operations.
This study discusses the China Incident and the
program of concurrent military operations and
negotiations undertaken to effect a termination of
hostilities. Covers the Canton and Hainan Island
Operations and the sinking of the U.S.S. Panay.
Included also is some slight coverage of the Manchuria and Nomonhan Incidents. Appendices contain statements of national and military policy as
well as an over-all plan for defeating the National-
ist Chinese Armies and overthrowing the Chungking
Government.

5788 JM-145. Navy: Plans and Preparations. Outline of
Naval Armament and Preparations for War, Part
I: (1922-1934). Edited translation, 61p.
Naval plans and preparations, including the construction of vessels and aircraft. Covers Japanese
participation in international conferences at Washington, Geneva, and London and the naval limita-
tions growing out of the meetings. Some information is also provided on the establishment of the
1st and 2nd Naval Armament Replenishment Plans.

5789 JM-146. Political Strategy Prior to the Outbreak of

War, Part II: (January-December 1940). Edited
translation, 56p.
A review of the situation in China and Japan's
deteriorating relations with America and Britain.
Some data on the Tripartite Pack and the political
maneuvering incident to the signing of that agreement with Germany and Italy.

5790 JM-147. Political Strategy Prior to the Outbreak of
War, Part III: January-December 1941). Edited
translation, 11p.
A detailed discussion of U. S. -Japanese negotia-
tions conducted prior to Pearl Harbor, which goes
on to explain Japan's occupation of French Indo-
China and gives a statement of Japan's Far East
Policy. Hideki Tojo's personal explanation of his
nation's decision to go to war with America,
Britain, and the Netherlands is appended.

5791 JM-148. Army: Defense Operations. Burma Area
Operations Record, 33rd Army Operations (Revised),
(April 1944-August 1945). Unedited translation,
unpaged (pamphlet size.)
An account of the formation of the 33rd to con-
duct operations against the Chinese Yunnan Expeditionary Force and to prevent the link-up of India
and China via an overland route.

5792 JM-149. Navy: Plans and Preparations. Outline of
Naval Armament and Preparations for War, Part
II: (1934-1939). Edited translation, 37p.
A continuation of JM-145 showing the accelera-
tion of naval construction programs due to the outbreak of the China Incident. Discusses the 3rd
and 4th Naval Armament Replenishment Plans.

5793 JM-150. Political Strategy Prior to the Outbreak of
War, Part IV: (January-December 1941.) Edited
translation, 121p.
Covers the same time span as JM-147, but
furnishes more details of Japanese Government conferences and discusses the decision for war in much
greater detail.

5794 JM-151. Army Air Force: Plans and Preparations.
Air Operations Record Against Soviet Russia (June
1941-September 1945). Edited translation, 65p.

The title is rather misleading in the preponderance of this work concerns the formation, buildup, and subsequent weakening through transfer of units of the 2nd Air Army in Manchuria. A small amount of data is, however, presented on operations against Soviet forces in August 1945.

5795   JM-152. Navy: Plans and Preparations. Political Strategy Prior to the Outbreak of War, Part V: (1940-1941). Edited translation, 148p.
       Although titled "political strategy," this study is in fact a review of the plans and preparations of the Imperial Navy for war in the Pacific. Only a few pages are devoted to a review of the political events of the period. It presents an excellent organizational chart of the Combined Fleet together with the complete Navy Plan for the conquest of the Southern and Central Pacific Ocean areas.

5796   JM-153. Army: Defense Operations. Homeland Operations Record, Volume IV: Operations in Karafutu and Chishima Area (9 August-22 August 1945). Edited translation, 69p.
       A description of minor engagements which developed when the Russians invaded Karafuto and the Kuril Islands. Information on the surrender, disarmament, and deportation of Japanese troops to Siberia is also given.

5797   JM-154. Army: Defense Operations. Record of Operations Against Soviet Russia, Eastern Front (August 1945). Rewritten translation, 346p.
       A series of studies covering plans and preparations of each of ten Kwantung Army units for the defense of Eastern Manchuria. Brief descriptions of defensive operations conducted against the Soviets are included.

5798   JM-155. Army: Defense Operations. Record of Operations Against Soviet Russia, Northern and Western Fronts (August-September 1945). Rewritten translation, 281p.
       Similar to JM-154, this account covers the plans, preparations, and cooperation of sixteen Kwantung Army units. The appendix contains lists of units and commanders, casualty and repatriation figures, and information on Soviet prison camps.

5799 JM-156. Army: Offensive Operations. Historical
      Review of Landing Operations and Japanese Forces
      (1904-1945). Edited translation, 50p.
      A general review of the principles and policies
      for the conduct of amphibious operations. No
      detailed information on any specific undertakings,
      but a broad discussion of types of transports re-
      quired, naval escorts needed, loading and unloading
      techniques, air cover, and organization of the
      Shipping Transport Command is presented.

5800 JM-157. Army Air Force: Defense Operations.
      Homeland Air Defense Operations Record (Revised),
      (July 1944-August 1945). Rewritten translation,
      167p.
      Covers the organization of the air defense forces,
      including the Air General Army. Special attention
      is given to a description of the efforts made to
      combat B-29 raids. Gives diagrams of radar nets
      and discusses the inability of Japanese radar equip-
      ment to adjust to the flexible operational methods
      of the U.S.A.A.F. Materials from JM-158 and
      JM-159 have been included here.

5801 JM-158. Army Air Force: Defense Operations.
      Homeland Air Defense Operations Record General
      Sector.
      Deleted and combined with JM-157.

5802 JM-159. Army Air Forces: Defense Operations.
      Homeland Air Defense Operations Record Western
      Sector.
      Deleted and combined with JM-157.

5803 JM-160. Navy: Plans and Preparations. Outline of
      Naval Armament and Preparations for War, Part
      III: (1939-1941). Edited translation, 46p.
      Follows JM-149 and describes the further accel-
      eration of Japanese naval construction programs due
      to the decision taken to engage in war with America
      and Britain. Discusses the 5th Naval Armament Re-
      plenishment Plan, as well as the Supplementary Naval
      Armament Plan.

5804 JM-161. Navy: Offensive Operations. Inner South Sea
      Islands Area Naval Operations, Part I: The Gilbert
      Islands (November 1941-November 1943). Edited
      translation, 17p.

Chronicles the South Seas Force (principally the
4th Fleet) in its capture of the Gilbert Islands and
the build-up of defenses there and in the Marshalls.
Covers the general naval operations undertaken in
the Central Pacific area and the defense of Making
and Tarawa. The appendix contains the Combined
Fleet's plans and orders for the initial Southern
Operations.

5805 JM-162. Army: Defense Operations. Southwest Area
Operations Record (April 1944-August 1945). Un-
edited translation, 186p.
An account of the establishment of the 7th Area
Army to control the Malaya, Borneo, Java, and
Sumatra areas with the 16th, 25th, 29th, and 39th
Armies. No military operations are described,
but detailed information is furnished on the use of
Malaya as a logistical base for the Southern Area.

5806 JM-163. Navy: Offensive Operations. Submarine
Operations in Third Phase Operations, Part I:
(March-November 1943). Unedited translation,
65p.
A look at Japanese silent service operations in
the Southeast Pacific, Indian Ocean, the Aleutians,
and U.S. coastal waters. The organization of the
submarine force, its missions and results, are
given as well as a brief account of the evacuation
of the Kiska Garrison and one submarine's meeting
with a German U-boat in the Indian Ocean.

5807 JM-164. Army: Transportation Operations. Railway
Operations Record (1941-1945). Unedited translation, 209p.
A general description of railway operations in
Japan and her occupied countries, including Korea
and Manchuria. Primarily devoted to describing
control agencies and the organization of the railways
for military use. Some information is given on the
construction of the infamous Burma-Siam Railroad.

5808 JM-165. Army: Plans and Preparations. Java Operations Record, Part II: (Early 1944-August 1945).
Unedited translation, 27p.
A summary of the 16th Army's plans and preparations for the defense of the Java area. As things
turned out, no defense was required.

5809 JM-166. Naval Air Force: Offensive Operations.
      China Incident Naval Air Operations (July-November
      1937). Unedited translation, 205p.
      Written in daily journal format, this study con-
      cerns the air operations of the 1st and 2nd Com-
      bined Naval Air Groups in support of ground troops
      in the China operation of 1937, especially in Cen-
      tral and Southern China. Contains data on the
      number of sorties flown, results of same, and
      losses incurred.

5810 JM-167. Army: Defense Preparations. Malay Opera-
      tions Record (January 1944-August 1945). Unedited
      translation, 52p.
      Covers the organization of the 29th Army and its
      mission of defending the Malay Peninsula. To this
      understanding we see Japanese plans and prepara-
      tions for defense, with emphasis on logistical prob-
      lems encountered, together with reorganization of
      forces, reinforcements, and the efforts of the In-
      spectorate of Military Administration to strengthen
      Nippon's position by winning the "hearts and minds"
      of the local populace.

5811 JM-168. Army: Defense Preparations. Homeland
      Antiaircraft Defense Operations Record, Tokai
      Sector (December 1944-August 1945). Unedited
      translations, 92p.
      Reviews the development of the AA defenses in
      Tokai (the East Coast) Sector from 1941 through
      the end of 1944. Looks at the plans made from
      late 1944 to the surrender for the defense of Nagoya
      and the surrounding territory.

5812 JM-169. Navy: Naval Construction. Outline of Naval
      Armament and Preparations for War, Part IV
      (1942). Edited translation, 62p.
      Gives details on wartime construction, including
      the build-up of naval air strength. Discusses plans
      for future naval bulding as seen by the 5th Naval
      Armament Replenishment Plan.

5813 JM-170. Army: Defense Preparations. Homeland
      Antiaircraft Defense Operations Record, Kanto
      Sector (June 1944-August 1945). Unedited transla-
      tion, 91p.
      Reviews the development of the AA defenses in

Kanto (Tokyo) Sector from 1941 thorugh mid-1944.
Particular emphasis is laid on plans, preparations,
and actual AA defenses of the Tokyo-Kawaski-Yoko-
hama industrial and governmental complex.

5814   JM-171. Navy: Offensive Operations. Submarine
Operations in Third Phase of Operations, Part II
(November 1943-March 1944). Unedited translation, 67p.
An account of Japanese silent service operations
in the Central and Southeast Pacific areas. Organ-
izations and dispositions of forces adopted in efforts
to cut U.S. supply lines and attack invasion forces
is examined as well as the attack on Truk by an
American task force and subsequent Japanese operations against that enemy force.

5815   JM-172. Navy: Naval Construction. Outline of Naval
Armament and Preparations for War, Part V (March
1943-April 1945). Edited translation, 79p.
Describes the efforts of the Imperial Navy to
effect replacement of materials and personnel losses.
Reviews warship production for 1942-1945.

5816   JM-173. Navy: Defense Operations. Inner South Seas
Islands Area Naval Operations, Part II: Marshall
Islands (December 1941-February 1944). Unedited
translation, 109p.
A description of efforts to defend this island
group against American air attacks. The appendix
contains a daily journal with entries from November
23, 1943 to March 1, 1944, also charts on ship
movements and losses in the area. A sequel to
JM-161.

5817   JM-174. Navy: Defense Operations. Outline of Naval
Armament and Preparations for War, Part VI (March-
June 1945). Edited translation, 108p.
A look at plans for the final defense of Japan
by the use of special attack (kamikaze) planes, boats,
manned torpedoes, and submarines. Cites construction figures for 1944 and 1945, showing estimates
for requirements of special attack equipment.

5818   JM-175. Army: Defense Preparations. Homeland
Antiaircraft Defense Operations Record, Central
Sector (September 1944-July 1945). Unedited

translation, 56p.

Traces the development of AA defenses in the
Central Sector from 1941 to 1944. Places particular emphasis on the defense of Osaka and Kobe.
Cites problems of radar, shortages of ammunition
and weapons.

5819 JM-176. Army: Defense Preparations. Homeland
Antiaircraft Defense Operations Record, Western
Sector (June 1944-August 1945). Unedited trans-
lation, 80p.

Reviews the development of AA defenses in the
Western Sector from 1941 to mid-1944. Places
particular emphasis on plans, preparations, and
actual defense of Kokura and Yawata. Some coverage of operations of the 4th AA Division in prepar-
ing to defend Kyushyu against invasion.

5820 JM-177. Army: Over-All Operations. Thailand
Operations Record (1941-1945). Rewritten translation, 37p.

Covers the relations between Japan and Thailand
before, during, and after the start of the Pacific
war. Describes Thailand's political strategy and
gives details of the Japanese use of that nation as
a logistical base for their Burma operations. Includes plans and preparations for defense and the
development of the Thailand Garrison Army, the
39th Army, and the 18th Area Army.

5821 JM-178. Army: Offensive Operations. North China
Area Operations Record (July 1937-May 1941).
Rewritten translation, 363p.

An account of the outbreak of the China Incident
and the efforts of the North China Area Army to
bring it to a speedy conclusion. Includes operations
in Northeast China and along the Mongolian border.
Punitive expeditions, mo-ups, and the formation of
garrison units are described in some detail.

5822 JM-179. Army: Offensive Operations. Central China
Area Operations Record (1937-1941). Rewritten
translation, 269p.

Chronicles the operations of the Central China
Area Army and its successor, the Central China
Expeditionary Army, in the area between Shanghai
and Hangkou. Gives details of more than twenty

operations conducted by the Japanese forces in
efforts to occupy and pacify the Central China Area.

5823   JM-180.   Army: Offensive Operations.   South China
       Area Operations Record (1937-1941).   Rewritten
       translation, 132p.
       Covers the invasion of Canton and Hainan Island
       by the 21st Army and includes subsequent operations
       conducted by that army and its successor unit, the
       South China Area Army, to cut Chiang Kai-shek's
       supply lines. Describes Japanese operations along
       the borders of Hong Kong, Macau, and French Indo-
       China culminating in the occupation of the latter
       area.

5824   JM-181.   Deleted.

5825   JM-182.   Deleted.

5826   JM-183.   Deleted.

5827   JM-184.   Navy: Defense Operations.   Submarine Oper-
       ations in Third Phase Operations, Parts III, IV, and
       V (March 1944-August 1945).   Partially edited
       translation, 237p.
       A detailed account of submarine operations in all
       areas of the Pacific with charts showing losses
       during quarterly periods. Some information is pro-
       vided on the reorganization of the Submarine Force
       and the employment of suicide tactics with midget
       submarines. The appendix contains much data on
       construction, losses, strength, and the final dis-
       positions of individual submarines after the termina-
       tion of hostilities.

5828   JM-185.   Army: Over-All Operations.   Sumatra Oper-
       ations Record, 25th Army (March 1942-August 1945).
       Edited translation, 18p.
       A brief, but fairly comprehensive, review of the
       operations of the Japanese 25th Army in Malaya and
       Sumatra. Covers the invasion of the latter and sub-
       sequent preparations for its defense.

ADDENDA

Each of the references following was uncovered too late for inclusion in the main body of the bibliography. A note in parentheses is given as to the section to which it belongs.

5828-1 Armstrong, David M. "Pearl Harbor: An Eye-witness Account." American History Illustrated, VIII (August 1974), 4-11, 41-48. (IIB-2).

5828-2 Barde, Robert E. "The Battle of Midway: A Study in Command." Unpublished PhD Dissertation, University of Maryland, 1971. (IIC-3).

5828-3 Bell, Charles. "Shoot-Out at Savo." American History Illustrated, IX (January 1975), 28-39. (IIC-5).
    The 1942 Battle of Savo Island.

5828-4 Blair, Clay. Silent Victory: The U.S. Submarine War Against Japan. Philadelphia: Lippincott, 1974. 1072p. (IID-6).
    Without a doubt, the definitive work for years to come.

5828-5 Burke, Arleigh. "Admiral Marc Mitscher: A Naval Aviator." USNIP, CI (April 1975), 53-63. (IIA).
    Much on his role in World War II.

5828-6 Byrd, Martha H. "Six Minutes to Victory: The Battle of Midway." American History Illustrated, X (May 1975), 32-49. (IIC-3).

5828-7 Dickson, W. D. The Battle of the Philippine Sea. Sea Battles in Close-up. London: Allan, 1975. 100p. (IID-4).

5828-8 Falk, Stanley L. Seventy Days to Singapore. New

York: Putnam, 1975. (IIB-4).
Much on the sinking of HMS Repulse and
Prince of Wales.

5828-9   Frank, Benis M. Halsey. Ballantine's Illustrated
History of World War II. New York: Ballantine
Books, 1974. 160p. (IIA).
A pictorial biography of the fighting American
admiral in the Pacific war.

5828-10   Furlong, William R. "A 'Sneak' Attack on Pearl
Harbor." In: Ray A. Billington, et al., eds.
The Making of American Democracy: Readings
and Documents. Rev. ed. 2 vols. New York:
Holt, 1962. II, 358-359. (IIB-2).
The after-action report of this rear admiral
commanding Pearl Harbor minecraft, who was
aboard his flagship U.S.S. Oglala, during the
raid.

5828-11   Hagoromo Society of Kamikaze Divine Thunderbolt
Corps Survivors. The Cherry Blossom Squadron:
Born to Die. Los Angeles: Okara Publications,
1974. 221p. (IIE-1).

5828-12   Hoehling, Adolph A. The Franklin Comes Home.
New York: Hawthorne Books, 1974. 132p.
(IIE-3).

5828-13   Hoyt, Edwin P. Blue Skies and Blood: The Battle
of the Coral Sea. New York: Eriksson, 1975.
217p. (IIC-2).

5828-14   Lott, Arnold S. and Robert F. Sumrall. Pearl
Harbor Attack: An Abbreviated History. Pomp-
ton Lakes, N.J.: Leeward Publications, 1974.
32p. (IIB-2).

5828-15   Lowder, Hughston E. Submarine Batfish. Balti-
more, Md.: Silent Service Books, 1974. 32p.
(IID-6).
The operational history of SS-310 in the Pacific.

5828-16   McDermott, Jon. "The Aleutian Campaign and the
Last Heavy Gun Naval Duel." World War Enthu-
siast, 1939-1945, I (September-October 1974),
137, 158. (IIC-4).

5828-17 _____. "Japanese Attack on the West Coast of
Canada's Vancouver Island." World War Enthu-
siast, 1939-1945, I (May-June 1974), 61-62.
(IID-6).
Shelling by the submarine I-26 on June 20,
1942.

5828-18 Millot, Bernard. The Battle of the Coral Sea.
Sea Battles in Close-up. Annapolis, Md.: U.S.
Naval Institute, 1974. 166p. (IIC-2).

5828-19 Milsop, John P. "Action Off Kon Chang." World
War II Journal, II (July-August 1975), 7-8.
(IIB-4).
Elements of the Vichy French Navy vs. vessels
of Thailand's fleet in September 1940.

5828-20 "Moment at Midway: [Clarence] McClusky's
Decision." USNIP, CI (April 1975), 64-66.
(IIC-3).
A USN air group commander not finding the
expected enemy carriers where they were supposed
to be, pressed on to their actual location--a
decision that altered the course of the war.

5828-21 Nagatsuka, Ryuji. I Was a Kamikaze. Translated
from the French by Nine Rootes. New York:
Macmillan, 1974. 212p. (IIE-1).

5828-22 "Pictorial History of Marine Airpower, 1937-1945."
Air Classics Quarterly Review, II (Fall 1975),
1-116. (IIA).
Almost exclusively devoted to the Pacific war.

5828-23 Richardson, James O. On the Treadmill to Pearl
Harbor: The Memoirs of Admiral James O.
Richardson. Washington: U.S. Government
Printing Office, 1973. 558p. (IIB-2).
In January 1941, the author was relieved of
his command of the U.S. Fleet by President
Roosevelt because of his strong objections to
basing the organization at Pearl Harbor.

5828-24 Russ, Martin. Line of Departure: Tarawa.
Garden City, N.Y.: Doubleday, 1975. (IID-2).

5828-25 Seno, Sadao. "A Chess Game with No Checkmate:

Admiral Inoue and the Pacific War. " Naval War
College Review, XXVI (January-February 1974),
26-39. (IIA).

5828-26   Sherrod, Robert L.   Tarawa: The Story of a
          Battle. Fredericksburg, Tex.: Admiral Nimitz
          Foundation, 1973. 206p. (IID-2).

5828-27   Simmons, Edwin H.   "The United States Marine
          Corps, 1941-1943. " Marine Corps Gazette,
          (August 1974), 39-46. (IIC).

5828-28   Skidmore, Ian.   Escape from the Rising Sun: The
          Incredible Voyage of the Sederhana Djohanis.
          London: Cooper, 1973. 198p. (IIB-4).

5828-29   Smith, Allan E.   "Battle of the Philippine Sea. "
          USNIP, C (November 1974), 102-103. (IIC-3).

5828-30   Speer, Richard T.   "Let Pass Safely the Awa
          Maru. " USNIP, C (April 1974), 69-76. (ID-6).
          A huge Japanese merchantman under safe
          conduct was torpedoed by a U.S. submarine on
          April 1, 1945.

5828-31   Stewart, A. J.   "Those Mysterious Midgets. "
          USNIP, C (December 1974), 54-63. (IID-6).
          Japanese mini-subs at Pearl Harbor on Decem-
          ber 7, 1941.

5828-32   Vanzant, Neil C.   "The Beachcomber and the Beach-
          head. " USNIP, CI (June 1975), 64-71. (IIA).

5828-33   Warrender, Simon G.   Score of Years.   Melbourne,
          Australia: Wren Publications, 1973.   235p.
          (IIA).
          Memoirs of service with the Royal Australian
          Navy.

5828-34   Webber, Ebbert.   Retaliation: Japanese Attacks
          and Allied Countermeasures on the Pacific Coast
          in World War II.   Studies in History, no. 6.
          Corvallis: Oregon State University Press, 1975.
          178p. (IIB-1).

5828-35   Weddle, Robert S.   "Texas to Tokyo Bay: Admiral
          Chester W. Nimitz. " American History Illustrated,
          X (August 1975), 4-10. (IIA).

5828-36   White, John A.   The United States Marines in North
          China.   Millbrae, Cal., 1974.   217p.   (IIE-6).

5828-37   Wolthuis, Robert K.   "United States Foreign Policy
          Towards the Netherland Indies, 1937-1945."
          Unpublished Phd Dissertation, Johns Hopkins
          University Press, 1968.   (IIB-5).

5828-38   Zehring, Robert.   "Coral Now Decks War Wreck-
          age in Truk Lagoon."   Smithsonian, VI (August
          1975), 76-81.   (IID-3).

AUTHOR INDEX
(including Addenda)

All vessels, engagements, and personnel referred to by name in the
Bibliography are cited in this index, keyed to entry numbers. Addi-
tionally, one will find index-keys to certain American and foreign
sea and air services, e. g. , the Royal Australian Air Force, the
Imperial Japanese Navy. These national forces are listed under
Navy, ... and under Air Force, ...

The American national designation for U. S. warships (USS or USCG)
has been dropped in favor of the hull-numbering system; thus the
battleship Missouri is entered here as Missouri (BB-63). National
designations are retained for foreign warships, e. g. , IJN Yamato.
A complete list of hull-designations for U. S. ships can be found in
the first volume of the U. S. Naval History Division's Dictionary of
American Naval Fighting Ships.

In order that one may associate certain persons or vessels with certain events or other figures, extensive cross-referencing will be
found among many of the entries below.